D1571177

Transitions Through Adolescence
Interpersonal Domains and Context

Transitions Through Adolescence
Interpersonal Domains and Context

edited by

Julia A. Graber
Jeanne Brooks-Gunn
Teachers College, Columbia University

Anne C. Petersen
University of Minnesota

LEA LAWRENCE ERLBAUM ASSOCIATES, PUBLISHERS
1996   Mahwah, New Jersey

Lawrence Erlbaum Associates, Inc., Publishers
10 Industrial Avenue
Mahwah, New Jersey 07430

cover design by Gail Silverman
cover photo courtesy of Darlene Rupinski,
Westwood High School, Westwood, New Jersey

Library of Congress Cataloging-in-Publication Data

Transitions through adolescence : interpersonal domains and context /
edited by Julia A. Graber, Jeanne Brooks-Gunn, Anne C. Petersen.
   p.   cm.
Includes bibliographical references and index.
ISBN 0-8058-1594-5 (alk. paper)
1. Adolescent psychology. I. Graber, Julia A. II. Brooks-Gunn,
Jeanne. III. Petersen, Anne C.
BF724.T64 1996
305.23′55—dc20   95-41221
                                                            CIP

Printed in the United States of America
10 9 8 7 6 5 4 3 2 1

Contents

Preface

Research on development during adolescence has flourished in the past decade. The adolescent period has attracted attention as an ideal period for investigating interactive models incorporating biological maturation with intra- and interpersonal development within different social contexts. Our focus is on adolescent transitions in three domains: the peer system, the family system, and school and work contexts. As other volumes have reviewed the status of research on adolescence in these and other domains, the goal of this volume is to highlight specific transitions that occur in the lives of adolescents with attention to innovative research programs and initiatives that look forward to future directions in ways of conceptualizing transitions and the nature of such transitions for adolescents.

Interest in adolescence has spanned disciplines; hence, this volume reflects a multidisciplinary perspective. Research and methods from life-span development, sociology, anthropology, and education provide exemplars of the range of approaches used in understanding the processes and transitions of adolescent development. These exemplars encompass the breadth not only of the investigation of adolescence (e.g., from survey research on drug use to ethnographic studies of involvement in criminal activities), but also of individual differences in the experience of adolescent transitions (e.g., from the transition to college and work in White, middle-class youth to the work experiences of urban, African American high school students). It would be impossible to cover the extent of multidisciplinary, multicontextual research on adolescence, rather through the contributions here a sample of the diversity of experience is presented with an emphasis on in-depth investigations of adolescent transitions. It is our hope that the volume will serve as a resource to investigators across several disciplines as it identifies approaches and recent findings from alternate fields.

The book is divided into four sections: (a) intrapersonal transitions, (b) transitions in the peer system and social behaviors, (c) transitions in the family system, and (d) school and work transitions, with a final summary chapter. It should be emphasized that these domains are interconnected and overlapping in shaping the lives of adolescents, and as such, chapters within a section frequently highlight the multiple contexts in which adolescents develop. For example, family influences are often discussed in the examinations of school success and work transitions just as perceptions of work and educational opportunities are factors in adolescent transitions in the family domain.

Part I of the book contains an overview of the concepts of adolescent transitions with an emphasis on continuity and change in developmental research, and an overview of the study of pubertal development. Part II is devoted to an overview of the nature of peer relationships during adolescence with several chapters on specific behaviors (e.g., sexual behaviors, drug use, and criminal activities) that frequently occur in the social realm. Part III focuses on the family system, again, beginning with a conceptual piece on transitions in parent–adolescent relationships. Two additional chapters are devoted to adolescent role transitions in the family domain as adolescents become parents themselves, and how such transitions and roles are defined and experienced intergenerationally. Part IV examines educational and work transitions of adolescence spanning the middle school experiences to entry into the workforce in late adolescence and young adulthood.

To reiterate, as previous volumes have provided review chapters on many of these topics in the past, it was not our goal to update literature reviews but rather explore in more depth how different transitions of adolescents are experienced by the adolescent with an emphasis on the social context in which transitions occur. The chapters reflect recent advances in conceptual thinking about transitions, in some cases strategies for intervention at times of transition (given the literature that has amassed on adolescence), and often policy implications for youth and families based on a better understanding of adolescent transitions.

Several individuals have assisted in the compilation of this book. First and foremost, we wish to thank the authors of the chapters in this volume for their thoughtful contributions. Other colleagues have also contributed to the development of the volume; we wish to thank Andrew Boxer and

Anita Greene for their contributions to this process. We also wish to acknowledge the influence of members of the Reproductive Transitions Working Group of the John D. and Catherine T. MacArthur Foundation Research Network on Health-Promoting and Disease-Preventing Behaviors, and the members of the W. T. Grant Foundation Consortium on Depression in Childhood and Adolescence in our work on this volume. We appreciate Tama Leventhal's technical assistance and the support of the staff of the Center for Children and Families and the Adolescent Study Program at Teachers College, Columbia University. We also greatly appreciate the support and encouragement of Judith Amsel and Kathleen Dolan at Lawrence Erlbaum Associates for their ongoing commitment to the publication of this book. Finally, Julia Graber and Jeanne Brooks-Gunn were supported by grants from the National Institute of Child Health and Development during the course of this project.

Julia A. Graber
Jeanne Brooks-Gunn
Anne C. Petersen

I

INTRAPERSONAL TRANSITIONS

1

Continuity and Discontinuity Across the Transition of Early Adolescence: A Developmental Contextual Perspective

Richard M. Lerner
Jacqueline V. Lerner
Alexander von Eye
Charles W. Ostrom
Michigan State University

Katherine Nitz
University of Maryland

Rachna Talwar-Soni
Long Beach, CA

Jonathan G. Tubman
Florida International University

Adolescence, and particularly early adolescence, is a period of multiple, and often rapid and profound changes and transitions (Brooks-Gunn & Petersen, 1983; Lerner & Foch, 1987; Lerner & Villarruel, 1994; Petersen, 1988; Stattin & Magnusson, 1990). Yet, these changes—involving the biological, psychological, and social characteristics of the person—are often coupled with constancies among variables associated with these same domains of characteristics. Because of the complex nature of these profound and interrelated changes that take place during early adolescent transitions, scientists have an opportunity to study the processes underlying continuity and discontinuity in intraindividual development.

For instance, despite changes in the nature of parent and peer relations, core values (e.g., regarding the value of education) seem to remain continuous from childhood through adolescence (e.g., Kandel & Lesser, 1969). Similarly, Fitzgerald, Nesselroade, and Baltes (1973) found that the structure of cognitive abilities remains continuous from childhood through at least early adolescence. Moreover, there is both developmental and demographic information indicating that problem behaviors often associated with development in the adolescent period (e.g., acts of violence or drug and alcohol use and abuse) are present as well in childhood (e.g., Bandura, 1964; Simons, Finlay, & Yang, 1991). In turn, multiple changes that take place, at both the individual and contextual level, present the adolescent with new challenges and constitute a basis of both risk and resiliency. It is through an examination of these changes, challenges, and individual trajectories that we can become more informed about the specific nature of continuity and discontinuity in development.

Indeed, to describe and to understand the character of behavior and development during early adolescence, both continuous and discontinuous phenomena must be studied. However, the identification of continuity and discontinuity in development is not just an empirical topic (Lerner, 1976, 1986; Werner, 1957). In addition, conceptual, theoretical, and metatheoretical issues are involved in understanding continuity and discontinuity. The latter, metatheoretical issues may be construed as superordinate, and as such, we focus first on metatheory in order to begin to discuss the role of issues of continuity and discontinuity in the structure of development during early adolescence.

METATHEORETICAL ISSUES IN THE STUDY OF CONTINUITY AND DISCONTINUITY IN DEVELOPMENT

The study of adolescent development or, more generally, human development, involves a concern with temporality (Baltes, Reese, & Nesselrode, 1977; Dixon & Lerner, 1992; Lerner, 1976, 1986). This focus obviously involves the study of change. Indeed, virtually all empirical studies, chapters, or books that focus on the adolescent period make mention of the concept of transition. The attention of researchers is continually called to the transition to puberty, and to related transitions involving schools, peer relationships, parent–child relationships, and cognitive abilities. Less apparent, however, is that the study of adolescence must equally be concerned with constancy. Temporal invariance of behavioral constructs (e.g., of temperament) is necessary as a baseline against which to gauge change. In addition, given that constancy and change both exist, unless one can partition human life into these two classes of components an inevitably incomplete depiction to the life course will result.

Given the goal of studying both constancy and change, then, several questions arise. First, it is clear that one must ask what features of the developmental system remain the same and what features change across life (Ford & Lerner, 1992). Second, one must inquire into the bases, the causes, of these constancies and changes. Addressing the issue of causality, however, raises both theoretical and metatheoretical issues (Lerner, 1986; Overton, 1984, 1991; Overton & Reese, 1973; Reese & Overton, 1970). To where does one look to explain constancy or change? Several prominent, metatheoretically shaped answers exist to this question.

For instance, some organismic accounts stress hereditary (e.g., Hamburger, 1957), maturation (e.g., Gesell, 1946), or other "predetermined epigenetic" (Gottlieb, 1983, 1992) factors (e.g., Freud, 1949); these accounts exclude, or assign secondary importance to, environmental or experiential factors. In turn, there are mechanistic-behavioristic ideas (e.g., Bijou, 1976) that stress behavior-theoretical mechanisms, to the exclusion of biological processes. There are also mechanistic-sociogenic formulations (e.g., Dannefer, 1984) that emphasize the sociocultural determination of individual constancy and change.

Finally, there is an emerging view based on a "probabilistic epigenetic" (Gottlieb, 1983, 1991, 1992), or a developmental systems (Ford & Lerner, 1992) conception; such a view stresses the reciprocal interdependence of biological and contextual variables. Within this conception, biological (or organism) and contextual variables are open to influence by the other, and thus each set of variables can both promote and/or constrain changes in the other (Lerner, 1984; Tobach & Greenberg, 1984; see also Lerner, 1986, 1991, 1992; Lerner, Jacobson, & Perkins, 1992). Lerner and Kauffman (1985; see also Lerner, 1986, 1991, 1992) termed this view *developmental contextualism*.

DEVELOPMENTAL CONTEXTUALISM
AND THE CONCEPTUALIZATION OF CONTINUITY
AND DISCONTINUITY

We believe that developmental contextualism involves the fullest and yet, admittedly, the most complex approach to understanding the conditions of constancy and change in human development. We adopt this approach in this chapter in order to illustrate its use, particularly in the context of an exploration of the transitionary period of early adolescence. From the perspective of a developmental contextual view of human development, the study of the human life span involves the appraisal of change and of the processes associated with biological, psychological, sociocultural, and physical ecological levels of organization that promote and/or constrain particular instances of change, that is, developmental ones. It is important to note that within developmental contextualism, levels:

> are conceived of as integrative organizations. That is, the concept of integrative levels recognizes as equally essential for the purpose of scientific

analysis both the isolation of parts of a whole and their integration into the structure of the whole. It neither reduces phenomena of a higher level to those of a lower one, as in mechanism, or describes the higher level in vague nonmaterial terms which are but substitutes for understanding, as in vitalism. Unlike other "holistic" theories, it never leaves the firm ground of material reality. . . . The concept points to the need to study the organizational interrelationships of parts and whole. (Novikoff, 1945, p. 209)

Moreover, Tobach and Greenberg (1984) stressed that "the interdependence among levels is of great significance. The dialectic nature of the relationship among levels is one in which lower levels are subsumed in higher levels so that any particular level is an integration of preceding levels. . . . In the process of integration, or fusion, *new* levels with their own characteristics result" (p. 2). If the course of human development is the product of the processes involved in the *fusions* (or "dynamic interactions"; Lerner, 1979, 1984; Lerner & Spanier, 1978) among integrative levels, then the processes of development are more plastic than often previously believed (cf. Brim & Kagan, 1980).

Given such a potential for plasticity, it is, then, a basic feature of the system of processes involved in human development that both constancy and change—both continuity and discontinuity—may exist across life. The presence of—or better, potentiality for—at least some plasticity means that the key way of casting the continuity–discontinuity issue is not a matter of deciding what exists for a given process or function; instead, the issue should be cast in terms of determining the patterns of fusions, or dynamic interactions, among levels that may promote continuity and/or discontinuity for a particular process or function at a given point in ontogeny and/or history. The same process may exhibit either continuity or discontinuity with earlier life periods, and/or may exhibit both some features of continuity and of discontinuity, depending on the particular fusion that exists among levels at a given point in historical time. Thus, neither continuity nor discontinuity is absolute. Both are features of change that have a greater than zero probability of existing, and the realization of either is dependent on prevailing organismic developmental and contextual conditions.

For example, Simmons and Blyth (e.g., Simmons & Blyth, 1987; Simmons, Carlton-Ford, & Blyth, 1987) illustrated that it is possible to find either continuity or discontinuity in females' self-esteem across early adolescence. Whether one finds continuity or discontinuity depends on the confluence of other organismic and contextual changes experienced by the females. For instance, discontinuity (in the direction of a decrement) of self-esteem is most likely when the early adolescent female is experiencing simultaneously the organismic changes associated with menarche and the contextual alterations associated with the transition from elementary school to junior high school. Again, the transition in the school context seems to be a marker for the relation between menarche and a decrease in self-esteem in young female adolescents. This sort of empirical association—between a biological characteristic (menarche), a psychological characteristic (self-esteem), and a contextual characteristic (change in school)—underscores the importance of examining multiple levels of functioning when assessing continuities and discontinuities in development.

Thus, the work of Simmons and her colleagues illustrates that changes in both organism and context contribute to development; but one needs to also appreciate that the organism as much shapes the context as the context shapes the organism, and that—at the same time—both organism and context constrain, or limit, the other. In sum, then, the processes that give humans their individuality and their plasticity are the same ones that provide their commonality and constancies (Lerner, 1984, 1988).

Accordingly, although there is some probability that any process or feature of development could show continuity or discontinuity, there are constraints on change, arising from both organism and context, making some constancies and changes more probable than others. This differential probability complicates the study of continuity and discontinuity, because it requires not only an indication of confidence intervals around particular instances of continuity and discontinuity but also a specification of the likely ordering of such instances. For instance, as Baltes (1987) noted, changes in human development across the life span have both normative and nonnormative features.

For example, it is less likely that a large and complex social institution such as a junior high school will alter its overall curriculum or educational policies to accommodate one child's individuality than it is that a single classroom will show such change in response to the child. Nevertheless, there is some possibility that a particular instance of child individuality (e.g., consider a child with AIDS) will evoke a general change in the junior high school. Conversely, it is less likely that the experience of instruction within a single course will alter the lives of an entire cohort of adolescents than it is that the experience of an overall high school curriculum will have that influence. Yet, as the case of East Los Angeles Garfield High School mathematics teacher Jaime Escalante illustrates (in the 1988 film *Stand and Deliver*), a single class, or in this case a single teacher, can indeed alter the educational lives of an entire cohort of students. Thus, although one would have to order the effects of a single child on a classroom as more likely than his or her effects on an entire school, and although one would similarly have to order changes on a cohort of high school students as more likely to be evoked by an entire school curriculum than by an individual course, there is nevertheless some probability in both cases that the less likely (lower order) change will occur.

One reason for the maintenance of some likelihood of such changes is that the person, as a consequence of his or her individuality, has a distinct influence on the multilevel context that is influencing him or her. In more general terms, the person is an active contributor to his or her own development (Lerner, 1982; Lerner & Busch-Rossnagel, 1981): The person can create the conditions of his or her own continuity or discontinuity.

To illustrate, the person's activity—for example, his or her cognitive control—can promote or constrain constancy or change in his or her development. Such cognitive and behavioral activity can be especially important in adolescence, when new cognitive abilities (formal operations) may broaden the person's perspective about the actions or life paths that are possible to pursue, and when new contexts of life (e.g., the workplace) become a frequent part of the ecology of many young people (Steinberg, 1983). Thus, how the developing person's activities interact with the changing context is a central feature of continuity and/or discontinuity across life.

Developmental contextualism is one framework that offers a rich but admittedly complex conceptualization of continuity–discontinuity in individual development (see also Baltes, Lindenberger, & Staudinger, in preparation; Brandtstädter, in preparation; Bronfenbrenner, in preparation; Elder, in preparation; Gottlieb, Wahlsten, & Lickliter, in preparation; Magnusson, in preparation, for others). However, developmental contextualism is made still more complicated for at least two reasons. First, the definition of developmental change, especially in regard to the intraindividual level, is itself a complex topic. Second, even after the concept of developmental change has been clearly delineated, one must decide when, within the life span, such change may be most usefully studied in order to understand the bases of constancy and change in development. It is useful to discuss these two issues separately.

INTRAINDIVIDUAL DEVELOPMENTAL CHANGE: DESCRIPTIVE AND EXPLANATORY ISSUES

Change per se, and developmental change in particular, can occur with variables at any level of analysis (Werner & Kaplan, 1963). In the study of human development, the individual level of analysis is the most typical focus of interest, but other levels of analysis—both more molecular (Lerner, 1984) and more molar (Featherman, 1985; Featherman & Lerner, 1985)—have been considered. However, at the individual level it is the case that issues of constancy and change as they pertain to alterations within the person have been confused with issues of constancy and change as they pertain to differences between people—in the extent to which they show within-person alteration over time. The former set of constancy versus change issues pertain to intraindividual change and to problems relating to the continuity–discontinuity of such changes. The latter set of constancy versus change issues pertain to interindividual difference in intraindividual change and to problems relating to the stability and instability of such differences over time.

For example, by again drawing on the research of Simmons et al. (1987), we can illustrate the distinction between intraindividual change and interindividual differences in intraindividual change. A given female's pattern of scores in self-esteem from Time 1 (e.g., the end of elementary school) to Time 2 (e.g., the beginning of junior high school) can involve a score of 8 (of 10) and a score of 6 (of 10) at each of these two times, respectively; these scores represent that female's intraindividual trajectory of change. Another older female's intraindividual change trajectory may involve scores of 9 and 8 at the two times, respectively. The two girls' respective Time 1 (or Time 2) scores represent, of course, interindividual differences; in each case, they constitute cross-sectional differences. In turn, the two girls' respective trajectories (i.e., their respective set of scores for Times 1 and 2) represent interindividual differences in intraindividual change; this comparison constitutes a difference in longitudinal change.

Defining Developmental Change

Complicating the definitional problem further is the fact that the concept of change, ubiquitous in developmental theory, is typically defined either in terms that describe functions of change or in terms that highlight evaluations associated with change. An example of the former is the description of change as either *elaborative* or *decremental* (Baltes, 1987; cf. Ford & Lerner, 1992). For instance, Ford and Lerner (1992) employed the following definitions: "An *elaborative change increases* the size, diversity, or complexity of organization of a person or of his or her characteristics, capabilities, and relationships with their environments" (p. 35) and "A *decremental change reduces* the size, diversity, or complexity of organization of a person or of his or her characteristics, capabilities, and relationships with their environments" (p. 35).

An example of the latter is the evaluation of changes as good or bad, where good typically is associated with increase and bad is associated with decrease (for counterexamples see Ford & Lerner, 1992, p. 36). Other examples of metatheoretical associations to change include teleological considerations that specify goals or end states for development, and balance concepts that discuss gains and losses as constituents of change (e.g., Baltes, 1987).

In the present context we attempt specificity at a different, yet complementary level. Rather than embedding concepts of change in metatheoretical systems, we propose a definition of change that operates at the level of variables observed. As such, this definition can be viewed as a precursor of definitions such as those already given.

We start with the assumption that, in empirical behavioral science, in order to depict change, variables are repeatedly observed. Thus, there is a minimum of two, preferably more, observation points in time. Suppose, we have T observation points with $T > 1$. Then, observing individual i T times in Variable Y yields the following series of measures:

$$y_{i,1}, y_{i,2}, \ldots, y_{i,T}, \tag{1}$$

where $i = 1, \ldots, N$, the sample size. Using this time series of measures, one can define univariate change as follows: *Univariate change* describes a significant increase or decrease in any of the parameters that can be estimated for a time series[1] of measures. This increase or decrease occurs relative to parameter values estimated (or known) for the time before the onset of the change.

Examples of univariate changes include changes in the mean. Suppose Equation 1 describes a successful learning process. As such, one might expect an increase in the amount of material mastered by the learner or, in more technical terms, a systematic mean shift or positive trend. In addition to the mean, slope characteristics may change. Suppose the learning curve is best described by an ogive. Then, the first rather flat slope is followed by a sharp increase that eventually levels out. Other parameters that may change include first order auto-correlations, higher order auto-correlations and auto-covariances, amplitude, and frequency of change. In addition, parameters that describe frequency distributions can be subject to change (cf. von Eye & Spiel, in press).

Researchers may focus on just one type of univariate change. Yet, several parameters that describe a time series may change at any time. For example, not only the slope but also the curvature of a time series may undergo significant changes. In addition, onset of change may not be the same for each parameter. Therefore, researchers often inspect more than one characteristic of a time series when they explore change.

To define multivariate change consider the following array of vectors, where the first subscript, i, denotes the ith individual, the second subscript, $j = 1, \ldots, D$, describes the number of variables under study ($D > 1$), and the third subscript counts observation points:

---

[1]At this point it should be noted that, although this chapter is concerned with temporal change, there is no need for change to be uniquely linked to time. Alternatively, and in accordance with Nesselroade's (1988) *selection* concept, change can be linked to concepts of location, social context, or, in general, any circumstance in which an individual may find himself or herself.

$$
\begin{array}{c}
y_{i,1,1} , y_{i,1,2}, \cdots , y_{i,1,T} \\
y_{i,2,1} , y_{i,2,2}, \cdots , y_{i,2,T} \\
. , \cdots , . \\
. , \cdots , . \\
. , \cdots , . \\
y_{i,D,1} , y_{i,D,2}, \cdots , y_{i,D,T}
\end{array}
\tag{2}
$$

Now, in a fashion analogous to univariate change, multivariate change can be defined as follows: *Multivariate change* describes a significant increase or decrease in any of the parameters that can be estimated for the measures in a time series[2] of a multiple of measures. This increase or decrease occurs relative to parameter values estimated (or known) for the time before the onset of the change.

Parameters that can be estimated for multivariate change include first the univariate parameters estimated for each individual. Comparisons of these parameters provide information about intraindividual differences in change across variables. In addition, relationships among variables may change over time. Consider the classical idea of intelligence divergence. If there is truth to this concept, the correlational structure of intelligence indicators should change over time or, more specifically, the correlations among factors of intelligence should decrease during adolescence. In a similar way, coping patterns of adolescents can be expected to become more sophisticated, and cognitive capacity in a Piagetian sense can be expected to accommodate more options. Other examples of parameters that may change in multivariate repeated measures include those that describe predictor–criteria relationships and covariance patterns.

One aspect of multivariate change concerns concepts of latent variables (von Eye & Clogg, 1994). Multivariate change often can be described from latent variable concepts that can include both continuous and categorical variables.

Descriptive and Explanatory Components of Change

Change—or constancy for that matter—has both descriptive and explanatory components, and continuity or discontinuity may be associated with either component; in addition, both continuity and discontinuity can occur in regard to quantitative and qualitative domains. For example, a phenomenon may remain descriptively the same over time (e.g., it may

---

[2]As was the case with the definition of univariate change, there is no need for multivariate change to be uniquely linked to time. Indeed, changes in location sometimes are associated with significant changes in time. Thus, changes in multiple parameters may face confounding problems similar to those encountered when decomposing age, time of measurement, and cohort effects.

be represented or depicted isomorphically at two different temporal points), and be therefore an instance of descriptive, qualitative continuity. However, more of this qualitatively invariant phenomenon may exist at Time 2 (e.g., there may be higher self-esteem scores) and thus descriptive quantitative discontinuity may be coupled with descriptive qualitative continuity. Moreover, either the descriptive quantitative discontinuity and/or the descriptive qualitative continuity may be explained by the same ideas (i.e., by explanatorily continuous principles) or by different ones (i.e., by explanatorily discontinuous principles). If different explanations are in fact evoked, they may involve statements that constitute either quantitatively or qualitatively altered processes.

For example, a phenomenon may remain descriptively the same over time (e.g., it may be represented or depicted isomorphically at two different temporal points), and may be therefore an instance of descriptive, qualitative continuity. For instance, the items or factors associated with particular measures of self-esteem (e.g., Harter, 1983), temperament (Windle & Lerner, 1986), or coping (Schwab, 1994) may remain constant from childhood into early adolescence.

However, more or less of this qualitatively invariant phenomenon may exist at Time 2 (e.g., factor scores may increase or decrease substantially for the same self-esteem dimension, as would occur, for instance, if females' general self-worth decreased precipitously across the transition to junior high school); thus descriptive quantitative discontinuity may be coupled with descriptive qualitative continuity.

Moreover, both descriptive quantitative discontinuity and descriptive qualitative continuity may be explained by the same ideas (i.e., by explanatorily continuous principles); or they may be explained by different ideas (i.e., by explanatorily discontinuous principles). For example, qualitative changes in knowledge from birth through adolescence may be explained by invariant (and continuous) principles of learning (e.g., Bijou, 1976) or by the positing of progression through a sequence of qualitatively distinct (and discontinuous) stages of cognitive development (e.g., Piaget, 1972).

If different explanations are in fact evoked they may involve statements that constitute either quantitatively or qualitatively altered processes. For example, and in regard to learning principles, quantitative alterations may be illustrated by the addition of similarly constituted connections among knowledge units; in regard to stage development, qualitative change in the structure of thought is the defining feature of the stage concept (McHale & Lerner, 1985).

In short, the study of intraindividual developmental change and of the processes that promote or constrain it are complicated, first, because intraindividual development involves simultaneous change along three

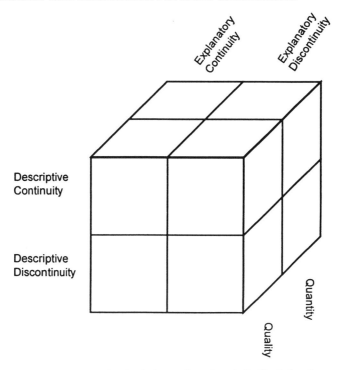

FIG. 1.1. The intraindividual change box. Intraindividual development involves change along three dimensions: descriptive continuity–discontinuity, explanatory continuity–discontinuity, and a quantitative-qualitative dimension. (From Lerner, 1986, p. 187.)

dimensions: descriptive continuity–discontinuity, explanatory continuity–discontinuity, and a quantitative–qualitative dimension. This complexity is illustrated in Fig. 1.1.

Stability Versus Instability

Second, however, the delineation of intraindividual developmental change is often complicated by—or, in this case it may be more accurately said, confused with—the stability or instability of interindividual differences in intraindividual change. Stability of interindividual differences refers to the across-time maintenance (or the correspondence in ordering) of interindividual differences; instability refers to the alteration over time in these between-people differences (in this ordering). However, the continuity or discontinuity of intraindividual change can be completely crossed with the stability or instability of interindividual differences. Stability can occur when there is either continuity or discontinuity in respect to a target person's change, if there is no alteration in the distribution of individual differences around the person. For instance, there can be a qualitative change in an adolescent's cognitive functioning (as he or she develops from concrete to formal operations). However, if the adolescent's reference group undergoes the same set of changes, and thus if the adolescent's standing relative to the reference group does not go either up or down, then despite this instance of qualitative discontinuity in cognition there is stability in cognitive development. Similarly, instability can occur where there is either continuity or discontinuity in respect to a target person's change, if there is an alteration in the distribution of individual differences around the person.

It is crucial that these distinctions be kept in mind in order to avoid making mistaken inferences about the absence or presence of intraindividual change on the basis of information about stability only (Baltes, Cornelius, & Nesselroade, 1977; Baltes & Nesselroade, 1973; Lerner, 1986). The scores of a group of individuals may show complete stability. For example, the correlation between scores on two occasions of measurement may be perfect; the rank-order of a group in regard to their scores on a dimension may not change from Time 1 to Time 2. Nevertheless, considerable intraindividual change may exist in regard to most if not all of the people in the group. This possibility is illustrated in Fig. 1.2, where, for a group of three people, there is complete stability in regard to rank-order and mean level and yet considerable intraindividual change in regard to two of the three people in the group. Indeed, directions of development (the trajectories of intraindividual change) are different for each of the people in this group.

Certainly, the change trajectories presented in Fig. 1.2 represent an "extreme" illustration of the point that potential problems might exist when a researcher uses either between-person group means and/or cross-time intraindividual correlations to represent intraindividual change without considering the limits of such statistics. However, this point should not be construed to mean that analyses using means or correlations should be exorcised from the armamentum of developmental researchers appraising change within or across ontogenetic periods. Indeed, there are at least two reasons why such an interpretation should not be made. First, it is not feasible to believe that a field trained for decades to rely on analytic techniques involving means and correlations will abruptly terminate their use—and perhaps rely instead on less familiar procedures emphasizing a focus on variance and change (e.g., Appelbaum, 1987; Nesselroade, 1988; Nesselroade & Ford, 1985). Second, there are analyses involving means and correlations that—if conducted in the context of appropriate cautions about what information the results of such analyses can provide about change—allow one to make useful assessments of intraindividual development.

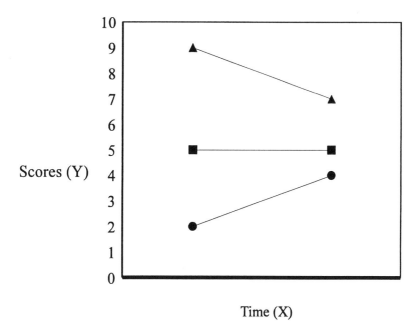

FIG. 1.2. An illustration of why stability does not mean the absence of intraindividual change. The rank-order position along the Y axis of all people studied at Times 1 and 2 remains stable, as does the group mean; however, this stability says nothing about whether intraindividual change has occurred or about the directions (the trajectories) of intraindividual change, which in this illustration are all different. (From Lerner, 1986, p. 214.)

Studying Continuity–Discontinuity at Different Periods of Life

However, this last requirement for understanding the continuity and discontinuity of intraindividual change is made more complicated when one recalls the second major problem that must be addressed in attempting to gain this understanding. What period or periods of life are most useful to study in order to understand the bases of intraindividual constancy and change? This problem is quite clearly a theoretical one. The period of life within which one focuses one's study of development involves the same sorts of metatheoretical and theoretical issues noted earlier, that is, about mechanism, predetermined epigenetic organicism, and probabilistic epigenetic organicism (or developmental contextualism). Here the issues become not only what variables provide the basis of developmental change but also when in ontogeny they act.

That is, if one believes that predetermined epigenetic variables (i.e., genetically fixed maturational processes; Gesell, 1946; Hamburger, 1957) are the basis of development, or if one believes that conditioning and learning processes are the basis of functioning, and as such that early learning significantly delimits later learning (e.g., Bijou & Baer, 1961; Thorndike, 1905; Watson, 1928), then one will look to the early portion of ontogeny (to assess either the key emergents in this period of life or the influences of shaping early experiences, respectively) in order to focus on the "important" portion of ontogeny. In turn, however, if one believes that the probabilistic epigenetic confluence of biological, psychological, and social variables provides a continuing basis of human functioning and change, then one would look across perhaps even the entire life span (e.g., see Baltes, 1987; Lerner, 1984; Schaie, 1979). One could then study development within portions of ontogeny wherein changes occur among variables from one or more levels of analysis, that is, wherein transitions occur in biological, psychological, and/or social/contextual variables.

In sum, then, the problem of deciding when in ontogeny it is best to study phenomena relating to continuity and discontinuity is a theoretically embedded issue. The developmental contextual perspective within which we approach this embeddedness leads us to believe that early adolescence is the exemplary period within the life span within which to understand the ontogenetic bases of continuity and discontinuity. Accordingly, we conclude this chapter with a specification of this role in developmental theory of the period of early adolescence.

CONCLUSION: THE DEVELOPMENTAL TRANSITIONS OF EARLY ADOLESCENCE AS WINDOWS TO CONTINUITY–DISCONTINUITY

In order to gain understanding of the biological, psychological, and sociocultural processes believed, within a developmental contextual perspective (Lerner, 1986, 1991, 1992; Lerner & Kauffman, 1985), to underlie such change, one must appraise periods of life when the processes undergo change at a level of magnitude sufficient to be detected, given available biopsychosocial measures; moreover, these changes must also be sufficiently dramatic in order for the separate and combined influences of the different processes to be gauged. Accordingly, periods of relative stasis in ontogeny may not be the ideal period of focus.

Thus, in order to understand the processes that promote and/or constrain developmental change, it is most useful to study a period of developmental transition, when that period involves significant biological, psychological, and sociocultural changes. Given the presence of such alterations, such periods of developmental transition become, then, natural ontogenetic "laboratories" for such study. Inevitably, such transition periods involve changes in both established, normative functions (Wohlwill, 1973) and in the distribution of interindividual differences around such functions. Thus, such periods afford knowledge not only of developmental functions but also of the range of systematic intraindividual variability—of plasticity (Lerner, 1984)—in general features of development.

However, interest in developmental transitions derives from more than a concern with the opportunities for and/or constraints on plasticity across ontogeny (Lerner, 1984, 1987). Plastic systems in the midst of change may be altered in multiple directions. As a consequence, periods of transition may involve changes that enhance adjustment and abilities to cope with life stressors or that diminish adjustment and coping. Thus, any period of transition represents a period of developmental opportunity—for continued or enhanced growth of psychological and social competencies; and it also represents a period of developmental risk—for diminution of physical and/or mental/behavioral health, of psychological resources, and of social support.

There are several reasons why the period of adolescence, and especially the transitionary period of early adolescence, represents an ideal time to investigate the bases and implications of continuity and discontinuity in intraindividual change. First, early adolescence is a period of several rapid and major biological, psychological, and sociocultural changes (Lerner, 1987; Petersen, 1985). Second, these sets of changes have been found to occur in an interrelated manner (Lerner & Foch, 1987; Petersen & Taylor, 1980).

Third, early adolescence represents just the sort of natural ontogenetic laboratory (Lerner & Foch, 1987) we seek for the appraisal of the developmental contextual conditions promoting continuity and/or discontinuity. For instance, at a descriptive level one can ask whether the changes seen in early adolescence represent qualitative, age-specific alterations, or continuations of early childhood phenomena, or a combination of both. In turn, at an explanatory level one can inquire into how the biological, psychological, and sociocultural changes of the period combine to foster descriptive continuity or discontinuity. Furthermore, comparable questions about descriptive and explanatory continuity and discontinuity may be raised in regard to the transition from adolescence into adulthood. As such, the changes of the early adolescent period can be used to model both transitions into and transitions out of particular portions of ontogeny.

Fourth, then, because of the profound character of the changes across the early adolescent period, this time of life—more so than other developmental transitions—represents a period of potential risk and of potential resiliency. It is a period wherein most youth find individual resources and contextual supports to cope adequately with and adjust successfully to the stressors they confront during this time of life; but early adolescence is also a period where alarmingly increasing numbers of youth do not cope or adjust successfully and where, as a consequence, such behaviors as suicide, drug use, violent crime, and teenage pregnancy and childbearing are dramatically on the rise (Dryfoos, 1990).

In essence, then, early adolescence provides an especially good scientific window for the study of the processes underlying continuity and discontinuity in intraindividual developmental functions and also of the plasticity involved in these functions. As such, this period is particularly useful for studying how individuals cope with normative and nonnormative stressors of life and of how they either weather the storms of change or succumb to its tribulations.

In sum, then, the study of early adolescent development may provide insight not only about a period of life having important social impacts on the vitality and health of our society, but also about key conceptual issues pertinent to the understanding of basic processes of human development across life. As such, early adolescence represents an exemplary period within life to integrate concerns of both basic and applied developmental psychology (Fisher & Lerner, 1994). It is a period of life that well illustrates Lewin's (1946) famous dictum that there is nothing as practical as a good theory.

ACKNOWLEDGMENT

The preparation of this chapter was supported in part by a grant from the W. K. Kellog Foundation.

REFERENCES

Appelbaum, M. (1987). *Methodological issues in research in child health and development*. Paper presented at Emotion and cognition in child and adolescent health and development: A two-way street, a conference at the Center for the Study of Child and Adolescent Development Conference, Pennsylvania State University, University Park.

Baltes, P. B. (1987). Theoretical propositions of life-span developmental psychology: On the dynamics between growth and decline. *Developmental Psychology, 23*, 611–626.

Baltes, P. B., Cornelius, S. W., & Nesselroade, J. R. (1977). Cohort effects in behavioral development: Theoretical and methodological perspectives. In W. A. Collins (Ed.), *Minnesota Symposia on Child Psychology* (Vol. 2, pp. 61–87). New York: Thomas Crowell.

Baltes, P. B., Lindenberger, V., & Staudinger, U. (in preparation). Life-span theories. In W. Damon (Ed. in Chief) & R. M. Lerner (Vol. Ed.), *Handbook of child psychology: Vol. 5. Theoretical models of human development* (5th ed.). New York: Wiley.

Baltes, P. B., & Nesselroade, J. R. (1973). The developmental analysis of individual differences on multiple measures. In J. R. Nesselroade & H. W. Reese (Eds.), *Life-span developmental psychology: Introduction to research methodological issues* (pp. 219–251). New York: Academic Press.

Baltes, P. B., Reese, H. W., & Nesselroade, J. R. (1977). *Life-span developmental psychology: Introduction to research methods.* Monterey, CA: Brooks/Cole.

Bandura, A. (1964). The stormy decade: Fact or fiction? *Psychology in the School, 1,* 224–231.

Bijou, S. W. (1976). *Child development: The basic stage of early childhood.* Englewood Cliffs, NJ: Prentice-Hall.

Bijou, S. W., & Baer, D. M. (Eds.). (1961). *Child development: A systematic and empirical theory.* New York: Appleton-Century-Crofts.

Brandtstädter, J. (in preparation). Action-theoretical perspectives on human development. In W. Damon (Ed. in Chief) & R. M. Lerner (Vol. Ed.), *Handbook of child psychology: Vol. 1. Theoretical models of human development* (5th ed.). New York: Wiley.

Brim, O. G., Jr., & Kagan, J. (Eds.). (1980). *Constancy and change in human development.* Cambridge, MA: Harvard University Press.

Bronfenbrenner, U. (in preparation). The ecology of developmental processes. In W. Damon (Ed. in Chief) & R. M. Lerner (Vol. Ed.), *Handbook of child psychology: Vol. 1. Theoretical models of human development* (5th ed.). New York: Wiley.

Brooks-Gunn, J., & Petersen, A. C. (Eds.). (1983). *Girls at puberty: Biological and psychosocial perspectives.* New York: Plenum.

Dannefer, D. (1984). Adult development and socialization theory: A paradigmatic reappraisal. *American Sociological Review, 49,* 100–116.

Dixon, R. A., & Lerner, R. M. (1992). A history of systems in developmental psychology. In M. H. Bornstein & M. E. Lamb (Eds.), *Developmental psychology: An advanced textbook* (pp. 3–58). Hillsdale, NJ: Lawrence Erlbaum Associates.

Dryfoos, J. G. (1990). *Adolescents at risk: Prevalence and prevention.* New York: Oxford University Press.

Elder, G. H., Jr. (in preparation). The life course paradigm and developmental science. In W. Damon (Ed. in Chief) & R. M. Lerner (Vol. Ed.), *Handbook of child psychology: Vol. 1. Theoretical models of human development* (5th ed.). New York: Wiley.

Featherman, D. L. (1985). Individual development and aging as a population process. In J. R. Nesselroade & A. von Eye (Eds.), *Individual development and social change: Explanatory analyses* (pp. 213–241). New York: Academic Press.

Featherman, D. L., & Lerner, R. M. (1985). Ontogenesis and sociogenesis: Problematics for theory about development across the lifespan. *American Sociological Review, 50,* 659–676.

Fisher, C. B., & Lerner, R. M. (Eds.). (1994). *Applied developmental psychology.* New York: McGraw-Hill.

Fitzgerald, J. M., Nesselroade, J. R., & Baltes, P. B. (1973). Emergence of adult intellectual structure. *Developmental Psychology, 9,* 114–119.

Ford, D. L., & Lerner, R. M. (1992). *Developmental systems theory: An integrative approach.* Newbury Park, CA: Sage.

Freud, S. (1949). *Outline of psychoanalysis.* New York: Norton.

Gesell, A. L. (1946). The ontogenesis of infant behavior. In L. Carmichael (Ed.), *Manual of child psychology* (pp. 295–331). New York: Wiley.

Gottlieb, G. (1983). The psychobiological approach to developmental issues. In M. M. Haith & J. J. Campos (Eds.), *Handbook of child psychology: Infancy and biological bases* (Vol. 2, pp. 1–26). New York: Wiley.

Gottlieb, G. (1991). The experiential canalization of behavioral development: Theory. *Developmental Psychology, 27,* 4–13.

Gottlieb, G. (1992). *Individual development and evolution: The genesis of novel behavior.* New York: Oxford University Press.

Gottlieb, G., Wahlsten, D., & Lickliter, R. (in preparation). The significance of biology for human development. In W. Damon (Ed. in Chief) & R. M. Lerner (Vol. Ed.), *Handbook of child psychology: Vol. 1. Theoretical models of human development* (5th ed.). New York: Wiley.

Hamburger, V. (1957). The concept of development in biology. In D. B. Harris (Ed.), *The concept of development* (pp. 49–58). Minneapolis: University of Minnesota Press.

Harter, S. (1983). *Supplementary description of the self-perception profile for child: Revision of the perceived competence scale for children.* Denver, CO: University of Denver.

Kandel, D. B., & Lesser, G. S. (1969). Paternal and peer influences on educational plans of adolescents. *American Sociological Review, 34,* 213–223.

Lerner, R. M. (1976). *Concepts and theories of human development.* Reading, MA: Addison-Wesley.

Lerner, R. M. (1979). A dynamic interactional concept of individual and social relationship development. In R. L. Burgess & T. L. Huston (Eds.), *Social exchange in developing relationships* (pp. 271–305). New York: Academic Press.

Lerner, R. M. (1982). Children and adolescents as producers of their own development. *Developmental Review, 2,* 342–370.

Lerner, R. M. (1984). *On the nature of human plasticity.* New York: Cambridge University Press.

Lerner, R. M. (1986). *Concepts and theories of human development* (2nd ed.). New York: Random House.

Lerner, R. M. (1987). The concept of plasticity in development. In J. Gallagher & C. T. Ramey (Eds.), *The malleability of children* (pp. 3–14). Baltimore, MD: Paul H. Brooks.

Lerner, R. M. (1988). Personality development: A life-span perspective. In E. M. Hetherington, R. M. Lerner, & M. Perlmutter (Eds.), *Child development in life-span perspective* (pp. 21–46). Hillsdale, NJ: Lawrence Erlbaum Associates.

Lerner, R. M. (1991). Changing organism-context relations as the basic process of development: A developmental contextual perspective. *Developmental Psychology, 27,* 27–32.

Lerner, R. M. (1992). *Final solutions: Biology, prejudice, and genocide.* University Park: The Pennsylvania State University.

Lerner, R. M., & Busch-Rossnagel, N. A. (Eds.). (1981). *Individuals as producers of their development: A life-span perspective.* New York: Academic Press.

Lerner, R. M., & Foch, T. T. (1987). Biological-psychosocial interactions in early adolescence: A view of the issues. In R. M. Lerner & T. T. Foch (Eds.), *Biological-psychosocial interactions in early adolescence* (pp. 1–6). Hillsdale, NJ: Lawrence Erlbaum Associates.

Lerner, R. M., Jacobson, L. P., & Perkins, D. F. (1992). Timing, process, and the diversity of developmental trajectories in human life: A developmental contextual perspective. In G. Turkewitz & D. Devenny (Eds.), *Developmental time and timing* (pp. 41–59). Hillsdale, NJ: Lawrence Erlbaum Associates.

Lerner, R. M., & Kauffman, M. B. (1985). The concept of development in contextualism. *Developmental Review, 5,* 309–333.

Lerner, R. M., & Spanier, G. B. (1978). A dynamic interactional view of child and family development. In R. M. Lerner & G. B. Spanier (Eds.), *Child influences on marital and family interaction: A life-span perspective* (pp. 1–22). New York: Academic Press.

Lerner, R. M., & Villarruel, F. A. (1994). Adolescence. In T. Husen & T. N. Postlethwaite (Eds.), *The international encyclopedia of education* (2nd ed., pp. 83–89). Oxford, UK: Pergamon.

Lewin, K. (1946). Action research and minority problems. *Journal of Social Issues, 2,* 34–46.

Magnusson, D. (in preparation). Person-context interaction theories. In W. Damon (Ed. in Chief) & R. M. Lerner (Vol. Ed.), *Handbook of child psychology: Vol. 1. Theoretical models of human development* (5th ed.). New York: Wiley.

McHale, S. M., & Lerner, R. M. (1985). Stages of human development. In T. Husen & T. N. Postlethwaite (Eds.), *The international encyclopedia of education* (pp. 2327–2331). Oxford, UK: Pergamon.

Nesselroade, J. R. (1988). Sampling and generalizability: Adult development and the aging research issues examined within the general methodological framework of selection. In K. W. Schaie, R. T. Campbell, W. M. Meredith, & S. C. Rawlings (Eds.), *Methodological issues in aging research* (pp. 13–42). New York: Springer.

Nesselroade, J. R., & Ford, D. H. (1985). Multivariate, replicated, single-subject designs for research on older adults: P technique comes of age. *Research on Aging, 7,* 46–80.

Novikoff, A. B. (1945). The concept of integrative levels of biology. *Science, 62,* 209–215.

Overton, W. F. (1984). World views and their influence on psychological theory and research: Kuhn-Kakatos-Lauden. In H. W. Reese (Ed.), *Advances in child development and behavior* (Vol. 18, pp. 191–225). New York: Academic Press.

Overton, W. F. (1991). The structure of developmental theory. In P. van Geert & L. P. Mos (Eds.), *Annals of theoretical psychology* (Vol. 6, pp. 191–235). New York: Plenum.

Overton, W. F., & Reese, H. W. (1973). Models of development: Methodological implications. In J. R. Nesselroade & H. W. Reese (Eds.), *Life-span developmental psychology: Methodological issues* (pp. 65–86). New York: Academic.

Petersen, A. C. (1985). Pubertal development as a cause of disturbance: Myths' realities, and unanswered questions. *Genetic Psychology Monographs, 111,* 207–231.

Petersen, A. C. (1988). Adolescent development. In M. R. Rosenzweig (Ed.), *Annual review of psychology* (pp. 583–607). Palo Alto, CA: Annual Reviews, Inc.

Petersen, A. C., & Taylor, B. (1980). The biological approach to adolescence: Biological change and psychological adaptation. In J. Adelson (Ed.), *Handbook of adolescent psychology* (pp. 117–155). New York: Wiley.

Piaget, J. (1972). Intellectual evolution from adolescence to adulthood. *Human Development, 15,* 1–12.

Reese, H. W., & Overton, W. F. (1970). Models of development and theories of development. In L. R. Goulet & P. B. Baltes (Eds.), *Life-span developmental psychology: Research and theory* (pp. 115–145). New York: Academic Press.

Schaie, K. W. (1979). The primary mental abilities in adulthood: An exploration in the development of psychometric intelligence. In P. B. Baltes & O. G. Brim, Jr. (Eds.), *Life-span development and behavior* (Vol. 2, pp. 67–115). New York: Academic Press.

Schwab, J. E. (1994). *The measurement of coping in early adolescence.* Unpublished doctoral dissertation, The Pennsylvania State University, University Park.

Simmons, R. G., & Blyth, D. A. (1987). *Moving into adolescence: The impact of pubertal change and school context.* Hawthorne, NJ: Aldine.

Simmons, R. G., Carlton-Ford, S. L., & Blyth, D. A. (1987). Predicting how a child will cope with the transition to junior high school. In R. M. Lerner & T. T. Foch (Eds.), *Biological-psychosocial interactions in early adolescence* (pp. 325–375). Hillsdale, NJ: Lawrence Erlbaum Associates.

Simons, J. M., Finlay, B., & Yang, A. (1991). *The adolescent and young adult fact book.* Washington, DC: Children's Defense Fund.

Stattin, H., & Magnusson, D. (1990). *Pubertal maturation in female development.* Hillsdale, NJ: Lawrence Erlbaum Associates.

Steinberg, L. (1983). The varieties and effects of work during adolescence. In M. Lamb, A. Brown, & B. Rogoff (Eds.), *Advances in developmental psychology* (Vol. 3, pp. 1–37). Hillsdale, NJ: Lawrence Erlbaum Associates.

Thorndike, E. L. (1905). *The elements of psychology.* New York: Seiler.

Tobach, E., & Greenberg, G. (1984). The significance of T. C. Schneirla's contribution to the concept of levels of integration. In G. Greenberg & E. Tobach (Eds.), *Behavioral evolution and integrative levels* (pp. 1–7). Hillsdale, NJ: Lawrence Erlbaum Associates.

von Eye, A., & Clogg, C. C. (Eds.). (1994). *Latent variables analysis: Applications for developmental research.* Thousand Oaks, CA: Sage.

von Eye, A., & Spiel, C. (in press). Nonstandard log-linear models for measuring change in categorical variables. In A. von Eye & C. C. Clogg (Eds.), *Categorical variables in developmental research.* San Diego, CA: Academic Press.

Watson, J. B. (1928). *Psychological care of infant and child.* New York: Norton.

Werner, H. (1957). The concept of development from a comparative and organismic point of view. In D. B. Harris (Ed.), *The concept of development* (pp. 125–148). Minneapolis: University of Minnesota.

Werner, H., & Kaplan, B. (1963). *Symbol formation: An organismic-developmental approach to language and the expression of thought.* New York: Wiley.

Windle, M., & Lerner, R. M. (1986). The goodness of fit model of temperament-context relations: Interaction or correlation? In J. V. Lerner & R. M. Lerner (Eds.), *Temperament and social interaction during infancy and childhood: New directions for child development* (Vol. 31, pp. 109–120). San Francisco: Jossey-Bass.

Wohlwill, J. F. (1973). *The study of behavioral development.* New York: Academic Press.

Pubertal Processes:
Methods, Measures, and Models

Julia A. Graber
Teachers College, Columbia University

Anne C. Petersen
University of Minnesota

Jeanne Brooks-Gunn
Teachers College, Columbia University

The interplay of constancy and change in development across the life span has been emphasized from both theoretical (Kagan, 1980; Overton & Reese, 1981; Rutter, 1989) and methodological perspectives (Nesselroade, 1984). The interactions among an individual's biological and psychological development and the social context of that development are examined simultaneously and longitudinally, in order to see what aspects of development are subject to continuity and change. Developmental transitions are believed to be of particular importance, in that periods when multiple changes converge allow for the study of both effects of different changes on life course trajectories and possible discontinuities in the trajectories themselves.

The onset of adolescence is considered a crucial developmental transition due to the confluence of changes across adolescence (Brooks-Gunn, 1984; Hamburg, 1974; Lewin, 1939). Entry into adolescence is marked by the physical changes of puberty; social changes in the family, peer group, and school environment; and concomitant individual changes in cognitive and socioemotional functioning, making it an excellent period in which to study the interaction of biological, psychological, and social components of development (Feldman & Elliott, 1990; Petersen, 1987). In addition, physical changes in adolescence are not only the indicator that adolescence has begun but are also causally linked to many of the other changes at this time (Petersen & Taylor, 1980).[1]

Another important point about development, and specifically puberty, is that the timing of transitions as well as the nature of the transition have an impact on the individual (Jones & Bayley, 1950; Petersen, Kennedy, & Sullivan, 1991; Rutter, 1989; Simmons, Blyth, & McKinney, 1983; Tanner, 1970). The focus of this chapter is on the methods and measurement tools used to study pubertal change and timing in particular and on models for understanding the nature of this transition.

Rutter (1989) provided three reasons why timing of a transition might be important; we illustrate these points with examples relating to the timing of puberty. First, any biological effects of the experience will be influenced by the level of development of the system at that time. For example, hormones influence the brain differently depending on the level of neural development present when the hormones are introduced (Meyer-Bahlburg, Ehrhardt, & Feldman, 1986). An example of a biological influence of pubertal timing was provided by Waber (1976, 1977), who developed a theory to explain individual differences in cognitive abilities based on how pubertal timing differences might affect the development of lateralization in the brain. Her main tenet was that puberty curtails lateralization; hence, the earlier individuals develop, the less lateralized they will be and the poorer their performance will be on tasks requiring more lateralized processing (e.g., spatial skills).

Second among Rutter's arguments about the importance of the timing of transitions was the point that any influences on the psychological state of the individual will be dependent on the "sensitivities and vulnerabilities deriving from the psychological processes that are emerging at the time" (Rutter, 1989, p. 25). For example, individuals who develop earlier might be less prepared cognitively and emotionally not only for puberty but also for the reaction of family and peers to their pubertal development (Brooks-Gunn, 1988; Paikoff & Brooks-Gunn, 1991). Pubertal development, in general, might also be difficult if pubertal change coincides with other important transitions. Coleman's (1978) focal theory suggested that many of the changes in adolescence are sequential, allowing the individual to cope and adapt to the most recent transition before the next challenge occurs. Coincidental challenges, however, such as pubertal development at the same time as school transitions (Petersen, Sarigiani, & Kennedy, 1991; Simmons & Blyth, 1987) or changes in family relationships might overtax the coping resources of the individual (Coleman, 1978).

---

[1]In fact, Tanner (1970) suggested that all behaviors of growing individuals are based in their physical structure, and that many of the implications of the level of rate of individual's development are overlooked by those around them.

Third, events are experienced differently in the social context depending on whether the event has occurred at a time that is considered "normative" versus "nonnormative" by the social referent. For example, in Western culture the prevalent ideal for appearance centers on a thin physique (Faust, 1983). Although adherence to this norm is difficult if not impossible for most girls, early-maturing girls gain weight at a time when most girls still have a childlike physical appearance. The fact that these girls do not fit the societal norm when other girls do has been suggested as one reason why early-maturing girls have reported poorer self-esteem especially as related to their body image (Brooks-Gunn & Warren, 1985a; Tobin-Richards, Boxer, & Petersen, 1983). The importance of experiencing normative development varies depending on the construct examined (Stattin & Magnusson, 1990).

The timing of pubertal development has been considered from each of these perspectives; however, pubertal timing effects have not been consistently demonstrated either in their existence or direction (Brooks-Gunn, Petersen, & Eichorn, 1985; Buchanan, Eccles, & Becker, 1992; Newcombe & Dubas, 1987; Susman et al., 1985; Tobin-Richards et al., 1983). A possible cause for the disparity of results is that different researchers have relied on different approaches to the measurement of pubertal timing (Brooks-Gunn et al., 1985; Susman et al., 1985). Puberty is not a singular process but a series of linked physical changes. In order to assess the impact of measurement differences, the various physical changes in pubertal development and how they relate to one another need to be described.

As an extensive literature exists on the processes of pubertal development, our discussion of puberty itself is brief. In addition, the psychosocial correlates of pubertal development and the timing of puberty are not reviewed extensively, but instead exemplars from the literature are used in order to highlight the influence of measurement and method when testing biopsychosocial models.

PUBERTAL DEVELOPMENT

Puberty has been defined from a medical perspective as the period of physical growth leading to the attainment of reproductive capability (Brooks-Gunn & Petersen, 1983). However, pubertal development includes physical changes not directly linked to reproductive functioning. Marshall and Tanner (1974) identified the internal and external changes at puberty, and grouped them into five general areas. These are: (a) the acceleration followed by the deceleration of skeletal growth (i.e., growth spurt), (b) the change in body composition and distribution of fat and muscle tissue, (c) development of the circulatory and respiratory systems resulting in greater strength and endurance, (d) maturation of the reproductive organs and secondary sexual characteristics, and (e) changes in the nervous and endocrine systems, which regulate and coordinate the other pubertal events. Pubertal development is controlled by an interaction of genetic, nutritional, and hormonal factors (Brooks-Gunn & Reiter, 1990; Reiter & Grumbach, 1982). The overall result of pubertal changes is the development of an individual's body from childhood appearance and functioning to the appearance and functioning of an adult body. With the possible exception of circulatory and respiratory changes, indicators have been used from each of these areas to measure pubertal development.

Although some studies have examined endocrine changes during puberty (e.g., Brooks-Gunn & Warren, 1989; Susman et al., 1985), most investigators have relied on other measurements of development as proxies for hormonal processes. These have included external physical changes (secondary sexual characteristics) either assessed by physicians or the adolescents themselves, or reports of events such as menarche (the first menses). The development of primary and secondary sexual characteristics and their temporal relation to one another was described by Marshall and Tanner (1969, 1970), who defined stages of development for key pubertal changes. The stages range from 1, no development, to 5, mature status, and describe different levels of growth in the continuous process of pubertal development. As such, they are not truly "stages" but reflect quantitative rather than qualitative change (Brooks-Gunn & Warren, 1985b).

For girls, breast and pubic hair development have been divided into stages for each with beginning breast development occurring at 10.5 years of age, on average, followed by the appearance of pubic hair (Marshall & Tanner, 1969, 1974). Substantial individual variations have been noted, with pubic hair appearing prior to breast budding for many girls (Warren, 1983). It takes girls approximately 4.5 years to traverse the stages of breast development, which span much of the pubertal process. Acceleration in growth in height begins 6 to 12 months before breast development and peaks during Stages 3 of breast and pubic hair development. Menarche occurs fairly late in the pubertal process, just after peak height velocity, at approximately 12.5 years of age in the United States (Brooks-Gunn & Reiter, 1990). (See Marshall & Tanner, 1969, 1974, for a more detailed description of these events.)

For boys, genital and pubic hair development have been divided into stages. The first sign of development is usually initial growth of the testes occurring around 11 to 11.5 years of age; it takes about 3 years to develop adult male genitalia. Pubic hair progresses at approximately a one-stage lag behind genital development. In boys, acceleration in growth begins shortly after initial testicle growth (around 11.7 years of age) and peaks around 14 years of age. (See Marshall & Tanner, 1970, 1974, again, for a more detailed description of these events.)

Boys' development is typically 1 to 2 years later than that of girls. This timing difference has implications for developmental outcomes. For example, gender differences in adult height are predominantly attributable to the difference in timing of growth spurt. The amount of growth (10–14 in.) during height velocity does not differ greatly between the sexes (Tanner, Whitehouse, & Takaishi, 1966). Rather, it is the amount of childhood growth that precedes the growth spurt that contributes most to overall size and appears to reflect the genetic component of adult height (Thissen & Bock, 1990). Adolescents who mature earlier than other adolescents (e.g., girls) have their childhood growth curtailed earlier and are on the average shorter than adolescents who mature later (e.g., boys).

Marshall and Tanner (1969, 1970) were careful to emphasize that although the progression of development of each indicator remains relatively stable across individuals, the timing of the onset of development and the rate at which individuals progress through puberty varies greatly among adolescents. In addition, asynchronies among indicators of pubertal development within individuals are not uncommon (Brooks-Gunn et al., 1985; Eichorn, 1975). The result of such variations is that it takes 10 or more years to follow a birth cohort through puberty (Petersen, 1987).

This imposes a substantial practical constraint on the investigation of puberty because most investigations of pubertal development and its association with other constructs do not have the time or funding to examine the entire process. Instead, in many studies, information on a single indicator or subset of indicators is collected either over a brief period of development or at a single point in time. Often, the indicators chosen are abstracted to represent the global pubertal process under the assumption that, within most individuals, different pubertal events have the same temporal relationship to one another. Thus, knowing when one or a few events occur, or how far advanced certain processes are, indicates the general level of development. As previously noted, this assumption is true for the majority of adolescents, but individual differences do occur (Eichorn, 1975).

PUBERTAL STATUS AND TIMING

The influence of pubertal development on behavior is usually examined in terms of either pubertal status or pubertal timing. Pubertal status refers to the level of development on a set of indicators at a single point in time, whereas timing refers to whether an individual's overall pubertal development occurs earlier, later, or at about the same time as most adolescents. Even though the conceptual distinction between the two is quite important, they are frequently confused in the literature. "Pubertal timing is an individual-differences variable that is often used in examining be-tween-subjects variations on some outcome variable. Pubertal status is a developmental variable that is used to examine whether a certain stage of development is needed before the occurrence of a certain behavior" (Dubas, Graber, & Petersen, 1991, pp. 583–584).

However, status and timing are by definition closely associated with one another during the pubertal process, but they may yield different informa-tion. For example, a boy may be undeveloped at age 12 but end up as on time in his timing of overall pubertal development. Often, pubertal timing categorizations are made by partitioning the distribution of scores on a pubertal status measure into multiple groups. Thus, when status changes, timing classifications may change rather than remain stable, as they should. Once pubertal development is completed, there are, of course, no status differences among individuals, whereas timing will always differ across individuals. The question is whether it continues to have an influence on development after the pubertal years. Status and timing are not con-founded in theory, but they are often confounded methodologically.

THE MEASUREMENT OF PUBERTAL STATUS

Measuring bone growth was previously considered one of the best ways to measure pubertal change (Petersen, 1983) and was commonly employed in the early longitudinal growth studies (Jones & Bayley, 1950; Jones & Mussen, 1958). Jones and Bayley (1950) noted that the advantages of skeletal age were that it was a common indicator for both girls and boys, was closely related to other aspects of physical maturation, and could be reliably assessed from birth to adulthood. Unfortunately, the method of assessment was the examination of x-rays of the long bones, usually in the hand or knee, in order to determine the level of development. Subsequent researchers (Roche, Wainer, & Thissen, 1975) have argued that x-rays have not been as easily rated as Jones and Bayley suggested. In addition, as the repeated use of x-rays is now known to involve risk to the individual, this practice has been discontinued in social science research (Petersen, 1983); physicians still employ this technique with patients to assess puberty in cases of abnormal development.

As an alternative, Marshall and Tanner (1969, 1970) devised a rating system for pubertal development that has become the standard for as-sessing pubertal status. They developed this system by examining nude photographs taken of adolescent boys and girls across adolescence and by defining common characteristics of each stage of development for each pubertal indicator, such as pubic hair or breast development. Implemen-tation of their approach has relied on trained health professionals to assess status during a physical examination. Both physical examinations and the scoring of photographs are quite intrusive for the adolescent, fairly labor intensive, and expensive for large-scale studies. Pubertal ratings of unclothed adolescents are also considered unacceptable by enough parents and school officials that such ratings are frequently not feasible for researchers interested in studying pubertal development, especially in school-based projects (Brooks-Gunn, Warren, Rosso, & Gargiulo, 1987).

For these reasons, self-report measures of pubertal status have been developed. Duke, Litt, and Gross (1980) had adolescents look at photographs depicting each level of development for each indicator and then code which level corresponded to their own development. These self-ratings, made after looking at photographs, have been found to correspond highly with physicians' ratings of pubertal status ($r = .80$ or higher; Duke et al., 1980). In another study, the correlation between girls' ratings and the ratings of health professionals was somewhat, yet significantly, higher than the corresponding correlation for boys for some pubertal indicators (Dorn, Susman, Nottelmann, Inoff-Germain, & Chrousos, 1990). Drawings, rather than photographs of actual adolescents, have also been used in examinations of adolescents' ratings of their pubertal status (Brooks-Gunn et al., 1987; Morris & Udry, 1980). Again, high correlations were found between self- and physician assessments.

Thus, ratings made after viewing visually depicted pubertal maturation have demonstrated accuracy. Unfortunately, school officials have not only objected to ratings by health practitioners, but also to visual depictions of pubertal development (Brooks-Gunn, 1990; Petersen, Crockett, Richards, & Boxer, 1988; Tobin-Richards et al., 1983). Hence, Petersen and her colleagues (Petersen et al., 1988) developed the Pubertal Development Scale (PDS), a verbal report of pubertal status obtained through interview or questionnaire. Using the PDS, adolescents rated their level of development for each indicator on a scale from 1 (*not begun*) to 4 (*development completed*). Adolescents of both genders rated body hair development, growth spurt, and skin changes. Boys also rated the development of facial hair and voice change, and girls rated breast development and whether they had begun to menstruate. Even without visual or verbal descriptions of the levels of development, the PDS has been found to be a reliable and valid measure of the status of pubertal development (Brooks-Gunn et al., 1987; Petersen et al., 1988).

Instead of obtaining self-reported pubertal development, Steinberg (1987) used ratings made by "trained observers" during the course of interviews conducted in the subjects' homes. These were single ratings from 1 to 5 of the level of overall development attained. Although inter-rater reliabilities were good, no assessments have been made comparing interviewer ratings with other methods of assessment, leaving the validity of this method virtually untested.

Of the single indicators of development, menarche has been used most extensively in research (Brooks-Gunn & Warren, 1985b; Petersen, 1983; Stattin & Magnusson, 1990). Adult women and adolescent girls are accurate and relatively uninhibited at providing information on their age of menarche for researchers and/or health professionals (Bean, Leeper, Wallace, Sherman, & Jagger, 1979; Brooks-Gunn et al., 1987; Rierdan & Koff, 1985). Inaccurate reporting of menarche has been found for some adolescent girls (Petersen, 1983). In the Petersen study, inaccurate reporting occurred in fewer than 10% of the girls. When it did occur, it was more often during the early adolescence years rather than retrospectively and was characterized by denial to the investigator of the event. These girls appeared to have difficulty accepting the change in their menarcheal status (Petersen, 1983). Most girls and women are accurate and reliable reporters of menarche, and may be more accurate retrospectively than during puberty (e.g., Dubas et al., 1991). Overall, menarche is a reliable measure for studies investigating the influence of pubertal development among adolescent girls and adult women. Because menarche occurs toward the end of pubertal development and has either occurred or not occurred, it has not been useful for differentiating stages of development, except to indicate that if menarche has occurred, then a girl has reached an advanced level of pubertal development.

An additional measure of physical development that has been closely linked with menarche is the ratio of total body water (TBW) to total weight (TW; Frisch, 1974). Mellits and Cheek (1970) derived regression equations to predict TBW using height and weight data. They also demonstrated that the ratio of TBW to TW was a useful index of fat in the body. Frisch (1974, 1983) suggested that a critical amount of body fat is necessary for the onset and maintenance of normal reproductive functioning in women. The higher proportion of body fat in mature women than in girls was hypothesized to be necessary in order to provide the metabolic support for pregnancy (Frisch, 1974, 1983).

Frisch and her colleagues used the Mellits and Cheek (1970) equations to estimate amount of body fat and found adolescent girls to have similar percentages of fat at the time of menarche regardless of their age at menarche (Frisch, Revelle, & Cook, 1973). Subsequently, other researchers have used the percentage of body fat as an indicator of pubertal development (Newcombe & Bandura, 1983; Waber, 1977). In these cases, it has been used as a continuous rather than dichotomous indicator (e.g., menarche); hence, it does not correspond to a specific level or status of development.

In general, the reliable and valid measurement of gender-appropriate indicators of pubertal development has been well established using a variety of measurement approaches. These indicators have been weighted and combined to form overall classifications of the stage of development (e.g., Crockett & Petersen, 1987) or have been examined individually (e.g., Brooks-Gunn, 1984) in relation to psychological variables of interest.

Limitations in Measurement Strategies

A few points are noteworthy in the discussion of pubertal status. First, in the investigation of pubertal status, often, the implied premise is that measurement of the observable physical changes of puberty is a "proxy" for the measurement of the hormonal changes. However, no one-to-one correspondence exists between hormonal level and secondary sexual characteristic development; although the latter is reflective of hormonal levels, correlations between Tanner breast stage and estradiol are in the 0.6 to 0.8 range, with similar associations between Tanner pubic hair stage and androgens for boys and girls. Additionally, the social stimulus value of a child's developing body is so great that no associated behavior changes may be attributed to hormones unless they are measured and the hormonal effects compared to those of physical changes with social or personal stimulus value. Indeed, in the few studies that have taken this approach, emotionality is related to current hormonal levels (Brooks-Gunn & Warren, 1989; Susman et al., 1987). In contrast, physical changes with social stimulus value do not influence emotionality per se, but interact with behavior carried out and shaped by the social world (e.g., leadership, school functioning, peer and parent relationships, dating, and experimentation with adult behaviors).

An additional consideration for studying pubertal status is that different indicators of development are often examined for girls and boys, by necessity in most cases. Furthermore, even though some indicators are the same or similar, such as growth spurt and body hair development, these are not necessarily the ones that are most salient for each gender or the easiest to measure (Brooks-Gunn & Warren, 1985b, 1988). For example, because body hair is not an outwardly visible sign of pubertal development, it has not been associated with psychological functioning as strongly as breast development has (Brooks-Gunn & Warren, 1988; Gargiulo, Attie, Brooks-Gunn, & Warren, 1987).

Although not an outwardly visible sign of maturity, menarche has often been considered the most salient indicator of pubertal development for girls from the perspective of reproductive maturity and psychological significance (Petersen, 1983; Stattin & Magnusson, 1990). Breast development has also been examined as a particularly socially salient indicator of development (Brooks-Gunn, 1984), but has not been used as frequently as menarche.

Unfortunately, no comparable events have been defined for boys. Some researchers have suggested that first nocturnal emission may be a comparable event to menarche in terms of reproductive capacity and psychological significance for boys (Sanders & Soares, 1986), but the same researchers found that many adult men were either reluctant or unable to recall when this event occurred. Few adolescent boys have been asked to report when they had their first ejaculation, so it is unclear whether it is a memory failure or an inhibition toward reporting.

One of the few studies of the psychological significance of first ejaculation examined only a small number of adolescent boys and found that most boys had their first ejaculation during masturbation rather than during sleep (Gaddis & Brooks-Gunn, 1985). Thus, asking about first nocturnal emission may have been misleading and not an accurate indicator of reproductive maturation. As yet, researchers have not determined which indicators of pubertal development may be most salient for boys.

More comparative research is necessary if we are to understand the psychological meaning of different pubertal processes (e.g., pubic hair growth, breast development, menarche) to the young adolescent, parents, peers, and society. One general caveat involves the use of global ratings of teens by adult observers. Results of these studies are sometimes interpreted as being due to processes that have not been measured (e.g., attributing links between affect and breast development to hormonal changes); studies need to be circumspect in their inferences.

One solution to the dilemma of how to examine puberty comparably in girls and boys using a nonintrusive method is to reconsider skeletal age, at least as approximated from height. Mathematical modeling (Bock et al., 1973; Thissen & Bock, 1990) has been used to obtain growth curves for individuals and to extract specific parameters from those curves such as the age at peak height velocity and expected adult height. The advantage of estimation is that it does not involve x-rays, but rather is derived from multiple measurements of height. Height is easily obtained in research settings and is often available from school records (Petersen & Crockett, 1985). Age at peak height velocity has the advantages of skeletal age noted by Jones and Bayley (1950) and is much like menarche in that it signifies a point in development that one has either reached or not reached. However, most attempts at fitting growth curves have used numerous points of data collection (Brooks-Gunn & Warren, 1985b). Establishing a method that uses measurements would increase the feasibility of this procedure.

Changes in body fat at puberty may also be comparable for boys and girls. Mellits and Cheek (1970) developed equations to estimate body fat for both boys and girls based on height and weight data. Like age at peak height velocity, the calculation of body fat can be constructed with little or no intrusion for the adolescents. Although body fat and pubertal development have not been linked as closely for boys as for girls, Frisch and Revelle (1971) suggested that the association may be similar for both genders. Frisch (1983) noted that extensive weight loss in men resulted in a loss of reproductive capacity similar to the cessation of menstruation observed with anorectic women. However, subsequent research (Graber, 1991) did not find strong correlations between the index of body fat and other indicators of pubertal development for boys. As yet, this index has been relatively unused for boys.

Both age at peak height velocity and the index of body fat have been used more often as measures of pubertal timing rather than of status. Height, in general, has demonstrated psychological significance for children (Brackbill & Nevill, 1981) and may be a salient measure for both girls and boys. Measures of height have also been more highly correlated with other pubertal indices than measures of weight for girls (Brooks-Gunn & Warren, 1985b; Petersen, 1973) and boys (Petersen, 1973). Whether both height and weight are comparably related to other developmental transitions in boys and girls has not been thoroughly tested.

THE MEASUREMENT OF PUBERTAL TIMING

The relative timing of an individual's pubertal development in relation to their peers or national averages is by definition derived from a measurement of status and the comparison of that level of development to what level is normative for the individual's age. Adolescents may be developing earlier, later, or at about the same time as their same-sex peers. Because of large gender differences in the nature and timing of pubertal development, timing groups are established within gender. Timing has been derived from nearly all of the previously mentioned indicators of development but typically a single study uses only one or two indicators.

In a meta-analysis of the association between cognitive abilities and pubertal timing, Newcombe and Dubas (1987) compiled listings of the pubertal indicator(s) used in each study in their sample. Although age at menarche was the most common indicator used to assess timing of maturation, a broad range of methods have been employed. Unfortunately, there were insufficient data to test the effect of the use of different measures across studies. Noncognitive studies have also used a diverse set of measures.

Pubertal timing has been associated with several aspects of psychosocial development and/or behavioral changes. Areas in which investigation has focused include self-esteem and body image, gender role, problem behaviors, heterosocial relations, and family relations (Brooks-Gunn, 1988; Duke et al., 1982; Newcombe & Bandura, 1983; Silbereisen, Petersen, Albrecht, & Kracke, 1989; Simmons, Blyth, Van Cleave, & Bush,

1979; Stattin & Magnusson, 1990; Steinberg, 1987; Tobin-Richards et al., 1983).

Table 2.1 shows a sampling of the pubertal indicators that have been used to investigate pubertal timing. Although this list is not exhaustive, it does indicate the variety of measures employed and how these measures were used to examine timing of maturation.

As previously noted, in order to assess the timing of the pubertal transition, a comparison of the level of development to some standard or group must be made. In some cases, developmental indicators were examined as continuous variables, as in the hormone study listed in Table 2.1 (Susman et al., 1985). In this study, if behavior was associated with hormone levels that were "high for one's age," then results were attrib-

TABLE 2.1
A Sampling of Pubertal Measures Used in Psychosocial Studies

Pubertal Indicator Study	Timing Categorization
Age of Menarche	
Caspi & Moffitt (1991)	% of sample, 4 groups, 20, 30, 30, 20
Simmons et al. (1979)	dichotomous, 2 groups; and % of sample, 3 groups, 20, 60, 20
Stattin & Magnusson (1990)	conceptual groupings, 4 groups
Brooks-Gunn & Warren (1985a)	age groupings, 3 groups
Age at Peak Height Velocity or Height	
Petersen & Crockett (1985)	trichotomized within sample, 3 groups
Simmons et al. (1979) (boys)	compared to national norms, dichotomous, 2 groups; and % of sample, 3 groups, 20, 60, 20
Body Fat	
Newcombe & Bandura (1983) (girls)	compared within sample, continuous
Hormones	
Susman et al. (1985)	compared level within age, continuous
Interviewer Rating	
Steinberg (1987)	compared within grade, 1 SD cutoffs, 3 groups
Skeletal Age	
Jones & Bayley (1950; boys)	extreme 20% of sample
Jones & Mussen (1958; girls)	2 groups
Tanner or Tanner-like Ratings	
Duke et al. (1982)[a]	% of sample within age, 3 groups, 20, 60, 20
Tobin-Richards et al. (1983)	compared level within grade, continuous
Self-Report of Timing	
Berzonsky & Lombardo (1983)	age of maturation, continuous
Dubas et al. (1991)	perceived timing, 3 groups
Silbereisen et al. (1989)	perceived timing, 3 groups

[a]For girls, breast and pubic hair development were averaged. For boys, pubic hair and genital development were averaged.

uted to individuals who were early maturers. This interpretation of hormone levels may confound possible individual differences in adult hormone levels with developmental change. In other studies, indicators have been divided into discrete groups, creating a categorical variable. Susman and colleagues (Susman et al., 1985) suggested that hormonal levels reflect the biological correlates of behavior whereas the meaning of timing based on the categorization of secondary sexual characteristics involves a social component. Because hormones not only influence behavior but also are influenced by behavior and the environment (Seyler & Reichlin, 1974; West, Mahajan, Chavre, Nabors, & Tyler, 1973), hormone levels cannot be assumed to reflect purely biological correlates of behavior.

The categorization of pubertal development into timing groups has, again, been made on several criteria, as can be seen in Table 2.1. Indicators of development have been compared with national norms and divisions have been based on cutoffs determined from the national averages (Simmons et al., 1979). Simmons and her colleagues compared the rate of growth of boys in their sample to growth rates observed by Stolz and Stolz (1951) for pubertal and nonpubertal boys in order to form dichotomous ratings of timing. If a boy's growth was within the range for pubertal in the seventh grade, then he was considered early; if he grew less than any of the pubertal boys in the Stolz and Stolz (1951) sample, then he was a late developer.

Similarly, divisions have been based on the distribution of the measured indicators within a sample (e.g., Caspi & Moffitt, 1991; Stattin & Magnusson, 1990). The choice of the division point in the distribution has depended on the conceptual issues of each study (Brooks-Gunn et al., 1985). Some criteria produce extreme groups. Several of the studies in Table 2.1 have defined the off-time groups as the 20% of the sample in each tail (e.g., Caspi & Moffitt, 1991; Duke et al., 1982; Jones & Bayley, 1950; Jones & Mussen, 1958). On the other hand, Simmons et al. (1979) used a dichotomous criterion; girls were early developers if they had reached menarche by the seventh grade and late developers if they had not. No standard method has been established across studies. By necessity, the conceptual questions as well as the practical constraints of each investigation have determined how timing should be classified. However, establishing a set of standard measures and methods may be desirable for the field.

The number of divisions or groups has also been determined by conceptual considerations. Whereas three groups—early, on time, and late— have been common (e.g., Caspi & Moffitt, 1991; Petersen & Crockett, 1985; Silbereisen et al., 1989), some investigations have further divided their samples for conceptual reasons. For example, Stattin and Magnusson (1990) divided their sample into extremely early, early, on time, and late maturation groups because they expected early maturation to have an influence on development and wanted to examine whether being extremely early in development had a greater influence on psychosocial functioning than being only somewhat earlier than peers. In contrast, Jones and colleagues (Jones & Bayley, 1950; Jones & Mussen, 1958) only compared early and late maturers (not including on-time maturers). Thus, they only investigated differences within off-time developers rather than comparing off-time to on-time developers. In addition, extreme group designs restrict the method of analysis. In these designs, because correlations (or regression approaches) would be inaccurately exaggerated, analysis of variance approaches are necessary.

An alternative to categorizing individuals based on some measure of pubertal development is to ask them to report their perceptions of their timing of maturation without collecting data on status. This is akin to self-report measures of status. Berzonsky and Lombardo (1983) asked college students to respond to the question(s) "With regard to your physical maturation, at what age would you say that you matured? At what age did you reach sexual maturation?" (p. 242). Males were told to use the appearance of pubic hair and girls were told to use age at menarche as a basis for answering the question only if the individual was puzzled by the question. It is unknown how many of the participants in this study used pubic hair or menarche as their basis for answering. The reported age was then used as a continuous measure with the direction of results discussed in terms of early or late maturation. Other researchers (Silbereisen et al., 1989; Tobin-Richards et al., 1983) have asked adolescents to report directly about their timing during the peak pubertal years. Thus, the adolescents themselves decided whether they were early, on-time, or late maturers relative to their peers.

Perceived pubertal timing has been considered useful especially when retrospective measures of pubertal development were the only measures available, as when postpubertal samples were being examined (Sanders & Soares, 1986). Even though retrospective accounts of age at menarche have been found to be fairly accurate and reliable (Bean et al., 1979) and have been useful for examining pubertal timing effects for women (Rierdan & Koff, 1985), identifying the indicator to use for men remains a problem. Having men and women provide their own ratings of pubertal timing circumvents this problem. However, it is unlikely that all adults will use similar criteria for making retrospective assessments of their pubertal timing.

The accuracy of perceptions of timing has only recently been investigated. Dubas and her colleagues (1991) examined perceptions of pubertal timing during 7th and 8th grades, the peak pubertal years, and in 12th grade, when puberty is completed or nearly completed for most adolescents. Perceptions were compared at each grade with an objective measure of timing. Correlations between perceived and objective measures were .28, .36, and .36 for boys, and .11, .38, and .56 for girls in 7th, 8th, and 12th grades, respectively. Hence, perceptions were most accurate after puberty was completed with a greater increase in accuracy for girls. As indicated by the size of the correlations, perceptions of pubertal timing were not based entirely on the actual timing of the individual's development, but included unidentified factors.

THE MEANING OF DIFFERENT MEASUREMENT APPROACHES

It is likely that the variety of pubertal measures and methods for determining timing of maturation affect the comparison of results across studies. Whereas some investigations of pubertal status have attempted to test whether using different pubertal indicators affected results (Gargiulo et al., 1987), very little has been done with measures of pubertal timing. In an investigation of problem behavior, perceived pubertal timing was associated with several norm-breaking behaviors, whereas an objective measure of timing was associated with a few behaviors (Petersen, Graber, & Sullivan, 1990). Of course, it has already been noted that perceived timing is only moderately related to objective timing. Returning to Rutter's conceptualization of the impact of the timing of transitions, perceived timing may reflect a different process than actual timing, possibly at the individual or social rather than biological level.

As noted, different indicators of development may have different meanings for some individuals, such as girls versus boys. Hence, categorizations of timing of puberty may relate to behaviors depending on the behavior under investigation and the pubertal status measure on which timing was based. In addition, different pubertal events are under the control of different hormones (Petersen & Taylor, 1980). Hence, a psychological construct may be associated with the timing of one indicator but not the timing of another even at the biological level.

This possibility merits further discussion. Because, as previously noted, puberty follows a similar progression for most individuals, despite differences in rate and onset of development, the timing of each pubertal indicator should be positively and highly correlated with the timing of all other pubertal indicators. Thus, examinations of the psychological significance of timing might be less affected by the choice of indicator than examinations of status.

Pubertal timing is not commonly conceptualized as a changing variable (Dubas et al., 1991). Theoretically, if timing is unchanging, not only should classifications of timing remain stable regardless of the indicator of development, but they should also remain stable regardless of the point in development at which they were obtained. If timing classifications are made in both seventh and eighth grades, each adolescent should be placed into the same timing category regardless of whether seventh or eighth grade data are used. In practice, very little attention has been given to this consideration, especially when status is used as a proxy for timing.

Discontinuities in classification may be attributable to the point in development at which measurements were made. The rate of passage through puberty or tempo of development varies across individuals (Marshall & Tanner, 1969, 1970), but little is known about the extent or nature of the variation (Brooks-Gunn et al., 1985). It is possible that if an individual began pubertal development at about the same time as peers and, at that time, was classified as on time, the same individual could be classified differently if he or she progressed more quickly or more slowly through puberty than peers. Subsequent observations may find this same adolescent to be much more developed than peers; thus, the adolescent might now be considered an early developer. Conversely, if the individual were progressing more slowly than others, he or she might be considered a late maturer at subsequent observations.

It is unclear how greatly outcomes have been affected by tempo variations. Is it more important to begin development at about the same time as others, to progress through puberty at the same time, or to complete development at about the same time? Most attention has focused on the early and middle pubertal periods rather than the completion of it. Although variations in rate of development are known to exist (Eichorn, 1975), if rate is normally distributed, variations that will produce differences in timing classifications should not be statistically common. The possibility of such variations, though, suggests that researchers should carefully consider the extent of stability of their method of measurement for timing of maturation and whether rate of development will influence this measurement. For example, in a 4-year longitudinal study of adolescent girls, rate of development was not associated with depressive symptoms, whereas timing of maturation was. The timing effect was more pronounced at ages 12 and 13 than earlier or later (Baydar, Brooks-Gunn, & Warren, 1992).

Time of measurement is also a factor if observations are made relatively early or late during development at times when some groups might be developmentally indistinguishable. For example, measurements of puberty obtained when children or adolescents were in the middle of fifth grade or commonly 10.5 years of age in a U.S. sample (extrapolating from Richardson, Galambos, Schulenberg, & Petersen, 1984) would clearly differentiate boys who were early developers. As most boys, on the average, would not begin puberty until a year later, boys who have begun to develop at this age would be earlier than most of their peers. However, boys who will be late maturers are indistinguishable from boys who will be on time at this age. The optimum period for differentiating timing groups differs by gender.

The extent to which time of measurement has affected classification remains unclear. Brooks-Gunn et al. (1985) encouraged researchers to reanalyze their data using alternate timing criteria. From a statistical perspective, if numerous investigations have been made on the effects of pubertal timing within a particular domain, and, if those effects are present within the population, minor variations in the classification of subjects should not consistently obscure the underlying effects. Because few studies have compared different measurement approaches, it is uncertain whether classification differences are, in fact, minor. A systematic investigation of pubertal measurement would be beneficial.

THE PSYCHOSOCIAL SIGNIFICANCE
OF PUBERTAL TIMING

In order to implement the strategy proposed by Brooks-Gunn et al. (1985), it would be desirable not only to have multiple measures of puberty but also to have measured a construct that has been prevalent in the literature on timing effects. Returning to Rutter's (1989) conceptualization of influences of timing, models for the developmental significance of timing of maturation have frequently fallen into the psychological and social influence areas.

Psychological influences of timing have been suggested in the stage termination hypothesis (Peskin & Livson, 1972; Petersen & Taylor, 1980). In this hypothesis, early maturation is disadvantageous because it interrupts the normal course of development. Because early-maturing girls develop earlier than any other girls or boys, they would be most at risk for encountering physical developments for which they are psychologically unprepared (Brooks-Gunn et al., 1985).

In contrast, social influences of timing as exemplified in the deviancy hypothesis (Neugarten, 1979; Petersen & Taylor, 1980) have also been posited. From a deviance approach, both early and late developers would be at risk, because their development is incongruent with the peer group. Because early-maturing girls develop earlier and late-maturing boys develop later than any other adolescents, these adolescents would be most socially deviant (Brooks-Gunn et al., 1985).

Support for either the stage termination or deviancy hypothesis has been mixed. As noted earlier, pubertal timing effects have not been

consistently demonstrated. For boys, when effects have occurred, researchers have generally found early maturation to be advantageous in
several aspects of social and emotional functioning (Duncan, Ritter, Dornbusch, Gross, & Carlsmith, 1985; Mussen & Jones, 1957; Simmons et al.,
1979). The advantages of early development for boys, especially in the
peer environment, have been attributed to the desirability of being taller
and stronger than one's peers, particularly in athletics (Jones, 1965; Susman et al., 1985). Advanced physical maturity has been associated with
popularity, and hence, more opportunities for heterosocial contacts. In
fact, a longitudinal examination into adulthood has found that men who
were early maturers during adolescence continue to be more poised and
confident than their late-maturing peers (Jones, 1965). Presumably, early
advantages led to the development of interpersonal skills that became a
lifelong advantage. Consistent findings for early-maturing boys have been
useful for hypothesis testing. Jones (1965) reported some negative effects
for late-maturing boys but support for the deviancy hypothesis with boys
has not been resounding.

In contrast, early maturation has been associated with several negative
outcomes for girls (Brooks-Gunn, 1988; Brooks-Gunn & Reiter, 1990; Jones
& Mussen, 1958; Stattin & Magnusson, 1990). This could be attributable to
either deviancy or stage termination models. The fact that early maturation
in a sample of Swedish girls was associated with lowered academic
achievement and less prestigious careers is supportive of both the deviancy
and stage termination hypotheses (Stattin & Magnusson, 1990); early girls
followed a different developmental trajectory from other girls.

Whether early maturation is advantageous for boys and disadvantageous for girls and whether differences have also been reported between
on-time and late developers fluctuates with the construct in question. In
order to understand how measurement differences in pubertal timing
might influence research results, it is useful to examine the results on a
single construct across a few of the primary studies of adolescent development. In the present case, we use body image as the construct of interest.

Body Image

Drastic changes in the body at puberty are thought to influence adolescents'
perceptions and feelings about their bodies. Changes in height and weight
are thought to be particularly salient to changes in body image. As
previously noted, increases in height and weight are often positive experiences for boys (Jones, 1965; Susman et al., 1985), but may be negative
experiences for girls, especially increases in weight (Faust, 1983). The
relationship between body image and pubertal timing has been investigated in several studies of adolescent development: Dornbusch and colleagues (Duncan et al., 1985), Brooks-Gunn and colleagues (Brooks-Gunn

& Warren, 1985a; Gargiulo et al., 1987), Simmons and Blyth (1987), Stattin and Magnusson (1990), and Petersen and colleagues (Tobin-Richards et al., 1983). Although each of these projects has examined adolescent development across a variety of domains, only the results for body image are reported here in order to illustrate issues of measurement.

Simmons and Blyth (1987) studied pubertal timing and body image in an urban, White sample of adolescents examined longitudinally in 6th, 7th, 9th and 10th grades. As indicated in Table 2.1, age at menarche was used to assess level of pubertal maturation for girls and estimated age at peak height velocity was used for boys. Analyses with body image use three timing groups, early, on time, and late, where the early and late groups each include 20% of the sample. Body image was assessed by having adolescents rate their satisfaction with their height, weight, overall appearance, figure for girls, and muscle development for boys.

In the National Health Examination Survey (NHES; Duncan et al., 1985), a nationally representative sample of adolescents aged 12 to 17 were studied cross-sectionally. Adolescents rated their pubertal development from photographs of Tanner stages. Scores for overall pubertal development were based on the average of breast and pubic hair development for girls and the average of pubic hair and genital development for boys. The upper and lower 20th percentiles for age and sex were used as the cutoffs for categorizing adolescents as early, on time, or late. (This information is shown in Table 2.1.) Satisfaction with height and weight were used as indicators of body image.

Stattin and Magnusson (1990) investigated pubertal timing and body image in a representative sample of Swedish girls followed from early adolescence into young adulthood. As previously noted, age at menarche was divided into four timing groups in order to differentiate very early development from early development. Body image was assessed through responses made to open-ended questions about whether and how the individual would like to change herself. Of particular salience to body image was the desire to change one's weight and/or physical appearance.

In the Adolescent Study Program, several samples of 5th- to 12th-grade girls were seen, both cross-sectionally and longitudinally (Brooks-Gunn, 1989). Additionally, girls from four different social contexts were assessed; the contexts varied with respect to athletic endeavor—girls either attended competitive private schools, attended national ballet company schools, participated in regional or national figure skating competitions, or participated in regional swimming competitions. Pubertal timing categories were based on Tanner stages or self-reported menarche. Early maturation was defined as menarche prior to 11.5 years of age, late maturation as menarche after 14 years of age. A shortened version of the Body Image Scale from the Self-Image Questionnaire for Young Adolescents (SIQYA) was used (Brooks-Gunn, Rock, & Warren, 1989; Petersen, Schulenberg, Abramowitz, Offer, & Jarcho, 1984).

Finally, in the Adolescent Mental Health Study (AMHS; Petersen, 1984), two successive birth cohorts of adolescents were followed longitudinally in sixth, seventh, and eighth grades with follow-up examinations at 12th grade and in young adulthood. Pubertal timing categories were based on trichotomized age at peak height velocity (Petersen & Crockett, 1985). The Body Image Scale from the SIQYA (Petersen et al., 1984) was used to measure adolescents' feelings about their development and their satisfaction with height, weight, and overall appearance.

Results across these studies are discussed separately for boys and girls because physical changes have been associated with gender-differential, psychosocial outcomes. Beginning with girls, both a stage termination and a deviancy hypothesis would suggest that early girls would have more difficulty adapting to the physical changes of puberty. In the Simmons and Blyth (1987) sample, early developers were less satisfied than other girls with their height, weight, and figures, whereas late developers were the most satisfied. Timing differences disappeared when analyses controlled for height and weight with one notable exception; at 10th grade, timing differences persisted with early-maturing girls experiencing the least satisfaction with their overall appearance. Interestingly, lowered satisfaction with appearance occurred for early-maturing girls after the peak pubertal years. In contrast, no pubertal timing effects on body image were found in the NHES. Even though early maturers reported the desire to be thinner more frequently than other girls, this association exhibited a developmental change; as girls became pubertal, they became less satisfied with their weight (Duncan et al., 1985). Thus, body image was associated with pubertal status rather than timing. Stattin and Magnusson (1990) also reported few effects. Very early maturers were less satisfied with their weight than other girls during early adolescence but this difference did not persist across time and was not associated with general self-evaluations of appearance. In the Adolescent Study Program, early developers had lower body image scores during junior and senior high school (Brooks-Gunn & Warren, 1985a; Gargiulo et al., 1987). Trends were more pronounced for ballet dancers and figure skaters (Brooks-Gunn et al., 1989).

Figure 2.1 shows the association of pubertal timing and body image for girls in the AMHS (Petersen, 1984) across early and midadolescence. As can be seen, early-maturing girls exhibit a marked decline in their body image across adolescence. In this sample, longitudinal analysis was essential to detect the increasing divergence of early girls' self-appraisals from the self-appraisals made by other girls. Across studies, results tended to follow expected patterns although effects were not uniform across samples. When timing effects were found, they were more likely to occur

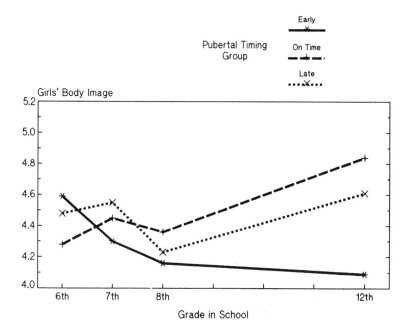

FIG. 2.1. The association between pubertal timing and body image in girls.

after the peak pubertal years rather than during periods of pubertal change.

Again, a deviancy hypothesis suggests that late boys would have more difficulty adapting to the physical changes of puberty, or lack of changes, than would other boys. Because early maturation is often advantageous for boys, neither a deviancy hypothesis nor a stage termination hypothesis would be applicable for this group.

Early-maturing boys in the Simmons and Blyth (1987) sample were more satisfied with their height, weight, and body build than were other boys, but this difference did not persist beyond early adolescence and did not occur for overall appearance. Late-maturing boys were not different in their satisfaction from other boys. In the NHES (Duncan et al., 1985), again, early boys were the most satisfied with their weight. In contrast, for height, late boys were distinguishable from other boys such that late-maturing boys were the least satisfied with their height. (Neither Stattin & Magnusson, 1990, nor The Adolescent Study Program, Brooks-Gunn, 1989, included boys in their studies.)

Figure 2.2 shows the association of pubertal timing and body image for boys in the AMHS (Petersen, 1984) across early and midadolescence. After early adolescence, no pubertal timing effects are found for boys. Across studies, little support is found for the hypothesis that late maturation is

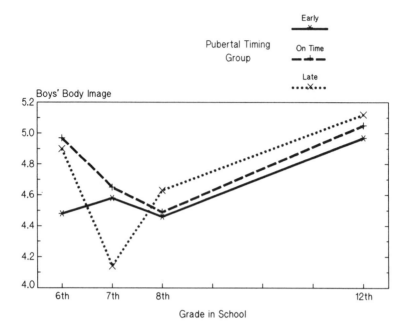

FIG. 2.2. The association between pubertal timing and body image in boys.

negative for boys; indeed, in Fig. 2.2 the later developing boys had the highest body image from 8th to 12th grade. In addition, the positive effects of early maturation in boys, when observed, did not persist into midadolescence. This is in contrast to the previously noted positive effects of early timing for boys in the Growth Studies (Jones, 1965).

Several factors could account for the variability among results: (a) sample differences such as socioeconomic status, (b) design differences such as cross-sectional versus longitudinal methods, and (c) differences in the measurement of pubertal development. Sample differences may be a factor but they would not explain all of the variations in effects. In fact, even though the Simmons and Blyth (1987) sample is predominantly urban with a broad range of socioeconomic backgrounds, the Petersen (1984) sample is suburban and middle to upper middle class, and the Brooks-Gunn (1989) sample is urban and upper-middle class, these studies report similar results for girls. Design characteristics are also important to consider. Notably, the NHES (Duncan et al., 1985) is the only cross-sectional investigation of these five; the rest employ a longitudinal or mixed approach. This difference could account for some of the difference in results that these or other investigations report. For example, in examining Fig. 2.2, it is clear that interpretation of the data would be quite different if only the seventh-grade data were available. Finally, as already noted, differences in the measurement of pubertal development have rarely been considered; hence, the extent of differences attributable to this factor is unknown.

MODELS FOR STUDYING BEHAVIORAL ASSOCIATIONS WITH PUBERTAL TRANSITIONS

Whereas much of the previous discussion has focused on how measurement and method are factors in the study of effects of pubertal development on behavior, in this section, we present several models that either have been or could be used to frame the study of the pubertal transition. As noted, some of the models used to study links between puberty and behavior focus primarily on pubertal processes; however, others examine the relative contribution of pubertal and social events to behavior, and still another set examines interactions between pubertal events and contextual factors. Each set of models is discussed.

Role of Pubertal and Social Events

At least three different models may be explicated to examine how both pubertal and environmental or social events work together in influencing behavior. As our chapter is on pubertal processes, we do not examine models that only consider social events or environmental factors.

Direct and Mediative Effects Models. Direct effects models are perhaps the most frequently tested but often the least likely to demonstrate effects (Brooks-Gunn, Graber, & Paikoff, 1994). Models postulating direct effects of puberty on behavior have usually focused on changes in secondary sexual characteristics or the direct effects of hormones on behavior. We noted in the prior discussion of pubertal status that the effects of pubertal changes vary by social stimulus value. Hormonal studies also need to compare direct and potentially mediated effect models. For example, levels of testosterone are related to sexual activity in boys, independent of secondary sexual development (Udry, Billy, Morris, Groff, & Raj, 1985). However, whether engagement in sexual intercourse increases androgen levels or androgen levels influence sexuality is not known. Additionally, contextual effects, if entered into the equation, might account for more of the variation in sexual activity than hormonal levels. Initiation of sexuality is highly associated with what is normative in one's peer groups (Furstenberg, Moore, & Peterson, 1986), so it is likely that although very early sexual initiations may in part be hormonally influenced, by the time the behavior is normative, social factors may account for sexual initiation (cf. Gargiulo et al., 1987, for a similar argument about dating behavior). Thus, even if hormonal effects are demonstrated, they must be evaluated relative to contextual and interactive effects before assuming a direct relation between hormones and behavior.

Bidirectional Models. Bidirectional models also may be postulated when studying hormonal activation effects. We know the hypothalamic-pituitary-gonadal axis is exquisitely sensitive to environmental conditions. For example, when weight loss is large (as in the case of anorexia nervosa), levels of gonadotropin secretions are suppressed in women, with the most obvious manifestations being amenorrhea and anovulatory cycles (Warren, 1985). In some adolescents with anorexia nervosa or exercise-induced weight loss, a reversion to the prepubertal pattern of low luteinizing hormone (LH) secretion, lowered amplitude secretion, and nocturnal LH spiking occurs. These changes are reversible with weight gain. Also, the genetic program for the timing of puberty may be partially overridden through environmental factors such as nutritional intake, weight, and extensivity of exercise (Brooks-Gunn, 1988; Malina, 1983).

Such bidirectional influences between behavior and/or environment and one's physiological functioning will potentially be demonstrated in pubertal status and potentially pubertal timing, depending on the extent of delay or acceleration induced via hormonal and environmental interactions. For example, recent research has demonstrated effects of family conflict and stress on the timing of pubertal development in girls, indicating that a broader range of contextual factors influence the developing system, in particular the developing reproductive system (Graber, Brooks-Gunn, & Warren, 1995; Moffitt, Caspi, Belsky, & Silva, 1992).

Interaction of Pubertal and Environmental Characteristics. Thus far, the proposed models have been additive. However, Bronfenbrenner (1986) conceptualized development as a function of person and environment, and several behavioral geneticists (Plomin, Loehlin, & DeFries, 1985; Scarr & McCartney, 1983) have proposed three different types of genotype–environment relations to describe development. Research using these frameworks has focused on early childhood, examining temperament or cognitive abilities as the "person characteristics." In early to middle adolescence, another set of personal characteristics may be examined, specifically pubertal processes or their timing. If behavioral correlates of puberty are studied in different environmental contexts, then it is possible to investigate physical characteristic–environment interactions.

First, personal characteristics may influence behavior differently depending on the environment in which they occur, given differences in expectations or demands that characterize a particular social milieu. An example is the findings of Simmons and her colleagues that being an early-maturing sixth-grade girl influences body image as a function of attendance at an elementary or middle school (Simmons & Blyth, 1987; Simmons et al., 1983). Second, an individual who possesses certain physical characteristics may actively seek or reject a certain social milieu. The work by Magnusson and his colleagues in Sweden is a case in point. Although early-maturing girls were more likely to drink and to be sexually active than later maturers, the effect was due to those early-maturing girls who had older friends, a phenomenon that was more prevalent in the early than later maturers (Magnusson, Stattin, & Allen, 1985). Presumably, early maturers actively sought, or were sought by older adolescents as friends. In Hill's work, one might hypothesize that early-maturing adolescents actively avoid spending time with their parents (Hill, Holmbeck, Marlow, Green, & Lynch, 1985). These data fit nicely the active or evocative genotype–environment effects described by Scarr and McCartney (1983).

Finally, pubertal children may have chosen environmental contexts that become inappropriate as their bodies grow; this is in contradistinction to the first example where contexts are not actively chosen (i.e., grade in which the transition to middle school occurs). In this instance, the match between individual and environment is altered as a function of changes beyond the control of the individual. The most obvious example of mismatches involves activities in which body shape and size are critical, as in athletics or modeling. An example is the influence of context and maturation on dating in seventh- to ninth-grade girls, some of whom were enrolled in national ballet company schools and some of whom were not. Dating was not related to menarcheal status in nondancers, but was related in dancers such that premenarcheal dancers dated less than postmenarcheal dancers (Gargiulo et al., 1987). It was hypothesized that in a context such as dancing, which negatively values a particular characteristic, such as pubertal growth, individuals who develop that characteristic may be more affected than similar individuals who are in a context that does not negatively value a particular characteristic.

CONCLUSION

Throughout the course of this discussion, several important issues in the measurement of pubertal development and timing have arisen. Research strategies that incorporate consideration of measurement and especially the multiplicity of processes involved in pubertal development, with models that delineate how and to what extent context interacts with individual development, hold promise for a better understanding of not only the unique biological and contextual interactions occurring at puberty, but also for developmental processes across the life span.

ACKNOWLEDGMENTS

This chapter was adapted from portions of Julia Graber's dissertation, The Pennsylvania State University, 1991. Research presented from the Adolescent Mental Health Study and support for this endeavor was provided by Grant No. MH 30252/38142 to Anne C. Petersen.

REFERENCES

Baydar, N., Brooks-Gunn, J., & Warren, M. P. (1992). *Changes of depressive symptoms in adolescent girls over four years: The effects of pubertal maturation and life events.* Manuscript submitted for publication.

Bean, J. A., Leeper, J. D., Wallace, R. B., Sherman, B. M., & Jagger, H. J. (1979). Variations in the reporting of menstrual histories. *American Journal of Epidemiology, 109,* 181–185.

Berzonsky, M. D., & Lombardo, J. P. (1983). Pubertal timing and identity crisis: A preliminary investigation. *Journal of Early Adolescence, 3,* 239–246.

Bock, R. D., Wainer, H., Petersen, A. C., Thissen, D., Murray, J. S., & Roche, A. (1973). A parameterization of human growth curves. *Human Biology, 45,* 63–80.

Brackbill, Y., & Nevill, D. (1981). Parental expectations of achievement as affected by children's height. *Merrill-Palmer Quarterly, 27,* 429–441.

Bronfenbrenner, U. (1986). Ecology of the family as a context for human development: Research perspectives. *Developmental Psychology, 22,* 723–742.

Brooks-Gunn, J. (1984). The psychological significance of different pubertal events to young girls. *Journal of Early Adolescence, 4,* 315–327.

Brooks-Gunn, J. (1988). Antecedents and consequences of variations in girls' maturational timing. *Journal of Adolescent Health Care, 9,* 365–373.

Brooks-Gunn, J. (1989). Adolescents as daughters and as mothers: A developmental perspective. In I. E. Sigel & G. H. Brody (Eds.), *Methods of family research: Biographies of research projects, Vol. I: Normal families* (pp. 213–248). Hillsdale, NJ: Lawrence Erlbaum Associates.

Brooks-Gunn, J. (1990). Overcoming barriers to adolescent research on pubertal and reproductive development. *Journal of Youth and Adolescence, 19*(5), 425–440.

Brooks-Gunn, J., Graber, J. A., & Paikoff, R. L. (1994). Studying links between hormones and negative affect: Models and measures. *Journal of Research on Adolescence, 4*(4), 469–486.

Brooks-Gunn, J., & Petersen, A. C. (1983). Introduction. In J. Brooks-Gunn & A. C. Petersen (Eds.), *Girls at puberty: Biological and psychosocial perspectives* (pp. xix–xxix). New York: Plenum.

Brooks-Gunn, J., Petersen, A. C., & Eichorn, D. (1985). The study of maturational timing effects in adolescence. *Journal of Youth and Adolescence, 14,* 149–161.

Brooks-Gunn, J., & Reiter, E. O. (1990). The role of pubertal processes in the early adolescent transition. In S. Feldman & G. Elliott (Eds.), *At the threshold: The developing adolescent* (pp. 16–53). Cambridge, MA: Harvard University Press.

Brooks-Gunn, J., Rock, D., & Warren, M. P. (1989). Comparability of constructs across the adolescent years. *Developmental Psychology, 25*(1), 51–60.

Brooks-Gunn, J., & Warren, M. P. (1985a). The effects of delayed menarche in different contexts: Dance and nondance students. *Journal of Youth and Adolescence, 14*(4), 285–300.

Brooks-Gunn, J., & Warren, M. P. (1985b). Measuring physical status and timing in early adolescence: A developmental perspective. *Journal of Youth and Adolescence, 14,* 163–189.

Brooks-Gunn, J., & Warren, M. P. (1988). The psychological significance of secondary sexual characteristics in 9- to 11-year-old girls. *Child Development, 59,* 161–169.

Brooks-Gunn, J., & Warren, M. P. (1989). Biological contributions to affective expression in young adolescent girls. *Child Development, 60,* 372–385.

Brooks-Gunn, J., Warren, M. P., Rosso, J., & Gargiulo, J. (1987). Validity of self-report measures of girls' pubertal status. *Child Development, 58,* 829–841.

Buchanan, C. M., Eccles, J. S., & Becker, J. B. (1992). Are adolescents the victims of raging hormones: Evidence for activational effects of hormones on moods and behavior at adolescence. *Psychological Bulletin, 111,* 62–107.

Caspi, A., & Moffitt, T. E. (1991). Individual differences are accentuated during periods of social change: The sample case of girls at puberty. *Journal of Personality and Social Psychology, 61,* 157–168.

Coleman, J. C. (1978). Current contradictions in adolescent theory. *Journal of Youth and Adolescence, 7,* 1–11.

Crockett, L. J., & Petersen, A. C. (1987). Pubertal status and psychosocial development: Findings from the Early Adolescence Study. In R. M. Lerner & T. T. Foch (Eds.), *Biological-psychosocial interactions in early adolescence: A life-span perspective* (pp. 173–188). Hillsdale, NJ: Lawrence Erlbaum Associates.

Dorn, L. D., Susman, E. J., Nottelmann, E. D., Inoff-Germain, G., & Chrousos, G. P. (1990). Perceptions of puberty: Adolescent, parent, and health care personnel. *Developmental Psychology, 26,* 322–329.

Dubas, J. S., Graber, J. A., & Petersen, A. C. (1991). A longitudinal investigation of adolescents' changing perceptions of pubertal timing. *Developmental Psychology, 27,* 580–586.

Duke, P. M., Carlsmith, J. M., Jennings, D., Martin, J. A., Dornbusch, S. M., Gross, R. T., & Siegel-Gorelick, B. (1982). Educational correlates of early and late sexual maturation in adolescence. *Journal of Pediatrics, 100,* 633–637.

Duke, P. M., Litt, I. F., & Gross, R. T. (1980). Adolescents' self-assessment of sexual maturation. *Pediatrics, 66,* 918–920.

Duncan, P. D., Ritter, P. L., Dornbusch, S. M., Gross, R. T., & Carlsmith, J. M. (1985). The effects of pubertal timing on body image, school behavior, and deviance. *Journal of Youth and Adolescence, 14,* 227–235.

Eichorn, D. H. (1975). Asynchronizations in adolescent development. In S. E. Dragastin & G. H. Elder, Jr. (Eds.), *Adolescence in the life cycle: Psychological change and social context* (pp. 81–96). Washington, DC: Hemisphere.

Faust, M. S. (1983). Alternative constructions of adolescent growth. In J. Brooks-Gunn & A. C. Petersen (Eds.), *Girls at puberty: Biological and psychosocial perspectives* (pp. 105–126). New York: Plenum.

Feldman, S., & Elliott, G. (Eds.). (1990). *At the threshold: The developing adolescent.* Cambridge, MA: Harvard University Press.

Frisch, R. E. (1974). A method of prediction of age of menarche from height and weight at ages 9 through 13 years. *Pediatrics, 53,* 384–390.

Frisch, R. E. (1983). Fatness, puberty, and fertility: The effects of nutrition and physical training on menarche and ovulation. In J. Brooks-Gunn & A. C. Petersen (Eds.), *Girls at puberty: Biological and psychosocial perspectives* (pp. 29–50). New York: Plenum.

Frisch, R. E., & Revelle, R. (1971). The height and weight of girls and boys at the time of initiation of adolescent growth spurt in height and weight and the relationship to menarche. *Human Biology, 43,* 140–159.

Frisch, R. E., Revelle, R., & Cook, S. (1973). Components of weight at menarche and the initiation of the adolescent growth spurt in girls: Estimated total water, lean body weight and fat. *Human Biology, 45,* 469–483.

Furstenberg, F. F., Moore, K. A., & Peterson, J. L. (1986). Sex education and sexual experience among adolescents. *American Journal of Public Health, 75,* 1331–1332.

Gaddis, A., & Brooks-Gunn, J. (1985). The male experience of pubertal change. *Journal of Youth and Adolescence, 14,* 61–69.

Gargiulo, J., Attie, I., Brooks-Gunn, J., & Warren, M. P. (1987). Girls' dating behavior as a function of social context and maturation. *Developmental Psychology, 23,* 730–737.

Graber, J. A. (1991). *The measurement of timing of pubertal development: Use of a triple-logistic growth function.* Unpublished doctoral dissertation, The Pennsylvania State University, University Park, PA.

Graber, J. A., Brooks-Gunn, J., & Warren, M. P. (1995). The antecedents of menarcheal age: Heredity, family environment, and stressful life events. *Child Development, 66,* 346–359.

Hamburg, B. A. (1974). Early adolescence: A specific and stressful stage of the life cycle. In G. V. Coelho, D. A. Hamburg, & J. E. Adams (Eds.), *Coping and adaptation* (pp. 101–124). New York: Basic Books.

Hill, J. P., Holmbeck, G. N., Marlow, L., Green, T. M., & Lynch, M. E. (1985). Menarcheal status and parent–child relations in families of seventh-grade girls. *Journal of Youth and Adolescence, 14,* 301–316.

Jones, M. C. (1965). Psychological correlates of somatic development. *Child Development, 56,* 899–911.

Jones, M. C., & Bayley, N. (1950). Physical maturing among boys as related to behavior. *Journal of Educational Psychology, 41,* 129–148.

Jones, M. C., & Mussen, P. H. (1958). Self-conceptions, motivations, and interpersonal attitudes of early- and late-maturing girls. *Child Development, 29,* 491–501.

Kagan, J. (1980). Perspectives on continuity. In O. G. Brim, Jr., & J. Kagan (Eds.), *Constancy and change in human development* (pp. 26–74). Cambridge, MA: Harvard University Press.

Lewin, K. (1939). Field theory and experiment in social psychology: Concepts and methods. *American Journal of Sociology, 44,* 868–896.

Magnusson, D., Stattin, H., & Allen, V. L. (1985). Biological maturation and social development: A longitudinal study of some adjustment processes from mid-adolescence to adulthood. *Journal of Youth and Adolescence, 14,* 267–283.

Malina, R. M. (1983). Menarche in athletes: A synthesis and hypothesis. *Annals of Human Biology, 10,* 1–24.

Marshall, W. A., & Tanner, J. M. (1969). Variations in the pattern of pubertal changes in girls. *Archives of Disease in Childhood, 44,* 291–303.

Marshall, W. A., & Tanner, J. M. (1970). Variations in the pattern of pubertal changes in boys. *Archives of Disease in Childhood, 45,* 13–23.

Marshall, W. A., & Tanner, J. M. (1974). Puberty. In J. D. Douvis & J. Drobeing (Eds.), *Scientific foundation of pediatrics* (pp. 124–151). London: Heinemann.

Mellits, B. D., & Cheek, D. G. (1970). Assessment of body water and fatness from infancy to childhood. *Monographs of the Society for Research in Child Development, 35* (7, Serial No. 140), 12–26.

Meyer-Bahlburg, H. F. L., Ehrhardt, A. A., & Feldman, J. F. (1986). Long-term implications of the prenatal endocrine milieu for sex-dimorphic behavior. In L. Erlenmeyer-Kimling & N. E. Miller (Eds.), *Life-span research on the prediction of psychopathology* (pp. 17–30). Hillsdale, NJ: Lawrence Erlbaum Associates.

Moffitt, T. E., Caspi, A., Belsky, J., & Silva, P. A. (1992). Childhood experience and the onset of menarche: A test of a sociobiological model. *Child Development, 63,* 47–58.

Morris, N. M., & Udry, J. R. (1980). Validation of a self-administered instrument to assess stage of adolescent development. *Journal of Youth and Adolescence, 9,* 271–280.

Mussen, P. H., & Jones, M. C. (1957). Self-conceptions, motivations, and interpersonal attitudes of late- and early-maturing boys. *Child Development, 28,* 243–256.

Nesselroade, J. R. (1984). Concepts of intraindividual variability and change: Impressions of Cattell's influence on lifespan developmental psychology. *Multivariate Behavioral Research, 19,* 269–286.

Neugarten, B. L. (1979). Time, age and life cycle. *American Journal of Psychiatry, 136,* 887–894.

Newcombe, N., & Bandura, M. M. (1983). Effect of age of puberty on spatial ability in girls: A question of mechanism. *Developmental Psychology, 19*, 215–224.

Newcombe, N., & Dubas, J. S. (1987). Individual differences in cognitive ability: Are they related to timing of puberty? In R. M. Lerner & T. T. Foch (Eds.), *Biological-psychosocial interactions in early adolescence: A life-span perspective* (pp. 249–302). Hillsdale, NJ: Lawrence Erlbaum Associates.

Overton, W. F., & Reese, H. W. (1981). Conceptual prerequisites for an understanding of stability-change and continuity-discontinuity. *International Journal of Behavioral Development, 4*, 99–123.

Paikoff, R., & Brooks-Gunn, J. (1991). Do parent–child relationships change during puberty? *Psychological Bulletin, 110*(1), 47–66.

Peskin, H., & Livson, N. (1972). Pre- and postpubertal personality and adult psychological functioning. *Seminars in Psychiatry, 4*, 343–353.

Petersen, A. C. (1973). *The relationship of androgenicity in males and females to spatial ability and fluent production.* Unpublished doctoral dissertation, University of Chicago.

Petersen, A. C. (1983). Menarche: Meaning of measures and measuring meaning. In S. Golub (Ed.), *Menarche: The transition from girl to woman* (pp. 63–76). Lexington, MA: Lexington.

Petersen, A. C. (1984). The Early Adolescence Study: An overview. *Journal of Early Adolescence, 4*, 103–106.

Petersen, A. C. (1987). The nature of biological-psychosocial interactions: The sample case of early adolescence. In R. M. Lerner & T. T. Foch (Eds.), *Biological-psychosocial interactions in early adolescence: A life-span perspective* (pp. 35–61). Hillsdale, NJ: Lawrence Erlbaum Associates.

Petersen, A. C., & Crockett, L. J. (1985). Pubertal timing and grade effects on adjustment. *Journal of Youth and Adolescence, 14*, 191–206.

Petersen, A. C., Crockett, L. J., Richards, M., & Boxer, A. (1988). A self-report measure of pubertal status: Reliability, validity, and initial norms. *Journal of Youth and Adolescence, 17*, 117–133.

Petersen, A. C., Graber, J. A., & Sullivan, P. (1990, March). *Pubertal timing and problem behavior: Variations in effects.* Paper presented in a symposium at the biennial meeting of the Society for Research on Adolescence, Atlanta, GA.

Petersen, A. C., Kennedy, R., & Sullivan, P. (1991). Coping with adolescence. In M. E. Colten & S. Gore (Eds.), *Adolescent stress: Causes and consequences* (pp. 93–110). New York: Aldine de Gruyter.

Petersen, A. C., Sarigiani, P. A., & Kennedy, R. E. (1991). Adolescent depression: Why more girls? *Journal of Youth and Adolescence, 20*, 247–271.

Petersen, A. C., Schulenberg, J. E., Abramowitz, R. H., Offer, D., & Jarcho, H. D. (1984). A Self-Image Questionnaire for Young Adolescents (SIQYA): Reliability and validity studies. *Journal of Youth and Adolescence, 13*, 93–111.

Petersen, A. C., & Taylor, B. (1980). The biological approach to adolescence: Biological change and psychological adaptation. In J. Adelson (Ed.), *Handbook of adolescent psychology* (pp. 117–155). New York: Wiley.

Plomin, R., Loehlin, J. C., & DeFries, J. C. (1985). Genetic and environmental components of "environmental" influences. *Developmental Psychology, 21*, 391–402.

Reiter, E. O., & Grumbach, M. M. (1982). Neuroendocrine control mechanisms and the onset of puberty. *Annual Review of Physiology, 44*, 595–613.

Richardson, R. A., Galambos, N. L., Schulenberg, J. E., & Petersen, A. C. (1984). Young adolescents' perceptions of the family environment. *Journal of Early Adolescence, 4*, 131–154.

Rierdan, J., & Koff, E. (1985). Timing of menarche and initial menstrual experience. *Journal of Youth and Adolescence, 14*, 237–244.

Roche, A. F., Wainer, H., & Thissen, D. (1975). The RWT method for the prediction of adult stature. *Pediatrics, 46*, 1016–1033.

Rutter, M. (1989). Pathways from childhood to adult life. *Journal of Child Psychology and Psychiatry and Applied Disciplines, 30*, 23–51.

Sanders, B., & Soares, M. P. (1986). Sexual maturation and spatial ability in college students. *Developmental Psychology, 22*, 199–203.

Scarr, S., & McCartney, K. (1983). How people make their own environments: A theory of genotype–environment effects. *Child Development, 54*, 424–435.

Seyler, L. E., & Reichlin, S. (1974). Episodic secretion of luteinizing hormone-releasing factor (LRF) in the human. *Journal of Clinical Endocrinology and Metabolism, 39*, 471–498.

Silbereisen, R. K., Petersen, A. C., Albrecht, H. T., & Kracke, B. (1989). Maturational timing and the development of problem behavior: Longitudinal studies in adolescence. *Journal of Early Adolescence, 9*, 247–268.

Simmons, R. G., & Blyth, D. A. (1987). *Moving into adolescence: The impact of pubertal change and school context.* New York: Aldine.

Simmons, R. G., Blyth, D. A., & McKinney, K. L. (1983). The social and psychological effects of puberty on white females. In J. Brooks-Gunn & A. C. Petersen (Eds.), *Girls at puberty: Biological and psychosocial perspectives* (pp. 229–272). New York: Plenum.

Simmons, R. G., Blyth, D. A., Van Cleave, E. F., & Bush, D. M. (1979). Entry into early adolescence: The impact of school structure, puberty, and early dating on self-esteem. *American Sociological Review, 44*, 948–967.

Stattin, H., & Magnusson, D. (1990). *Paths through life: Vol. 2. Pubertal maturation in female development.* Hillsdale, NJ: Lawrence Erlbaum Associates.

Steinberg, L. (1987). Impact of puberty on family relations: Effects of pubertal status and pubertal timing. *Developmental Psychology, 23*, 451–460.

Stolz, H. R., & Stolz, L. M. (1951). *Somatic development of adolescent boys.* New York: Macmillan.

Susman, E. J., Inoff-Germain, G. E., Nottelmann, E. D., Cutler, G. B., Jr., Loriaux, D. L., & Chrousos, G. P. (1987). Hormones, emotional dispositions, and aggressive attributes in early adolescents. *Child Development, 58*, 1114–1134.

Susman, E. J., Nottelmann, E. D., Inoff, G. E., Dorn, L. D., Cutler, G. B., Jr., Loriaux, D. L., & Chrousos, G. P. (1985). The relation of relative hormone levels and physical development and social-emotional behavior in young adolescents. *Journal of Youth and Adolescence, 14*, 245–264.

Tanner, J. M. (1970). Physical growth. In P. H. Mussen (Ed.), *Carmichael's manual of child psychology* (pp. 77–155). New York: Wiley.

Tanner, J. M., Whitehouse, R. H., & Takaishi, M. (1966). Standards from birth to maturity for height, weight, height velocity, and weight velocity: British Children, 1965. *Archives of Disease in Childhood, 41*, 613–635.

Thissen, D., & Bock, R. D. (1990). Linear and nonlinear curve fitting. In A. von Eye (Ed.), *Statistical methods in longitudinal research: Vol. II. Time series and categorical longitudinal data* (pp. 289–318). New York: Academic Press.

Tobin-Richards, M. H., Boxer, A. M., & Petersen, A. C. (1983). The psychological significance of pubertal change: Sex differences in perceptions of self during early adolescence. In J. Brooks-Gunn & A. C. Petersen (Eds.), *Girls at puberty: Biological and psychosocial perspectives* (pp. 127–154). New York: Plenum.

Udry, J. R., Billy, J. O. G., Morris, N. M., Groff, T. R., & Raj, M. H. (1985). Serum androgenic hormones motivate sexual behavior in adolescent boys. *Fertility and Sterility, 43*, 90–94.

Waber, D. P. (1976). Sex differences in cognition: A function of maturation rate? *Science, 192*, 572–574.

Waber, D. P. (1977). Sex differences in mental abilities, hemispheric lateralization, and rate of physical growth at adolescence. *Developmental Psychology, 13*, 29–38.

Warren, M. P. (1983). Physical and biological aspects of puberty. In J. Brooks-Gunn & A. C. Petersen (Eds.), *Girls at puberty: Biological and psychosocial perspectives* (pp. 3–28). New York: Plenum.

Warren, M. P. (1985). When weight loss accompanies amenorrhea. *Contemporary Obstetrics and Gynecology, 28,* 588–597.

West, C. D., Mahajan, D. K., Chavre, V. J., Nabors, C. J., & Tyler, F. H. (1973). Simultaneous measurement of multiple plasma steroids by radio-immunoassay demonstrating episodic secretion. *Journal of Clinical Endocrinology and Metabolism, 36,* 1230–1236.

II

*TRANSITIONS IN THE
PEER SYSTEM AND
SOCIAL BEHAVIORS*

3

*Transitions in Friendship
and Friends' Influence*

Thomas J. Berndt
Purdue University

As children move into adolescence, they spend increasing amounts of time interacting with peers (Csikszentmihalyi & Larson, 1984; Larson & Richards, 1991). The features of the closest peer relationships, those between best friends, also change during the transition to adolescence. The most important change is the emergence of intimate friendships characterized by open disclosure of personal information (Berndt & Savin-Williams, 1993). Moreover, the changes in friendships are accompanied by increases in friends' influence.

TWO PERSPECTIVES ON FRIENDS' INFLUENCE

The effects of friends' influence on adolescents' attitudes and behavior are controversial. One perspective that is accepted by many researchers, parents, and other adults can be illustrated—or, perhaps, caricatured—by the following fictional vignette.

> Joe, who is 15 years old and in the ninth grade, got a phone call one evening from his friend Mike. Mike said that he and a few other friends were having a party at his house because his parents were out for the evening. He invited Joe to come over and Joe agreed. When Joe arrived, he found Mike and the others were smoking marijuana and acting kind of crazy. Mike asked Joe if he wanted to join them. When Joe hesitated, Mike said, "What's the matter? Are you afraid of it?" The other kids said, "Come on, get high, it's really wild." So Joe sat down and started smoking with them.

A radically different perspective on friends' influence is accepted by other psychologists. The alternative perspective is also accepted by many parents and other adults who, on occasion, take the first perspective. To illustrate this alternative, a fictional vignette is again useful.

> Mary, who is 14 years old and in the eighth grade, came home one Friday evening after cheerleading practice to find her parents in a big argument. Her parents quarrel often, but this time they were really shouting and her mother started throwing things. Mary left the house as soon as she could and went to the home of her best friend Jane. Jane invited Mary up to her room. Then they talked for hours about how hard it is to live with parents sometimes, and how to handle it when parents are fighting. When Mary went home, she felt much better and thought of some things she could do to help her parents get along with each other.

The most obvious difference between the two vignettes is the apparent effect of friends' influence. In the first vignette, friends' teasing and encouragement led to Joe's initiation into the use of illicit drugs. In the second vignette, a conversation with a close friend helped Mary to understand and cope with the problems in her family. Stated more generally, the two vignettes contrast negative and positive outcomes of friends' influence.

The vignettes also differ in other respects. The influence in the first vignette is exerted by a group of friends. Their mode of influence is often described as "social pressure" or "peer pressure." The influence in the second vignette comes from a single close friend. What happened in that vignette might not even be described as influence, because Jane probably did not set out to persuade Mary to do anything in particular. The outcome of their conversation might instead be described as a consequence of their relationship with each other.

The negative perspective on friends' influence illustrated by the first vignette has a long history. Bronfenbrenner (1970) argued that peer groups in the United States contribute to antisocial behavior by adolescents. During the 1980s, many researchers argued that friends' influence was a major factor in adolescents' alcohol use, use of other illegal drugs, and delinquent behavior (Barrett, Simpson, & Lehman, 1988; Brook, Whiteman, & Gordon, 1983; Steinberg & Silverberg, 1986).

The positive perspective on friends' influence also has a long history. Piaget (1932/1965) argued that interactions with peers are critical for the development of a mature morality based on justice and benevolence. Sullivan (1953) proposed that intimate friendships among adolescents are critical for high self-esteem and accurate understanding of other people. More recently, several researchers have suggested that supportive friendships enhance adolescents' self-esteem and help them cope more effectively with stressful life events (see Berndt & Savin-Williams, 1993; Hartup, 1993).

Despite the sharp contrast between the two perspectives, few writers have discussed it directly. The primary goal of this chapter is to evaluate both the similarities and the differences between the two perspectives. The chapter is organized in terms of a prototypical question about peer influence: Who influences whom, about what, and how? This question captures most elements in the journalist's formula for a story. The same elements are emphasized in theories of attitude formation and change (McGuire, 1985). Organizing the chapter around the question makes sense because friends' influence can be viewed as one instance of attitude formation and change (Sherif & Sherif, 1964).

The focus of the first section is on *who*, the friends who influence adolescents. Theories and empirical research suggest that adolescents are most influenced by the few peers they consider best friends. The focus of the second section is on *whom*, the characteristics of adolescents that affect their susceptibility to friends' influence. One of these characteristics is age. Friends' influence seems not to increase steadily during adolescence, but to peak in middle adolescence.

The third section deals with *what*. In this chapter, *what* refers to the outcomes of friends' influence—an increase in socially desirable behaviors and psychological adjustment or the reverse. Currently available data suggest that both outcomes are possible, but for most adolescents, positive outcomes outweigh negative ones.

The fourth section of the chapter deals with *how*, the processes by which friends influence adolescents. Social pressure is not the primary process by which friends influence adolescents' behavior. Instead, friends rely on rewards, reasoning, and many other influence techniques. In addition, the effects of a friendship depend partly on its features, as the example of Mary and Jane implies.

In each section of the chapter, the two perspectives on friendship are examined separately, but connections between them are discussed explicitly. All sections also include evidence on the changes in friendships and friends' influence between childhood and adolescence. When available, evidence on changes during the adolescent years is included. In other words, the chapter provides information about the transitions to adolescence and through adolescence.

WHO ARE THE PEERS WHO INFLUENCE ADOLESCENTS?

Judging which peers have the most influence on adolescents is not a simple task. Researchers have used different methods to estimate friends' influence. Researchers have also proposed different definitions of friendship itself.

Sources of Peer Pressure

Writers who emphasize the negative outcomes of peer pressure rarely state precisely who these peers are. Some researchers have used peer pressure to refer to the influence of the entire peer group in a particular setting. For example, Bronfenbrenner (1970) described the pressure on Soviet adolescents that comes from the group of other adolescents who live at the same boarding school. However, the effects of an entire peer group are weak.

Several decades ago, Coleman (1961) suggested that adolescents' educational aspirations and academic achievement are strongly influenced by the social class of the peers in their high school. Later research has shown, however, that Coleman exaggerated the effects of the social class of the students in a school (see Cohen, 1983). Adolescents' aspirations and achievement are much more strongly affected by the aspirations and achievement of their close friends. Friends' influence actually accounts for the effects Coleman attributed to the social class of the entire peer group.

More recently, researchers examined the influence of adolescents' best friends on their cigarette smoking, drinking, and use of other drugs (Morgan & Grube, 1991). The researchers compared the influence of an adolescent's best friend with that of other friends and peers in general. On all behaviors, the best friends' influence seemed greater than that of other friends, and other friends' influence seemed greater than that of peers in general. These findings confirm Cohen's (1983) conclusion that "most peer influence exists in practice as the mutual influence of close friends" (p. 166).

Conclusions about the influence of close friends must be stated cautiously, because the techniques most often used to assess friends' influence are problematic. Researchers have usually asked adolescents to report on their own behavior and their friends' behavior. Then the researchers have compared adolescents' self-reports to their reports on friends. For example, variations in adolescents' cigarette smoking have been related to variations in their reports on their friends' smoking (Chassin, Presson, Montello, Sherman, & McGrew, 1986). The strength of these relations is used to estimate the strength of friends' influence.

One problem with this assessment technique is that adolescents are usually asked to report on their friends in general, rather than on specific friends. However, most adolescents have several best friends (Hartup, 1993) and these friends are likely to differ in their attitudes and behaviors. Adolescents must average across these differences when they answer general questions about their friends' behavior. Whether adolescents can accurately do this kind of mental averaging is doubtful.

To avoid this problem, a few researchers have obtained specific information about each of several friends. One team of researchers asked adolescents to report how often each of four best friends got into trouble at school (Gillmore, Hawkins, Day, & Catalano, 1992). Other researchers independently assessed the school involvement, alcohol use, and cigarette smoking of up to three friends named by the adolescents in their samples (Berndt & Keefe, 1994; Graham, Marks, & Hansen, 1991). Obtaining separate assessments of multiple friends' behavior takes more time than using general questions about all friends, but the extra time should assure more valid measures.

Another issue concerned the definition of a best friendship. Most researchers consider two adolescents as best friends if one of them names the other as a best friend. However, some writers have argued that a nomination by one adolescent does not identify a friendship unless the peer who is nominated reciprocates the nomination (Bukowski & Hoza, 1989). Data on the degree of reciprocity in adolescents' friendship nominations are limited, but reciprocity may be lower than 50% (Kandel, 1978b) and is rarely higher than 60% (Epstein, 1986).

A peer named as a best friend might be expected to have more influence when the friendship nomination is reciprocated than when it is not. This expectation has not been strongly supported in research (Epstein, 1986). Hirsch and Renders (1986) reported an intriguing case study that illustrates why nonreciprocal friendships sometimes have a powerful influence.

The researchers interviewed an adolescent girl several times over 2 years. When first interviewed, the girl said that she was trying to make friends with a more popular group of older students by acting and dressing as they did. Eventually, her strategy worked and she became a member of that group. This girl was probably more calculating in making friends than most adolescents, but she is not unique. Many adolescents are influenced by more popular peers they would like to have as friends. Most adolescents are influenced by peers they view as close friends but who do not feel exactly the same way about them.

Sources of Social Support

Writers who emphasize the benefits of supportive friendships often focus on the closest friendship of an adolescent. A few researchers have adopted Sullivan's (1953) terminology and referred to this friend as a "chum." Then the researchers have compared the personality and social behavior of adolescents who do and do not have a chum (e.g., Townsend, McCracken, & Wilton, 1988).

The benefits of a supportive relationship with one other person have also been emphasized in research with adults (Cohen & Wills, 1985;

Sarason, Sarason, & Pierce, 1990). The type of support that seems most important is that provided by a confidant. Adults who have a confidant with whom they can share their thoughts and feelings cope more successfully with stressful events than do adults without such an intimate relationship. Some researchers have also suggested that having several friends may not help a person cope with stress better than having one intimate relationship (see Cohen & Wills, 1985).

Nevertheless, hypotheses about the value of a single best friendship represent a misreading of Sullivan (1953) and a narrow view of supportive relationships. Although Sullivan (1953) wrote about the relationship between two chums, he commented that these pairs of chums often became part of larger groups. That is, he recognized that adolescents often have more than one friend with whom they form close relationships. Moreover, limited data suggest that adolescents' social adjustment is better when they have more than one close and supportive friendship (Renshaw & Brown, 1993).

Finally, the quality of adolescents' relationships with nonfriends can also affect their adjustment. Rejection by peers, in particular, is associated with loneliness, anxiety, and low self-esteem even among adolescents who have good friendships (Coie, 1990; Renshaw & Brown, 1993). Peer rejection and poor friendships also overlap. Adolescents who are disliked by most of their peers often have friendships low in support (Parker & Asher, 1993). Yet little is known about why these two aspects of peer relationships are related, or how they differ in the effects on adolescents' development (but see Hanna, 1994).

Transitions in Sources of Friends' Influence

The two perspectives on friends' influence lead to the same conclusion about major sources of influence. The peers who have the greatest influence on adolescents and those whose support is most important to adolescents are their closest friends. Between childhood and adolescence, the frequency of interactions with close friends increases (Larson & Richards, 1991). Increased interaction frequency is one sign of an increase in the cohesiveness of friendship groups. Another sign is that cliques are better defined and become more important as children move into adolescence (Crockett, Losoff, & Petersen, 1984).

In addition, adolescents differentiate more sharply among their peer relationships than children do. School-age children often name several best friends and think of all these friends as equally close. Adolescents may name as many best friends as children do, but adolescents begin to regard only one or two friends as especially close. Other friends are perceived as more peripheral (Berndt & Hoyle, 1985).

Changes in friendship groups may affect the sources of friends' influence. For example, adolescents who make sharp distinctions among their friends may be more influenced by their closest friends and less influenced by other friends than children are (cf. Downs, 1987). Changes in the cohesiveness of friendship groups also may contribute to changes in the magnitude of friends' influence. This hypothesis has been examined in a few studies, but those studies focused less on the sources of friends' influence than on the adolescents who were its targets. Therefore, they are discussed in the next section.

WHO IS MOST INFLUENCED BY FRIENDS?

Adolescents differ in how much they are influenced by friends. Understanding these differences might allow adults to predict which adolescents would be most negatively influenced by friends' suggestions, and which would be most positively affected by supportive friendships.

Individual Differences in Susceptibility to Friends' Influence

At least three types of variables affect adolescents' susceptibility to friends' influence. The first involves adolescents' position in their friendship group. Adolescents who are lower in the pecking order, or whose status is more marginal, are more susceptible to influence than are adolescents higher in status (Hartup, 1983; Sherif & Sherif, 1964). Lower status adolescents usually comply with more dominant friends to retain their membership in the group.

Leaders of friendship groups are not impervious to influence attempts. Effective leaders are influential partly because they anticipate what the other members of the group would like to do (Sherif & Sherif, 1964). Thus when they seem to be leading, they are merely taking the group in the direction that most people wanted to go. But when leaders feel strongly about a decision, they are more able to sway the rest of the group than are low-status members.

A second variable that affects adolescents' susceptibility to friends' influence is the quality of their relationships with other people. Friends have more influence on adolescents whose other relationships are less satisfying. The most significant of these relationships are with parents. Adolescents are less influenced by friends when they have close and involving relationships with parents (Steinberg & Silverberg, 1986). Adolescents are more influenced by friends when their parents are neglecting or rejecting (Dishion, 1990).

The third type of variable that affects susceptibility to friends' influence is the importance that adolescents attach to activities that conflict with friendships. Adolescents are less influenced by friends when they invest more energy in other activities such as academic work or athletics. Bloom (1985) described adolescents who spent hours each day practicing for swimming tournaments. The primary goal of these adolescents was to excel in swimming, not to have close friends. Therefore, these adolescents placed a lower priority on doing activities with friends than on keeping to their schedule of training.

However, Bloom studied only exceptional athletes. For most adolescents, having intimate and supportive friendships is extremely important. Thus, most adolescents attach great value to their interactions with friends; they also have the potential to be highly influenced by friends.

Individual Differences in the Effects of Supportive Friendships

Adolescents can only receive the benefits of supportive friendships if their actual friendships are high in support. Thus individual differences in the effects of supportive friendships can be partially understood by finding which adolescents are most and least likely to have supportive friendships.

During adolescence, girls typically have more intimate and supportive friendships than boys (Hartup, 1993). Girls are more willing than boys to engage in intimate self-disclosure by talking about their worries and fears with best friends. Girls' friendships are also higher in emotional closeness than boys' friendships. This difference can be partly attributed to the gender difference in intimate self-disclosure (Bukowski, Hoza, & Boivin, 1994; Camarena, Sarigiani, & Petersen, 1990). Explorations of the reasons for the gender differences have not gone far beyond sheer speculation, but both genetic differences and socialization practices may play a role (Berndt, 1994).

The quality of adolescents' friendships is also related to their psychological adjustment (Berndt & Savin-Williams, 1993). Adolescents with supportive friendships tend to have high self-esteem, not to be lonely or depressed, to have positive reputations with peers, and to be high in academic achievement. These data have often been taken as evidence that supportive friendships enhance psychological adjustment. However, the data come mainly from correlational studies, so other interpretations are possible.

Several studies have shown that adolescents' psychological adjustment affects their involvement in supportive friendships (Berndt, 1989; DuBois, Felner, Brand, Adan, & Evans, 1992). The reasons are easy to understand. Adolescents who are low in self-esteem, lonely, and depressed are not especially enjoyable companions. Adolescents who have a reputation for aggressive or weird behavior or who do poorly at school are not likely to be preferred as friends. These adolescents often have difficulty forming supportive friendships. Therefore, they receive fewer of the benefits of supportive friendships than do better adjusted adolescents.

Adolescents with equally supportive friendships may still differ in how much they are affected by them. The adolescent girls in one recent study not only described their friendships as more supportive than boys did; they also were more affected by the quality of their friendships than boys were (Slavin & Rainer, 1990). Variations in friends' support were significantly related to the changes over time in girls' symptoms of depression. These variations were not related to the changes over time in boys' symptoms. In other studies, however, the apparent effects of supportive friendships were comparable for boys and for girls (e.g., Berndt & Keefe, 1994).

As the examples imply, researchers have only begun to explore the variations in the effects of friends' support. These variations might depend on the same variables that affect adolescents' susceptibility to friends' influence. This connection between the two perspectives on friends' influence should be examined directly in future research.

Transitions in the Strength of Friends' Influence

Because adolescents interact with friends more often than children do, they might be expected to be more susceptible to friends' influence than children are. Because adolescents' friendships are more supportive than those of children, friends' support might be expected to have a greater effect on adolescents. These expectations have been only partially confirmed by research.

One method of assessing friends' influence is to ask adolescents how they would respond to situations in which their friends urged them to do something. Responses to these situations show modest variations with age (Berndt, 1979; Brown, Clasen, & Eicher, 1986; Steinberg & Silverberg, 1986). Between middle childhood and middle adolescence (or about age 15), willingness to comply with friends' suggestions increases. Between middle and late adolescence, willingness to comply decreases. Researchers using other assessment techniques have reached similar conclusions about the age changes in friends' influence (Urberg, Cheng, & Shyu, 1991).

Age changes in the effects of supportive friendships have rarely been examined. Buhrmester (1990) found that the intimacy of adolescents' friendships was more strongly correlated with their socioemotional adjustment in middle adolescence (14–16 years) than in early adolescence (10–13 years). These findings suggest that either the effects of supportive friendships on adjustment or the effects of adjustment on friendship formation increase with age. Unfortunately, the correlational design of this study makes it impossible to distinguish between these two possibilities.

Nevertheless, there are good reasons to assume that susceptibility to friends' influence and responsiveness to friends' support both peak in middle adolescence. Before that age, ties to parents are strong, and parental influence is often greater than friends' influence. After that age, true autonomy shown by independence from both parents and friends first becomes evident (Berndt, 1979; Steinberg & Silverberg, 1986).

As adolescents move toward adulthood, they spend less time with same-gender friends and more time with romantic partners. Boyfriends or girlfriends then begin to fill some roles that earlier were filled by same-gender best friends (Savin-Williams & Berndt, 1990). Romantic relationships do not supplant same-gender friendships, however. Data from two studies suggest that same-gender best friendships and romantic relationships are perceived by late adolescents and young adults as equally intimate and supportive (Furman & Buhrmester, 1992; Sharabany, Gershoni, & Hofman, 1981). Near the end of high school, both same-gender friends and girlfriends influence the career aspirations of adolescent males (Otto, 1977).

Nevertheless, the age changes are significant. At the transition to adulthood, most individuals attach importance to suggestions from their best friends and from girlfriends or boyfriends. Romantic partners vie with friends for late adolescents' attention; they also claim the right to advise late adolescents on how to behave and direct their lives (Horowitz & Schwartz, 1974). Consequently, the influence of same-gender friends lessens somewhat.

WHAT ARE THE OUTCOMES
OF FRIENDS' INTERACTIONS?

Bronfenbrenner's (1970) hypotheses about peer influence were widely cited because he argued forcefully that this influence leads to antisocial behavior by U.S. adolescents. His writings were especially provocative because he asserted that officials in the Soviet Union (which many Americans viewed as a hostile and inferior nation) had structured peer influence to enhance socially desirable behavior during adolescence. By contrast, adults in the United States paid too little attention to peer influence, and so put our country in danger. Bronfenbrenner (1970) wrote that unless adolescents increased their involvement with adults and reduced their involvement with peers, "we can anticipate increased alienation, indifference, antagonism, and violence on the part of the younger generation in all segments of our society—middle-class children as well as the disadvantaged" (p. 121).

Sullivan's (1953) hypotheses about intimate friendships were provocative because he argued that these friendships could correct earlier deviations from normal development. He suggested, in particular, that intimate friendships could reduce adolescents' egocentrism, increase their maturity, and enhance their understanding of their responsibilities to other people. Sullivan mentioned commonsense ideas about possible negative effects of close friendships, but he concluded these ideas were mistaken or that negative effects were atypical. He instead suggested that negative effects occur mainly when an adolescent never finds a chum, or the chumship never becomes intense.

Recent research has shown that the hypotheses of both Bronfenbrenner and Sullivan are incomplete and, therefore, misleading. Even in the United States, peer influence does not invariably, or even typically, have the negative consequences suggested by Bronfenbrenner. Close friendships can have positive effects, as Sullivan believed, but they can also have negative effects on adolescents' attitudes and behavior. In short, the outcomes of friends' influence differ importantly from those assumed by Bronfenbrenner and by Sullivan.

Outcomes of Friends' Influence

During adolescence, friends significantly influence a wide range of attitudes and behavior. Friends influence adolescents' educational aspirations and their use of alcohol, marijuana, and other illicit drugs (Fisher & Bauman, 1988; Kandel, 1978a). Friends influence adolescents' attitudes toward school and their grades on school work (Epstein, 1983). Friends influence many attitudes and behaviors that affect the physical and mental health of adolescents, including their nutrition, sexual behavior, physical activity, and tendencies toward risky driving (Millstein, Petersen, & Nightingale, 1993).

However, previous research has led to serious misinterpretations of both the strength and the outcomes of friends' influence. As mentioned earlier, researchers have often estimated friends' influence from the similarity between adolescents' self-reports and their reports on friends. The problem that adolescents might have in calculating the average behavior of multiple friends was discussed previously. Yet even if adolescents report on several friends separately, this method is likely to overestimate the strength of friends' influence.

Adolescents do not have full knowledge of their friends' behavior. When their knowledge is limited, they usually assume that their friends' behavior matches their own. In other words, adolescents project their own characteristics onto friends. Moreover, the degree of projection can be substantial. Adolescents in one study assumed that their friends' attitudes toward sexuality were similar to their own, when their actual similarity was low (Wilcox & Udry, 1986). Adolescents also perceive themselves as more similar to friends than they actually are in cigarette smoking and alcohol use (Bauman & Fisher, 1986; Graham et al., 1991), in use of illegal drugs (Iannotti & Bush, 1992), in behavior at school (Berndt & Keefe, 1994), and in academic achievement (Ide, Parkerson, Haertel, & Walberg, 1981).

Even when projection is not a problem, and adolescents accurately report their friends' behavior, their similarity to friends cannot be used to judge the friends' influence on them. Adolescents often select friends to whom they are already similar. To assess friends' influence, researchers need to see whether the similarity between friends increases over time. In one longitudinal study, Kandel (1978a) found that friends' similarity in drug use and educational aspirations was due as much to friendship selection as to friends' influence. In another longitudinal study (Fisher & Bauman, 1988), friends' similarity in cigarette smoking and alcohol use was due far more to selection than to influence. These and other studies establish that friends' influence on adolescents is much weaker than most writers have assumed.

The outcomes of friends' influence have also been misinterpreted because of a subtle bias in research reporting. Most researchers describe their results as if adolescents became delinquent, began using drugs, or started to drive recklessly because of their friends' influence. However, when friends' influence is estimated from increases in friends' similarity over time, judging whether this influence has led to desirable or undesirable behavior is impossible.

Recall the fictional vignette involving Joe and Mike. Although Joe supposedly became more similar to Mike because he started smoking marijuana, the influence could have gone in the opposite direction. That is, Joe might have convinced Mike to stop smoking marijuana. Both outcomes reflect an increase in friends' similarity because of their influence on each other. The two outcomes cannot be distinguished when only the magnitude of the increase in friends' similarity is reported. Yet those are the only data provided in recent studies. Despite this crucial ambiguity in research, many intervention programs for adolescents rest on the assumption that friends' influence usually leads to undesirable behaviors (see Millstein et al., 1993).

For most adolescents, this assumption is probably false. For example, adolescents in one study reported that their friends put little or no pressure on them to smoke cigarettes (Urberg, Shyu, & Liang, 1990). Adolescents who did not smoke cigarettes believed that their friends would disapprove if they started smoking. Adolescents who were already smokers believed that their friends tolerated their smoking but did not approve of it. The adolescents in another study (Keefe, 1994) said that their friends pressured them not to use alcohol rather than pressuring them to drink. Adolescents in a third study (Brown et al., 1986) perceived their friends as putting more pressure on them to study hard and get good grades than to shirk their academic work.

Viewed more broadly, any generalization about the outcomes of friends' influence must be questioned. Friends' influence is a mutual process: Adolescents influence their friends as the friends influence them (Downs, 1987). The usual outcome of this process is a compromise that increases friends' similarity without changing their average position. Adolescents who initially felt more positively than their friends about an issue become less positive; those who initially felt less positively than their friends become more positive. This model of friends' influence accounts for most findings in recent studies (Berndt, Laychak, & Park, 1990).

Under some conditions, friends' discussions lead not only to an increase in their similarity, but also to changes in their average position (Isenberg, 1986). However, even in these cases, discussions with friends do not invariably have negative outcomes. For example, these discussions can increase adolescents' willingness to endorse prosocial behavior as the proper response to a social dilemma (Berndt, McCartney, Caparulo, & Moore, 1983–1984). Unfortunately, the conditions responsible for these positive outcomes are not well understood.

Outcomes of Supportive Friendships

Sullivan (1953) emphasized the impact of intimate friendships on many aspects of social and personality development, including self-esteem, understanding of social reality, and the healthy development of heterosexual relationships. Other researchers have speculated about the effects of supportive friendships on adolescents' social development (Youniss, 1980), psychological adjustment (Goodyer, Wright, & Altham, 1989), and social skills (Hartup, 1993).

Direct tests of these hypotheses have yielded inconsistent results. In several longitudinal studies, measures of supportive friendships did not predict the changes over time in adolescents' self-esteem, depression, drug use, and academic achievement (DuBois et al., 1992; Vernberg, 1990; Windle, 1992). By contrast, in a study mentioned earlier, friends' support predicted changes in the depressive symptoms of girls but not boys (Slavin & Rainer, 1990). In other studies, having supportive friendships was related to improvements in boys' and girls' attitudes toward classmates (Berndt, 1989) and their positive involvement in schoolwork (Berndt & Keefe, 1994).

These mixed findings suggest that friends' support has weaker and more specific effects than some theorists have assumed. The findings, and other research with adults, suggest that friends' support may be most valuable for retaining a positive self-concept (Sarason, Pierce, Bannerman, & Sarason, 1993) and a positive view of other people.

Finally, Sullivan (1953) and later writers ignored the possibility that friendships might have negative effects on adolescents' adjustment. Sullivan discussed the negative effects of competitiveness and rivalry with peers during middle childhood, but he implied that negative interactions do not occur in intimate friendships during adolescence. Both casual observations and systematic research suggest the opposite. Friends have conflicts with each other (Hartup, 1992), and they often engage in rivalry or competition (Berndt & Savin-Williams, 1993; Youniss, 1980). Moreover, friendships that involve more negative interactions are not necessarily lacking in positive features. During adolescence, measures of the negative and the positive features of best friendships are largely independent (Berndt & Keefe, 1994; Berndt & Perry, 1986).

In studies of adults, the negative qualities of social relationships sometimes have stronger effects on psychological adjustment than do their positive qualities (Schuster, Kessler, & Aseltine, 1990). That may also be true in adolescents. In one study (Berndt & Keefe, 1994), seventh and eighth graders reported on their best friendships in both the fall and the spring of a school year. At both times students also reported their involvement in schoolwork and their disruptive behavior in classrooms. Adolescents whose friendships in the fall had more negative features—who reported more conflict and rivalry with friends—also reported more disruptive behavior in the spring than in the fall. The change over time suggests that conflicts and rivalry with friends contributed to an antagonistic style of social interaction. Negative interactions with friends apparently spilled over to affect adolescents' behavior toward other peers and teachers. In a balanced portrait of the effects of friendships, such negative effects of close friendships need to be acknowledged and examined further.

Transitions in the Outcomes of Friendship and Friends' Influence

Writers who emphasize the negative effects of friends' influence always focus on adolescents, not on younger children. This emphasis may seem sensible, but it involves an empirical question: Are the outcomes of friends' influence actually more negative during adolescence than during childhood?

The best answer to this question comes from research in which children and adolescents responded to hypothetical dilemmas. Bronfenbrenner

(1970) created brief dilemmas in which friends supposedly encouraged adolescents to engage in antisocial behaviors like cheating on a test. When asked how they would respond, children rarely say they will do what friends suggested. Conformity to friends increases during middle childhood, peaks in middle adolescence, and then decreases (Berndt, 1979; Brown et al., 1986; Steinberg & Silverberg, 1986)

These data do not prove that friends' influence is especially negative during middle adolescence, because the same age trends have been found for friends' influence on neutral and prosocial behaviors (Berndt, 1979). In other words, middle adolescents are more responsive to all influence attempts by friends, not merely to negative influence.

In addition, adolescents' responses to the antisocial situations are strongly related to their evaluations of those behaviors. Adolescents who evaluate the behaviors more negatively are less likely to say that they will conform to friends who suggest them (Berndt, 1979). Adolescents also evaluate the behaviors less negatively than younger children. The age changes in apparent conformity to friends can thus be attributed partly to age changes in standards for behavior.

The age change in standards is not simply a methodological artifact. As individuals' standards for behavior change between childhood and adolescence, so do the standards of the individuals' friends. Children who are fairly accepting of antisocial behavior are likely to have friends who encourage them to reject it. Adolescents who are equally accepting of antisocial behavior are more likely to find friends who agree with them. The net result of the change in individuals' standards, therefore, is that friends are less likely to have a positive influence on adolescents than on children.

Other data suggests that even in adolescence, friends' influence typically is more positive than negative. Adolescents report more pressure to engage in undesirable behaviors such as drinking, smoking, and sexual activity at 18 years of age than at 12 (Brown et al., 1986). However, these behaviors are legal or normative for adults, so the age change could reflect attempts to model adult behavior rather than a rise in negative peer influence.

In contrast to the literature on friends' influence, few writers suggest any age changes in the outcomes of supportive friendships. As noted earlier, researchers have emphasized the impact of supportive friendships on adolescents more than on children because they assume adolescents have more supportive friendships (Berndt, 1989; Youniss, 1980). Yet after granting this point, most researchers implicitly or explicitly assume that support from friends is as valuable for children and adults as for adolescents (but see Buhrmester, 1990). Conversely, most researchers assume that conflicts with friends have as negative effects on children and adults as they do on adolescents.

Could these assumptions be wrong? Is there any age period, for example, in which some types of conflicts with friends contribute to social maturity and the development of social skills? Is there any age period in which some types of support from friends reduce social adjustment or psychological well-being? Although a few writers have speculated that the answers to these questions may be "yes" (see Berndt, 1989; Hartup, 1992), relevant data are limited.

Another possibility is that the effects of supportive friendships and of negative interactions with friends change in their magnitude. These changes could alter the balance between positive and negative effects of friendship. Suppose, for example, that conflicts with friends are less intense, and more quickly forgotten, during childhood than during adolescence. Then friends' conflicts might have little effect on children's psychological adjustment, so the net effect of friendship might be more positive during childhood than during adolescence. The data needed to test this hypothesis are unavailable, but it should be kept in mind when questions about the effects of friendship are considered.

HOW DO FRIENDS INFLUENCE ADOLESCENTS?

Questions about *how* refer to the processes that explain an effect. Unfortunately, few writers have tried to specify the processes by which interactions with friends affect adolescents' behavior and development, and still fewer have attempted to measure these processes directly. Processes have been largely ignored in research on both friends' influence and supportive friendship. Yet in each area, data valuable for drawing conclusions about processes are available.

Peer Pressure and the Multiple Processes of Friends' Influence

Few writers who express concern about the negative effects of peer pressure state directly when or how this pressure is applied. Ideas about peer pressure can be greatly enriched by linking them to social-psychological theories of interpersonal influence. To illustrate this point, French and Raven's (1959) classic analysis of social power can be applied to the question of friends' influence.

French and Raven identified five types of power that can give one person influence over another. The first is *coercive power*. People have coercive power when they can punish others for noncompliance with a suggestion or command. Writers who focus on peer pressure seem to assume that coercive power is the primary basis for friends' influence on adolescents. This assumption is also accepted by researchers who have devised intervention to promote adolescent health. For example, training in the social and cognitive skills necessary to resist peer pressure is part of the Life Skills Training program for smoking prevention (Botvin & Tortu, 1988). The skills needed to resist influences to use drugs are part of the Midwestern Prevention Project (Pentz et al., 1989).

By contrast, observations in natural settings have shown that coercive power is rarely employed in adolescents' friendship groups. In Sherif and Sherif's (1964) long-term observations of adolescents' groups, coercion was common only when all members of the group needed to join in a fight. In those circumstances, coercive power was necessary because some group members feared for their safety and so wanted to avoid the fight. However, if part of the group was absent, the rest were more likely to lose the fight and suffer personal injury. Only in such cases, when the safety and reputation of the entire group were at stake, did group members apply coercive power to get compliance.

Coercion is uncommon in adolescents' friendship groups because it can often be resisted. Membership in friendship groups is entirely voluntary, so an adolescent can easily escape from pressure in one group by leaving that group and joining another. Adolescents' freedom to withdraw from a friendship group partly explains why friends usually rely on forms of power other than coercion.

If coercive pressure is rarely used in friendship groups, are researchers interested in health promotion making an error when they try to train adolescents to resist peer pressure? Some evaluations of successful health promotion programs suggest that they are (Cook, Anson, & Walchli, 1993). Although the Life Skills Training program has been effective in reducing cigarette smoking by adolescents, improvements in adolescents' skills in resisting peer influence seem not to be the cause. Similarly, the Midwestern Prevention Project has been effective in reducing adolescents' drug use, but changes in adolescents' resistance skills seem not to be significant mediators of these effects. Taken together, these evaluations suggest that "resistance skills have not been demonstrated to play the crucial mediating role commonly ascribed to them in theories about preventing drug abuse" (Cook et al., 1993, p. 364). The most likely reason is that coercive pressure from peers is not a major factor in adolescent drug abuse.

French and Raven (1959) defined a second type of power that is crucial to friends' influence during adolescence. *Reward power* refers to friends' control over resources that adolescents value. In friendship groups, the most important rewards are companionship and support. Adolescents enjoy opportunities to go places with friends; they rely on friends for help when they are in need. Friends' ability to dispense or withdraw these rewards gives them power to influence adolescents' behavior.

Reward power is transformed into persuasive force when friends encourage an adolescent to engage in a specific behavior. As noted earlier, most adolescents say that their friends encourage them to study hard in school (Brown et al., 1986), and that friends encourage them not to start smoking or drinking (Keefe, 1994; Urberg et al., 1990). However, the effects of friends' encouragement have been assessed directly in very few studies. In one study (Graham et al., 1991), seventh graders were asked how often their friends or other peers invited them to drink alcohol. Few of the seventh graders said they received such invitations, but those few were especially likely to show an increase in alcohol use a few months later. These findings confirm that friends' encouragement can alter adolescents' behavior. This evidence from a naturalistic study is bolstered by that from many laboratory studies of peer reinforcement (Hartup, 1983).

Friends have a third type of social power, called *referent power*, when adolescents admire them and want to be like them. Adolescents often try to become friends with other adolescents they perceive as popular, skilled in athletics, or outstanding in another way (Epstein, 1983; Sherif & Sherif, 1964). After these friendships are formed, adolescents continue to use the friends as referent others. That is, adolescents take the friends' behavior as a guide for their behavior. In Bandura's (1977) social learning theory, this phenomenon would be described as observational learning from friends.

The idea of referent power is especially intriguing because it contrasts so sharply with hypotheses about peer pressure. When friends have referent power, adolescents accept their suggestions without any need for coercion. Adolescents are influenced even when their friends make no suggestions, and put no pressure of any kind on them.

Referent power may be the most significant source of friends' influence in adolescence. This type of power encompasses not only modeling by friends, but also cases in which adolescents perceive their friends as engaging in certain behaviors, even when those perceptions are inaccurate. Such misperceptions affect adolescents' cigarette smoking and alcohol use (Graham et al., 1991; Prentice & Miller, 1993), their use of other drugs (Iannotti & Bush, 1992), and their sexual behavior (Gibson & Kempf, 1990). Moreover, interventions to prevent smoking and drug use in adolescence are effective partly because they reduce adolescents' misperceptions of their friends' attitudes toward drugs and actual drug use (Cook et al., 1993).

French and Raven's (1959) fourth type of power is *expert power*, the power of a person with special knowledge of some subject to influence other people. This type of power may seem irrelevant to friends' influence because friends view one another as equals (Youniss, 1980). However, two friends may view each other as equal overall, yet still assume that each has special expertise in certain areas (see Sherif & Sherif, 1964; Tesser, Campbell, & Smith, 1984). One friend may be better at playing basketball, for example, whereas the other is better at arranging a party. When a decision concerns one friend's area of expertise, that friend's ideas may be especially influential.

Even if adolescents deny that their friends are experts on a topic, they can acknowledge that the friends might have good ideas. That is, adolescents will be persuaded by friends if the friends offer convincing arguments. Interpreted this way, expert power becomes a form of informational influence (Isenberg, 1986). Like adults, adolescents are often influenced by the information exchanged during a discussion. Reasons and arguments stated by friends can change adolescents' ideas about moral dilemmas, cognitive problems, and school-related decisions (Berndt et al., 1990; Berndt et al., 1983–1984; Nelson & Aboud, 1985). Because adolescents get much of their information about health issues from friends (Millstein et al., 1993), friends' reasoning during discussions is likely to affect health-related behaviors, too.

The last type of social power described by French and Raven (1959) is *legitimate power*. Legitimate power exists in formally established, hierarchically organized social institutions. In such institutions, individuals who occupy positions higher in the hierarchy have a recognized right to control the behavior of individuals lower in the hierarchy. Adolescents' friendship groups do not have these characteristics. Therefore, legitimate power is the only one of French and Raven's types of social power that does not apply to friends' influence during adolescence.

The preceding examples suggest the value of French and Raven's typology for explaining friends' influence in adolescence, but additional research is needed to clarify its limits. Most needed are direct observations of friends' interactions in natural or laboratory settings. These observations could show how often and why friends use specific processes of influence on one another.

Features of Supportive Friendships

Questions about how supportive friendships affect adolescents can be partly answered by describing the support that friends give each other (Berndt, 1989; Cohen & Wills, 1985). Theorists have identified four types of support that overlap with the features of close friendships (Berndt, 1989; Parker & Asher, 1993).

First, friends provide each other with *informational support*, or advice and guidance in solving personal problems. This type of support is often provided during intimate conversations. When friends have an intimate relationship, they freely share their most personal thoughts and feelings with each other. They also work together on tasks that give them a deep understanding of each other. Intimacy enhances friends' support because it makes people feel comfortable talking about personal problems with friends. During problem-focused conversations, adolescents obtain useful advice, as Mary did in the earlier vignette.

Second, friends provide each other with *instrumental support,* or help one another with various tasks. The corresponding feature of friendship is prosocial behavior. Many proverbs and sayings emphasize friends' obligations to act prosocially toward each other. This feature of friendship differs from the first because prosocial behavior refers to help with practical problems (e.g., how to do a homework assignment) rather than personal problems.

Third, friends provide each other with *companionship support,* or do many activities together. Having companions is inherently supportive because it gives people a sense of belonging to a social unit. Also, many activities such as going to the movies and playing tennis are less enjoyable or even impossible for a single adolescent. Rook (1987) suggested that companionship may affect psychological health more than do problem-focused supportive interactions. During adolescence, however, friends' interaction frequency is less strongly related to their psychological adjustment than are the positive and negative features of their friendship (Berndt, 1989).

Fourth, friends provide each other with *esteem support,* or try to bolster each other's self-esteem. Adolescents receive esteem support from friends when the friends congratulate them on their achievements or give them other kinds of encouragement. Esteem support can also overlap with other types of support. For example, intimate conversations about personal problems can lead both to useful advice and to heightened self-esteem. In the earlier vignette, Mary's conversation with Jane probably made her feel more in control of her situation. Her sense of control may not only have enhanced her ability to adapt to her family situation, but also have boosted her sense of self-worth.

Defining social support and its related friendship features helps to explain why supportive friendships contribute to adolescents' development. However, the task of definition is different from an analysis of underlying processes. Two hypotheses about these processes have been proposed (see Berndt, 1989). Some theorists have hypothesized that the benefits of supportive friendship derive from deliberate efforts by friends to help each other. For example, Mary might have gone to Jane's house because she wanted Jane to give her advice in handling her parents' fights. In other words, Mary may have wanted to obtain the support that Jane could give her. Jane, in turn, may have tried explicitly to help Mary solve this personal problem.

Other theorists have hypothesized that social support is most often gained simply from participation in close relationships (e.g., Thoits, 1985). Having a close friend gives adolescents a sense of belonging that enhances their sense of well-being. Having a companion for activities makes adolescents' lives more enjoyable. In these and other ways, a close friend enhances adolescents' well-being. Stated more formally, this hypothesis attributes the benefits of supportive friendship simply to having a close and satisfying relationship.

The contrasting hypotheses suggest alternative strategies for research. If the positive effects of friendship are a consequence of deliberate attempts by friends to give and receive support, then research on supportive transitions would be valuable. If these effects are by-products of involvement in good friendships, then research on casual, routine interactions with friends would be more appropriate. Of course, this issue need not be settled before research is done. Some researchers might choose the first strategy of exploration whereas others choose the second. The combination of strategies might lead more quickly to an explanation of how supportive friendships foster adolescents' development.

Transitions in Influence Processes and Friendship Features

One stereotype about adolescents is that they are preoccupied with looking and acting exactly like their peers. If the stereotype was accurate, peers would have greater referent power during adolescence than during childhood. That is, adolescents would be especially likely to take peers, and friends in particular, as models for their behavior.

Little evidence on this hypothesis exists. Although researchers have studied observational learning from peers (see Hartup, 1983), few studies have included multiple age groups. Therefore, age changes in the effects of peer models cannot be documented. Research that examines the truth of the stereotype about adolescents' attention to peer models is greatly needed.

Piaget's (1926/1955) early theory of egocentrism also included hypotheses about age changes in influence processes. Piaget argued that children under about 7 years of age are egocentric, so they cannot engage in a true discussion of ideas. Their discussions involve a clash of assertions, with little reasoning. After 7 years of age, children can understand their peers' ideas, so influence via reasoning is possible.

Piaget's hypothesis implies that the use of reasoning to justify opinions should increase with age, as egocentrism decreases. Evidence consistent with this hypothesis was obtained in one study (Berndt et al., 1983–1984), but more evidence is needed. Additional evidence for the hypothesis would cast greater doubt on the notion that friends' influence on adolescents is due mainly to coercive pressure. This evidence would also suggest that cognitive development affects social influence as much as it affects individual problem solving. That is, the logical reasoning and hypothesis testing that is apparent when adolescents work on cognitive tasks (Keating, 1990) might also be apparent in friends' discussions.

Age changes in friends' support, and related friendship features, can be identified more confidently than age changes in influence processes. Friends' informational support increases between childhood and adolescence as intimacy becomes a central feature of friendships (Berndt & Savin-Williams, 1993). Companionship support also increases, as friends begin to spend more time together (Larson & Richards, 1991). Evidence on the age changes in friends' instrumental support, or prosocial behavior, is not entirely consistent (Berndt, Hawkins, & Hoyle, 1986; Berndt & Perry, 1986). Little direct evidence on friends' esteem support is available (but see Berndt & Perry, 1986). When all types of support are taken together, a dramatic increase in the degree to which friendships are supportive relationships is apparent (Furman & Buhrmester, 1992).

As friendships become more supportive, ideas about the role of friendships might also change. More than children, adolescents might deliberately set out to provide emotional support to friends. Between childhood and adolescence, both planning of one's activities and understanding of other people increase greatly (Keating, 1990). Adolescents should, therefore, plan their interactions with friends and understand a friend's needs for support better than children do. Consequently, intentionally supportive interactions may occur more often during adolescence than during childhood. To test this hypothesis, researchers might interview children and adolescents about their interactions with friends, and see if they report explicit attempts to offer support to friends.

CONCLUSIONS

Adults often hold contradictory beliefs about the influence of friends during adolescence. On the one hand, adults worry that adolescents will be negatively influenced by their friends. In particular, adults believe that friends' pressure may lead to delinquent behavior, drug use, early sexual intercourse, risky driving, or other kinds of undesirable behavior. On the other hand, adults encourage the formation of supportive friendships between adolescents. Adults believe that these friendships contribute to adolescents' self-esteem and psychological adjustment.

In the scientific literature, a comparable division exists. Some scholars emphasize the negative effects of conformity to peer pressure; others emphasize the positive effects of supportive friendships. The division has persisted in part because writers who emphasize the negative effects of friends' influence ignore theories of the positive effects of friends' support and vice versa.

Both views of friends' influence are partly correct but both are oversimplified. Friends' influence can contribute to undesirable behaviors by adolescents, but it can also contribute to desirable behaviors like putting effort into school work. Moreover, coercive pressure is not the primary means by which friends influence each other. Adolescents often adopt friends' suggestions because they value the rewards of membership in a friendship group. Adolescents also listen to friends' reasons for their opinions, and accept opinions that are supported by convincing reasons. Perhaps most important, adolescents admire their best friends and respect their opinions. Consequently, adolescents often behave the way they perceive their friends as behaving. Unfortunately, adolescents often perceive their friends as engaging in socially undesirable behaviors (e.g., using drugs) more often than the friends actually do.

Supportive friendships have positive effects on adolescents, but these effects probably are more limited than previous hypotheses have suggested. One plausible hypothesis is that supportive friendships most strongly affect adolescents' self-concepts and their sense of well-being. However, even supportive friendships have negative features that contribute to a negative style of social interaction. Unfortunately, little is known about the processes by which the features of adolescents' friendships affect their psychological adjustment.

Friendships change during the transitions to adolescence and through adolescence to adulthood. Susceptibility to friends' influence seems to peak in middle adolescence. Friends' support may also have stronger effects after the transition to adolescence, as intimacy becomes a central feature of friendship. Evidence for these conclusions is limited, however, and the age changes are modest in size.

The transition to adolescence may be accompanied by changes in the outcomes of friends' influence. Changes between childhood and adolescence in individuals' standards for behavior may shift friends' influence in a more negative direction. Yet for most adolescents, the outcomes of friends' influence seem more positive than negative. Changes in thinking and reasoning may also increase the degree to which friends' influence depends on a rational discussion of arguments.

Finally, the transition to adolescence may be accompanied by changes in the effects of supportive friendships. The emergence of intimate friendships and increases in friends' interaction frequency change the types of support that friends provide. Adolescents may also be more aware than children of the value of friends' support, and so try more consciously to provide support to friends. Research on these hypotheses would be valuable in refining interventions to enhance the positive effects of friendships on adolescents' behavior and development.

ACKNOWLEDGMENTS

Some research reported in this chapter was supported by grants from the Spencer Foundation, the National Science Foundation, and the National Institute of Mental Health.

REFERENCES

Bandura, A. (1977). *Social learning theory*. Englewood Cliffs, NJ: Prentice-Hall.

Barrett, M. E., Simpson, D. D., & Lehman, W. E. (1988). Behavioral changes of adolescents in drug abuse intervention programs. *Journal of Clinical Psychology, 44*, 461–473.

Bauman, K. E., & Fisher, L. A. (1986). On the measurement of friend behavior in research on friend influence and selection: Findings from longitudinal studies of adolescent smoking and drinking. *Journal of Youth and Adolescence, 15*, 345–353.

Berndt, T. J. (1979). Developmental changes in conformity to peers and parents. *Developmental Psychology, 15*, 608–616.

Berndt, T. J. (1989). Obtaining support from friends during childhood and adolescence. In D. Belle (Ed.), *Children's social networks and social supports* (pp. 308–331). New York: Wiley.

Berndt, T. J. (1994). Intimacy and competition in the friendships of adolescent boys and girls. In M. R. Stevenson (Ed.), *Gender roles through the life span*. Muncie, IN: Ball State University Press.

Berndt, T. J., Hawkins, J. A., & Hoyle, S. G. (1986). Changes in friendship during a school year: Effects on children's and adolescents' impressions of friendship and sharing with friends. *Child Development, 57*, 1284–1297.

Berndt, T. J., & Hoyle, S. G. (1985). Stability and change in childhood and adolescent friendships. *Developmental Psychology, 21*, 1007–1015.

Berndt, T. J., & Keefe, K. (1995). Friends' influence on adolescents' adjustment to school. *Child Development, 66*, 1312–1329.

Berndt, T. J., Laychak, A. E., & Park, K. (1990). Friends' influence on adolescents' academic achievement motivation: An experimental study. *Journal of Educational Psychology, 82*, 664–670.

Berndt, T. J., McCartney, K. A., Caparulo, B. K., & Moore, A. M. (1983–1984). The effects of group discussions on children's moral decisions. *Social Cognition, 2*, 343–360.

Berndt, T. J., & Perry, T. B. (1986). Children's perceptions of friendships as supportive relationships. *Developmental Psychology, 22*, 640–648.

Berndt, T. J., & Savin-Williams, R. C. (1993). Variations in friendships and peer-group relationships in adolescence. In P. Tolan & B. Cohler (Eds.), *Handbook of clinical research and practice with adolescents* (pp. 203–219). New York: Wiley.

Bloom, B. S. (Ed.). (1985). *Developing talent in young people*. New York: Ballantine Books.

Botvin, G. J., & Tortu, S. (1988). Preventing adolescent substance abuse through life skills training. In R. H. Price, E. L. Cowen, R. P. Lorion, & J. Ramos-McKay (Eds.), *Fourteen ounces of prevention* (pp. 98–110). Washington, DC: American Psychological Association.

Bronfenbrenner, U. (1970). *Two worlds of childhood*. New York: Sage.

Brook, J. S., Whiteman, M., & Gordon, A. S. (1983). Stages of drug use in adolescence: Personality, peer, and family correlates. *Developmental Psychology, 19,* 269–277.

Brown, B. B., Clasen, D. R., & Eicher, S. A. (1986). Perceptions of peer pressure, peer conformity dispositions, and self-reported behavior among adolescents. *Developmental Psychology, 22,* 521–530.

Buhrmester, D. (1990). Intimacy of friendship, interpersonal competence, and adjustment during preadolescence and adolescence. *Child Development, 61,* 1101–1111.

Bukowski, W. M., & Hoza, B. (1989). Popularity and friendship: Issues in theory, measurement, and outcome. In T. J. Berndt & G. W. Ladd (Eds.), *Peer relationships in child development* (pp. 15–45). New York: Wiley.

Bukowski, W. M., Hoza, B., & Boivin, M. (1994). Measuring friendship quality during pre- and early adolescence: The development and psychometric properties of the Friendship Qualities Scale. *Journal of Social and Personal Relationships, 11,* 471–484.

Camarena, P. M., Sarigiani, P. A., & Petersen, A. C. (1990). Gender-specific pathways to intimacy in early adolescence. *Journal of Youth and Adolescence, 19,* 19–32.

Chassin, L., Presson, C. C., Montello, D., Sherman, S. J., & McGrew, J. (1986). Changes in peer and parent influence during adolescence: Longitudinal versus cross-sectional perspectives on smoking initiation. *Developmental Psychology, 22,* 327–334.

Cohen, J. (1983). Commentary: The relationship between friendship selection and peer influence. In J. L. Epstein & N. Karweit (Eds.), *Friends in school* (pp. 163–174). New York: Academic Press.

Cohen, S., & Wills, T. A. (1985). Stress, social support, and the buffering hypothesis. *Psychological Bulletin, 98,* 310–357.

Coie, J. (1990). Toward a theory of peer rejection. In S. R. Asher & J. D. Coie (Eds.), *Peer rejection in childhood* (pp. 365–402). New York: Cambridge University Press.

Coleman, J. S. (1961). *The adolescent society.* New York: The Free Press.

Cook, T. D., Anson, A. R., & Walchli, S. B. (1993). From causal description to causal explanation: Improving three already good evaluations of adolescent health program. In S. G. Millstein, A. C. Petersen, & E. O. Nightingale (Eds.), *Promoting the health of adolescents* (pp. 339–374). New York: Oxford University Press.

Crockett, L., Losoff, M., & Petersen, A. C. (1984). Perceptions of the peer group and friendship in early adolescence. *Journal of Early Adolescence, 4,* 155–181.

Csikszentmihalyi, M., & Larson, R. (1984). *Being adolescent.* New York: Basic Books.

Dishion, T. J. (1990). The family ecology of boys' peer relations in middle childhood. *Child Development, 61,* 874–892.

Downs, W. R. (1987). A panel study of normative structure, adolescent alcohol use and peer alcohol use. *Journal of Studies on Alcohol, 48,* 167–175.

DuBois, D. L., Felner, R. D., Brand, S., Adan, A. M., & Evans, E. G. (1992). A prospective study of life stress, social support, and adaptation in early adolescence. *Child Development, 63,* 542–557.

Epstein, J. L. (1983). The influence of friends on achievement and affective outcomes. In J. L. Epstein & N. Karweit (Eds.), *Friends in school: Patterns of selection and influence in secondary schools* (pp. 177–200). New York: Academic Press.

Epstein, J. L. (1986). Friendship selection: Developmental and environmental influences. In E. C. Mueller & C. R. Cooper (Eds.), *Process and outcome in peer relationships* (pp. 129–160). New York: Academic Press.

Fisher, L. A., & Bauman, K. E. (1988). Influence and selection in the friend–adolescent relationship: Findings from studies of adolescent smoking and drinking. *Journal of Applied Social Psychology, 18,* 289–314.

French, J. R. P., & Raven, B. (1959). The bases of social power. In D. C. Cartwright (Ed.), *Studies in social power* (pp. 150–167). Ann Arbor: University of Michigan.

Furman, W., & Buhrmester, D. (1992). Age and sex differences in perceptions of networks of personal relationships. *Child Development, 63*, 103–115.

Gibson, J. W., & Kempf, J. (1990). Attitudinal predictors of sexual activity in Hispanic adolescent females. *Journal of Adolescent Research, 5*, 414–430.

Gillmore, M. R., Hawkins, J. D., Day, L. E., & Catalano, R. F. (1992). Friendship and deviance: New evidence on an old controversy. *Journal of Early Adolescence, 12*, 80–95.

Goodyer, I. M., Wright, C., & Altham, P. M. (1989). Recent friendships in anxious and depressed school age children. *Psychological Medicine, 19*, 165–174.

Graham, J. W., Marks, G., & Hansen, W. B. (1991). Social influence processes affecting adolescent substance abuse. *Journal of Applied Psychology, 76*, 291–298.

Hanna, N. H. (1994). *Predictors of peer relationships and adaptation to summer camp.* Unpublished doctoral dissertation, Purdue University, West Lafayette, IN.

Hartup, W. W. (1983). Peer relations. In P. H. Mussen (Series Ed.) & E. M. Hetherington (Vol. Ed.), *Handbook of child psychology: Vol. 4. Socialization, personality, and social development* (4th ed., pp. 103–196). New York: Wiley.

Hartup, W. W. (1992). Conflict and friendship relations. In C. U. Shantz & W. W. Hartup (Eds.), *Conflict in child and adolescent development* (pp. 186–215). Cambridge, UK: Cambridge University Press.

Hartup, W. W. (1993). Adolescents and their friends. In B. Laursen (Ed.), *New directions for child development: Close friendships in adolescence* (pp. 3–22). San Francisco: Jossey-Bass.

Hirsch, B. J., & Renders, R. J. (1986). The challenge of adolescent friendships: A study of Lisa and her friends. In S. E. Hobfoll (Ed.), *Stress, social support, and women* (pp. 17–27). Washington, DC: Hemisphere.

Horowitz, R., & Schwartz, G. (1974). Honor, normative ambiguity, and gang violence. *American Sociological Review, 39*, 238–251.

Iannotti, R. J., & Bush, P. J. (1992). Perceived vs. actual friends' use of alcohol, cigarettes, marijuana, and cocaine: Which has the most influence? *Journal of Youth and Adolescence, 21*, 375–389.

Ide, J. K., Parkerson, J., Haertel, G. D., & Walberg, H. J. (1981). Peer group influence on educational outcomes: A quantitative synthesis. *Journal of Educational Psychology, 73*, 472–484.

Isenberg, D. J. (1986). Group polarization: A critical review and meta-analysis. *Journal of Personality and Social Psychology, 50*, 1141–1151.

Kandel, D. B. (1978a). Homophily, selection, and socialization in adolescent friendships. *American Journal of Sociology, 84*, 427–436.

Kandel, D. B. (1978b). Similarity in real-life adolescent friendship pairs. *Journal of Personality and Social Psychology, 36*, 306–312.

Keating, D. P. (1990). Adolescent thinking. In S. S. Felman & G. R. Elliott (Eds.), *At the threshold: The developing adolescent* (pp. 54–89). Cambridge, MA: Harvard University Press.

Keefe, K. (1994). Perceptions of normative social pressure and attitudes toward alcohol use: Changes during adolescence. *Journal of Studies in Alcohol, 55*, 46–54.

Larson, R., & Richards, M. H. (1991). Daily companionship in late childhood and early adolescence: Changing developmental contexts. *Child Development, 62*, 284–300.

McGuire, W. J. (1985). Attitudes and attitude change. In G. Lindzey & E. Aronson (Eds.), *Handbook of social psychology: Vol. II* (3rd ed., pp. 233–346). New York: Random House.

Millstein, S. G., Petersen, A. C., & Nightingale, E. O. (Eds.). (1993). *Promoting the health of adolescents: New directions for the twenty-first century.* New York: Oxford University Press.

Morgan, M., & Grube, J. W. (1991). Closeness and peer group influence. *British Journal of Social Psychology, 30*, 159–169.

Nelson, J., & Aboud, F. E. (1985). The resolution of social conflict between friends. *Child Development, 56*, 1009–1017.

Otto, L. B. (1977). Girlfriends as significant others: Their influence on young men's career aspirations and achievements. *Sociometry, 40,* 287–293.

Parker, J. G., & Asher, S. R. (1993). Friendship and friendship quality in middle childhood: Links with peer group acceptance and feelings of loneliness and social dissatisfaction. *Developmental Psychology, 29,* 611–621.

Pentz, M. A., Dwyer, J. H., MacKinnon, D. P., Flay, B. R., Hansen, W. B., Wang, E. Y. I., & Johnson, C. A. (1989). A multicommunity trial for primary prevention of adolescent drug abuse. *Journal of the American Medical Association, 261,* 3259–3266.

Piaget, J. (1955). *The language and thought of the child.* New York: Harcourt. (Original work published 1926)

Piaget, J. (1965). *The moral judgment of the child.* New York: The Free Press. (Original work published 1932)

Prentice, D. A., & Miller, D. T. (1993). Pluralistic ignorance and alcohol use on campus: Some consequences of misperceiving the social norm. *Journal of Personality and Social Psychology, 64,* 243–256.

Renshaw, P. D., & Brown, P. J. (1993). Loneliness in middle childhood: Concurrent and longitudinal predictors. *Child Development, 64,* 1271–1284.

Rook, K. S. (1987). Social support versus companionship: Effects on life stress, loneliness, and evaluations by others. *Journal of Personality and Social Psychology, 52,* 1132–1147.

Sarason, B. R., Pierce, G. R., Bannerman, A., & Sarason, I. G. (1993). Investigating the antecedents of perceived social support: Parents' views of and behavior toward their children. *Journal of Personality and Social Psychology, 65,* 1071–1085.

Sarason, B. R., Sarason, I. G., & Pierce, G. R. (Eds.). (1990). *Social support: An interactional view.* New York: Wiley.

Savin-Williams, R. C., & Berndt, T. J. (1990). Friendships and peer relations during adolescence. In S. S. S. Feldman & G. Elliott (Eds.), *At the threshold: The developing adolescent* (pp. 277–307). Cambridge, MA: Harvard University Press.

Schuster, T. L., Kessler, R. C., & Aseltine, R. H. (1990). Supportive interactions, negative interactions, and depressive mood. *American Journal of Community Psychology, 18,* 423–438.

Sharabany, R., Gershoni, R., & Hofman, J. E. (1981). Girlfriend, boyfriend: Age and sex differences in intimate friendship. *Developmental Psychology, 17,* 800–808.

Sherif, M., & Sherif, C. (1964). *Reference groups: Exploration into conformity and deviance of adolescents.* New York: Harper & Row.

Slavin, L. A., & Rainer, K. L. (1990). Gender differences in emotional support and depressive symptoms among adolescents: A prospective analysis. *American Journal of Community Psychology, 18,* 407–421.

Steinberg, L., & Silverberg, S. B. (1986). The vicissitudes of autonomy in early adolescence. *Child Development, 57,* 841–851.

Sullivan, H. S. (1953). *The interpersonal theory of psychiatry.* New York: Norton.

Tesser, A., Campbell, J., & Smith, M. (1984). Friendship choice and performance: Self-esteem maintenance in children. *Journal of Personality and Social Psychology, 46,* 561–574.

Thoits, P. A. (1985). Social support and psychological well-being: Theoretical possibilities. In I. G. Sarason & B. R. Sarason (Eds.), *Social support: Theory, research, and applications* (pp. 51–72). Dordrecht, The Netherlands: Martinus Nijhoff.

Townsend, M. A. R., McCracken, H. E., & Wilton, K. M. (1988). Popularity and intimacy as determinants of psychological well-being in adolescent friendships. *Journal of Early Adolescence, 8,* 421–436.

Urberg, K. A., Cheng, C.-H., & Shyu, S.-J. (1991). Grade changes in peer influence on adolescent cigarette smoking: A comparison of two measures. *Addictive Behaviors, 16,* 21–28.

Urberg, K. A., Shyu, S.-J., & Liang, J. (1990). Peer influence in adolescent cigarette smoking. *Addictive Behavior, 15,* 247–255.

Vernberg, E. M. (1990). Psychological adjustment and experiences with peers during early adolescence: Reciprocal, incidental, or unidirectional relationships? *Journal of Abnormal Child Psychology, 18,* 187–198.

Wilcox, S., & Udry, J. R. (1986). Autism and accuracy in adolescent perceptions of friends' sexual attitudes and behavior. *Journal of Applied Social Psychology, 16,* 361–374.

Windle, M. (1992). A longitudinal study of stress buffering for adolescent problem behaviors. *Developmental Psychology, 28,* 522–530.

Youniss, J. (1980). *Parents and peers in social development.* Chicago: University of Chicago Press.

4

Sexual Transitions in Adolescence

Joseph Lee Rodgers
University of Oklahoma

At Sunday lunch several years ago, my then 92-year-old grandmother—who married and raised a family in a different age and time—asked me a question: "Joe, do the boys and girls today who—you know—live together, live like—well, you know—husbands and wives?" I did understand what she was asking, and I told her "Yes, many of them do." I did not tell her that, in fact, many young teenagers in the United States are also doing things together like—well, you know—husbands and wives.

Many adolescents—who are still half children—are remarkably candid and interpersonally revealing. One 14-year-old girl was asked by an interviewer, "Are you sexually active?" "No," she said, "I just lie there." A 15-year-old boy was asked for demographic information about his parents. "How far did your mom and dad go in school?" Without a pause, he responded "I think they went all the way." Rodgers, Billy, and Udry (1982) reported that over a 2-year period, about one sixth of the nonvirgin adolescents in the North Carolina ADSEX survey "regained their virginity": Of the 111 adolescents who said they were nonvirgins in 1978, 21 reported that they were virgins in 1980.

Certainly some of these inconsistent responders were just rowdy adolescents playing games with nosy social science researchers. Just as certainly, some were not. Besides fibs and random responses, these data must reflect a substantial amount of confusion by boys and girls who are anything but well-educated about reproductive and maturational processes. Despite the careful efforts to pilot questions and test instruments, adolescent sexuality data are certainly affected by naiveté, confusion, duplicity, and evasion. How do we ask 12-year-olds what their virginity status is, when the words used to ask such questions are to some of them unknown or traumatic? Clearly, studying adolescent sexuality requires delicacy, sensitivity, and both theoretical and analytic models to handle data problems like these.

Popular literature has characterized adolescent sexual behavior as a national "epidemic." The epidemic metaphor is strained and forced in at least two senses. First, it suggests that teenage sexual activity might be considered a biological disease, an obvious overstatement (although the link between sexual behavior and sexually transmitted disease suggests that sexual activity is a primary part of the causal structure of STD epidemics). Second, the epidemic metaphor suggests that many or most adolescents are very sexually active (or becoming such), which is a belief that is largely incorrect (as shown later in this chapter). However, there is another level of the epidemic metaphor that has proven to be very powerful, and that provides some of the motivation for this chapter. Adolescent sexual behavior is, in several senses, a social epidemic. Like other social epidemics (e.g., cigarette smoking, using a particular brand of detergent, supporting a certain professional football team), a driving force in the spread of adolescent sexual behavior is one-to-one transmission of opinion and information. Further, social processes that drive the development of sexual attitudes and behavior interact in subtle and intricate ways with other social and biological transitions that occur during and around puberty.

This chapter is organized into four sections. I begin with a discussion casting adolescent sexual behavior within a broad framework of adolescent transition behaviors. In the next section, I review a number of theories that have been presented in the literature that can help organize and motivate research on sexual transitions during adolescence, particularly the "transition to nonvirginity." Next I present some previously unpublished empirical data concerning social and environmental characteristics of the most highly studied sexual transition during adolescence, the loss of virginity. Finally, I present and discuss a social contagion theory of adolescent sexual development that has come from my own research program in collaboration with David Rowe at the University of Arizona. This presentation focuses interest on the way potential sexual partners interact with and influence one another, and develops a broader and more complex transitional process than the usual "two-state model" of virgin–nonvirgin status.

SEXUALITY AS AN ADOLESCENT TRANSITION BEHAVIOR

Adolescent sexual behavior is a domain of study perhaps best cast within a broader framework of adolescent transition behaviors. Despite singular and focused cultural fascination—even fixation—with the subject, sexuality is not a single independent domain of behavior. It is one of many behaviors that are suddenly available in the behavioral repertoire of developing adolescents. Some of these behaviors are ones that, by virtue of social or cultural norms, or biological prerequisite, are "age graded" (Udry, 1988).

Transition behaviors are ones in which adolescents participate, the purpose of which—at least in part—is to signal transition from childhood into adulthood. When young teenagers first begin to smoke or drink, it is for reasons other than physiological addiction; some of those reasons will be social in nature. Not all transition behaviors have negative connotations for adolescents. For example, playing in the school band or beginning to focus study on a subject of interest are socially positive transition behaviors. Ensminger (1987) proposed sexuality as one member of the package of transition behaviors, and Rodgers and Rowe (1993) presented a taxonomy of transition behaviors based on societal perception of their propriety.

Conceptualizing developing sexuality as a transition behavior has at least three advantages. First, it supports that sexuality (and particularly sexual intercourse) is not a single act, but rather the gradual development of a whole repertoire of attitudes and behavior. Second, it casts sexual activity in the context of other behaviors, motivating interest in overlap between transition behaviors. Third, if sexual activity signals transition from childhood to adulthood, its seeds must exist within childhood, and its consequences must cross the boundary into adulthood, providing a life-course perspective in which to view behaviors that come into sharp focus with the biological changes that occur during puberty.

THEORIES OF ADOLESCENT SEXUAL TRANSITION

Several careful and systematic reviews of the adolescent sexuality literature have been published (Chilman, 1980; Clayton & Bokemeier, 1980; Hayes, 1987; Miller & Fox, 1987; Miller & Moore, 1990). In this section, I focus on theories that have been proposed in the social science literature that help explain transitions of adolescent sexual behavior, particularly the onset of adolescent sexuality as reflected in the first intercourse experience. Loss of virginity holds a notable status within our culture. For many, it is the ultimate marker for the onset of adulthood. Its date is personally noted, the social setting surrounding its occurrence is discussed, and the cultural role it plays in U.S. society is reflected in songs and movies. For demographers and psychologists, loss of virginity signals another important milestone. With sexual debut, fertility behavior officially begins. Except for unusual circumstances, intercourse is a prerequisite for conception is a prerequisite for pregnancy is a prerequisite for birth. One of the aggregate predictors of fertility rates is the amount of time that females are at risk of pregnancy. Obviously, the younger intercourse begins, the longer the at-risk period will be.

Many different theoretical perspectives have been used to explain and model adolescent sexuality in general and the transition to nonvirginity more particularly. Seventeen of those theories are listed in Table 4.1. The number next to each theory gives the approximate chronology, ordered by the article(s) that first applied the theory to studying adolescent sexuality. The theories are organized into three categories: social theories, cognitive theories, and component theories.

TABLE 4.1
A Substantive Taxonomy of Theories of Adolescent Sexual Transitions
(Numbers Refer to the Approximate Chronology
of the Development of the Theories)

Social Theories
1. Theory of Sexual Permissiveness (Reiss, 1967; Reiss & Miller, 1979)
2. Reference Group Theory (Mirande, 1968)
3. Theory of Relative Consequences (Christensen, 1969)
5. Socialization Theory (Spanier, 1975)
7. Differential Opportunity Theory (Schulz, Bohrnstedt, Borgatta, & Evans, 1977)
9. Exchange Theory (Davidson & Leslie, 1977)
10. Equity Theory (Walster, Walster, & Traupmann, 1978)

Cognitive Theories
4. The Contingent Consistency Model (Clayton, 1972)
6. Morality Theory (D'Augelli & Cross, 1975; D'Augelli & D'Augelli, 1977)
11. Reinforcement Theory (Kelley, 1978)
13. Subjective Expected Utility Model (Bauman & Udry, 1981; Gilbert, Bauman, & Udry, 1986)

Component Theories
8. Problem Behavior Theory (Jessor, Costa, Jessor, & Donovan, 1983; Jessor & Jessor, 1975, 1977)
12. Developmental Sociopsychology Theory (DeLamater & MacCorquodale, 1979)
14. The Health Belief Model (Eisen, Zellman, & McAlister, 1985)
15. Domain Theory (Newcomb, Huba, & Bentler, 1986)
16. Biosocial Models (Hofferth, 1987; Smith, Udry, & Morris, 1985; Udry, 1988)
17. Epidemic (EMOSA) Models (Rodgers & Rowe, 1993; Rowe, Rodgers, & Meseck-Bushey, 1989)

This list is certainly not exhaustive, although it is extensive. The metaperspective that I use is that no theory is ultimately the wrong or right one; rather, each simplifies the reality that it attempts to model in a different way. Social theories focus on social influences that affect adolescent sexual behavior. Cognitive theories focus on attitudes and decision making. Component theories use modeling from multiple perspectives; in particular, many approaches in this category add a biological component. Naturally, with time, theories have become more complicated—that is, less parsimonious—but also more complete in matching the reality being modeled.

Each of the 17 theories listed are briefly reviewed and illustrated in a short vignette. Each vignette focuses on the interaction between two adolescents, given the basic premise of the theory. The hypothetical players within each vignette are those well-known adolescents, Jack and Jill. There is a popular ditty that seems apropos and helps to motivate the choice of these players:

> Jack and Jill went up the hill
> To do what they shouldn't oughta;
> They both came down with smiles on their faces
> They didn't go up for water!
> (And soon they'll have a daughter!!)

Social Theories

Seven theories are predominantly social. Some are social at the institutional setting—relying on the family or religion—whereas others are social at the individual level. Jack and Jill's families and friends will help illustrate each theory.

Reiss' (1967) theory of sexual permissiveness linked a number of social institutions—including the family and friendship groups—to sexual permissiveness. Notably, these were defined in a time-dynamic fashion, focusing on how sexual permissiveness changes in relation to social influence (emphasizing the importance of adolescent sexual behavior as a process of transition).

> Jack and Jill arrive at the hill. Jill says, "Jack, we've been dating a long time. What about the sex thing?" They discuss pros and cons. Jill's family wouldn't like it if they became sexually involved; Jack's family has religious objections. But most of their friends are pretty liberal about sex. So they decide on the middle ground; they'll begin a sexual relationship, but not have intercourse for awhile.

Mirande's (1968) reference group theory suggested that reference groups—in particular the peer group and the family—have important social influences. The "groups of which one is a member and other important groups become a point of reference for the shaping of attitudes, values, and behavior" (Davidson & Leslie, 1977, p. 20).

> Jack and Jill are at a party. The student council president is in the corner making out with her new boyfriend, who's captain of the men's cheerleading squad. Everyone in the room is trying not to look, but is intrigued by this latest "pairing up." Three other couples follow their lead. Jack and Jill go off in search of their own corner.

Christensen's (1969) theory of relative consequences invoked cultural norms to develop propositions stating relationships between these norms and sexual permissiveness. The consequences of sexual activity are accounted for carefully in this theory. He viewed some sexual variables as universal, and others to be culture bound.

> Jack and Jill go up the hill. Jack says "Jill, we really like each other. We love each other. Let's fool around." Jill says, "Jack, I'd love to fool with you, but we're pretty young. Remember the 'Just Say No' program from school yesterday? And what if I got pregnant? Our parents would never forgive us!"

Socialization theory is based on the notion that "attitudes and behavior carried into adulthood are learned early in life" (Philliber, 1980, p. 3). Thus, an adolescent's behavior can be predicted from knowledge of how the adolescent was socialized as a child. Spanier (1975) proposed the idea of *sexualization* (sexual socialization), using a developmental perspective tied to gender identity, gender role development, development of sex object preference, acquisition of sexual skills and knowledge, and development of sexual values.

> Jill and Jack are on the couch, making out, but fully clothed. Jack wants more intimacy. Jill says, "Jack, you know I love you, but we've been through this before. Because of my family and my religious beliefs, I've always planned to remain a virgin until I marry. Please try to understand."

Schulz, Bohrnstedt, Borgotta, and Evans (1977) borrowed the theoretical notion of "opportunity" from the deviance literature to suggest differential opportunity theory. In this theory, potential partners and conducive settings are prerequisite for adolescent sexual behavior to occur.

> Jack and Jill live in highly supervised family and neighborhood environments. Their parents chaperone all social gatherings, and dating is discouraged until age 16. After that, socializing in group settings is encouraged. Jack and Jill like each other a lot, but are not sexually intimate.

Exchange theory suggests that one "gives something of value in order to get something in return" (Davidson & Leslie, 1977, p. 20). Sexual expression may be exchanged for different (and overlapping) things, including affection, popularity, physical stimulation, power, and expression of adulthood. Abstaining from sexual behavior also returns benefits, including avoidance of sexually transmitted disease and pregnancy, maintenance of reputation, social support from family and friends, and feelings of morality. Exchange theory involves a whole network of costs and benefits.

> Jack has been pressuring Jill to have sex with him. Jill loves their intimacy, but isn't sure she's ready. Jack says, "Jill, there are lots of girls in our school. I love you, but I don't want to wait around forever." Jill has resisted, because of fear of losing her moral reputation, and fear of pregnancy. But Jill finally gives in, because losing Jack as her boyfriend would be worse.

Equity theory suggests that couples in inequitable relationships become distressed and will behave so as to reduce unhappiness. Walster, Walster, and Traupmann (1978) used this theory and the double standard of gender-appropriate sexual behavior to generate a set of predictions: Underbenefitted men should demand sex of their female partner; underbenefitted women should insist that their partner wait for sex.

> Jack and Jill haven't been getting along very well. Jack wants to have sex to try to "mend their relationship." Jill thinks having sex would be the worst thing they could do while they're quarreling.

Cognitive Theories

Four theories draw on cognitive processes to explain sexual transition among adolescents. Jack and Jill's thoughts, attitudes, intentions, and feelings are important within these theories.

The contingent consistency model, developed by Warner and DeFleur (1969) and first applied to adolescent sexuality by Clayton (1972), was developed to model the relationship between attitudes and behaviors (work that eventually led to the theory of reasoned action; Fishbein & Ajzen, 1979). Clayton proposed that the attitude–behavior link is mediated by contingent factors, including cultural norms, individual differences, personal perceptions, and opportunities.

> Jack's head feels like it's swirling around. He thinks Jill wants to have sexual intercourse on their next date (although they haven't really discussed it much). It would be the first time for both of them. He's never had to decide how he feels about sex before. What would his parents and friends

think? What about his religious training? How would he feel about himself afterward? How would he feel about Jill? Where would they go? Could they be discovered? Is he reading Jill's signals right? There are so many things to weigh.

Morality theory is a simple theoretical perspective suggesting that an adolescent's internal sense of morality will have a relationship to sexual behavior. D'Augelli and Cross (1975) suggested that "two factors related to the [sexual] decision making process would seem to be sex guilt . . . and moral reasoning" (p. 40).

Jill feels like it's time to lose her virginity. What better partner than her best friend, Jack? But she knows it won't work. She knows that Jack's sense of morality is strong, and that he feels sexual intercourse at their age is wrong. She wonders if Jack's moral stance is the right one? It does give a simple and clear answer to what she perceives as a very difficult problem.

Reinforcement theory is among the simplest (and therefore, in the sense of parsimony, most elegant) of the theories that is reviewed here. It suggests that "sex is highly pleasurable and therefore reinforcing" (Kelley, 1978, p. 455); such behavior will therefore occur and increase in frequency. Hardy's (1964) appetitional theory of sexual motivation—a cognitive-affective model of motivation—overlaps with reinforcement theory, in that an "appetite" is developed for sexuality through the reinforcement properties of the positive social and biological effects of sexuality.

Jack is good looking, and he knows it. He often goes out on the town to try and pick up women; often he finds a willing sex partner. Tonight he's working on Jill, who knows and likes him, but also knows his reputation. "What makes boys like Jack always out for sex?" she wonders. "I didn't come here looking for sex, and I don't have any intention of having sex with Jack." But then, almost subconsciously, she reflects on the good times she had with one of her past boyfriends, and begins to take Jack's attention more seriously.

The subjective expected utility (SEU) model is a cognitively based decision-making model that posits that individuals behave to maximize their personal and subjectively computed utility (Bauman & Udry, 1981). The SEU model assumes that adolescents (implicitly) compute trade-offs between costs and benefits. When the computation gives a positive utility for making the transition to nonvirginity or for continued sexual activity, they will behave accordingly.

Jill is one of the most logical people Jack has ever met; that's part of what he loves about her. But now she's gone way overboard. When he told her last week that he wanted to have sex with her, she took out her notebook and started making a list of the pluses and minuses. He was sorry when the minuses outweighed the pluses, but secretly he knew that she was right.

Component Theories

Six theories combine features from different domains. These correspond to the "theoretical integration" called for by Clayton and Bokemeier in their 1980 review. The component theories represent an increase in conceptual sophistication; thus, they are closer to the reality that they are modeling, but they are also less parsimonious. Loss of parsimony is justified to the extent that such component approaches realistically capture within their theoretical structure the complicated interactive processes that we know actually occur.

Problem behavior theory (Jessor & Jessor, 1977) was the first complete statement that adolescent sexual behavior co-occurs with other problem behaviors. This theoretical perspective had been anticipated by Reiss (1970). Problem behavior theory was originally applied to drug use and delinquency, as well as onset of adolescent sexuality (Jessor, Costa, Jessor, & Donovan, 1983; Jessor & Jessor, 1975). The theory is composed of three systems: the personality system, the perceived environment system, and the behavior system.

Jack wants to lose his virginity. But he's naive, and doesn't know how to find a girl in his school who will have sex with him. His friend suggests that he pursue Jill. "After all," his friend says, "she smokes and drinks. And she's pretty wild-acting when she's drunk. So she's probably not a virgin. Why don't you make your move at the school party on Friday?"

DeLamater and MacCorquodale (1979) presented work that gives a careful blend of theory, method, and empirical research in explaining adolescent sexuality. (Because their work has, apparently, never been given a name, I have taken the liberty of naming this approach developmental sociopsychology theory.) This method used linear structural modeling methods to link sexual behavior to measures of socializing influences (peers, parents, and partners), sociopsychological characteristics, past sexual behavior, and sexual attitudes. In later work, DeLamater (1981) linked Hirschi's (1969) social control theory to sexuality for the first time.

Jack and Jill are sitting around a campfire with teenage friends. Not so surprisingly, they start talking about sex. "It's all so complicated," says Jill. "Yeah," responds Jack, "your friends want you to, but your family doesn't." Someone else answers, "Yeah, and some people our age just do it a lot and don't worry about it, but others either don't at all, or do and feel guilty."

Jack says, "Wouldn't it be nice if sex were just no big deal, like running track. Some do, some don't, and it's no big deal." "Don't count on it," says Jill. "Running track doesn't spread AIDS or get you pregnant."

The health belief model (Janz & Becker, 1984) has been applied to fertility control in adolescents (Eisen, Zellman, & McAlister, 1985). This model proposes that engaging in a health-promoting behavior (or abstaining from ones that hurt health, e.g., early sexuality) depends on the trade-offs among: (a) perceived seriousness of negative health consequences (e.g., does a teenage girl feel like a pregnancy would harm her health?), (b) perceived likelihood of negative health consequences (e.g., does a girl think that a pregnancy is likely to result from intercourse?), (c) perceived benefits (e.g., affection, physical pleasure), and (d) perceived costs of the health-promoting behavior (e.g., loss of physical or emotional outlet). This theory shares features of the cost–benefit models given earlier, except with stronger biological and health orientation.

Jack and Jill are older now, and are still together. They still haven't had sex, and Jack is still trying to convince her that now's the time. "I agree that we're old enough, Jack," Jill tells him, "and you know how much I love you. But if we have sex, I guarantee that I'll get pregnant. That will ruin our educational plans, and might damage our relationship. We just can't risk it until we're married and ready to start a family." Jack takes that opportunity to propose.

Newcomb, Huba, and Bentler (1986) suggested domain theory in which "13 general domains are hypothesized that represent biological, intrapersonal, interpersonal, and sociocultural dimensions" (p. 429). Like Jessor and Jessor (1977), they developed their domain perspective to account for general types of adolescent deviance, including especially drug use.

Back to the campfire conversation. Jack says, "You know, having sex isn't just a single thing like our parents and teachers make it." "Yeah," says Jill, "it's like drugs. There's more to it than just doing it or not doing it. Either way you can feel good or bad physically, you can feel right or wrong ethically, and you can feel like you've done what others want you to do or just the totally wrong thing, all at the same time."

Udry and his colleagues recently introduced biological components into models of adolescent sexuality. Their empirical motivation was the demonstration of a relationship between androgenic hormones and adolescent sexual behavior in both males (Udry, Billy, Morris, Groff, & Raj, 1985) and females (Udry, Talbert, & Morris, 1986). Udry (1988) presented "biosocial models of adolescent sexuality that combine traditional sociological models with models derived from a biological theory of hormone effects" (p. 709). Hofferth (1987) also developed a model that combined biological and psychosocial domains into a framework to predict onset of adolescent sexuality.

> Jack and Jill have been dating for a long time. They feel in love, intimate, and they've openly discussed intercourse. They know that some people— like Jill's best friend—think they should; other people—like Jack's youth counselor—think they shouldn't. Most of the time they limit their sexual interactions to making out and petting. A few times, when they've been especially aroused, they've had manual and oral sex. Twice recently, their passion was more than they could stand, and they had sexual intercourse.

The final theoretical formulation is the newest of the theories. The social contagion model of sexual transition (Rodgers & Rowe, 1993; Rowe & Rodgers, 1994; Rowe, Rodgers, & Meseck-Bushey, 1989) has both social and biological features. The theory posits that sexuality is "transmitted" through a social network according to a social contagion process, with a maturational screen for pubertal development. I discuss this model in more detail in a later section.

> "All the other couples are doing it," Jill says. "Take it from me, it's the most fun we could possibly have." Jack is still a virgin, and reluctant. But he doesn't want to be the only virgin left in the school, and Jill is certainly attractive. It's almost like she's trying to sell him a product; he's thinking seriously of buying.

THE FIRST INTERCOURSE EXPERIENCE: EMPIRICAL RESULTS

The theoretical models just discussed are only a part of the adolescent sexuality research enterprise. Several taxonomies of this research arena (e.g., Clayton & Bokemeier, 1980; Hayes, 1987) divide the study into two components, epidemiology (incidence) and etiology (causal structure). The review already given concerns etiology; the theories propose causal factors surrounding sexual transitions. The second half of the study pertains to the incidence of adolescent sexuality (and, more specifically, onset of sexual intercourse). This descriptive research has a large supporting literature that is of particular value to public health experts, family planning clinic workers, medical personnel working on AIDS and sexually transmitted disease, and other applied researchers, practitioners, and policymakers. Important contributions within this domain have been made by Zelnick and his colleagues in a series of *Family Planning Perspec-*

tives articles in the late 1970s and early 1980s (e.g., Zelnik & Kantner, 1977; Zelnik & Shah, 1983), Furstenberg's longitudinal study of teenage childbearing in Baltimore (Furstenberg, 1976; Furstenberg, Brooks-Gunn, & Morgan, 1987), and Hofferth (1987).

Relatively little attention has been devoted to the structural features of the first intercourse experience itself. Ironically, adolescent sexuality researchers have given more research attention to the characteristics of same-gender peers than to the characteristics of the actual opposite-gender partners. A notable exception to this lack of attention is a paper by Hofferth (1987), which used a number of different studies to define descriptive portrayals of intercourse rates, the age and race structure, relationship to first sexual partner (acquaintance, friend, steady, fiancé), location of first intercourse, and additional sexual activity with first partner.

A unique study conducted around 1980 contains a great deal of still-unpublished information about the structural features of the first intercourse experience. The original ADSEX data were collected between 1978 and 1982 in two metropolitan areas in the southeastern United States: Raleigh, North Carolina, and Tallahassee, Florida. The study, supervised by J. Richard Udry and conducted out of the UNC Carolina Population Center, was unique in that complete intact schools of adolescents were surveyed, and then followed longitudinally (for three waves in Raleigh and two in Tallahassee). This mechanism provided information about friends (and potential sex partners) of adolescents in the survey. The ADSEX data have provided the basis for dozens of studies of adolescent sexual behavior. In the following section, I present empirical results from the ADSEX data that provide information about social and environmental characteristics of the first intercourse experience.

The ADSEX results partially overlap those from Hofferth's (1987) review. The studies that she reviewed used more representative data than are used here. However, the ADSEX data have more breadth of treatment, and have the particular attraction of being drawn from intact school settings. Thus, they reflect the interaction of friends, siblings who go to the same school (there were a surprising number of these—around one third of the respondents also had siblings in the study), and, in fact, their sexual partners (although partners are not explicitly identified, but rather described by the respondents).

My goal is to give as complete a description as possible of the social and physical environment surrounding the onset of intercourse. This includes consideration of the respondent at the time of first intercourse, the partner's characteristics, the relationship between them, and aspects of the social environment. A small subset of the descriptive results reported here was published in Rodgers (1992), although few specific percentages were given in that source.

The ADSEX data came from a longitudinal study of junior high students in two communities and four different schools between 1978 and 1982. The total sample size was slightly greater than 1,900, with some attrition by the later rounds of the study. The subset of the data I will use are the "last round" data, which have as many adolescents as possible who have become sexually active. These data reflect all of the original junior high students, aged by 2 to 3 years. Thus, the respondents supporting the following descriptive results were in Grades 10 to 12 (along with a very few ninth graders). Thus, the frequencies presented should be considered a "snapshop" of a group of high school students. The tables differ in total sample sizes because of substantial differences in rates of nonresponse across different questions (as indicated within each table).

Characteristics of Respondents at First Intercourse

As shown in Table 4.2, almost exactly one half of the sample reported that they were nonvirgins, with different distributions by race–sex subgroups. The distribution of age at first intercourse in Table 4.3 shows the bulk of the distribution for all race–sex categories between ages 12 and 16 (the upper age limit for most of the sample). Males, and especially Black males, reported very young ages at first intercourse (many, in fact, reported prepubertal intercourse). There is reason to doubt the veracity of these reports, although they are not idiosyncratic among a very few respondents (and are, furthermore, consistent with results from other surveys; e.g., Clark, Zabin, & Hardy, 1984; Rosenbaum & Kandel, 1990). I elaborate on the logic of this concern later in the chapter. The Black and White females had similar distributions, although a higher percentage of Black females reported being sexually active than White females, matching results found in previous studies (e.g., Furstenberg, Morgan, Moore, & Peterson, 1987).

Most of these adolescents reported some use of contraception at first intercourse, and these percentages are higher than in most other sexuality surveys (creating some doubt concerning the validity of the contraceptive

TABLE 4.2
Intercourse Prevalence, ADSEX Data, Grades 9–12

	White Males	Black Males	White Females	Black Females	Total
Frequency "No"	266	29	382	94	771
(Column %)	(55)	(12)	(71)	(41)	(52)
Frequency "Yes"	215	215	160	136	726
(Column %)	(45)	(88)	(30)	(59)	(48)
Frequency Missing	180	56	150	55	441

TABLE 4.3
Age at First Intercourse, ADSEX Data (Column Percentages)

	White Males	Black Males	White Females	Black Females	Total
<6	1	5	–	–	2
6	1	9	1	–	3
7	2	6	–	–	2
8	1	9	–	–	3
9	1	9	–	–	3
10	4	14	1	5	6
11	4	6	3	2	4
12	13	16	4	8	11
13	24	14	14	17	17
14	18	7	27	29	19
15	18	4	29	22	17
16	12	3	21	15	12
17	1	–	1	1	1
>17	–	–	–	2	0
Column N	207	199	159	131	696

responses). The condom was the most popular "first contraceptive," and withdrawal, pills, and rhythm were also used often. The reason for first intercourse was given by the ADSEX respondents. The modal response for both males and females was "So that my partner would love me more" (from approximately 43% of the respondents of each gender). Other responses were "To please the partner" (16% of the females and 12% of the males), because the "partner forced me" (18% of the females and 9% of the males) and "not to hurt the partner" (14% of the females and 8% of the males).

Around two thirds of these adolescents reported sex again with their first partner. By race–sex subgroups, a "yes" response was given for repeated intercourse with the first partner by 59% of the White males, 67% of the Black males, 72% of the White females, and 67% of the Black females. However, few engaged in consistent repeated coital activity with their first partner (Table 4.4). More than half of those answering the question about additional intercourse with first partner indicated that they had sex three or fewer additional times after the first one. A large majority of those who did report many additional coital acts with their first partner were females, and almost no Black males reported more than just a few. Two thirds of the respondents reported sex partners other than their first one. At least one additional partner was reported by 65% of White males, 85% of Black males, 53% of White females, and 58% of

TABLE 4.4
Number of Times Had Sex Again with First Partner, ADSEX Data
(Column Percentages)

	White Males	Black Males	White Females	Black Females	Total
1	16	4	14	14	12
2	22	17	14	22	19
3	22	28	8	17	20
4–7	17	36	17	18	23
8–15	10	16	20	19	16
16–25	7	0	13	8	7
>25	4	0	15	3	6
Column N	98	102	88	64	352

Black females. However, the modal number of additional partners was one (Table 4.5; note that Table 4.5 gives the total partners, and because two is the mode, this corresponds to one additional partner besides the first). Very few had more than 10 partners, and of those who did, virtually all were males. Of those who were nonvirgins, around three quarters reported zero or one sexual partner in the month preceding the interview (Table 4.6), and most had engaged in three or fewer coital acts in the last month, with zero being the modal number (Table 4.7).

The location of first intercourse in this sample matches those in previous surveys (Table 4.8). Around one third lost their virginity in their partner's home, with another one third in either their home or a friend's home. In a car, outside, at school, in a hotel, or other unspecified locations accounted for the additional third. The seasonality of first intercourse in

TABLE 4.5
Number of Total Sex Partners, ADSEX Data (Column Percentages)

	White Males	Black Males	White Females	Black Females	Total
1	5	1	6	15	5
2	29	10	26	29	22
3	19	9	32	18	18
4	11	8	10	20	11
5–9	19	36	20	9	33
10–15	8	25	3	4	12
16–25	6	6	3	0	4
>25	4	5	0	3	3
Column N	128	140	78	75	421

TABLE 4.6
Number of Partners Last Month, ADSEX Data (Column Percentages)

	White Males	Black Males	White Females	Black Females	Total
0	43	26	44	43	37
1	35	24	54	45	37
2	9	18	1	7	11
3	4	14	0	3	6
4	3	5	0	1	3
5	3	5	0	0	3
6–10	1	7	0	0	2
11–25	0	3	0	0	1
>25	1	1	0	0	1
Column N	127	154	81	73	435

TABLE 4.7
Number of Coital Acts in the Last Month, ADSEX Data
(Column Percentages)

	White Males	Black Males	White Females	Black Females	Total
0	43	24	41	28	33
1	19	15	19	28	19
2	11	15	5	12	12
3	9	15	6	15	12
4–5	6	15	6	5	7
6–10	4	12	14	6	10
11–15	2	2	4	4	3
16–25	4	3	5	1	3
>25	3	0	0	1	1
Column N	130	146	79	76	441

TABLE 4.8
Location of First Intercourse, ADSEX Data (Column Percentages)

	White Males	Black Males	White Females	Black Females	Total
Partner's home	26	35	35	39	33
My home	20	19	18	19	19
Friend's home	8	10	16	10	11
Outdoors	22	17	10	4	15
In a car	10	5	12	11	9
At school	0	6	0	2	2
Hotel or motel	5	1	3	5	3
Other	10	9	7	11	9
Column N	200	198	147	123	668

the ADSEX data has been studied previously (Rodgers, Harris, & Vickers, 1992). In the second round, the Tallahassee respondents filled out an "intercourse calendar." By selecting those who made the transition between the first and second round, and noting the month of first occurrence of intercourse on their calendar, we constructed a distribution of first intercourse by month of its occurrence. The summer was a popular time to lose one's virginity in this sample, with a June or July peak. Rodgers et al. (1992) presented a large national sample that replicated this pattern.

Characteristics of the First Partner

A number of characteristics of first partner were indicated by ADSEX respondents. Table 4.9 shows "relationship to the first partner;" slightly over two thirds of the respondents lost their virginity with someone they knew well, either a fiancé, steady, or close friend (matching results in Zelnik & Shah, 1983). Slightly under 20% lost their virginity with someone they had met recently. The distribution of age of first partner is shown in Table 4.10. A bivariate table of age of respondent by age of first partner (respondent report) is shown in Table 4.11 for the race–sex categories combined. The mean difference between the age of the first sex partner and the age of the respondent was +2.6 years for Black females, +1.5 years for Black males, +2.8 years for White females, and +1.4 years for White males. Thus, respondents in all four categories reported an older first partner.

A number of males (particularly Black males) reported that their partners were prepubertal (which often matched the report for themselves). An age of first intercourse of under 10 was given by 84 males (21%). Of these 84, 54 (64%) reported that their first partner was also 10 or younger. This identifies a potential logical impossibility, because in the whole

TABLE 4.9
Relationship to the First Partner, ADSEX Data (Column Percentages)

	White Males	Black Males	White Females	Black Females	Total
Met a little while before first sex	25	22	13	12	19
Knew a little and was friendly with	12	21	5	9	12
Knew well, liked a lot, but no steady	29	38	23	32	31
Going steady with, no plans to marry	25	13	32	25	23
Going steady with, planned to marry	8	5	26	21	14
Husband/wife, after marriage	0	0	0	2	0
Prostitute (male) or rape (female)	1	1	1	0	1
Column N	206	197	159	127	689

TABLE 4.10
Age of First Partner, ADSEX Data (Column Percentages)

	White Males	Black Males	White Females	Black Females	Total
4–6	0	8	0	0	2
7–9	3	18	1	0	6
10	3	11	0	1	4
11	2	10	0	0	3
12	7	8	0	4	5
13	16	16	3	4	11
14	23	12	11	10	15
15	20	9	18	17	16
16	15	5	20	19	14
17	6	4	19	14	10
18–20	3	1	24	28	13
>20	2	1	4	4	2
Column N	206	197	158	130	691

TABLE 4.11
Age of First Partner by Age of Respondent, ADSEX Data
(Column Percentages)

Age of First Partner	Age of Respondent							
	≤10	11	12	13	14	15	16	Total
≤10	.62[*]	.19	.04	.01	.01	.00	.00	.13
11	.10	.23	.06	.01	.00	.00	.00	.03
12	.10	.23	.18	.04	.00	.00	.00	.05
13	.07	.12	.28	.30	.05	.01	.00	.11
14	.03	.08	.15	.26	.30	.05	.08	.15
15	.02	.08	.11	.19	.21	.28	.12	.16
16	.03	.00	.10	.06	.16	.32	.20	.14
17	.02	.08	.03	.03	.13	.16	.22	.10
≥18	.02	.00	.06	.09	.15	.18	.37	.13
Column N	120	26	72	118	131	120	83	670

Note. Within the category of respondent and partner ≤10, the 74 responses broke down as follows: partner 2 years younger, 3%; partner 1 year younger, 11%; partner same age, 50%; partner 1 year older, 19%; partner 2 years older, 9%; others, 8%.

sample only a single White female reported intercourse at less than age 10, and no Black females reported intercourse at less than age 10; thus, none of the girls in this sample could have been the young partners reported by a large number of boys. This suggests that either all these males were finding other young girls than those with whom they went to school (an unlikely interpretation), or that systematic and sex-related

TABLE 4.12
Were You the First Boy/Girl That Your First Partner
Ever Had Sex With? (Column Percentages)

	White Males	Black Males	White Females	Black Females	Total
I was the first boy/girl	43	29	22	6	27
Maybe I was the first boy/girl	11	19	4	5	11
I don't know whether I was the first	22	40	12	39	28
Maybe I was not the first boy/girl	2	3	3	4	3
I was not the first boy/girl	23	9	59	47	31
Column N	209	209	159	132	709

misresponding is occurring (i.e., overreporting of sex by males and/or underreporting of sex by females). Alternatively, it is possible that males and females differ in how they remember and report prepubertal sex play, or even in their definition of first intercourse.

Around 40% of the respondents were sure or thought that their first partner was also a virgin (Table 4.12). Around 35% were sure or thought that their partner was not a virgin. There was a large gender difference in these responses. A disproportionate number of females thought their partner was not a virgin and a disproportionate number of males thought their partner was a virgin.

These results should certainly not be considered a veridical portrayal of the first intercourse experience. Rather, they are self-reports of that experience, and must be highly affected by the various data problems discussed in the introduction to this chapter (see also Rodgers et al., 1982). Further, the data supporting these analyses are around 15 years old, and becoming outdated. Data collection efforts that are currently underway (e.g., the Adolescent Health Project, like the ADSEX project directed by Udry) have the potential to update and extend descriptive results presented here. Despite their weaknesses, the results suggest several useful patterns, summarized in the following statements:

1. The majority of nonvirgin adolescents did not report being very sexually active. A "typical" (modal) nonvirgin ADSEX adolescent had zero or one partner with whom he or she occasionally had sex (no more than a couple of times a month and often less).

2. A very few adolescents reported being very sexually active, especially males and especially Black males.

3. Most of these adolescents reported using some type of birth control at first intercourse (although most did not report continuing reliable contraception).

4. Internal patterns of reported ages of first partner cast doubt on the validity of some of the responses regarding themselves and their partners. Inconsistency of reports about prepubertal intercourse between males and females suggests systematic misreporting by one or both sexes.

5. The majority of first partners were close friends or steady boyfriends or girlfriends, typically somewhat older than the respondent. First intercourse was reported to occur in the home of one of the participants or the home of a friend; the summer months of June and July were the periods of "peak" first intercourse experience. A majority of first partners of females were believed by the respondent to already be nonvirgins, whereas a majority of first partners of males were believed to be virgins.

SEXUAL TRANSITIONS IN ADOLESCENCE—
A DEVELOPMENTAL EMOSA MODEL

My colleague David Rowe and I recently published a general theoretical statement of how social influences affect transitions through stages of adolescent sexual behavior (Rodgers & Rowe, 1993). Several features of that paper make it particularly relevant for a chapter treating sexual transitions during adolescence. First, it extends work by Smith, Udry, and Morris (1985) that treats adolescent sexual transitions as a multistage process, rather than focusing exclusively on virginity status. Second, it accounts for such transitions in a whole intact population of interacting adolescents, with particular attention to the specific interactions between potential and actual sexual partners. Third, the model is nonlinear and time dynamic (as are sexual transitions).

In this section, I briefly review the social contagion theory that underlies this work, and some empirical results that we obtained when we fit the mathematical model implied by this theory to empirical data. The approach falls within a broader perspective that we call Epidemic Modeling of the Onset of Social Activities (EMOSA Modeling), which we have applied to smoking (Rowe & Rodgers, 1991a; Rowe, Chassin, Presson, Edwards, & Sherman, 1992), drinking (Rowe & Rodgers, 1991a), sexuality (Rodgers & Rowe, 1993; Rowe & Rodgers, 1991b, 1994; Rowe, Rodgers, & Meseck-Bushey, 1989), and criminal behavior (Rowe, Gulley, & Rodgers, 1994).

To define EMOSA models, we posit an intact and interacting population of adolescents. We assume that during the course of a fixed time period (e.g., a calendar year, an age period, etc.) these adolescents come in contact with one another in social settings, and that those settings are ones in which they exert various types of mutual influence on one another. Certain behaviors are particularly susceptible to being spread through (at least part of) an adolescent network by the process of social contagion that such mutual influence can bring about. Transition behaviors, because they help signal that the adolescent is approaching adulthood, are ones to which most of the EMOSA models we have developed have been applied.

Our EMOSA sexuality models posit two sexes, males and females, and have only treated heterosexual development (although homosexual and bisexual models could be developed as well). During the course of a time period, males and females are paired up by the model, and are assumed to potentially exert influence on one another to engage or not to engage in new sexual behaviors. Whether the potential is realized or not is probabilistic, and depends on several features, the most notable of which is the status of the two opposite-gender adolescents in regard to the behavior. Thus, for example, a 12-year-old boy who is paired up with a 12-year-old girl, neither of whom has ever kissed a member of the opposite sex, is treated differently by the model than two 12-year-olds, both of whom are "kissing nonvirgins." Another feature of the adolescent that is accounted for by the model is whether he or she is pubertally mature or not. In most of our analyses, maturity has been a useful screen for transition to intercourse (in particular for females), but not for transitions into less intimate forms of sexual behavior (specifically, kissing and petting).

I have already discussed how the model "treats" a particular adolescent pair. More specifically, the model estimates transition rates to indicate likelihood (or speed) of transition through different levels of sexual intimacy. Thus, for example, the model permits different rates of transition from a kissing stage into a light petting stage than from a heavy petting stage into an intercourse stage. Furthermore, each transition rate may be different for males than for females, and may be "filtered" based on pubertal maturity of one or both members of the couple.

These transition rates are parameters in the model that are estimated by fitting the model to prevalence data. In other words, when the age by sex by race prevalence curves that the model produces are matched (with a fitting routine) to the age by sex by race prevalence curves that come from real interacting adolescents, that process produces estimates of these transition rates that can be interpreted for what they say about the interacting adolescents.

A simple two-stage model is used to illustrate this process. The first EMOSA model (Rowe et al., 1989) was based on the following interacting and time-dynamic equations, the first for males and the second for females:

$$Pm_{a+1} = Pm_a + Tm(1 - Pm_a)Pf_a + kM_a(1 - Pm_a)(1 - Pf_a)$$
$$Pf_{a+1} = Pf_a + TfM_a(1 - Pf_a)Pm_a + kM_a(1 - Pf_a)(1 - Pm_a)$$

The first equation models the proportion of nonvirgin males at Age a + 1 from three components: (a) the carry-over from Age a of males who were already nonvirgins, (b) the proportion of virgin males $(1 - Pm)$ at Age a who came in contact with one of the nonvirgin females (with probability Pf), and who made the transition to nonvirginity (with transition rate Tm), and (c) the proportion of virgin males who came in contact with virgin females $(1 - Pf)$ who were also pubertally mature (with probability M) at Age a, and who made the transition to nonvirginity (with probability k). The second equation shows how the proportion of nonvirgin females is defined at Age a + 1, through the same three components. The equations interact with one another, because the overlapping proportions of male and female virgins and nonvirgins are accounted for in each equation. Further, the results of the process for one age are used in the model at the next age, the time-dynamic component of the model.

More complicated EMOSA sexuality models have been written and fit to data. Rowe and Rodgers (1994) defined an intercohort contagion model that accounted for mixing sex partners of different ages (whereas the original model assumed that all partners were of the same age). Rodgers and Rowe (1993) defined four transitions between five stages (rather than the one transition between two stages in the previous model). The stages they used were complete naïveté, kissing, light petting, heavy petting, and sexual intercourse.

In much of this work, the empirical data to which these models were fit was the same ADSEX data for which descriptive results are presented in an earlier section of this chapter. Because the ADSEX data contained an approximately intact group of interacting adolescents who aged across the different waves of the study, these data provide a very clean match to the requirements for fitting the models. In Rowe and Rodgers (1991b), we fit the same equations to national data, a process that assumed all adolescents were one intact interacting population. Although this assumption is clearly unrealistic, the estimated transition rates were very similar to those obtained using the (approximately) intact ADSEX sample. The references listed in this section may be consulted for complete presentation of transition rates and goodness-of-fit statistics. I summarize one set of these results to give a flavor of the type of information that can be "extracted" from the data with this type of modeling.

When the simple 2-stage model defined in the two equations was fit to the ADSEX data accounting for virginity status across age, the model estimated the following transition rates: For virgin males who were paired with nonvirgin females, $T_m = 1.00$; for virgin females who were paired with nonvirgin males, $T_f = .33$; for pairing a nonvirgin male and female, $k = .08$. Verbally, this suggests that the information in the prevalence curves combined with the process of social contagion assumed by the model predicted that three times as many males will become nonvirgins if they are paired with a nonvirgin female as the reverse situation when a virgin female is paired with a nonvirgin male. Furthermore, if two virgin adolescents are paired, their rate of transition into nonvirginity is only around one quarter of that for the females (and less than one tenth that of males). When these models were fit separately by race, transition rates were estimated to be almost identical for White and Black males and for White and Black females. The rather substantial difference in empirical rates of nonvirginity across race were absorbed by the maturity filters in the model (because Black females were, on the average, more likely to be pubertally mature than White females).

We have obtained more complex, but equally interpretable, results when we have fit the more complicated models described earlier. Careful examination of those results is beyond the scope of this chapter, although summary comments about what we reported in Rodgers and Rowe (1993) provide a useful conclusion to this section. When equations were written to extend the model in the two equations to five stages, and these were fit to 5-stage empirical data from the ADSEX survey, we found that the rates from light petting to heavy petting were by far the highest transition rates, for both sexes, both races, and in both cities. This is quite interpretable, because the psychological difference between this transition appears smaller than for others. The lowest transition rates were for the transition from naïveté to kissing status, suggesting that there is a greater barrier to beginning intimate behavior than there is to making transitions to more intimate behavior once the initial stage has been entered. As in the simpler model, males had higher transition rates than females (i.e., it was easier for a nonvirgin female to "convert" a male than vice versa), and this result held for all transitions for both races in both cities. Finally, one of the most interesting race–sex differences occurred in the transition rates for White females. Rates were moderate for transitions into the first three categories, but dropped to virtually zero for transitions into intercourse with a nonvirgin male. However, the transition rate for White females with a virgin male was much higher, approaching that of the transition rate of White males with nonvirgin females. However, this result suggested by the model was inconsistent with the empirical results shown in Table 4.12, in which the majority of White females suggested that their first partner was not a virgin.

CONCLUSION

Only recently have theoretical models of sexual transitions during adolescence begun to account for multiple stages, for partner interaction, and for the process of social influence. EMOSA models are an early stage in the development of more formal models of these processes. Other time-dynamic and nonlinear models will certainly follow to extend understanding of social and biological processes, and these will better capture the influences that affect adolescent decision making. Thus, despite a number of different theoretical successes, the research community still has much work to do.

Even after two decades of careful research, lots of theorizing, and dozens of innovative programs aimed at reducing levels of adolescent sexual activity, pregnancy, and sexually transmitted disease, Jack and Jill are still going up that proverbial hill. We understand more about how often, with whom, why, and what they do when they get there. We now know quite a lot about Jack and Jill, their parents, siblings, and friends. We know some things about Jack and Jill as a couple. We even know that Jack and Jill are not always honest with us. However, Jack and Jill's behavior is subtle, complicated, and time dynamic, as our models must be as well.

REFERENCES

Bauman, K. E., & Udry, J. R. (1981). Subjective expected utility and adolescent sexual behavior. *Adolescence, 63*, 527–535.

Chilman, C. S. (1980). Social and psychological research concerning adolescent childbearing: 1970–1980. *Journal of Marriage and the Family, 42*, 793–805.

Christensen, H. T. (1969). Normative theory derived from cross-cultural family research. *Journal of Marriage and the Family, 31*, 209–222.

Clark, S., Zabin, L., & Hardy, J. (1984). Sex, contraception, and parenthood: Experience and attitudes among urban Black young men. *Family Planning Perspectives, 16*, 77–82.

Clayton, R. R. (1972). Premarital sexual intercourse: A substantive test of the contingent consistency model. *Journal of Marriage and the Family, 34*, 273–281.

Clayton, R. R., & Bokemeier, J. L. (1980). Premarital sex in the seventies. *Journal of Marriage and the Family, 42*, 759–775.

D'Augelli, J. F., & Cross, H. J. (1975). Relationship of sex guilt and moral reasoning to premarital sex in college women and in couples. *Journal of Consulting and Clinical Psychology, 43*, 40–47.

D'Augelli, J. F., & D'Augelli, A. R. (1977). Moral reasoning and premarital sexual behavior: Toward reasoning about relationships. *Journal of Social Issues, 33*, 46–66.

Davidson, J. K., & Leslie, G. R. (1977). Premarital sexual intercourse: An application of axiomatic theory construction. *Journal of Marriage and the Family, 39*, 15–25.

DeLamater, J. (1981). The social control of sexuality. *Annual Review of Sociology, 7*, 263–290.

DeLamater, J., & MacCorquodale, P. (1979). *Premarital sexuality: Attitudes, relationships, behavior.* Madison: The University of Wisconsin Press.

Eisen, M., Zellman, G. L., & McAlister, A. L. (1985). A health belief model approach to adolescents' fertility control: Some pilot program findings. *Health Education Quarterly, 12*, 185–210.

Ensminger, M. E. (1987). Adolescent sexual behavior as it relates to other transition behaviors in youth. In S. Hofferth & C. Hayes (Eds.), *Risking the future* (Vol. II, pp. 36–55). Washington, DC: National Academy Press.

Fishbein, M., & Ajzen, I. (1979). *Belief, attitude, intention, and behavior: An introduction to theory and research.* Reading, MA: Addison-Wesley.

Furstenberg, F. F. (1976). *Unplanned parenthood: The social consequences of teenage childbearing.* New York: The Free Press.

Furstenberg, F. F., Brooks-Gunn, J., & Morgan, S. P. (1987). *Adolescent mothers in later life.* New York: Cambridge University Press.

Furstenberg, F. F., Morgan, S. P., Moore, K. A., & Peterson, J. L. (1987). Race differences in the timing of adolescent intercourse. *American Sociological Review, 52*, 511–518.

Gilbert, M. A., Bauman, K. E., & Udry, J. R. (1986). A panel study of subjective expected utility for adolescent sexual behavior. *Journal of Applied Social Psychology, 16*, 745–756.

Hardy, K. R. (1964). An appetitional theory of sexual motivation. *Psychological Review, 71*, 1–18.

Hayes, C. D. (1987). *Risking the future: Adolescent sexuality pregnancy, and childbearing* (Vol. I). Washington, DC: National Academy Press.

Hirschi, T. (1969). *Causes of delinquency.* Berkeley: University of California.

Hofferth, S. L. (1987). Factors affecting initiation of sexual intercourse. In S. Hofferth & C. D. Hayes (Eds.), *Risking the future: Adolescent sexuality, pregnancy, and childbearing* (Vol. II, pp. 56–77). Washington, DC: National Academy Press.

Janz, N., & Becker, M. (1984). The health belief model: A decade later. *Health Education Quarterly, 1*, 1–47.

Jessor, R., Costa, F., Jessor, L., & Donovan, J. E. (1983). Time of first intercourse: A prospective study. *Journal of Personality and Social Psychology, 44*, 608–626.

Jessor, R., & Jessor, S. L. (1977). *Problem behavior and psycho-social development: A longitudinal study of youth.* New York: Academic Press.

Jessor, S. L., & Jessor, R. (1975). Transition from virginity to nonvirginity among youth: A social-psychological study over time. *Developmental Psychology, 11*, 473–484.

Kelley, J. (1978). Sexual permissiveness: Evidence for a theory. *Journal of Marriage and the Family, 40*, 455–468.

Miller, B. C., & Fox, G. L. (1987). Theories of adolescent heterosexual behavior. *Journal of Adolescent Research, 2*, 269–282.

Miller, B. C., & Moore, K. A. (1990). Adolescent sexual behavior, pregnancy, and parenting: Research through the 1980's. *Journal of Marriage and the Family, 52*, 1025–1044.

Mirande, A. M. (1968). Reference group theory and adolescent sexual behavior. *Journal of Marriage and the Family, 30*, 572–577.

Newcomb, M. D., Huba, G., & Bentler, P. M. (1986). Determinants of sexual and dating behavior among adolescents. *Journal of Personality and Social Psychology, 50*, 428–438.

Philliber, S. G. (1980). A conceptual framework for population socialization. *Population and Environment, 3*, 3–9.

Reiss, I. L. (1967). *The social context of premarital sexual permissiveness.* New York: Holt, Rinehart, & Winston.

Reiss, I. L. (1970). Premarital sex as deviant behavior: An application of current approaches to deviance. *American Sociological Review, 35*, 78–87.

Reiss, I. L., & Miller, B. C. (1979). Heterosexual permissiveness: A theoretical analysis. In W. R. Burr, R. Hill, F. I. Nye, & I. L. Reiss (Eds.), *Contemporary theories about the family* (pp. 57–100). New York: The Free Press.

Rodgers, J. L. (1992). Development of sexual behavior. In S. B. Friedman, M. Fisher, & S. K. Schonberg (Eds.), *Comprehensive adolescent health care* (pp. 39–43). St. Louis, MO: Quality Medical Publishing.

Rodgers, J. L., Billy, J. O. G., & Udry, J. R. (1982). The rescission of behaviors: Inconsistent responses in adolescent sexuality data. *Social Sciences Research, 11*, 280–296.

Rodgers, J. L., Harris, D., & Vickers, K. B. (1992). Seasonality of first coitus in the United States. *Social Biology, 39*, 1–14.

Rodgers, J. L., & Rowe, D. C. (1993). Social contagion and adolescent sexual behavior: A developmental EMOSA model. *Psychological Review, 100*, 479–510.

Rosenbaum, E., & Kandel, D. B. (1990). Early onset of adolescent sexual behavior and drug involvement. *Journal of Marriage and the Family, 52*, 783–798.

Rowe, D. C., Chassin, L., Presson, C. C., Edwards, D., & Sherman, S. J. (1992). An "epidemic" model of adolescent cigarette smoking. *Journal of Applied Social Psychology, 22*, 261–285.

Rowe, D. C., Gulley, B. L., & Rodgers, J. L. (1994). *An epidemic model of the post-war crime wave, 1950–1987*. Manuscript under review.

Rowe, D. C., & Rodgers, J. L. (1991a). Adolescent smoking and drinking: Are they "epidemics"? *Journal of Studies in Alcohol, 52*, 110–117.

Rowe, D. C., & Rodgers, J. L. (1991b). An "epidemic" model of adolescent sexual intercourse prevalences: Applications to national survey data. *Journal of Biosocial Science, 23*, 211–219.

Rowe, D. C., & Rodgers, J. L. (1994). A social contagion model of adolescent sexual behavior: Explaining race differences. *Social Biology, 41*, 1–18.

Rowe, D. C., Rodgers, J. L., & Meseck-Bushey, S. (1989). An "epidemic" model of sexual intercourse prevalences for Black and White adolescents. *Social Biology, 36*, 127–145.

Schulz, B., Bohrnstedt, G. W., Borgatta, E., & Evans, R. (1977). Explaining premarital sexual intercourse among college students: A causal model. *Social Forces, 56*, 148–165.

Smith, E. A., Udry, J. R., & Morris, N. M. (1985). Pubertal development and friends: A biosocial explanation of adolescents sexual behavior. *Journal of Health and Social Behavior, 26*, 183–192.

Spanier, G. B. (1975). Formal and informal sex education as determinants of premarital sexual behavior. *Archives of Sexual Behavior, 5*, 39–67.

Udry, J. R. (1988). Biological predispositions and social control in adolescent sexual behavior. *American Sociological Review, 53*, 709–722.

Udry, J. R., Billy, J. O. G., Morris, N. M., Groff, T. R., & Raj, M. H. (1985). Serum androgenic hormones motivate sexual behavior in adolescent boys. *Fertility and Sterility, 43*, 90–94.

Udry, J. R., Talbert, L. M., & Morris, N. M. (1986). Biosocial foundations for adolescent female sexuality. *Demography, 23*, 217–230.

Walster, E., Walster, G., & Traupmann, J. (1978). Equity and premarital sex. *Journal of Personality and Social Psychology, 36*, 82–92.

Warner, L., & DeFleur, M. L. (1969). Attitude as an interacting concept: Social constraint and social distance as intervening variables between attitudes and action. *American Sociological Review, 34*, 153–169.

Zelnik, M., & Kantner, J. F. (1977). Sexual and contraceptive experience of young unmarried women in the United States, 1976 and 1971. *Family Planning Perspectives, 9*, 55–71.

Zelnik, M., & Shah, F. K. (1983). First intercourse among young Americans. *Family Planning Perspectives, 15*, 64–70.

5

Transitions in Drug Use During Late Adolescence and Young Adulthood

Jerald G. Bachman
Lloyd D. Johnston
Patrick M. O'Malley
John Schulenberg
Institute for Social Research
University of Michigan

This chapter is concerned with drug use and abuse among young people, a topic that has gained considerable importance and attention in the last two decades because of dramatic rises in the use of various illicit drugs. The "drug scene" in the United States has undergone pronounced changes in recent years, and those changes continue. There are important inter-relationships among several dimensions of drug use, but there are also substantial differences among drugs in their recent history of use and in their links with individual characteristics of users. Accordingly, we prefer not to speak of drug use or drug abuse as a single dimension; instead, we look at several kinds of drug use, noting in what ways they differ from each other and in what ways they are similar.

There are a number of kinds of transitions or changes one could consider in looking at drug use. For one thing, there have been large shifts in the "popularity" of various drugs, reflected in the changing proportions of young people using them. Such overall trends upward and downward provide the context within which we can look at other kinds of transitions at the individual level; these include (a) transitions into use of particular drugs (i.e., "initiation"), and (b) later changes in drug use linked to particular roles and experiences during the years following high school.

We begin this chapter with a brief conceptual overview. Following that, we present findings from the Monitoring the Future project. The first set of data focuses on the recent histories of young people's use of four important types of drugs: cigarettes, alcohol, marijuana, and cocaine. We then examine the kinds of individual differences in background and early experience, plus current lifestyle, that relate to differences in high school seniors' use of these and other drugs. Finally, we turn our attention to the ways in which different post-high-school experiences have an impact on drug use.

CONCEPTUAL OVERVIEW

Our approach in this chapter is informed by several conceptualizations consistent with a life-span perspective on human development (e.g., Baltes, 1987; Baltes, Reese, & Lipsett, 1980; Featherman, 1983; Lerner, 1984, 1986; Pandina, Labouvie, & White, 1984). In addition to subscribing to the basic tenet of the life-span perspective that "humans have the capacity for change across the entire life-span" (Brim & Kagan, 1980, p. 1), we believe that the explanation for change and stability is not necessarily located in the distal developmental past, but rather in the more proximal developmental past and present circumstances. We envision intraindividual change and stability to be a function of both individual and contextual factors—the individual acting on and reacting to the environmental system in which he or she is embedded (Bronfenbrenner, 1979; Lerner, 1986).

Our general concern is with change and stability in drug-related behaviors and attitudes during the transition to young adulthood. In many respects, change in drug-related behaviors and attitudes should be expected. In particular, new immediate contexts (e.g., new school, new job, new home, marriage) emerge during the transition that can alter patterns of use or nonuse of substances.

In several other respects, however, stability of drug use patterns can be expected during the transition to young adulthood. Many individual characteristics (e.g., personality, coping styles) are quite robust and stable, perhaps more a match for the forces of change that are evident during the transition. In addition, it is likely that drug and alcohol use patterns for some adolescents and young adults reflect dependency. Moreover, many young adults experience relatively little change in friendship groups, and a number of them remain living in the same parental home environment well past their completion of secondary school, holding constant many of the social forces that can influence drug use.

It has long been recognized that drug and alcohol use tend to decline during the middle to late 20s, about the same time when individuals typically assume adulthood roles related to marriage, parenthood, and full-time employment, suggesting a causal relationship between the successful assumption of adulthood roles and decline in drug use (e.g., Bachman, O'Malley, & Johnston, 1981, 1984; Donovan, Jessor, & Jessor, 1983; Jessor, Donovan, & Costa, 1991; Kandel, 1984; O'Malley, Bachman, & Johnston, 1984, 1988; Zucker, 1979, 1987). Although the transition to young adulthood may begin with more freedom than responsibility, the actual assumption of adulthood roles is likely to involve the opposite—more responsibility than freedom.

A number of longitudinal studies have followed young people from adolescence into young adulthood and looked at changes in drug use; these include the Youth in Transition study (Bachman, O'Malley, & Johnston, 1978; Johnston, 1973), and studies by Brunswick, Messeri, and Titus (1992), Jessor and colleagues (Donovan et al., 1983; Jessor et al., 1991), Kandel and colleagues (e.g., Yamaguchi & Kandel, 1985), Kaplan and colleagues (e.g., Johnson & Kaplan, 1991), Newcomb and Bentler (1987), Elliott, Huizinga, and Menard (1989), O'Donnell, Voss, Clayton, Slatin, and Room (1976), and Robins (1974). One consistent finding is that drug use tends to be lower after marriage (Brunswick et al., 1992; Donovan et al., 1983; Horwitz & White, 1991; Miller-Tutzauer, Leonard, & Windle, 1991; Newcomb & Bentler, 1987; Yamaguchi & Kandel, 1985). Another important finding is that more young women are taking seriously the message about drug use and possible effects on a fetus, consequently reducing their use during pregnancy (e.g., Fried, Barnes, & Drake, 1985; Ihlen, Amundsen, Sande, & Daae, 1990; Yamaguchi & Kandel, 1985). However, many of these studies generally have been based on small and sometimes nonrepresentative samples. Here we look at the issue using large nationally representative samples.

MONITORING THE FUTURE PROJECT: RESEARCH DESIGN

All findings presented here are drawn from the Monitoring the Future project, which has been studying high school seniors and young adults, beginning in 1975. A detailed discussion of the research design is available elsewhere (Bachman, Johnston, & O'Malley, 1991). Briefly, nationally representative samples of about 16,000 to 18,000 seniors are surveyed each year using in-school administered questionnaires; then smaller subsamples from each senior cohort are followed using mailed questionnaires (sent on a rotating, every-2-year schedule) throughout their late teens and their 20s. Most of the findings reported here are summaries of original reports available elsewhere (see citations).

AGE OF "INITIATION" INTO USE OF VARIOUS DRUGS

The likelihood of having tried cigarettes, alcohol, marijuana, and other drugs increases with each year of age during adolescence and young adulthood. Figure 5.1, based on retrospective reports by high school seniors in the graduating classes of 1975 to 1992, shows patterns of first use of alcohol, first use of marijuana, first use of cocaine, and first regular use of cigarettes on a daily basis (all data in this and the next section are adapted from Johnston, O'Malley, & Bachman, 1993).

As shown in Fig. 5.1, by the senior year of high school very few students had not tried alcohol at least once. These first experiences with alcohol occur at younger ages than society approves, and thus are generally viewed as problematic. Nevertheless, if most high school students only tried alcohol a few times it would probably not be viewed as a basis for serious concern. A much more worrisome finding is that substantial proportions of students report having had five or more drinks in a row on at least one occasion during the preceding 2 weeks; specifically, in 1992 the proportions were 14% of male and 13% of female 8th-graders, 24% of male and 19% of female 10th-graders, and 36% of male and 20% of female 12th-graders. The fact that large numbers of students report drinking this much on a frequent basis is consistent with the finding that alcohol-related accidents are a leading cause of death among teenagers and young adults.

As Fig. 5.1a suggests, the story for alcohol has not changed a great deal during the past two decades. For other drugs, however, there was a good deal more change. There have been distinct shifts in the popularity of marijuana (Fig. 5.1b) and cocaine (Fig. 5.1c) as well as most other illicit drugs. There was also a decline some years ago in the proportions of young people who were cigarette smokers (Fig. 5.1d) although here the story is more complicated, as we will see.

Figure 5.1b shows that very few students had tried marijuana as early as sixth grade; however, each year thereafter an additional 5% to 10% had their first experience with this drug.

Much less widely used than marijuana is cocaine. Figure 5.1c shows that at each grade level there were far fewer young people involved with cocaine than with marijuana. Also, initiation rates for cocaine tended to increase most in the later grades, whereas for marijuana the largest increases occurred earlier. Note also that the historical trends for these drugs are not parallel: (a) the numbers of cocaine users increased at a more rapid rate than the numbers of marijuana users during the late 1970s, (b) cocaine use did not decline during the first half of the 1980s, whereas marijuana use did, but then (c) cocaine use dropped sharply

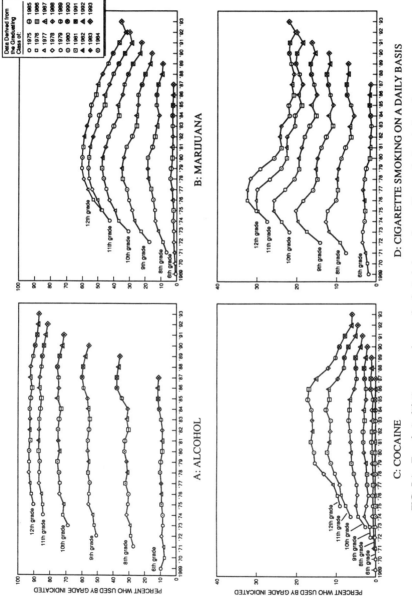

FIG. 5.1. Trends in lifetime prevalence of selected drugs for earlier grade levels based on retrospective reports from 12th graders.

115

after 1986. Later in this chapter we discuss why these historical trends are distinctly different.

We turn next to cigarette smoking, but this time we focus on regular use rather than just trying the substance. Figure 5.1d shows the proportions of young people at each grade level who first used cigarettes on a regular daily basis. Here, as in the case of marijuana, the trends peaked during the 1970s and were lower during the 1980s; however, there is an important difference between the trends in daily cigarette use and trends in the use of the other drugs. Close inspection of Fig. 5.1d reveals that the peak occurred nearly 1 year later for each higher grade level: For 8th graders the peak year was 1974, for 9th graders it was 1975, for 10th graders it was 1975 to 1976, for 11th graders it was 1975 to 1977, and for 12th graders it was 1976 to 1978.

It seems clear to us that it is the addictive nature of cigarette smoking that accounts for the pattern shown in Fig. 5.1d; the peak years for new "recruits" into the ranks of daily smokers were 1973 to 1975; and most continued the habit once they were hooked.

There are two general conclusions we can draw from the age of onset data presented thus far. First, it is clear from the data shown here for cigarettes, alcohol, marijuana, and cocaine, plus our findings about other illicit drugs (not shown, see Johnston et al., 1993), that the further young people progress through adolescence, the more likely it is that they will have tried various drugs. We should add that rates of regular use of most drugs also increase with age during adolescence; an important exception is inhalants, which tend to be discontinued as adolescents grow older.

A second general conclusion is that different drugs have shown distinctly different historical trend patterns during the past two decades. We have seen this illustrated for cigarettes, alcohol, marijuana, and cocaine; the conclusion also holds true for other illicit drugs. There are times when it is appropriate and useful to speak of drug use in general, and there are certainly important similarities and commonalities across many categories of drug use. Nevertheless, one of the important lessons to be drawn from this section, and the next one as well, is that specific drugs have risen and fallen in popularity at different times during the past several decades.

AGE TRENDS IN DRUG USE DURING YOUNG ADULTHOOD

Throughout the remainder of this chapter we deal with drug use during the senior year of high school and the years that follow. We begin by examining age differences and trends, in ways somewhat parallel to the age of onset data shown earlier. From now on, however, we deal with current use rather than first instance of use.

Turning first to alcohol use, Fig. 5.2 shows that monthly use rises during the first few years after high school and then drops off a bit during the late 20s and early 30s. (Although these age differences are taken from cross-sectional surveys of students in a given year, we know from other panel analyses that they are linked to age rather than cohort differences.)

As we noted earlier, a more worrisome matter is the consumption of more than one or two drinks at a time, with one in three males and one in five females in the high school class of 1992 reporting that at least once during the preceding 2 weeks they had five or more drinks in a row. Figure 5.3 indicates that the proportion reporting this level of drinking increases until ages 21 to 22, and decreases steadily thereafter. We see later that certain roles and experiences associated with late adolescence and adulthood seem to influence these rates of heavy drinking.

The age trends shown in Figs. 5.2 and 5.3 were less strongly in evidence 5 or more years ago. The change in recent years is that both monthly use of alcohol and instances of heavy drinking have declined among those under the age of 21. This trend for 30-day prevalence is illustrated in Fig.

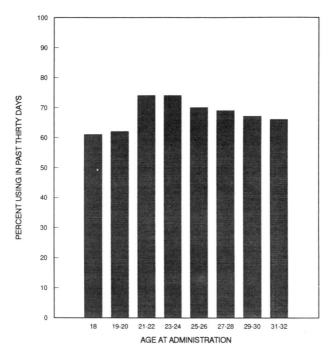

FIG. 5.2. Alcohol: 30-day prevalence rate among young adults, 1993, by age group.

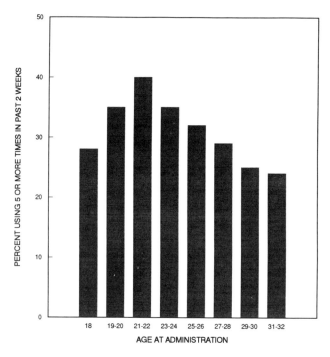

FIG. 5.3.   Alcohol: 2-week prevalence of five or more drinks in a row among
young adults, 1993, by age group.

5.4, and the trend for occasions of heavy drinking is similar. The decline
in drinking among those under age 21 is due in part to the effects of
changes in minimum drinking laws in many states (O'Malley &
Wagenaar, 1991).

When we turn to marijuana use during the senior year and afterward,
the age distinctions are easier to describe: At any given year there simply
are no meaningful differences among the various age groups after high
school graduation (see Fig. 5.5). However, in the presence of a historical
trend such as that shown for marijuana, it is not strictly accurate to say
that there are no differences associated with age. For example, for the
high school class of 1980, average marijuana use went down each year
after graduation, whereas for the class of 1976 use went up each year
until about age 21 (i.e., 1979) and thereafter declined. Thus, age-related
differences will appear in any cohort that is tracked through a period of
historical change; however, those differences are not a function of age
per se, and the age-related changes observed for one cohort may not be
generalizable to other cohorts.

There is an important lesson in these findings for those interested in
developmental patterns, especially in an area as volatile as drug use has

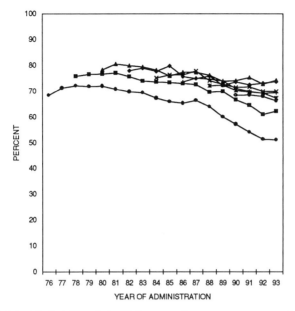

FIG. 5.4. Alcohol: Trends in 30-day prevalence among young adults by age group.

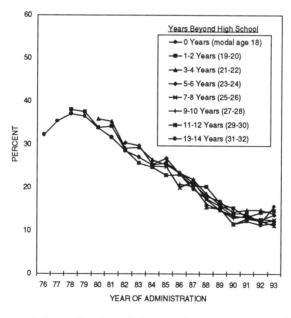

FIG. 5.5. Marijuana: Trends in 30-day prevalence among young adults by age group.

119

been during the past two decades: Following a single cohort across time (as is often done) runs the risk of confusing historical trends with maturational change. As our examples show, tracking a cohort from age 18 to age 28 could suggest very different conclusions about age trends in marijuana use, depending on whether one started in 1976 or 1980. Moreover, each one of these different conclusions would be accurate only in a very limited sense, and thus misleading. The much more general conclusion is that marijuana use peaked around 1979, at least for late adolescents or young adults, no matter what age or cohort we consider. When we try to sort out the causes of these changes, it becomes quite important to distinguish between age-related trends and those that are more appropriately viewed as historical trends.

Turning now to cocaine use, we see evidence for both kinds of trends. Figure 5.6 shows that annual prevalence of cocaine use by high school seniors rose from less than 6% in 1976 to 12% in 1979, changed relatively little from 1980 through 1986, and thereafter declined sharply. These data are fully consistent with those shown in Fig. 5.1c; they indicate a historical trend upward during the late 1970s, and then a sharp decline after 1986.

An important additional finding shown in Fig. 5.6 is that annual prevalence of cocaine use rises with age during the late teens and early 20s, so that by age 23 to 24 it is nearly double the rate for high school seniors.

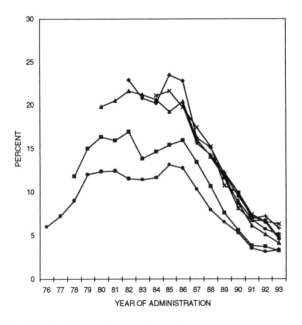

FIG. 5.6. Cocaine: Trends in annual prevalence among young adults by age group.

None of the other illicit drugs we have examined has shown such increases during early adulthood (Johnston et al., 1993).

The pattern of findings for cigarette use during senior year and beyond is different from that for the other drugs; however, it is fully consistent with the data we reported earlier. Figure 5.1d showed that the bulge in daily smokers among eighth and ninth graders in the mid-1970s moved on to be a bulge in smokers among seniors graduating in the later 1970s. Figure 5.7 shows that this bulge extended into early adulthood a few years later; we can see, for example, that those who graduated in 1976 to 1978 (and thus reached age 21 or 22 in 1980 or 1981) were more likely to be half-pack-a-day smokers than those who graduated in later years.

In addition to showing stable cohort differences in smoking, Fig. 5.7 also shows an age-linked shift in half-pack-a-day smoking. During the first 1 to 3 years after graduation, each class has shown about a 5% or 6% increase in half-pack-a-day smokers, with little change thereafter (see also O'Malley et al., 1984, 1988). More detailed analyses of the data indicate that this change is not primarily due to new recruits into the ranks of smokers; rather, some who smoked at lower rates raised their cigarette consumption soon after leaving high school. Attending high school no doubt constrains some individuals from smoking as often as they wish, so when they enter less restrictive environments after graduation their rates of smoking rise.

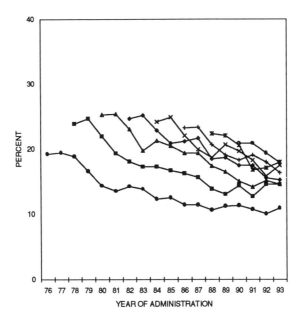

FIG. 5.7. Cigarettes: Trends in 30-day prevalence of smoking a half-pack or more daily among young adults by age group.

Summarizing briefly the findings from this section, our first observation is that in recent years there have been several fairly consistent age-related changes in drug use. Nearly all of these changes involve an increase after high school, although the likely explanations are somewhat different. Alcohol use in general, and instances of heavy drinking in particular, rise as young people reach and surpass the legal drinking age of 21; however, heavy drinking tends to decrease thereafter (see Fig. 5.3), for reasons discussed in a later section. Cocaine use also rose after high school, at least for those who graduated during the early 1980s. (The cocaine findings stand in contrast to those for marijuana, where no such general increase after high school was evident.) Rates of half-pack or more daily cigarette use also increase during the first several years after high school, probably because the reduced constraints in most post-high-school environments permitted those already "hooked" on cigarettes to increase their daily rates of consumption.

A second summary observation is that there have been several historical trends in recent years that are, of course, confounded with age. In other words, not all changes that occur as members of a particular cohort move from one age to another should be thought of as influenced by age, or by factors related to age. In particular, major changes in usage rates for marijuana and cocaine during the 1980s can be attributed to a variety of historical events that had their impact across a wide range of ages. In the next section we turn our attention to some of these events, and what they may be able to tell us about the factors that contribute to drug use by youth and young adults.

EXPLAINING RECENT HISTORICAL TRENDS IN DRUG USE

The changes in marijuana and cocaine use during the 1980s were really quite striking, in part because they were distinctly different from each other. Although the declines in marijuana use and cocaine use had different trajectories and starting times, they were similar in two important respects: (a) each was marked by a clear shift in attitudes about the drug, and (b) neither was accompanied by any appreciable decline in the perceived availability of the drug.

We have long argued that the more danger young people associate with a drug, the less likely they will be to use it (Johnston, 1982, 1985; Johnston, Bachman, & O'Malley, 1981). Indeed, the national trend data on use and perceived risk certainly supported such an interpretation, as did the increasing frequency of mentioning health concerns as reasons for abstaining from, or quitting, marijuana use. However, Jessor (1985) suggested a possible alternative explanation for the decline in marijuana use—that young people had undergone a more general change in the direction of being more "conservative" and less "trouble-prone."

We carried out detailed explorations of these two competing explanations, first with respect to marijuana use (Bachman, Johnston, O'Malley, & Humphrey, 1988) and later with respect to cocaine use (Bachman, Johnston, & O'Malley, 1990). The findings clearly showed that neither of the declines in use could be attributed to overall shifts in lifestyle factors. Instead, our findings suggested that drug-specific factors such as perceived risk and disapproval can act to limit the use of a drug. Importantly, perceptions of availability seemed unrelated to the declines in use. We view this combination of findings as indicating that reductions in demand (rather than supply) were the key factors in the declines in marijuana and cocaine use that took place during the 1980s.

What are the dynamics of changing attitudes about particular drugs? We believe that perceptions about the risks associated with use of any drug are a fundamental factor, and that these perceptions in turn influence disapproval at both individual and peer group levels (see Johnston, 1991, for an elaboration of the underlying theoretical perspective).

However, that leaves us with a further question: What causes the changing perceptions of risk? In the case of marijuana, we suggested that at least two kinds of social change were involved: First, there was better research and media reporting on the physical and psychological consequences of marijuana use; second, long-term heavy marijuana use had become common enough that students' firsthand perceptions provided some validation of the "burnout" descriptions being carried in the media. In the case of cocaine, it seemed again that information provided via the media was a key factor prompting changes in attitudes. In the late spring of 1986, two popular young athletes, Len Bias and Don Rogers, died as a result of cocaine use. These talented and successful young men in prime physical condition were the kinds of individuals with whom high school students could readily identify—and thus their deaths, within weeks of each other, no doubt had some of the same impact as would a classmate's death due to cocaine (Bachman et al., 1990). Johnston (1991) referred to such individuals as "unfortunate role models." Others can learn vicariously of the dangers of a drug from their tragic experiences.

With respect to prevention efforts, the findings already summarized strongly suggest that young people do pay attention to new information about the risks associated with using particular drugs; therefore, such information, when presented realistically and credibly, can contribute importantly to demand reduction.

There can be other reasons for the decline in popularity of a drug. A change in any of the five conditions Johnston (1991) posited as giving rise to an epidemic in use could, in theory, cause a decline. These conditions are: awareness of the drug and its psychoactive potential, access to the drug, motivation to use, a willingness to violate social norms (and perhaps laws), and reassurance about the safety of the drug. We believe that a loss of reassurance about safety probably was key to declines in the use of LSD, PCP, and methamphetamines, as well as marijuana and cocaine.

We have thus far reviewed several different historical trends in the use of various drugs, and we have seen several different patterns of age-linked changes in proportions of users or rates of use. Based on this diversity of patterns, we have cautioned against treating drug use or drug abuse as a single dimension. We must also note, however, that there are factors that make some adolescents and young adults more likely than others to initiate, increase, or decrease their involvement with any of a variety of drugs. We turn next to an examination of some of these individual differences in background and experiences that are related to drug use.

INDIVIDUAL DIFFERENCES PREDICTING ADOLESCENTS' DRUG USE

What characteristics lead some adolescents to become regular smokers, or use alcohol in large quantities, or use marijuana? How consistent are these factors across different drugs and across different times? After examining a number of background and lifestyle factors correlated with the use of cigarettes, alcohol, marijuana, and other illicit drugs, we concluded that some individuals seem especially disposed toward deviant or problem behavior (Jessor, Chase, & Donovan, 1980; Jessor & Jessor, 1977; Johnston, O'Malley, & Eveland, 1978; Smith & Fogg, 1978), although the particular forms of behavior chosen vary over different historical periods (as well as from one school or region to another). Thus in the 1960s and 1970s illicit drug use emerged as an increasingly "popular" form of deviance, so instead of simply smoking cigarettes and using alcohol, many teenagers also used marijuana, and some used other illicit drugs (Bachman, Johnston, & O'Malley, 1991). We have found consistently that those dimensions of background and lifestyle that correlate with one kind of drug use (e.g., heavy drinking) also correlate with most other kinds of drug use (e.g., use of marijuana, use of other illicit drugs). We also have found that these patterns of correlation changed rather little over time. It continues to be true that drug use is above average among those less successful in adapting to the educational environment (as indicated by truancy and low grades), those who spend many evenings out for recreation, those with heavy time commitments to a part-time job, and those with relatively high incomes. It also continues to be true that drug use is below average among those with strong religious commitments and those with conservative political views; however, the links with religious and political views grew somewhat weaker during the 1980s (see Bachman, O'Malley, & Johnston, 1986).

Still another analysis was carried out in order to assess the relative importance of shared causes, specific causes, and influences of one form of deviant behavior on another. The analysis employed three waves of panel data ranging from senior year to 4 years beyond high school, and examined self-reported measures of heavy alcohol use, marijuana use, use of other illicit drugs, problem driving, and other illegal behavior (including interpersonal aggression, theft, and vandalism). We summarized our results as showing that "a general tendency toward deviance could explain the positive correlations between different deviant behaviors. Indeed, a single latent variable can account for virtually all of their cross-sectional and longitudinal relationships" (Osgood, Johnston, O'Malley, & Bachman, 1988, p. 91). In other words, it appears that the correlations between different types of deviance are largely due to a single set of shared causes.

But does that mean that the various forms of drug use and other deviant behaviors are all simply manifestations of the same general tendency toward unconventionality or criminality? No, the findings are not that simple. Although a general tendency can account for why different forms of deviance are correlated with each other, and although that tendency shows much stability across time, there remains a good deal of additional stability in each of the deviant behaviors. This suggests that in addition to the general or shared causes, there are equally important and stable specific causes for each of the deviant behaviors. Indeed, we have already noted the highly addictive properties of nicotine as one source of stability in the case of cigarette use.

STABILITY IN INDIVIDUAL PATTERNS OF DRUG USE

How stable or consistent across time is drug-using behavior in late adolescence and early adulthood? The answer to this question, based on our own research as well as the work of others (Donovan et al., 1983; Elliott et al., 1989; Grant, Harford, & Grigson, 1988; Kandel, Yamaguchi, & Chen, 1992; Newcomb & Bentler, 1987), is that drug use shows a considerable degree of continuity across time. Indeed, by far the best predictor of drug use in young adulthood is drug use during high school. Table 5.1 shows patterns of cross-time correlations for use of cigarettes, alcohol, marijuana,

TABLE 5.1

Autocorrelations (Base Year With Follow-Up) for Drug Use Measures

Drug Use Measure	Estimated Reliability	Correlations With Base Year		
		1-Year Follow-Up	2-Year Follow-Up	3-Year Follow-Up
Cigarette use in past month	.89			
Autocorrelations		.79	.73	.70
Stability estimates		.89	.82	.79
Heavy drinking in past 2 weeks	.64			
Autocorrelations		.51	.46	.42
Stability estimates		.80	.72	.65
Alcohol use in past year	.87			
Autocorrelations		.70	.65	.58
Stability estimates		.81	.75	.67
Marijuana use in past	.90			
Autocorrelations		.76	.66	.59
Stability estimates		.85	.73	.66
Other illicit drug use in past year	.73			
Autocorrelations		.60	.48	.42
Stability estimates		.82	.66	.58

Note. Autocorrelations = correlations between drug use during high school and use of the same category of drug during the first several years after high school. Stability estimates = autocorrelations adjusted for reliability. Adapted by permission from Bachman, J. G., O'Malley, P. M., & Johnston, L. D. (1984). Drug use among young adults: The impacts of role status and social environment. *Journal of Personality and Social Psychology, 47,* 629–645.

and other illicit drugs. Particularly after adjustments for measurement unreliability, the relationships across time are impressively high.

Why are there such high levels of stability for the various types of drug use? There are a variety of plausible explanations. In the case of cigarette use, which shows distinctly higher stability than any other form of drug use we have studied, we believe physical addiction plays a very strong role, even at these young ages. The majority of smokers in our surveys would prefer not to smoke, and many have tried unsuccessfully to quit. In the case of most other drug use in the samples we have studied, we suspect that physical dependency is not usually the primary factor in sustaining the behavior; however the actual physical effects experienced as a result of using the drug must certainly have some influence on an individual's desire to repeat the experience.

With the possible exception of habitual cigarette use, we suspect that factors in the social environment contribute most heavily to drug use. Moreover, it seems likely that the same social factors that influenced use during high school continue to be influential during the post-high-school years. One very important set of factors influencing drug use consists of peer attitudes, pressures, and practices. Those most involved with drug use in high school were also most likely to have friends who used drugs and who held relatively uncritical attitudes about drugs. Although most young people leaving high school take on some new roles, experience new social environments, and make some new friends, they also tend to hold on to old friends and social habits. Parental attitudes and practices are another important influence on youthful drug use, and although there may be some changes in parents' views and actions, especially with respect to legal substances such as cigarettes and alcohol, it is also highly likely that parental values continue to have some influence on the behaviors of young adults. (This is especially true, as shown later, for those young adults who continue to live in their parents' homes.) Religious commitment is still another important influence on drug use; those with the highest involvement in religion during high school were least likely to use drugs, and religious commitment remains relatively stable during the post-high-school years.

As we see in the next section, there are several key changes in roles and social environments that tend to change following high school and that can have substantial impacts on drug use. Changes such as moving out of the parental home, becoming engaged, and marrying all seem to influence drug use. However, it is worth adding that even among mobile young adults these really important transitions occur relatively infrequently; during any 1-year interval, for example, relatively few make the transition from unmarried to married, whereas the great majority retain the same marital status.

In sum, we think that a broad range of factors in the social environment affect drug use, and many of these factors are relatively stable. This in turn means that patterns of drug use that are established during high school will continue with a good deal of stability into the years beyond high school. With each additional year after high school the likelihood increases that an individual will have made one or more important transitions in status (e.g., have become married); and thus the longer intervals in Table 5.1 show lower stability. Nevertheless, even among those in their mid-20s (which goes well beyond the 3-year interval shown in Table 5.1), young adult drug use is still quite well predicted by senior year use.

CHANGES IN DRUG USE LINKED TO POST-HIGH-SCHOOL EXPERIENCES

Against the backdrop of considerable stability in individual patterns of drug use, we have nevertheless found some systematic changes in drug use linked to post-high-school experiences. Extensive analyses of the first 3 years following high school (Bachman et al., 1984) revealed that instances of heavy drinking, marijuana use, and use of other illicit drugs tended to decrease among those who married, remained much the same (on average) among the unmarrieds who continued to live in their parents' homes, and increased among other unmarrieds who left the parental home.

The findings for marijuana use, shown in Fig. 5.8, illustrate these effects of living arrangements clearly. When we look at the follow-up (or "after") data in the figure, we see distinctly different proportions of marijuana users among those living with a spouse, those living with parents, and those in other living arrangements. If our information were limited to these post-high-school data, we might be hard put to decide whether they reflect differential effects of living arrangements, or simply longer standing differences among those who enter these different situations during the first few years after high school. Fortunately, the senior year (or "before") data are available, and they clearly indicate that the three major subgroups started out with virtually identical proportions of marijuana users. This close similarity at the end of high school, coupled with distinct differences observed during the next several years, provide strong support for the interpretation that living arrangements do influence the use of marijuana.

The one other subgroup shown in Fig. 5.8 is comprised of those few (3% of the males, 5% of the females) who at the time of the follow-up survey reported that they were cohabiting with a partner of the opposite sex. This subgroup showed much higher proportions of marijuana users both as seniors and during the post-high-school years; that is, the high

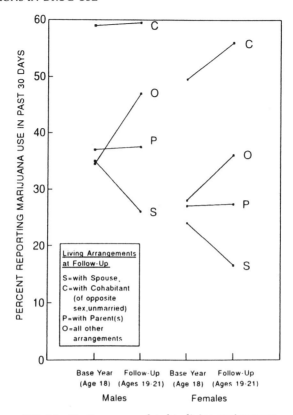

FIG. 5.8. Marijuana use related to living environment.

rates of marijuana use preceded entrance into the social role of cohabitant. We need not conclude from this that marijuana use directly increases the likelihood that someone will later become a cohabitant; a broader and more parsimonious interpretation is that those individuals more willing to undertake one "unconventional" and widely disapproved behavior in high school are also more willing to undertake other such behaviors in the years following high school.

The findings for heavy drinking and for use of other illicit drugs closely match those for marijuana shown in Fig. 5.8. Along each of these dimensions of drug use, those who married showed a decrease in use, on average, whereas others who left the parental home showed an increase. Thus it is clear that living arrangements and marital status are aspects of post-high-school experience that have implications for a number of dimensions of drug use.

Another important aspect of post-high-school experience involves taking on new roles as college students and/or as employees. There are many possible combinations of these two role dimensions, but for the present we simply distinguish between those who at the time of the follow-up survey were (a) full-time students, (b) employed full-time in civilian occupations, or (c) unemployed and not a student or homemaker. Figure 5.9 shows that the proportions of marijuana users increased among both males and females who were full-time students, whereas among the other subgroups the proportions did not increase. Heavy drinking was also more likely to increase among the students, as was use of other illicit drugs. In this figure, unlike the earlier one, we do not see the several subgroups starting from much the same point and then diverging; instead, it appears that the college students tend to "catch up" with the levels of drug use shown earlier by their non-college-bound high school classmates (see also Schulenberg, Bachman, O'Malley, & Johnston, 1994).

What is it about being a college student that leads to the upturn in heavy drinking and use of illicit drugs? One of the most important aspects of college life is that it often involves leaving the parental home and moving to a dormitory or other student housing situation; also, relatively few college students are married and living with a spouse. In other words,

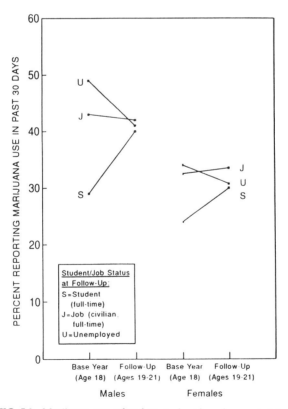

FIG. 5.9. Marijuana use related to student/employment status.

the living arrangements associated with college are conducive to increased drug use, and this suggests that what at first blush appear to be
simply "college effects" may be explainable in terms of the living arrangements we saw earlier. Multivariate regression analyses indicate that indeed this is the case; once living arrangements are entered into the
equation, there is little remaining effect that could be attributed to something unique about the student role. The reverse is not true; if we control
first for student and employment status, substantial effects remain that
are attributable to marriage and living arrangements. What causal interpretation is suggested by this overlap between college attendance and
living arrangements? In our view, the most appropriate causal interpretation is that college attendance has indirect effects on drug use, because
going to college influences living arrangements (including marriage),
which in turn have more direct effects on drug use.

In sum, the analyses summarized here suggest that marital status and
living arrangements are among the most important factors influencing
changes in drug use, at least during the first few years after high school.
In a later section, we examine whether the same kinds of changes in drug
use appear when marriage occurs a bit later in young adulthood. First,
however, we consider how the findings for cigarette smoking differ from
those we have just reviewed.

Figures 5.10 and 5.11 show changes in half-pack-a-day cigarette smoking during the first few years after high school, as related to marital status
and living arrangements, and to student and employment status. We
noted earlier that smoking at the half-pack or more rate increased during
the first several years after high school, and that increase is evident for
each of the groups shown in these figures. The figures do not show much
in the way of differential change among the several subgroups; instead,
they show differences among the groups that were evident before they
left high school. Most striking is the fact that those headed for college
were less than half as likely to be regular smokers—either during high
school or afterward—as were their non-college-bound classmates.

We noted earlier that those with a poor adjustment to school, as
reflected in low grades, truancy, and so on, were most likely to use drugs.
That relationship is especially strong in the case of cigarette use. In a
study of young men who were in high school during 1966 to 1969, we
found that among all their drug-using behaviors, cigarette use was by
far the most strongly linked with (actually, "predictive" of) the amount
of education they eventually attained (Bachman et al., 1978). This does
not mean, of course, that cigarette use "stunted their intellectual
growth"—even though the differences in smoking clearly preceded the
differences in educational attainment. Instead, we interpret the correlation
as reflecting a common set of prior causes: Young people who do poorly

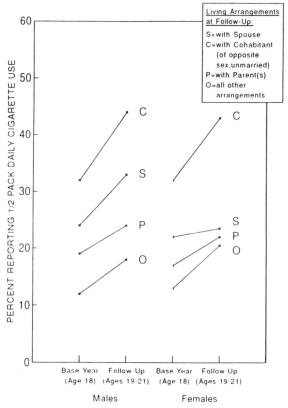

FIG. 5.10. Cigarette use related to living environment.

in the earlier years of school (elementary school, middle school, and/or junior high school) are more likely to become smokers during adolescence, and they also are less likely to go to college. The fact that the relationship between smoking and eventual educational attainment is so strong can be seen as evidence for two rather different ways in which early educational successes and failures can have long-term impacts: (a) they shape later educational aptitudes and aspirations, and (b) they affect the likelihood of involvement with a highly addictive substance—nicotine. Having said that, we can add that to some extent, at least, smoking might actually have some indirect causal impacts on educational attainment; because adolescent smokers tend to associate with each other, and because smoking is relatively rare among the college bound, the teenager who smokes is less likely to associate with college-bound classmates, and thus less likely to feel any peer pressure or encouragement to go on to college.

Some of our recent longitudinal evidence based on structural equation modeling underscores the importance of earlier educational success (high school grade point average [GPA] and college plans) on changes in drug

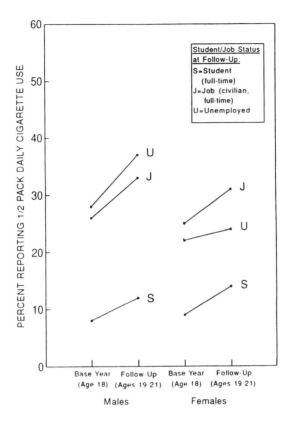

FIG. 5.11. Cigarette use related to student/employment status.

use during the transition to young adulthood (Schulenberg et al., 1994). As has been well documented over the years, educational commitment and success in school are negatively related to substance use during high school. Our findings show that high school GPA continues to exert a negative influence on the use of cigarettes, alcohol, and illicit drugs 3 to 4 years after high school. This influence is largely indirect, operating via senior year substance use, indicating that the effect of GPA operates regardless of post-high-school contexts and experiences. Similarly, college plans during high school had a negative indirect effect on post-high-school cigarette use that operated largely via senior year cigarette use. In contrast, however, college plans had an indirect positive effect on post-high-school alcohol use, and this effect operated largely via post-high-school experiences (student and marital status)—that is, compared to their classmates, those with college plans in high school were more likely to increase their alcohol use after high school because they were more likely to be college students and less likely to be married, a causal chain consistent with our earlier work. We also found that college plans had no total effect on post-high-school illicit drug use (i.e., the indirect negative effect via senior year drug use was "cancelled out" by the indirect positive effect via post-high-school experiences).

Thus far in this section we have summarized analyses of changes in drug use during the first few years after high school. More recent work (Bachman, O'Malley, Johnston, Rodgers, & Schulenberg, 1992) has extended the panel analyses up to 10 years beyond high school, with results that replicated our earlier findings quite closely. Perhaps the most important and consistent of these findings is the decline in drug use associated with the transition into marriage. Figures 5.12 and 5.13 display percentages of males and females using marijuana at various points throughout an 8-year interval, looking separately at those who married prior to the first follow-up, prior to the second, third, fourth, as well as those who remained unmarried at the time of the fourth follow-up. It can readily be seen that in each of the intervals of transition into marriage (marked by heavy lines) there are sharp declines in the proportions of

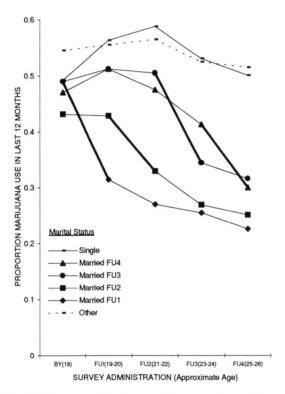

FIG. 5.12.   Marijuana use related to marital status, males. Bold line indicates the time interval during which marriage occurred. From Bachman (1987).

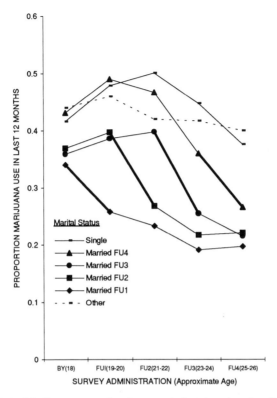

FIG. 5.13. Marijuana use related to marital status, females. Bold line indicates the time interval during which marriage occurred. From Bachman (1987).

both males and females involved in marijuana use. The findings for heavy drinking (not shown) are quite similar to those for marijuana use; in the interval during which marriage occurs, the likelihood of heavy drinking declines. The data for cocaine show the pattern less clearly; actually, the pattern for this drug is better described as marriage seeming to prevent (and sometimes reverse) the increasing proportions of young adults becoming involved with cocaine.

We can note briefly a number of other findings that have emerged in other analyses of our follow-up surveys of young adults, and that are closely related to the marriage findings. First, the relatively small numbers who were married and then divorced were excluded from Figs. 5.12 and 5.13; however, when we looked at them separately it appeared that during the interval when they made the transition out of marriage they also tended to increase their drug use. Second, when we examined those who indicated that they were engaged, we found that their drug use had declined somewhat—in other words, it appears that the total effect of marriage, including some experiences that may precede the actual exchange of vows, works predominantly in the direction of reducing drug use. Third, when we looked separately at the transition from nonparent to parent, we found an additional decline in drug use. This appears to be largely independent of the marriage effects displayed in Figs. 5.12 and 5.13, because most make the transition into parenthood somewhat later than the transition into marriage. In any case, regression analyses that distinguish the two effects indicate that both are important (Bachman et al., 1992). Finally, it appears that during pregnancy women very sharply reduce their use of alcohol, and even reduce their use of cigarettes (a behavior that changed very little in connection with other post-high-school experiences); incidentally, the husbands of pregnant women reduce their alcohol use somewhat, but not their cigarette use (Bachman et al., 1992).

CONCLUDING COMMENTS

What are the developmental implications of the findings summarized here? Certainly one important implication is that there is considerable evidence of continuity over time and across behavioral domains in terms of the general factors that seem to predispose to deviant behaviors; the kinds of individuals likely to get involved with a whole range of troublesome behaviors were much the same in the 1980s as they were in 1975. However, insofar as drug use is concerned, the particular types of troublesome behavior have shifted somewhat during the past decade, and the shifts have not all been the same; thus, they cannot be explained simply in terms of changes in general predisposing factors. Instead, it appears that we must look to more specific factors to account for the rise and fall in popularity of particular forms of deviance.

That last conclusion may have practical implications for drug prevention efforts; it suggests that we do not necessarily have to "cure" or "prevent" general trouble-proneness in order to deal with particular drugs. We seem to be in the midst of a particularly exciting period of social change in which many of the effects of various forms of risky behavior are examined, widely reported, and incorporated into the perceptions of young people, all within the space of a few years. We think that sequence of phenomena accounts for many of the recent trends in marijuana use and in cocaine use. Based on experiences in prior years, it seems unlikely that scare tactics will work, particularly when contradicted by personal experiences. However, we believe that realistic information about the risks of a given type of deviant behavior, communicated by a credible source, can be persuasive and can play an important role in what must ultimately be the most effective means of reducing drug use—reducing demand.

The implications of these findings for theory would seem to be that any effort to account for the totality of deviance in adolescence and young adulthood will have to take into account both the general factors and those specific to particular deviant behaviors. Moreover, there will need to be a recognition that some forms of deviance may remain largely dependent on early experiences and current social factors, whereas others are more addictive and thus are much more resistant to change. Taking account of all these factors is a tall order indeed. In the meantime, we do well to keep in mind that our theorizing is usually about only a portion of a complex and ever-changing domain of behaviors.

ACKNOWLEDGMENT

Data are drawn from the Monitoring the Future project, a study supported by a grant from the National Institute on Drug Abuse (R01-DA-01411).

REFERENCES

Bachman, J. G. (1987, July). *Changes in deviant behavior during late adolescence and early adulthood.* Paper presented at the ninth biennial meeting of the International Society for the Study of Behavioral Development, Tokyo, Japan. (ERIC Document No. ED 309365)

Bachman, J. G., Johnston, L. D., & O'Malley, P. M. (1990). Explaining the recent decline in cocaine use among young adults: Further evidence that perceived risks and disapproval lead to reduced drug use. *Journal of Health and Social Behavior, 31,* 173–184.

Bachman, J. G., Johnston, L. D., & O'Malley, P. M. (1991). *Monitoring the Future project after seventeen years: Design and procedures* (Monitoring the Future Occasional Paper No. 33). Ann Arbor, MI: Institute for Social Research.

Bachman, J. G., Johnston, L. D., O'Malley, P. M., & Humphrey, R. H. (1988). Explaining the recent decline in marijuana use: Differentiating the effects of perceived risks, disapproval, and general lifestyle factors. *Journal of Health and Social Behavior, 29,* 92–112.

Bachman, J. G., O'Malley, P. M., & Johnston, J. (1978). *Youth in transition: Vol. 6. Adolescence to adulthood—A study of change and stability in the lives of young men.* Ann Arbor, MI: Institute for Social Research.

Bachman, J. G., O'Malley, P. M., & Johnston, L. D. (1981). *Changes in drug use after high school as a function of role status and social environment* (Monitoring the Future Occasional Paper No. 11). Ann Arbor, MI: Institute for Social Research.

Bachman, J. G., O'Malley, P. M., & Johnston, L. D. (1984). Drug use among young adults: The impacts of role status and social environments. *Journal of Personality and Social Psychology, 47,* 629–645.

Bachman, J. G., O'Malley, P. M., & Johnston, L. D. (1986). *Change and consistency in the correlates of drug use among high school seniors: 1976–1986* (Monitoring the Future Occasional Paper No. 21). Ann Arbor, MI: Institute for Social Research.

Bachman, J. G., O'Malley, P. M., Johnston, L. D., Rodgers, W. L., & Schulenberg, J. (1992). *Changes in drug use during the post-high school years* (Monitoring the Future Occasional Paper No. 35). Ann Arbor, MI: Institute for Social Research.

Baltes, P. B. (1987). Theoretical propositions of life-span developmental psychology: On the dynamics between growth and decline. *Developmental Psychology, 23,* 611–626.

Baltes, P. B., Reese, H. W., & Lipsett, L. P. (1980). Life-span developmental psychology. *Annual Review of Psychology, 31,* 65–110.

Brim, O. G., Jr., & Kagan, J. (1980). Constancy and change: A view of the issues. In O. G. Brim, Jr. & J. Kagan (Eds.), *Constancy and change in human development* (pp. 1–25). Cambridge, MA: Harvard University Press.

Bronfenbrenner, U. (1979). *The ecology of human development.* Cambridge, MA: Harvard University Press.

Brunswick, A. F., Messeri, P. A., & Titus, S. P. (1992). Predictive factors in adult substance abuse: A prospective study of African American adolescents. In M. Glantz & R. Pickens (Eds.), *Vulnerability to drug abuse* (pp. 419–472). Washington, DC: American Psychological Association.

Donovan, J. E., Jessor, R., & Jessor, L. (1983). Problem drinking in adolescence and young adulthood: A follow-up study. *Journal of Studies on Alcohol, 44,* 109–137.

Elliott, D. S., Huizinga, D., & Menard, S. (1989). *Multiple problem youth: Delinquency, substance use, and mental health problems.* New York: Springer-Verlag.

Featherman, D. L. (1983). Life-span perspectives in social science research. In P. B. Baltes & O. G. Brim, Jr. (Eds.), *Life-span development and behavior* (Vol. 5, pp. 1–59). New York: Academic Press.

Fried, P. A., Barnes, M. V., & Drake, E. R. (1985). Soft drug use after pregnancy compared to use before and during pregnancy. *American Journal of Obstetrics and Gynecology, 151,* 787–792.

Grant, B. F., Harford, T. C., & Grigson, M. B. (1988). Stability of alcohol consumption among youth: A national longitudinal survey. *Journal of Studies on Alcohol, 49,* 253–260.

Horwitz, A. V., & White, H. R. (1991). Becoming married, depression, and alcohol problems among young adults. *Journal of Health and Social Behavior, 32,* 221–237.

Ihlen, B. M., Amundsen, A., Sande, H. A., & Daae, L. (1990). Changes in the use of intoxicants after onset of pregnancy. *British Journal of Addictions, 85,* 1627–1631.

Jessor, R. (1985). Bridging etiology and prevention in drug abuse research. In C. J. Jones & R. J. Battjes (Eds.), *Etiology of drug abuse: Implications for prevention* (NIDA Research Monograph No. 56, DHHS Publication No. ADM-85-1335, pp. 257–268). Washington, DC: U.S. Government Printing Office.

Jessor, R., Chase, J. A., & Donovan, J. E. (1980). Psychosocial correlates of marijuana use and problem drinking in a national sample of adolescents. *American Journal of Public Health, 70,* 604–613.

Jessor, R., Donovan, J. E., & Costa, F. M. (1991). *Beyond adolescence: Problem behavior and young adult development.* New York: Cambridge University Press.

Jessor, R., & Jessor, S. L. (1977). *Problem behavior and psychological development: A longitudinal study of youth.* New York: Academic Press.

Johnson, R. J., & Kaplan, H. B. (1991). Developmental processes leading to marijuana use: Comparing civilians and the military. *Youth & Society, 23,* 3–30.

Johnston, L. D. (1973). *Drugs and American youth.* Ann Arbor, MI: Institute for Social Research.

Johnston, L. D. (1982). A review and analysis of recent changes in marijuana use by American young people. In *Marijuana: The national impact on education* (pp. 8–13). New York: American Council on Marijuana.

Johnston, L. D. (1985). The etiology and prevention of substance use: What can we learn from recent historical changes? In C. L. Jones & R. J. Battjes (Eds.), *Etiology of drug abuse:*

Implications for prevention (pp. 155–177). Washington, DC: U.S. Government Printing Office.

Johnston, L. D. (1991). Toward a theory of drug epidemics. In R. L. Donohew, H. Sypher, & W. Bukoski (Eds.), *Persuasive communication and drug abuse prevention* (pp. 93–132). Hillsdale, NJ: Lawrence Erlbaum Associates.

Johnston, L. D., Bachman, J. G., & O'Malley, P. M. (1981). *Highlights from student drug use in America, 1975–1980* (DHHS Publication No. ADM-81-1066). Washington, DC: U.S. Government Printing Office.

Johnston, L. D., O'Malley, P. M., & Bachman, J. G. (1993). *National survey results on drug use from the Monitoring the Future study, 1975–1992* (NIH Pub. Nos. 93-3597, 93-3598). Rockville, MD: National Institute on Drug Abuse.

Johnston, L. D., O'Malley, P. M., & Eveland L. K. (1978). Drugs and delinquency: A search for causal connections. In D. B. Kandel (Ed.), *Longitudinal research on drug use: Empirical findings and methodological issues* (pp. 137–156). Washington, DC: Hemisphere.

Kandel, D. (1984). Marijuana users in young adulthood. *Archives of General Psychiatry, 41,* 200–209.

Kandel, D., Yamaguchi, K., & Chen, K. (1992). Stages in drug involvement from adolescence to adulthood: Further evidence for the gateway theory. *Journal of Studies on Alcohol, 53,* 447–457.

Lerner, R. M. (1984). *On the nature of human plasticity.* New York: Cambridge University Press.

Lerner, R. M. (1986). *Concepts and theories of human development* (2nd ed.). New York: Random House.

Miller-Tutzauer, C., Leonard, K. E., & Windle, M. (1991). Marriage and alcohol use: A longitudinal study of "maturing out." *Journal of Studies on Alcohol, 52,* 434–440.

Newcomb, M. D., & Bentler, P. M. (1987). Changes in drug use from high school to young adulthood: Effects of living arrangement and current life pursuit. *Journal of Applied Developmental Psychology, 8,* 221–246.

O'Donnell, J. A., Voss, H. L., Clayton, R. R., Slatin, G. T., & Room, R. (1976). *Young men and drugs—A nationwide survey* (NIDA Monograph No. 5, DHEW Publication No. ADM-76-311). Rockville, MD: Alcohol, Drug Abuse, and Mental Health Administration.

O'Malley, P. M., Bachman, J. G., & Johnston, L. D. (1984). Period, age, and cohort effects on substance use among American youth. *American Journal of Public Health, 74,* 682–688.

O'Malley, P. M., Bachman, J. G., & Johnston, L. D. (1988). Period, age, and cohort effects on substance use among young Americans: A decade of change, 1976–1986. *American Journal of Public Health, 78,* 1315–1321.

O'Malley, P. M., & Wagenaar, A. C. (1991). Effects of minimum drinking age laws on alcohol use, related behaviors, and traffic crash involvement among American youth: 1976–1987. *Journal of Studies on Alcohol, 52,* 478–491.

Osgood, D. W., Johnston, L. D., O'Malley, P. M., & Bachman, J. G. (1988). The generality of deviance in late adolescence and early adulthood. *American Sociological Review, 53,* 81–93.

Pandina, R. J., Labouvie, E. W., & White, H. R. (1984). Potential contributions of the life span developmental approach to the study of adolescent alcohol and drug use. *Journal of Drug Issues, 14,* 253–270.

Robins, L. N. (1974). The Vietnam drug user returns. (Special Action Office Monograph, Series A, No. 2). Washington, DC: Executive Office of the President (Special Action Office for Drug Abuse Prevention).

Schulenberg, J., Bachman, J. G., O'Malley, P. M., & Johnston, L. D. (1994). High school educational success and subsequent substance use: A panel analysis following adolescents into young adulthood. *Journal of Health and Social Behavior, 35,* 45–62.

Smith, G. M., & Fogg, C. P. (1978). Psychological predictors of early use, late use, and nonuse of marijuana among teenage students. In D. B. Kandel (Ed.), *Longitudinal research on drug use: Empirical findings and methodological issues* (pp. 101–113). Washington, DC: Hemisphere.

Yamaguchi, K., & Kandel, D. (1985). On the resolution of role incompatibility: Life event history analysis of family roles and marijuana use. *American Journal of Sociology, 90,* 1284–1325.

Zucker, R. A. (1979). Developmental aspects of drinking through the young adult years. In H. T. Blane & M. E. Chafetz (Eds.), *Youth, alcohol, and social policy* (pp. 91–146). New York: Plenum.

Zucker, R. A. (1987). The four alcoholisms: A developmental account of the etiologic process. In P. C. Rivers (Ed.), *Nebraska Symposium on Motivation, 1987: Alcohol and addictive behavior* (pp. 27–83). Lincoln: University of Nebraska Press.

6

Developmental Transitions in Poor Youth: Delinquency and Crime

Mercer L. Sullivan
Vera Institute of Justice, Rutgers University

Involvement in delinquent activity during adolescence is relatively common among young males but does not generally lead to a life of serious crime. For those who do become involved in delinquency, the timing and manner of their transitions into and out of delinquent and criminal activity can have profound consequences for their entry into adult roles. This chapter explores research and theories dealing with patterns of delinquent and antisocial behavior, focusing on continuities and discontinuities over the life course and the roles played by personality and social context in shaping these transitions.

The relationship of age to criminality is quite strong. Whether one looks at crimes detected by the police or at self-report measures, criminal activity peaks sharply between the midteens and the mid-20s (Greenberg, 1977, 1985; Hirschi & Gottfredson, 1983). This age pattern appears to be quite stable across different social contexts and is evident, for example, in 19th-century Wales and England as well as the contemporary United States. Explanations for this strong association between age and crime, however, have been and remain controversial, seesawing over several generations of social scientific research between explanations based on stable and enduring differences between individuals and those rooted in theories of socialization.

Perhaps nowhere in the social sciences has the relationship between nature and nurture been more vigorously debated than in studies of crime and delinquency. Oddly, despite the obvious close relationship between processes of human development and patterns of criminal behavior, studies of the etiology of crime and delinquency have until recently tended not to pose questions directly in terms of developmental processes (Sampson, 1992). Research has more often attempted to identify factors differentiating criminals from noncriminals than to study in depth the developmental processes through which varying patterns of delinquent and criminal behaviors become manifest. Recent research, although still fraught with controversy, has seen a convergence from different theoretical and methodological perspectives on the question of the relationship of developmental processes to patterns of criminal and deviant behavior. Current thinking credits both individual-level characteristics and social context as having important roles in the etiology of crime and delinquency.

This chapter reviews briefly the history of research leading to recent convergent theories of crime and human development and identifies key findings and theoretical questions guiding current work in this field. Based on this review, the argument is advanced that although developmental patterns in deviant and criminal careers are becoming more clearly understood, further understanding of these processes requires greater knowledge and more clearly articulated theories of the relationship between context and development. Examples from ethnographic research are examined in some detail in order to explore questions of social context, including how context affects developmental transitions during adolescence and how these transitions are related to adult outcomes.

THEORY AND RESEARCH ON CRIME
AND ANTISOCIAL BEHAVIOR

The earliest attempts at scientific explanation of criminality relied on now-discredited classifications of criminals as throwbacks to an earlier stage of physical evolution (Lombroso, 1911). The attitudes of criminologists toward the role of the family in the genesis of criminality, in contrast, have undergone a series of shifts back and forth between ontogenetic and sociogenic paradigms (Dannefer, 1984; Sullivan, 1989b). Theorists nearer the ontogenetic end of this spectrum have placed far greater emphasis on the family. Broken homes were widely assumed to be primary causes of delinquency in the early 20th century, but the pioneering work of Shaw and McKay (1931) discredited that body of theories and research, substituting residence in poor neighborhoods in place of broken families as the primary causal factor. The success of Shaw and McKay in demonstrating the striking concentration of officially recorded delinquency in inner-city areas along with the methodological inadequacies of previous attempts to correlate broken homes with delinquency was such that scientific interest in the relation of family relationships to delinquency remained in abeyance for decades (Wilkinson, 1974).

Along with the ecological studies of Shaw and McKay and their successors (Chilton, 1964; Shevky & Bell, 1955), ethnographic studies, beginning with Whyte's (1943) classic *Street Corner Society*, also played a prominent role in linking delinquency to the environment of poor neighborhoods more strongly than to family relationships. The dominant criminological paradigms from the 1940s through the 1960s were those of *differential association*, emphasizing processes of direct recruitment (Sutherland, 1937) and *subculture*, emphasizing the alienation of working-class boys from school discipline (Cohen, 1955). These theories culminated in the influential work of Cloward and Ohlin (1960). Following Merton (1938), Cloward and Ohlin linked the notion of delinquent subcultures to the structural concept of blocked opportunities to explain the still evident concentration of official delinquency in poor neighborhoods. The fact that delinquent acts are usually committed in groups, to a far greater extent than adult criminal acts, added weight to the emphasis on delinquency as collective, learned behavior (Erickson & Jensen, 1977).

Beginning in the late 1950s, however, new methods in the study of delinquency led to a shift toward renewed emphasis on individual factors in the etiology of delinquency. Ethnographic studies of poor neighborhoods and ecological studies based on official police records began to be supplanted by the newly developed use of self-report surveys (Short & Nye, 1958). This shift led in turn to a theoretical shift away from emphasis on social class and neighborhood ecology back to a renewed emphasis on psychological and even biological causation. After it was discovered that high school students were not hesitant to report a variety of delinquent behaviors on confidential survey questionnaires, a great number of these studies were conducted and their results indicated high levels of reliability. The self-report data overturned some long-held assumptions about delinquency, particularly concerning its concentration in poor areas. It quickly became apparent that delinquency is much more widely distributed throughout the class structure than was previously suspected, at least the relatively minor offenses tapped by these instruments (Hindelang, Hirschi, & Weis, 1979).

The development of self-report methods also provided the opportunity to conduct multivariate analyses on large, systematically selected samples. A variety of new theoretical approaches emerged from these studies. Control theory (Hirschi, 1969) emphasized the comparatively weaker attachments of delinquents to family, school, and peers. Older theories were also tested with these methods, such as Akers' (1973) test of social learning theory, a direct descendant of differential association theory. This phase of research culminated in the mid-1980s with the work of

Elliott, Huizinga, and Ageton (1985), which combined control theory with social learning theory and strain theory (Cloward and Ohlin's emphasis on blocked opportunities) and found that the theories predicted delinquent behavior better in combination than separately.

All of these studies, however, were essentially concentrating on social psychology. Although control theory, for example, leaned heavily in the direction of the ontogenetic paradigm and strain theory toward sociogenic causation, the operationalization of these theories through cross-sectional self-report studies meant that data on personal development and data on social context played minor roles in the analysis. Individual attitudes, as revealed in questionnaire responses, were correlated with delinquent activity, but little attention was paid either to the contexts in which these attitudes developed or to how these attitudes evolved over time.

Although research based on cross-sectional self-report data was successful in establishing the existence of middle-class delinquency and re-establishing the importance of psychological factors that differentiate delinquents from nondelinquents, other important questions began to fade from view. Because self-reports are not as successful at tapping more serious offenses, for example, they have not been as useful for understanding patterns of more serious criminality. The widely reported finding from these studies that there is no correlation between social class and delinquency (Tittle, Villemez, & Smith, 1978) must be understood as referring primarily to the distribution of relatively minor offenses. A second problem is that self-reports provide little direct information on social context, of the type so characteristic of the older tradition of ethnographic studies. A third problem is that cross-sectional studies provide very little information about processes of development.

Since the mid-1980s, a new emphasis on developmental issues and a resurgence of ethnographic studies have addressed these issues. The prior single-minded focus of etiological inquiries on the factors differentiating criminals from noncriminals has given way to a new emphasis on the relation of juvenile delinquency to both antecedent and subsequent antisocial behavior. At the same time, there has been renewed concern about the role of context in shaping developmental sequences of antisocial and criminal behavior.

Wilson and Herrnstein's (1985) *Crime and Human Nature* reviews a wide range of prior studies in a systematic attempt to debunk virtually all sociogenic explanations of crime in favor of what they referred to as *constitutional* factors, by which they referred to a series of individual characteristics, chiefly temperament and intelligence, that could be rooted in either biology, through genetic inheritance or prenatal and infant health, or early childhood socialization. Gottfredson and Hirschi's (1990) *A General Theory of Crime* takes a similarly individual-level approach to explaining the etiology of criminal behavior; however, where Wilson and Herrnstein's constitutional factors include both differences rooted in biology and differences rooted in early childhood socialization, Gottfredson and Hirschi firmly rejected biological explanations and placed all explanatory power on early childhood socialization.

Although both of these comprehensive re-examinations of the criminological literature remain controversial, they have forced a return to fundamental questions. Whereas the trend had been in a direction from straightforwardly sociogenic explanations—couched in terms of differential association, labeling, subculture and the like—toward social psychological explanations, these two works have focused attention on continuities in antisocial behavior from early childhood through adulthood, thus reviving and promoting an ontogenetic paradigm.

Some of the strongest arguments mustered by these theorists have derived from their demonstration of the early childhood roots of much severe antisocial behavior. Prior theories of criminality had focused primarily on the high-crime period extending from adolescence through young adulthood. When the inquiry is extended beyond criminal behavior to the broader category of antisocial behavior and such behavior is examined over a wider age range, previously obscure continuities emerge. A number of longitudinal studies, conducted by both criminologists (Elliott et al., 1985; Shannon, 1988; West & Farrington, 1977; Wolfgang, Thornberry, & Figlio, 1987) and developmentalists (Caspi, Bem, & Elder, 1987; Huesmann, Eron, Lefkowitz, & Walder, 1984; Jessor, Donovan, & Costa, 1991; Jessor & Jessor, 1977; Loeber, 1982; Olweus, 1979; Robins, 1966) have demonstrated strong continuities between antisocial behavior in early childhood and later juvenile delinquency and adult criminality. These studies have tended to support the plausibility of explanations of crime and antisocial behavior that emphasize individual rather than social factors.

Yet, these continuities exist along with significant discontinuities. Not every troubled child becomes a delinquent; not every juvenile who commits a legal infraction becomes a persistent offender; and not every persistent juvenile offender becomes an adult criminal. Despite the now widespread recognition of significant developmental continuities in antisocial and criminal behavior, the nature of these continuities and of significant discontinuities remains subject to debate. In more recent work, Elliott (1993) cited the lack of knowledge about why individuals do or do not make the transition out of dangerous and antisocial lifestyles as a major gap in the literature.

Recently, Sampson and Laub (1993) demonstrated significant discontinuities even among serious persistent delinquents. Reanalyzing the classic longitudinal work of Glueck and Glueck (1950, 1968) that provided much of the grist for Wilson and Herrnstein's revival of the ontogenetic paradigm, Sampson and Laub demonstrated that the Gluecks' own data document change as well as continuity. According to their reanalysis, even though serious delinquents are much more likely than others from similar backgrounds to become adult criminals, ties to work and marriage in young adulthood are associated with a turn toward conformity even among this group. In other recent work, Moffitt (1993) suggested that there are two different developmental patterns of antisocial behavior, a "life-course persistent" pattern that begins in early childhood, develops to a high degree of severity, and persists well into adulthood; and an "adolescence-limited" pattern that begins later and is more restricted in severity and duration.

Whereas these studies point to the limits of the revived ontogenetic paradigm, a number of recent ethnographic studies provide strong support for a renewal of a sociogenic paradigm. Although ethnographic studies were of fundamental importance for the construction of the sociogenic theories from the 1930s through the 1960s, few important ethnographic studies of crime emerged in the 1970s and 1980s. Since then, however, there has been a resurgence of ethnographic studies of crime in poor, urban neighborhoods (Anderson, 1990; Hagedorn, 1988; MacLeod, 1987; Moore, 1978, 1991; Padilla, 1992; Sullivan, 1989b; Taylor, 1989; Vigil, 1988; Williams, 1989).

These studies are not united by a particularly well-developed body of theory, and they do not provide information on the life course of the delinquents and young criminals that would allow systematic comparison with quantitative, longitudinal studies. Nonetheless, all these studies attribute criminogenic significance to the developmental context of growing up in poor neighborhoods.

Further, even a cursory comparison of these studies with the older studies such as those of Whyte (1943) or even Suttles (1968) quickly reveals dramatic differences in the severity of the delinquent and criminal behavior being discussed. The older studies portrayed delinquents engaged in petty theft, acting as street agents for corrupt machine politicians, or engaged in gang fights with fists, bludgeons, knives, and homemade guns. The more recent studies portray teenagers engaged in serious and sustained crime, using sophisticated weapons, controlling their local areas without direction by adults, and sometimes succeeding in earning regular income over a period of time through theft and drug dealing. As Hagan (1993) noted in a recent review, these studies provide the basis for a historical and political economic perspective on crime and delinquency that has been absent from a criminology focused at the level of social psychology.

A historical perspective also raises specifically developmental questions concerning changes in the context of development that have not received much attention in the recent discussions of continuities and change over the life course. Even to the extent that there do exist significant ontogenetic roots of antisocial behavior, these individual-level differences do not readily explain the great discrepancies between the United States and other developed nations in rates of crime and incarceration (Currie, 1985), nor do they explain the sharp increases in aggregate crime that occurred in the late 1960s in the United States, giving rise to the high rates that persist to the present. The ontogenetic paradigm is of little help in explaining why there is so much more crime in the United States in the period since the late 1960s. Whatever the individual-level processes leading to the development of serious criminality, there have clearly been aggregate-level changes in the extent to which this happens.

It is true that family structure also changed during the same period in which crime increased, but so did many other things. Higher rates of crime, higher rates of female-headed households, and fundamental restructuring of the economy all came about during the same general time frame. Although it is possible to argue that family breakdown caused higher rates of crime, it is difficult to connect those two things without also bringing in related changes in social context such as the disappearance of manufacturing jobs and the increased difficulty of labor market entry for those without extensive education and training. During this period, large classes of young people are said to have become marginal to social production in a historically unprecedented way (Petersen & Mortimer, 1994). Both recent ethnographic studies and the dramatic changes over time in aggregate crime rates direct continued attention to sociogenic factors in the development of criminality and antisocial behavior.

ONTOGENETIC AND SOCIOGENIC FACTORS IN THE DEVELOPMENT OF CRIME AND ANTISOCIAL BEHAVIOR: THEORETICAL ISSUES

In order to untangle some of these issues, it is first necessary to ask to what extent ontogenetic and sociogenic approaches to the etiology of crime and antisocial behavior are inherently incompatible. One remarkable aspect of the debates among criminologists has been the extent to which these two approaches have been seen as irreconcilable. This tendency is evident in the criminological literature in the wide historical pendulum shifts in emphasis between the two, most recently in the polemical tone of the controversial volumes by Wilson and Herrnstein and Gottfredson and Hirschi. Most developmentalists, in contrast, treat the assumption that development is a function of both person and environment as axiomatic (Bronfenbrenner, 1992; Jessor et al., 1992; Vygotsky, 1978). Although the kinds of data developmentalists deal with are typically more focused on sequences of individual experiences and outcomes than on characteristics of their environments, the importance of environment is nonetheless routinely affirmed at the level of theory (Bronfenbrenner, 1992; Jessor et al., 1991). The kind of extreme ontogenetic position espoused in recent criminology appears somewhat naive from this perspective.

Consider, for example, the relation of family to social class and neighborhood. Family factors are usually associated with an ontogenetic emphasis and social class and neighborhood with a sociogenic emphasis, but poverty and the environments of poverty put enormous stress on families and children. As a result, trying to separate the effects of family from those of neighborhood and class is a difficult and rather arbitrary undertaking, particularly in a society in which imposed residential segregation has severely limited families' choice of residence (Massey & Denton, 1993).

An even more fundamental problem with the extreme ontogenetic position is the assumption that individual continuities in antisocial behavior over the life course are attributable only to unchanging individual characteristics. A number of theorists have recently addressed this problem, and it is these arguments that are developed more fully in the rest of this chapter, both theoretically and with reference to ethnographic data relating development to context.

Beginning from the Vygotskian axiom that development is a function of both person and environment, continuities in development could logically be related to continuities in environment as well as in person. In this context, Laub and Sampson (1993) noted that ecological continuity may play an important role in progressions from early childhood antisocial behavior to adult criminality. Some data from key studies would appear to support this view. For example, in their longitudinal study of delinquency among working-class boys in London, West and Farrington (1977) found that moving out of the neighborhood was strongly related to desistance from delinquency. Similarly, the Job Corps is virtually the only intervention program to have shown crime reduction effects on the basis of rigorous evaluation (Mallar et al., 1980), and the Job Corps is notable not only for the intensity and expense of its efforts but also because it moves participants out of their normal environments to residential training centers. In both examples, a break in ecological continuity is associated with a break in developmental continuity.

Sampson and Laub (1993) developed this logic further, using the more general concept of cumulative continuity to denote the fact that experiences in the course of development are not just epiphenomena of pre-existing innate dispositions but themselves have consequences. They elaborate this notion in terms of labeling theory (Becker, 1963; Lemert, 1967;

Tannenbaum, 1938), noting that prior delinquencies can call forth stig-matizing reactions that are then amplified from primary to secondary deviance. In a related theoretical vein, Nagin and Paternoster (1991) used the concept of state dependence to refer to the relation of prior to sub-sequent states of being. They attempted empirically to separate prior heterogeneity in propensity to commit crimes from the subsequent effects of having actually committed a crime. They advanced cautious claims to having demonstrated the existence of state dependence, showing conti-nuity to be the result not only of innate characteristics but also, separately, of the experience of committing crimes. Stated more succinctly, they concluded that persons do not begin to commit crimes because they were already criminals who had not yet committed crimes so much as they become criminals by committing crimes.

If these theories of cumulative continuity and state dependence are correct, they raise significant questions about the process through which participation in crime becomes self-perpetuating. Sampson and Laub (1993) suggested that such effects may be due to labeling, by which they mean the stigmatizing reactions of others such as neighbors, parents, police, courts, and schools. The next section of this chapter examines some ethnographic materials in an effort to unpack the notions of cumulative continuity and state dependence further, examining not just stigmatizing reactions but also the ways in which these are internalized and the role of the environment in presenting continued incentives to engage in crime to the individual who has already begun a deviant developmental trajectory.

ETHNOGRAPHIC PERSPECTIVES
ON PERSON–ENVIRONMENT INTERACTIONS

The ethnographic examples discussed here are drawn from Sullivan's fieldwork over a 10-year period in three low-income neighborhoods of Brooklyn. Full descriptions of the neighborhoods and the findings are available elsewhere (Sullivan, 1989a, 1989b, 1991, 1993a, 1993b). For pur-poses of this discussion, the following background descriptions should suffice. The three neighborhoods differ in race and ethnicity, social class, and family structure. They are predominantly Black, Latino, and White, respectively. The White neighborhood is predominantly working class and the two minority neighborhoods are characterized by concentrated pov-erty. The rates of female-headed households in the two minority neighbor-hoods are over 40%, compared to about 10% in the White working-class area.

Ethnographic samples of about a dozen young males were initially recruited in each area. Their ages ranged between 15 and 19 at the time of contact, and these samples were intentionally recruited from among criminally active youths. The samples were thus not typical of the general population nor even of the populations of these low-income neighborhoods. Later research on teenage pregnancy within these areas generated samples including noncriminally active youths. Even among the criminally active youths, however, there was considerable variation in the extent and eventual duration of criminal involvement. Further, criminal activity for most individuals waned over time. Researchers followed these groups for periods of a year or more, and ongoing contacts with some members of the groups provided information on their life situations over a period of years. Retrospective life histories provided information on their lives back to their early teens, the period of their initial delinquent involvements.

No claims are made for systematic sample selection that would make these data comparable to longitudinal studies. Further, no information on early childhood experiences was collected. As a result of small sample sizes and information restricted primarily to experiences during adolescence and young adulthood, therefore, these data cannot directly address many of the questions raised in recent research on crime and the life course. The methodological disadvantages of these data, however, are offset to some extent by the intensive nature of the data and the fact that these were interactive samples in which members knew each other. These youths shared the same neighborhood environments and many common experiences within those environments.

Comparison among these young males of developmental sequences of involvement in criminal activities reveal a number a distinct patterns, both within and between groups. The single most striking difference was the greater degree of involvement over time of the youths in the two poorer, minority neighborhoods as compared to the White, working-class youths. By the time they reached their early 20s, many of the minority youths had become seriously involved in crime and had been incarcerated several times, in some cases having done prison terms of more than a year. None of the White youths had progressed to this level of seriousness. Yet, these differences emerged only over time and at least in part as a result of neighborhood-specific environments and experiences.

Comparison of early criminal experiences across these three neighborhood-based groups selected because of their criminal involvements reveal few differences. All of these youths reported qualitatively similar experiences of getting into fights and engaging in nonviolent acts of theft, such as burglary and shoplifting. The greater involvement in crime over time of the minority youths and the relatively more cautious ongoing criminal activities of the White youths were clearly related to aspects of their physical and social environments.

The progression from early exploratory crimes beginning in their early teens to more sustained criminal activities in their later teens was a movement from activities motivated by thrills to activities more and more motivated by a sustained quest for income. Many of the minority youths became what West (1974) termed *serious thieves*, relying on crime as a fairly regular source of income. West referred to involvement in serious theft as a short-term career, because it is difficult to sustain for long periods of time. Nonetheless, for some youths, crime can become a regular way to make money.

With continued involvement, however, the costs in terms of mounting criminal penalties become excessive. In addition, other kinds of jobs become more available. The differences between the neighborhoods were due to precisely these two factors: the rate at which the costs of crime mounted and the extent to which legitimate jobs became available. Social control in the White, working-class neighborhood worked much more effectively. Local households had many more adult males present, and these males exercised much tighter control of neighborhood streets, either directly disciplining local youths who stole or working with the local police precinct. In addition, households had much stronger labor market networks through which local youths could obtain jobs, both part-time jobs while they were still of school age and relatively high-wage, unionized, blue-collar jobs as they got older. The White youths effectively learned both not to steal in their own neighborhood and also that they had other ways to obtain money.

Lacking these controls and these resources, the minority youths were more likely to become serious thieves or serious drug dealers. The White youths, in contrast, although not entirely law abiding by any means, were much more cautious in the crimes they committed. For example, when they sold drugs, the White, working-class youths usually did so within their own neighborhood to people they knew. The minority youths, in contrast, worked the streets in commercial areas or worked in specialized, high-volume retail locations that were highly vulnerable both to local predators and the police. Similarly, the White youths engaged in a very specific form of robbery, taking money from drunken undocumented immigrants who were afraid to go to the police. Some of the minority youths did this also, but a number of them began mugging ordinary citizens who could and did report them to the police, eventually resulting in severe penalties.

Although these comparisons across neighborhoods were quite striking, it was also true that there were differences within each of the peer groups. In each of the three peer groups, there were one or two individuals who were seen, by their own peers, as irrational in the kinds of risks they took for highly uncertain rewards. These individuals did not seem to learn how to engage in crime as efficiently as their peers, and this fact was remarked on within their neighborhoods. Certain individuals were de-

scribed as "crazy" in this way, unlike others who might do the same sorts
of things but who would not take risks that seemed almost certain to
result in extremely unpleasant consequences, such as retaliation and
incarceration. Interestingly, their own peers tended to describe the problems of these extreme risk takers as related to their family situations. One
such youth in the African American neighborhood lived with a mother
who was often gone from home for days at a time. Another moved back
and forth between his father, who was very strict and physically abused
him when he got in trouble, and his mother, who drank heavily and was
said to engage in sexual relations with her son's friends. Another such
youth in the White, working-class neighborhood was the son of a father
who had spent many years in prison himself. This youth was the subject
of astonishment in the neighborhood because his father gave him a gun
on his 18th birthday, which he proceeded to try out by engaging in a
gratuitous shooting in a distant neighborhood on that same day.

Although the methodological approach involved here differs substantially from that of quantitative longitudinal studies, it is noteworthy that
these youths themselves appeared to differentiate between sociogenic and
ontogenetic patterns of criminality; that is, between relatively rational
approaches to crime that have some kind of status of normality, at least
within the collective construction of reality and shared circumstances of
these peer groups, and crimes that appear to be willfully self-destructive.
Although this research did not collect systematic information on early
childhood patterns of antisocial behavior, it did appear that the extreme
risk takers were headed for long careers of criminality and incarceration.
These data would thus appear to be at least consistent with the notion
of a difference between a more sociogenic "adolescence-limited" pattern
of criminality and a more ontogenetic "life-course-persistent" pattern.

The comparisons across neighborhoods also suggest that criminal involvements stemming from context-specific configurations of stresses and
opportunities can have long-term consequences. The youths from the two
poor minority neighborhoods who became involved in crime on a regular
basis as a fairly regular source of income found it more difficult than
they had anticipated to avoid having their lives disrupted. As they
reached their later teens, many of these youths reported themselves to
be much more interested in regular employment and began to seek jobs
on a sustained basis. Although they faced many difficulties in the labor
market, they generally found that they could get jobs, albeit often low-
wage and insecure jobs that they had to replace constantly. They were
hindered in this process, however, by their backlog of arrests and court
cases. Having found a new job, an individual would discover that he
either had to risk losing the job because he had to go to court or he had
to risk re-arrest if he missed the court date.

Similarly, some individuals decided to resume schooling and found that court appearances interfered with that process. Because the criminal justice system allows for second chances for youths still of school age, the problems they faced at this point sometimes had less to do with whether they could "beat the rap" than with the turmoil created in the wake of their earlier criminal involvements. They discovered that a criminal career involves not just engaging in crime but, after a period of sustained involvement, spending a lot of time with police, courts, and probation and parole officers. In extreme cases, extended incarceration becomes a serious deficit in future attempts to acquire education and training or find employment. As these stigmata of criminality mount up, returning to criminal involvement becomes more likely, because they already know that lifestyle and are having difficulty changing to a different lifestyle.

These accumulations of stigmata, of course, are the classic processes described in labeling theory, the amplification of deviance from primary to secondary (Lemert, 1967). What these comparative ethnographic data show, however, are some of the ways in which labeling processes are specific to local neighborhood environments. The White, working-class youths, for example, had knowledge and attitudes about the criminal justice system that were quite different from their minority peers. A number of police officers and criminal justice system personnel lived in their neighborhood, and some of the youths were related to these people. When the youths got into trouble, their families dealt with the problem in a personalistic way. As a result, these youths were simultaneously more likely to be apprehended earlier in their explorations of criminality, due to a more effective local social control environment, and less likely to be formally arrested and charged, due to personal relationships between local residents and local police. These factors, combined with their simultaneous greater access to jobs through family- and neighborhood-based social networks, gave them advantages over their minority peers in avoiding cumulative stigmata.

The developmental process by which these youths progressed from the similar, early, exploratory criminal acts to the later patterns of criminality that differed so strikingly across the three neighborhoods, however, cannot be attributed entirely to labeling processes, at least not if labeling is narrowly defined as the reactions of official institutions such as the criminal justice system, the schools, and the labor market. More sustained involvement in particular types of criminal activities required not just stigmatizing reactions from others, but also an ongoing process of internalization of these roles, a key aspect of West's characterization of the development of serious thieves. The youths learned to think systematically about various criminal opportunities: which factories could be broken into most easily, which subway riders were the most likely "vics" (victims) for snatching gold chains or purses, or how to sell drugs with maximum profit and minimum risk. Individuals who did not learn these things both accumulated criminal justice sanctions more rapidly and also became known to their peers as unreliable partners in crime. This is in fact exactly what happened to one or two members of each of the three peer groups.

The extreme ontogenetic position within criminology has acknowledged the group nature of delinquency and the fact that social learning takes place, but has tended to dismiss the etiological significance of these phenomena by claiming that "birds of feather flock together" and denying that "flocking" precedes "feathering" (Hirschi, 1969). Although this position is logically tenable, it is also controversial. The comparative ethnographic data discussed here put this venerable dispute in rather a different light, because the units of comparison are delinquent peer groups in specific, described neighborhood contexts. This contextual argument shows some of the limits of attempts to discount the influence of delinquent groups by deferring to claims about self-selection.

These three neighborhood-based samples were recruited on the basis of active criminal involvement; these clearly were the local bad boys. They described themselves that way and were so described by others. Later work on young fathers in these neighborhoods led to contacts with other young males who had far less involvement in crime along with different self-concepts and social reputations. From this perspective, the comparisons between neighborhoods suggest that local context makes a difference in how severe the activities of local delinquent groups become. The White, working-class youths committed many illegal acts, and, through group process, learned to define themselves for a few years as persons who knew how to steal, rob, and sell drugs. Yet, they learned, not just from their peers but also from others in the neighborhood, to place certain limits on these activities that made the activities less visible and disruptive for their neighbors and also less risky for themselves and less disruptive of their later transitions into the labor market.

Neighborhood social context offers a much more persuasive explanation than innate individual-level differences for these flock or group differences in the extent to which exploratory delinquency develops into ongoing criminality. Adolescents spend a great deal of time in their local environments, and most delinquent acts occur close to the residence of the offender (Turner, 1969). Even a troubled individual seeking a group with whom to act out antisocial impulses is not free to join any group in any neighborhood, certainly not in a place like Brooklyn that is subdivided into a patchwork of racial and ethnic enclave neighborhoods. The extent to which local neighborhood social control environments are able to restrain and channel delinquent activities has important implications not just for neighborhood safety but also for the development of local youths.

Together, these comparative ethnographic observations of differences within and between neighborhood-based male peer groups support the notion that the development of delinquent and criminal behavior is a function of neighborhood environment as well as individual propensities to engage in crime. In particular, they support the notion of cumulative continuity and the related notion of ecological continuity. Continued residence in an environment where many local youths are involved in crime and social control is lax provides ongoing reinforcement for evolving criminal behavior.

This does not imply that every youth in that environment will become delinquent, only that initial explorations of delinquency, which self-reports reveal to be fairly common across the class structure, are more likely to receive both positive reinforcement from criminally active peers and irregular negative sanctions, from the local social control environment, in poor and socially disorganized neighborhoods. Nor is this to deny the importance of individual factors and family support systems, for the delinquents in this study clearly attributed importance to these factors in assessing the behavior of their own peers. Rather, the interaction of person and environment on a continuous basis comes to the fore as the most appropriate framework for explanation. In adverse environments, negative developmental trajectories become much harder to alter.

The person–environment developmental perspective points to a resolution of one of the deepest contradictions in research on crime and delinquency: the lack of a strong correlation between social class and crime at the level of the individual (Tittle et al., 1978), on the one hand, and the persistent evidence of strong ecological correlations between poor, urban neighborhoods and high crime rates on the other. Self-report studies show wide distribution of relatively minor delinquent acts across the class structure but do not effectively tap participation in more serious crimes. This is one reason that the link between social class and crime appears weak at the level of the individual. Another reason is that involvement in serious crime is not characteristic of most poor people. The person–environment developmental perspective, in contrast, suggests that troubled persons in adverse environments are the most likely individuals to become heavily involved in sustained, serious criminality.

The ethnographic comparisons of neighborhood contexts explored here represent one avenue for assessing the relationship of developmental processes to social context. Examining the effects of different historical contexts on development, in the manner of developmentalists such as Elder (1974) is another. Whereas the age distribution of criminal activity appears to have remained stable over time and across societies, the amount and severity of criminal activity manifestly have not. Older images of juvenile delinquency as getting into fistfights and stealing hubcaps seem quaint in an era of crack and drive-by shootings. Just as the cross-sectional ethnographic comparisons cited earlier show differences in the amount and severity of criminality and point to the role of social context, secular changes in social context provide another opportunity to examine the effects of context on the development of criminal behavior. The Brooklyn studies under discussion provided just that opportunity with the advent of crack cocaine in the mid-1980s.

Most of the data discussed so far were collected in the early 1980s. Although most of the youths in the study used alcohol and soft drugs, principally marijuana, most of them had never become regular users of hard drugs. The only exceptions were two of the White, working-class youths, who had begun to use heroin. Most of the youths in all three neighborhoods, however, had steered away from heroin. They knew about it and were aware of older heroin users in their neighborhoods, and, for some, in their own families. They had seen the effects of heroin addiction as young children and reported that this experience kept them from being interested in it, because heroin addicts were sources of contempt. In the mid-1980s, however, cocaine became much more popular, first inhaled in powdered form, and then smoked in the form of crack. During this time, the effects of crack on the neighborhoods became dramatically apparent.

One of the most surprising effects of the introduction of crack in these neighborhoods was its sudden impact on the development of youths who had previously been involved in crime but had either ceased committing crimes for money or significantly scaled back their activities. Some youths who had been stealing regularly at the ages of 15 and 16 had, by their early 20s, gotten regular jobs and appeared to be well past their involvement with crime. They were thus typical of the well-documented age–crime curve that declines sharply in young adulthood. Then they discovered crack and regressed very rapidly.

One such youth in the African American neighborhood had established his own family and had lived with his child and the mother of the child on a fairly regular basis, although they had had to move separately back in with relatives when he was out of work. Still, he eventually found other employment and they had reestablished a common household. After being introduced to crack by his older sister, however, these arrangements fell apart entirely. He ceased to support his family altogether and spent all his money on drugs. He still worked sporadically, but was less and less able to show up reliably. Researchers eventually lost direct contact with him, but reports from others indicated that he was spending short periods in jail for minor drug-related offenses.

Another individual, in the White, working-class neighborhood, had married and fathered a child and was working steadily in a good, unionized job, when the family had a financial windfall. He and his wife received a sum of around $75,000 as a result of a lawsuit following an automobile accident. Instead of using the money for the plastic surgery and dental work for which the money had been awarded, they began to smoke crack and eventually smoked up all the money. As a result of their drug use, her family had their child removed from their custody, he lost his job, and they had no regular residence. In this case, they eventually stopped their use and began to put things back together, but at high costs in terms of money, health, job continuity, and nurture for their child. Family supports were crucial to their ability to recover.

These are only two case histories, but much other evidence, including the many recent ethnographic studies cited earlier, also points to the advent of crack cocaine in the mid-1980s as a historical event that severely disrupted both individual lives and the social dynamics of entire neighborhoods. In a longer historical frame, the sharp, steady rise in crime rates from the mid-1960s through the mid-1970s and continued high crime rates since that time points to a significant transformation of social context with severe consequences for child and adolescent development in those areas.

TRANSITIONS DURING ADOLESCENCE AND ADULT OUTCOMES

Most of the discussion thus far has been devoted to an attempt to reconcile seemingly inconsistent bodies of research, emphasizing either ontogenetic or sociogenic factors in the development of antisocial and criminal behavior over the life course. Older criminological studies showing the concentration of criminality in poor neighborhoods as well as more recent ethnographic work have emphasized the importance of social context, often implying or even stating directly (Cohen, 1955; Tannenbaum, 1938) that criminality in some contexts is developmentally normal. This assertion of normality was contested by Matza (1964) and Kornhauser (1978), among others, who pointed out that the decline of criminality with age is itself strong evidence that criminality is not sustained by culture but should be viewed as situationally induced and rationalized. It is not necessary, however, to assert that delinquency is either tied to lifelong nihilistic attitudes or is without ambiguities and tensions in the minds of those who engage in it in order to acknowledge that, within some adolescent groups for a period of time, delinquency is socially valued and reinforced by peers.

Quantitative longitudinal studies by criminologists and developmentalists, in contrast, have emphasized the continuity from antisocial behavior in childhood through juvenile delinquency and into adult criminality or other antisocial behavior. The concept of cumulative continuity has been suggested as a theoretical bridge that helps resolve this contradiction, acknowledging continuities in the psychological characteristics of individuals but pointing also to the importance of interactions with continuous features of the environment in generating continuities in behavior.

At this point, it is useful to summarize the principal research findings on crime and antisocial behavior that characterize the transitions during adolescence linking earlier stages of development to subsequent outcomes. Further discussion of ethnographic data then explores the role of neighborhood social context in defining these transitions.

First, the commission of illegal acts is more common during adolescence than during any other portion of the life course (Greenberg, 1977, 1985; Hirschi & Gottfredson, 1983) and this age-specific peak is widely distributed throughout the population. Estimates of the proportion of males who have been arrested before the age of 18 range between 25% and 45% (Blumstein, Cohen, Roth, & Vishers, 1986).

Second, most juvenile delinquents do not go on to become high-rate offenders. Wolfgang, Figlio, and Sellin's (1972) widely cited birth cohort study showed that nearly half of those ever arrested by the age of 18 were one-time offenders, whereas 18% of the cohort members were responsible for over half of the arrests for the entire cohort. There is thus a sharp distinction between those who are ever arrested and those who go on to become chronic offenders during their teens.

Third, as shown by a wide variety of longitudinal studies, severe delinquency and adult criminality as well as the more general category of chronic antisocial behavior often have roots in early childhood. Most men who have severe behavioral problems during adolescence and adulthood probably also had behavioral problems as young children. The initiation of chronic criminal or antisocial behavior after adolescence is extremely rare (Robins & Rutter, 1990).

These findings all point to the crucial importance of understanding the processes through which large proportions of the male population make the transitions both into and out of delinquent behavior. Various etiological positions for the genesis of delinquent behavior have been suggested, and important roles are indicated both for individual characteristics identifiable in early childhood and for social context. The transition out of delinquency is also of crucial importance, particularly because it is a transition experienced by such a large proportion of all those who ever experience behavioral problems.

Robins and Rutter (1990), summarizing major longitudinal studies, stated that: "Many difficult children turn out to be normal adults, and a minority of very difficult children become apparently normal adults" (p.

xiv). They went on to note the crucial importance of environment in these transitions away from deviant behavior, noting that "environments that have been implicated in increasing the risk of nonconformity in adulthood for antisocial children are broken homes, institutionalization, bad neighborhoods, deviant peers, and easy availability of psychoactive substances" (p. xiv). Given the sharp peak of criminality during adolescence, the presence of these contextual factors during adolescence thus appears to play a major role in determining the adult outcomes of childhood and adolescent deviance. Referring to lifestyles associated with a wide range of delinquent and otherwise dangerous behaviors, Elliott (1993) also stressed the importance of environment, noting that "those in disadvantaged social environments are less likely to mature out of these lifestyle behaviors than are adolescents from more advantaged social contexts, an outcome that may reflect the differences in access to jobs and other conventional roles associated with the transition from adolescence to adulthood" (p. 134).

The comparative ethnographic data from Brooklyn discussed here have focused on the role of neighborhood social context in fostering transitions from early exploratory criminal activity to more sustained criminal activity. Neighborhood context appears to play a role both in fostering this transition and also in influencing the extent to which youths become formally labeled by the criminal justice system for their misdeeds. In addition to labeling, other aspects of neighborhood context also play a role in the cumulative continuity of criminal involvements, notably the ecological continuity of short-term incentives for continued involvement in crime and the extent to which deviant roles become internalized through peer group interactions within these ecological niches.

Other ethnographic studies of poor and working-class neighborhoods shed further light on the social processes through which deviant behavior in adolescence leads to adverse adult outcomes such as low levels of formal education, low occupational achievement, and family instability (Anderson, 1990; Hagedorn, 1988; MacLeod, 1987; Moore, 1978, 1991; Padilla, 1992; Taylor, 1989; Vigil, 1988; Williams, 1989). These studies suggest that delinquency and criminality lead to long-term outcomes not merely in and of themselves but through disruption of normative transitions to adulthood defined at the societal level but differentially achievable within different types of local communities. For example, it is not just labeling that leads to long-term adverse consequences from sustained adolescent criminality but the fact that such criminality is usually embedded in a lifestyle that disrupts education and labor force entry in multiple ways.

Developmentalists have also pointed to adverse consequences of the disruption of normatively defined transitions to adulthood. For example, Caspi, Elder, and Herbener (1990), citing Hogan (1980), noted that "the timing of role transitions represents an important contingency in the life-course that has implications for subsequent achievement and behavior" (p. 25). The role played by the social context of poor communities in disrupting normative role transitions is discussed further in the following with reference to ethnographic materials.

Willis' (1977) ethnographic study of working-class boys in Britain, for example, found that those who participated in what he termed a culture of opposition within their schools achieved some adult roles, in sexuality and in the workplace, earlier than their more conforming and studious peers. The price of early initiation into sexuality and work, however, is longer term stagnation in occupational mobility. Rebellious in school, they barely manage to finish, go immediately into factory work, and are stuck there. The ingenious aspect of Willis' analysis is his demonstration that what usually appears to be anomalous, self-destructive behavior— acting out in school—is part of a culturally patterned process of transition from school to work. This patterned transition is in turn a key aspect of the social process of reproducing the class structure.

In poor, inner-city neighborhoods of the United States, high levels of involvement in crime—along with precocious sexuality and early parenthood, leaving school early and erratic entry into and exit from the labor force—serve to disrupt normative transitions to adulthood, in which completed schooling is supposed to precede entry into the labor force and the establishment of stable employment is supposed to precede parenthood. Ianni's (1989) comparisons of inner-city with middle-class suburban neighborhoods have pointed out the contrast between the coordinated messages, opportunities, and social controls perceived by suburban youth and the mixed messages received by inner-city youth. Inner-city youth, for example, often feel pressure to earn income from their parents that conflicts with encouragement to stay in school from their teachers. When they get into trouble, police, social workers, school officials, and parents convey very different messages and work at cross-purposes in trying to deal with the problem. Similarly, Burton, Allison, and Obeidallah (1994) noted the early demands for household responsibility faced by poor, African American youth and the contrast with the expectations of dependency and subordination they encounter in school. Treated as children in school and adults at home, they become cynical about school and overburdened at home.

These ethnographic materials illustrate different aspects of the social context of growing up in poor neighborhoods. Poor youths often encounter a profound dissonance between the short-term demands of survival and gaining social respect in their home and community environments and the normatively age-graded expectations of behavior of the larger society that are conveyed to them through school, the mass media, and, indeed, other residents of their own communities, most of whom are aware of these demands but many of whom have not been able to live up to them.

Some individuals who become involved in serious criminality probably are acting out conflicts established at a very early age. For many inner-city youths, however, involvement in criminality also accomplishes certain normal developmental tasks, such as testing limits, learning to take risks, and establishing competence, autonomy, and social affiliation in a manner continuously reinforced by social context. Accomplishing these developmental tasks in this manner then takes on a momentum of its own that becomes self-destructive over time. Whereas the in-school pranks of Willis' working-class British boys are part of a culturally patterned reproduction of a manual labor force, crime and delinquency in the inner cities of the United States have become part of the culturally patterned reproduction of a way of life that includes high rates of early, violent death; incarceration; long-term weak attachment to the labor force; and family instability.

This chapter has explored the continuities and discontinuities in progressions from early childhood antisocial behavior through juvenile delinquency to adult criminality. Particular attention has been focused on the role of social context, particularly the social context of growing up in poor, inner-city neighborhoods, in affecting these continuities and discontinuities. Developmental research, particularly longitudinal studies of crime and antisocial behavior, have added much to our knowledge of these processes. Although developmental theory has consistently pointed to the important role of social context in these processes, longitudinal methodologies have been able to incorporate contextual data only to a limited extent. Ethnographic studies, in contrast, provide rich contextual data but have not been able to follow developmental processes with the same rigor as quantitative, longitudinal studies. Although the methodological gap between these approaches remains formidable, continued rapprochement between the two appears to be necessary for addressing fundamental theoretical and substantive questions about the interaction of person and environment that emerge whenever one begins to address these questions.

REFERENCES

Akers, R. L. (1973). *Deviant behavior: A social learning approach.* Belmont, CA: Wadsworth.
Anderson, E. (1990). *Streetwise: Race, class, and change in an urban community.* Chicago: University of Chicago Press.
Becker, H. S. (1963). *The outsiders: Studies in the sociology of deviance.* New York: The Free Press.
Blumstein, A., Cohen, J., Roth, J. A., & Vishers, C. A. (Eds.). (1986). *Criminal careers and "career criminals"* (Vol. 1). Washington, DC: National Academy Press.

Bronfenbrenner, U. (1992). Ecological systems theory. In R. Vasta (Ed.), *Six theories of child development: Revised formulations and current issues.* Philadelphia: Jessica Kingsley.

Burton, L. M., Allison, K., & Obeidallah, D. (1994). *Social context and adolescence: Perspectives on development among inner-city African-American teens.* Unpublished manuscript, Pennsylvania State University, University Park.

Caspi, A., Bem, D. J., & Elder, G. H. (1987). Moving against the world: Life course patterns of explosive children. *Developmental Psychology, 23,* 308–313.

Caspi, A., Elder, G. H., & Herbener, E. S. (1990). Childhood personality and the prediction of life-course patterns. In L. N. Robins & M. Rutter (Eds.), *Straight and devious pathways from childhood to adulthood* (pp. 13–35). Cambridge, UK: Cambridge University Press.

Chilton, R. (1964). Continuity in delinquency area research: A comparison of studies for Baltimore, Detroit, and Indianapolis. *American Sociological Review, 20,* 71–83.

Cloward, R. A., & Ohlin, L. (1960). *Delinquency and opportunity: A theory of delinquent gangs.* New York: The Free Press.

Cohen, A. K. (1955). *Delinquent boys.* New York: The Free Press.

Currie, E. (1985). *Confronting crime: An American challenge.* New York: Pantheon.

Dannefer, D. (1984). Adult development and social theory: A paradigmatic reappraisal. *American Sociological Review, 49,* 100–116.

Elder, G. H., Jr. (1974). *Children of the great depression.* Chicago: University of Chicago Press.

Elliott, D. S. (1993). Health-enhancing and health-compromising lifestyles. In S. G. Millstein, A. C. Petersen, & E. O. Nightingale (Eds.), *Promoting the health of adolescents: New directions for the twenty-first century* (pp. 119–145). New York: Oxford University Press.

Elliott, D., Huizinga, D., & Ageton, S. (1985). *Explaining delinquency and drug use.* Beverly Hills, CA: Russell Sage.

Erickson, M. L., & Jensen, G. F. (197). Delinquency is still group behavior: Toward revitalizing the group premise in the sociology of deviance. *Journal of Criminal Law and Criminology, 68,* 262–73.

Glueck, S., & Glueck, E. (1950). *Unravelling juvenile delinquency.* New York: The Commonwealth Fund.

Glueck, S., & Glueck, E. (1968). *Delinquents and nondelinquents in perspective.* Cambridge, MA: Harvard University Press.

Gottfredson, M. R., & Hirschi, T. (1990). *A general theory of crime.* Stanford, CA: Stanford University Press.

Greenberg, D. F. (1977). Delinquency and the age structure of society. *Contemporary Crises, 1,* 189–223.

Greenberg, D. F. (1985). Age, crime, and social explanation. *American Journal of Sociology, 91,* 1–21.

Hagan, J. (1993). Structural and cultural disinvestment and the new ethnographies of poverty and crime. *Contemporary Sociology, 22,* 327–331.

Hagedorn, J. M. (1988). *People and folks: Gangs and crime in a rustbelt city.* Chicago: Lakeview Press.

Hindelang, M. J., Hirschi, T., & Weis, J. G. (1979). Correlates of delinquency: The illusion of discrepancy between self-report and official measures. *American Sociological Review, 44,* 995–1014.

Hirschi, T. (1969). *Causes of delinquency.* Berkeley: University of California Press.

Hirschi, T., & Gottfredson, M. R. (1983). Age and the explanation of crime. *American Journal of Sociology, 89,* 552–584.

Hogan, D. P. (1980). *Transitions and social change.* New York: Academic Press.

Huesmann, L. R., Eron, L. D., Lefkowitz, M. M., & Walder, L. O. (1984). Stability of aggression over time and generations. *Developmental Psychology, 20,* 1120–1134.

Ianni, F. A. J. (1989). *The search for structure: A report on American youth today.* New York: The Free Press.

Jessor, R., Donovan, J. E., & Costa, F. M. (1991). *Beyond adolescence: Problem behavior and young adult development.* Cambridge, UK: Cambridge Univesity Press.

Jessor, R., & Jessor, S. (1977). *Problem behavior and psychosocial development: A longitudinal study of youth.* New York: Academic Press.

Kornhauser, R. (1978). *Social sources of delinquency.* Chicago: University of Chicago Press.

Laub, J. H., & Sampson, R. J. (1993). Turning points in the life course: Why change matters to the study of crime. *Criminology, 31,* 301–325.

Lemert, E. (1967). *Human deviance, social problems, and social control.* Englewood Cliffs, NJ: Prentice-Hall.

Loeber, R. (1982). The stability of antisocial child behavior: A review. *Child Development, 53,* 1431–1446.

Lombroso, C. (1911). *Crime, its causes and remedies.* Boston: Little, Brown.

MacLeod, J. (1987). *Ain't no makin' it: Leveled aspirations in a low-income neighborhood.* Boulder, CO: Westview Press.

Mallar, C. S., Kerachsky, T. C., Donihue, M., Jones, C., Long, D., Noggoh, E., & Schore, J. (1980). *Evaluation of the economic impact of the job corps program: Second follow-up report.* Princeton, NJ: Mathematica Policy Research.

Massey, D. S., & Denton, N. A. (1993). *American apartheid: Segregation and the making of the underclass.* Cambridge, MA: Harvard University Press.

Matza, D. (1964). *Delinquency and drift.* New York: Wiley.

Merton, R. K. (1938). Social structure and anomie. *American Sociological Review, 3,* 672–682.

Moffitt, T. E. (1993). Adolescence-limited and life-course-persistent antisocial behavior: A developmental taxonomy. *Psychological Review, 100,* 674–701.

Moore, J. W. (1978). *Homeboys.* Philadelphia: Temple University Press.

Moore, J. W. (1991). *Going down to the barrio: Homeboys and homegirls in change.* Philadelphia: Temple University Press.

Nagin, D. S., & Paternoster, R. (1991). On the relationship of past to future participation in delinquency. *Criminology, 29,* 163–189.

Olweus, D. (1979). Stability of aggressive reaction patterns in males: A review. *Psychological Bulletin, 86,* 852–875.

Padilla, F. M. (1992). *The gang as an American enterprise.* New Brunswick, NJ: Rutgers University Press.

Petersen, A. C., & Mortimer, J. T. (Eds.). (1994). *Youth unemployment and society.* Cambridge, UK: Cambridge University Press.

Robins, L. N. (1966). *Deviant children grown up.* Baltimore, MD: Williams & Wilkins.

Robins, L. N., & Rutter, M. (1990). Introduction. In L. N. Robins & M. Rutter (Eds.), *Straight and devious pathways from childhood to adulthood* (pp. xiii–xix). Cambridge, UK: Cambridge University Press.

Sampson, R. J. (1992). Family management and child development: Insights from social disorganization theory. In J. McCord (Ed.), *Advances in criminological theory* (Vol. 3, pp. 63–93). New Brunswick, NJ: Transaction.

Sampson, R. J., & Laub, J. H. (1993). *Crime in the making: Pathways and turning points through life.* Cambridge, MA: Harvard University Press.

Shannon, L. (1988). *Criminal career continuity: Its social context.* New York: Human Sciences Press.

Shaw, C. R., & McKay, H. D. (1931). *Social factors in juvenile delinquency.* (Report to the National Commission on Law Observance and Enforcement, Wickersham Commission, Vol. 13, no. 2). Washington, DC: U.S. Government Printing Office.

Shevky, E., & Bell, W. (1955). *Social area analysis: Theory, illustration, application and computational procedures.* Stanford, CA: Stanford University Press.

Short, J. F., Jr., & Nye, F. I. (1958). Extent of unrecorded delinquency: Tentative conclusions. *Journal of Criminal Law, Criminology, and Police Science, 49,* 296–302.

Sullivan, M. L. (1989a). Absent fathers in the inner city. *Annals of the American Academy of Political and Social Science, 501,* 48–58.

Sullivan, M. L. (1989b). *Getting paid: Youth crime and work in the inner city.* Ithaca, NY: Cornell University Press.

Sullivan, M. L. (1991). Crime and the social fabric. In J. H. Mollenkopf & M. Castells (Eds.), *Dual city: Restructuring New York* (pp. 225–244). New York: Russell Sage Foundation.

Sullivan, M. L. (1993a). Culture and class as determinants of out-of-wedlock childbearing. *Journal of Research on Adolescence, 3,* 295–316.

Sullivan, M. L. (1993b). Young fathers and parenting in two inner-city neighborhoods. In R. I. Lerman & T. J. Ooms (Eds.), *Young unwed fathers: Changing roles and emerging policies* (pp. 52–73). Philadelphia: Temple University Press.

Sutherland, E. (1937). *The professional thief.* Chicago: University of Chicago Press.

Suttles, G. D. (1968). *The social order of the slum: Ethnicity and territory in the inner city.* Chicago: University of Chicago Press.

Tannenbaum, F. (1938). *Crime and the community.* New York: Columbia University Press.

Taylor, C. S. (1989). *Dangerous society.* East Lansing: Michigan State University Press.

Tittle, C., Villemez, W., & Smith, D. (1978). The myth of social class and criminality. *American Sociological Review, 43,* 643–656.

Turner, S. (1969). Delinquency and distance. In T. Sellin & M. Wolfgang (Eds.), *Delinquency: Selected studies* (pp. 11–27). New York: Wiley.

Vigil, D. (1988). *Barrio gangs.* Austin: University of Texas Press.

Vygotsky, L. S. (1978). *Mind in society.* Cambridge, MA: Harvard University Press.

West, D. J., & Farrington, D. P. (1977). *The delinquent way of life.* London: Heinemann.

West, W. G. (1974). Serious thieves: Lower-class adolescent males in a short-term deviant occupation. Unpublished doctoral dissertation, Northwestern University, Evanston, IL.

Whyte, W. F. (1943). *Street corner society.* Chicago: University of Chicago Press.

Wilkinson, K. (1974). The broken family and juvenile delinquency: Scientific explanation or ideology? *Social Problems, 21,* 726–739.

Williams, T. (1989). *The cocaine kids: The inside story of a teenage drug ring.* Reading, MA: Addison-Wesley.

Willis, P. (1977). *Learning to labour.* Farnborough, UK: Saxon House.

Wilson, J. Q., & Herrnstein, R. J. (1985). *Crime and human nature.* New York: Simon & Schuster.

Wolfgang, M. E., Figlio, R. M., & Sellin, T. (1972). *Delinquency in a birth cohort.* Chicago: University of Chicago Press.

Wolfgang, M. E., Thornberry, T. P., & Figlio, R. (1987). *From boy to man: From delinquency to crime.* Chicago: University of Chicago Press.

III

TRANSITIONS IN THE
FAMILY SYSTEM

7

A Model of Family Relational Transformations During the Transition to Adolescence: Parent–Adolescent Conflict and Adaptation

Grayson N. Holmbeck
Loyola University of Chicago

The relative dearth of published research on family relations during adolescence prior to 1980 stands in sharp contrast to the dramatic increase in both the quantity and quality of research on parent–adolescent relationships during the 1980s and early 1990s. Indeed, the state of the field is such that several scholars have been able to provide integrative reviews of this literature (e.g., Collins, 1990, 1995; Collins & Laursen, 1992; Collins & Russell, 1991; Hauser & Greene, 1991; Hill, 1980a, 1985, 1987; Hill & Holmbeck, 1986; Holmbeck, Paikoff, & Brooks-Gunn, 1995; Laursen & Collins, 1994; Leigh & Peterson, 1986; Paikoff & Brooks-Gunn, 1991; Powers, Hauser, & Kilner, 1989; Steinberg, 1990). Given the impressive level of agreement among the existing reviews, it is not my goal to provide another comprehensive survey of this literature. Instead, the conclusions from these reviews are summarized, examining the premise that parent–adolescent relationships, relative to parent–child relationships, endure a period of transformation and redefinition during early adolescence (Collins, 1990, 1995).

The bulk of this chapter is devoted to a consideration of process. Thus far, research on the nature of parent–adolescent relationships has detailed the types of changes that do (and do not) occur in families during the transition to adolescence (Collins, 1990; Holmbeck et al., 1995; Laursen & Collins, 1994; Steinberg, 1990). We know, for example, that the early adolescent period is often a time of increased emotional distance and mild disruption in familial relationships (Hill & Holmbeck, 1987; Holmbeck & Hill, 1991; Paikoff & Brooks-Gunn, 1991; Steinberg, 1989; although see Laursen & Collins, 1994, for an opposing view). As yet, however, little is known about the processes that underlie these relational transformations (Brooks-Gunn & Zahaykevich, 1989; Collins, 1990, 1995; Holmbeck et al., 1995; Paikoff & Brooks-Gunn, 1991; Smetana, 1995; Steinberg, 1989, 1990). For example, we do not know very much about the mechanisms that produce familial disruptions nor do we know very much about the developmental role of such disruptions. More generally, "the complex interplay among context, maturation, and relationship characteristics is poorly understood" (Laursen & Collins, 1994, p. 206).

To illustrate some of the mechanisms by which transformations in parent–child relationships occur during the transition to adolescence, this chapter focuses specifically on the role of conflict in the redefinition of the parent–adolescent relationship. Although it is assumed that relationships are transformed along multiple behavioral, cognitive, and affective dimensions (Collins, 1990; Collins & Russell, 1991), this chapter focuses more narrowly on parent–adolescent conflict because considerable theoretical and empirical work has accumulated on this topic (see Collins & Laursen, 1992; Laursen & Collins, 1994, for reviews) and because conflict has considerable clinical significance (Robin & Foster, 1989).

To understand the role of conflict in the transition to adolescence, the developmental antecedents of increases in parent–child conflict are described, as well as how parents' and adolescents' responses to relational conflict determine whether outcomes of conflict are adaptive (and facilitative of individual and relational growth) or maladaptive. A framework is proposed that includes the following components: (a) biological, cognitive, and social role changes; (b) responses of the adolescent and significant others to these changes; (c) discrepancies in the perceptions and expectations of parents and adolescents; (d) moderating variables at each stage of the model; and (e) specification of adaptive and dysfunctional relationship outcomes. Prior to discussing the specifics of this framework, the literature on parent–child relationships during the transition to adolescence is reviewed. Previous attempts to discuss relational transformations from a process perspective are also summarized.

PARENT–CHILD RELATIONSHIPS DURING
THE TRANSITION TO ADOLESCENCE

The summary that follows is not intended to be an exhaustive discussion of all findings in the area of parent–adolescent research. Rather, it is a summary of general conclusions, drawn from past reviews of the literature. Most of the conclusions that are discussed have been replicated. Citations in this section are, for the most part, reviews rather than specific studies. The reader is referred to these reviews for more detailed accounts of the studies that contributed to each conclusion. The topics to be discussed in this section include: (a) storm and stress theory and the incidence of parent–adolescent conflict, (b) emotional distance and temporary perturbations in family relationships, (c) relational continuity and authoritative parenting, and (d) reciprocity of causality between adolescent development and family relationships. Finally, past reviewers' recommendations for future research are discussed; these recommendations were used as a basis for developing the model described later in this chapter.

Storm and Stress Theory and the Incidence of Parent–Adolescent Conflict

Contrary to the beliefs of the general public (Holmbeck & Hill, 1988) and reports in the media, little empirical support exists for the contention that extreme levels of conflictive engagement ("storm and stress"; e.g., Freud, 1958) characterize parent–adolescent relationships. In fact, in those rare instances where high levels of conflict in the parent–adolescent relationship are found, they are predictive of less desirable early adolescent adjustment outcomes (Montemayor, 1983, 1986). The notion that preadolescent parent–child attachments are significantly disrupted or severed during the adolescent period also has not been verified by empirical research (Collins, 1990; Hill, 1980a, 1985, 1987; Hill & Holmbeck, 1986; Powers et al., 1989; Steinberg, 1990).

It appears that less than 10% of families endure serious relationship difficulties during adolescence (i.e., parent–adolescent relationships characterized by chronic and escalating levels of conflict and repeated arguments over serious, rather than mundane, issues). Of these families, however, a sizable proportion present with problems that are continuations of difficulties encountered in childhood—before the transition to adolescence (Collins, 1990; Collins & Laursen, 1992; Hill, 1985, 1987; Montemayor, 1983; Rutter, Graham, Chadwick, & Yule, 1976; Steinberg, 1990). As Hill (1985) noted, although the percentages for extreme levels of conflict represent a sizable number of families, the rates are "not large enough to be the basis for a general developmental theory" (p. 235). When parents and adolescents disagree, these conflicts are over rather mundane issues involving household responsibilities and privileges; arguments over religious, political, or social issues are less common (Hill, 1985, 1987; Hill & Holmbeck, 1986; Montemayor, 1983, 1986; Steinberg, 1990). On the other hand, arguments between parents and adolescents tend to occur at a rate of about one every 3 days (Montemayor, 1982), which is similar to the rate found in distressed marital dyads (Montemayor, 1986). Given the likely differences in the issues under discussion in these two types of dyads, it may be that conflicts are more intense and have different meanings in distressed marital dyads than in typical parent–adolescent dyads. As yet, however, comparisons between these types of dyads have not been made.

Emotional Distance and Temporary Perturbations in Family Relationships

Despite the lack of serious relationship trauma during early adolescence, a period of increased emotional distance or temporary perturbations in parent–adolescent relationships (e.g., less closeness, less positive affect, moderate levels of conflictive engagement, less acceptance, changes in the nature of rules and standards, less adolescent involvement in family activities) appears to follow shortly after the onset of pubertal development in boys and girls and especially in mother–daughter dyads (see Collins, 1990; Collins & Russell, 1991; Hill, 1987, 1988; Hill & Holmbeck, 1987; Holmbeck & Hill, 1991; Holmbeck et al., 1995; Larson, Richards, Moneta, Holmbeck, & Duckett, in press; Montemayor, 1983; Paikoff & Brooks-Gunn, 1991; Powers et al., 1989; Steinberg, 1989, 1990, for reviews; see Laursen & Collins, 1994, and Laursen & Ferreira, 1994, for an alternative interpretation of these data). An increase in the time spent with peers during the transition to adolescence (Hill, 1987) and an increase in discrepancies between parents' and adolescents' perceptions of important family issues also emerge (Collins, 1990; Holmbeck & O'Donnell, 1991; Smetana, 1988b). Moreover, parents are deidealized by their offspring during early adolescence (Steinberg, 1990).

Relational Continuity and Authoritative Parenting

Although the changes just described can be stressful for the adolescent and the family, they typically do not undermine the quality of the relationship between parent and adolescent (Steinberg, 1990). As children manage the transition to adolescence, close relationships between parents and offspring are maintained for the majority of families (Brooks-Gunn & Zahaykevich, 1989; Collins, 1990; Hill, 1987; Powers et al., 1989; Steinberg, 1990). Authoritative parenting—a form of parenting that combines high levels of warmth, demandingness, and democracy—continues to be beneficial for young adolescents (as it was during childhood; Maccoby & Martin, 1983) and is related to a variety of desirable psychosocial outcomes (e.g., self-esteem, self-governance; Hill, 1980a, 1987; Hill & Holmbeck, 1986; Holmbeck et al., 1995; Steinberg, 1990). Value sharing is common between parents and adolescents, with adolescents tending to select as friends peers that have the same values as their parents (Collins,

1990; Hill, 1980a, 1985, 1987; Steinberg, 1990). Moreover, parental disapproval is anticipated to be more difficult than peer disapproval by most adolescents (Hill, 1987). Discontinuities in the parent–child relationship during the transition to adolescence tend to occur against a backdrop of relational continuity (with respect to the level of connectedness, warmth, and cohesiveness between parents and adolescents; Brooks-Gunn & Zahaykevich, 1989; Collins, 1990). Over the course of adolescence, the relationship between adolescent and parent tends to be transformed from one of unilateral authority to one of mutuality and cooperation (Steinberg, 1990; White, Speisman, & Costos, 1983; Youniss & Smollar, 1985).

Reciprocity of Causality

Not only does adolescent development (e.g., pubertal status) appear to have an impact on family relationships, but family relationships also appear to have an impact on the development of adolescents (e.g., pubertal development, ego development, identity development, role-taking skills; Brooks-Gunn, Graber, & Paikoff, 1994; Graber, Brooks-Gunn, & Warren, 1995; Hauser, 1991; Hill, 1985; Paikoff & Brooks-Gunn, 1991; Powers et al., 1989; Steinberg, 1988, 1990) and the development of parents (e.g., satisfaction with parenting, work status and vocational aspirations, body image and dieting behavior; Hill, 1980a; Paikoff & Brooks-Gunn, 1991; Steinberg, 1990). For example, Steinberg (1988) found (for girls only) that distance in the mother–daughter relationship may serve to accelerate pubertal development and that closeness may slow such development. With respect to other types of developmental outcomes, Cooper, Grotevant, and Condon (1983) found that certain types of disagreements within family interaction are associated with more advanced levels of adolescent identity exploration. Thus, in some instances, causal relations between individual development and parent–adolescent interactions may be bidirectional.

Past Reviewers' Recommendations for Future Research

In addition to these conclusions, reviewers of this literature have also advanced a number of recommendations for future research on parent–child relationships during early adolescence. These recommendations are reviewed here because they proved useful in developing the proposed framework that is described later in this chapter.

1. Most of what we know about parent–adolescent relationships is based on research involving White, middle-class, and intact families (Barber, 1994; Collins, 1990, 1995; Hill, 1987; Paikoff & Brooks-Gunn, 1991;

Powers et al., 1989; Sessa & Steinberg, 1991; Smetana, 1995; Spencer & Dornbusch, 1990; Steinberg, 1990; see McAdoo, 1988; McAdoo & McAdoo, 1985; Spencer & Dornbusch, 1990; Spencer & McLoyd, 1990, for exceptions). Little is known about the transformations that occur in families who come from other social classes, family structures, or ethnic backgrounds. Even less is known about how families from various backgrounds differ prior to making the transition to adolescence; such information is needed if we are to determine the differential impact of early adolescence on various subpopulations.

2. An increase in the number of longitudinal investigations would enable researchers to examine the causal patterning of the effects. Several reviewers have suggested that researchers examine how the nature of preadolescent parent–child relationships impacts future parent–adolescent relationships (Paikoff & Brooks-Gunn, 1991; Powers et al., 1989; Smetana, 1995; Steinberg, 1990).

3. Researchers should give more careful attention to gender differences in both the child and parent generations. More specifically, we need more information about differences between different parent–child dyads (e.g., mother–son, mother–daughter, etc.). Studies that include parental developmental issues, such as midlife identity concerns, orientation toward work, and life satisfaction, would also be useful (Collins, 1990, 1995; Silverberg & Steinberg, 1987; Steinberg, 1987, 1990).

4. Researchers in this area have tended to focus on pubertal change to the exclusion of other developmental (e.g., social-cognitive changes, social role changes) and contextual (e.g., school transitions) changes (e.g., Brooks-Gunn & Zahaykevich, 1989; Collins, 1990; Collins & Russell, 1991; Laursen & Collins, 1994; Paikoff & Brooks-Gunn, 1991; Powers et al., 1989; Smetana, 1995). It may be that each of these developmental and contextual changes is linked with different types of changes within the family. It has also been suggested that it would be helpful if researchers examined (simultaneously) transformations across multiple behaviors (e.g., interactions, affect, cognitions; Collins & Russell, 1991) as well as the impact of transformations in one relational context on relationships in another context (e.g., relationships with parents impacting on relationships with peers; Paikoff & Brooks-Gunn, 1991).

5. More work is needed on the processes that underlie the observed transformations in parent–adolescent relationships (e.g., changes in parents' and adolescents' expectations; Collins, 1990, 1995; also see Brooks-Gunn & Zahaykevich, 1989; Holmbeck et al., 1995; Paikoff & Brooks-Gunn, 1991; Powers et al., 1989; Smetana, 1995; Steinberg, 1989, 1990).

6. Families should be studied from a systems perspective rather than only being viewed as sets of parent–child and parent–parent dyads

(Paikoff & Brooks-Gunn, 1991; Steinberg, 1990). Analyses of triadic interactions (mother–father–adolescent) have been rare (Smetana, Yau, Restrepo, & Braeges, 1991; Vuchinich, Emery, & Cassidy, 1988); comparisons of dyadic and triadic interactions and the development of systems-level coding approaches will be a first step in the study of the family as a "system."

7. Regarding the observed associations between pubertal change and family relationships, more attention should be paid to variables that moderate the effects of biological change on relational outcomes (e.g., parent and adolescent responses to pubertal change, demographic characteristics, peer factors; Paikoff & Brooks-Gunn, 1991).

8. The conditions under which conflict is adaptive versus when it is dysfunctional need to be studied (Ellis, 1986; Powers et al., 1989; Steinberg, 1990).

PROCESS-ORIENTED APPROACHES TO THE STUDY OF FAMILY RELATIONAL TRANSFORMATIONS DURING THE TRANSITION TO ADOLESCENCE

Although we now understand much more about family relationships than we did 15 years ago, a large gap in our knowledge about the transformations that occur during the transition to adolescence still remains. At present, we know very little about how relationships come to be transformed. What processes underlie the relational transformations that occur in response to adolescent developmental change? What happens day to day between parents and adolescents that allows for such transformations? How do parents decide when to alter their parenting behaviors? How are significant others outside of the home implicated in the process? Why are some dimensions of the relationship altered whereas others remain unchanged? Is the process the same for all adolescents or does it vary depending on the family's background? What conditions determine whether the relationship that parents and adolescents end up with after the transformation is functional and healthy or dysfunctional and highly conflictive?

What these questions have in common is that they all address the processes that underlie the transformations discussed earlier. They are not new questions; concerns with these issues were echoed already in the suggestions for future research. Reviewers of this literature have suggested, for example, that more studies need to be conducted on the causal patterning of the effects of developmental change on relational transformations as well as the moderators of these effects (e.g., gender, ethnicity, social class, family structure differences, changing expectations of parents and adolescents; see Paikoff & Brooks-Gunn, 1991).

Despite the lack of attention to underlying process, several attempts to describe family processes that promote relational transformations have appeared in the literature. These include: (a) Petersen and Taylor's (1980) mediated-effects model, (b) Paikoff and Brooks-Gunn's (1991; also see Paikoff & Brooks-Gunn, 1990) discussion of variables that mediate effects of biological change on family relationships during adolescence, (c) Robin and Foster's (1989) behavioral-family systems model of parent–adolescent conflict, (d) Collins' (1990, 1992, 1995) studies of changes in adolescent and parent expectations during early adolescence, (e) Smetana's (1988a, 1988b, 1989, 1995) studies of adolescent–parent reasoning about conflict issues, (f) Steinberg's (1989) evolutionary perspective on parent–adolescent conflict, and (g) Holmbeck and Hill's (1991) discussion of the role of interpersonal and intrapsychic factors in the onset of parent–adolescent conflict.

Petersen and Taylor

Petersen and Taylor's (1980) mediated-effects model (see also Brooks-Gunn et al., 1994; Paikoff & Brooks-Gunn, 1990; Petersen, 1985) describes the likely causal pathways between biological change and changes in adolescent and family behavior. These authors argued that a mediated-effects model can be distinguished from a direct-effects model insofar as intervening variables (personality and contextual factors) influence associations between changes in the biological system and psychological outcomes. Although these authors were among the first to discuss underlying process, this model has proven to be lacking in specificity (Paikoff & Brooks-Gunn, 1990, 1991; also, see later discussion on distinctions between mediated and moderated effects).

Paikoff and Brooks-Gunn

Building on the work of Peterson and Taylor (1980), Paikoff and Brooks-Gunn (1991; see also Brooks-Gunn & Zahaykevich, 1989; Paikoff & Brooks-Gunn, 1990) suggested that researchers in this area have consistently ignored variables that mediate the effects of biological change on family relationships. They provided a useful review of many of the likely contributors, namely, adolescent and parental responses to biological change; changes in social cognition and self-definition; pre-existing characteristics of adolescents and parents; ethnicity, peer, and school factors; and other major life events. Many of the underlying processes discussed by Paikoff and Brooks-Gunn (1991) are expected to have their own direct effects on changes in parent–child relationships during the transition to adolescence and each may mediate and interact with the effects of the other processes.

Robin and Foster

Robin and Foster (1989) provided a behavioral-family systems model of parent–adolescent conflict. Although the underlying processes linking biological change and changes in parent–adolescent relationships are not well delineated, the model does specify moderating variables (e.g., problem-solving abilities, communication patterns, belief systems, and the structural nature of the family system) that determine whether normative levels of conflict remain normative or escalate to levels characteristic of distressed family systems.

Collins

Collins (1990, 1992, 1995) argued that rapid developmental change during early adolescence sets the stage for changes in the expectations that parents and adolescents have for each other; violations of expectations are particularly likely during periods of rapid change. In one of the few examples of empirical work that attempts to address process issues, Collins (1990, 1995) provided some preliminary evidence that discrepancies between family members' perceptions of "what is" and their expectations of "what could be" are greater during early adolescence (8th grade) than before (5th grade) or after (11th grade). Finally, he argued that such discrepancies have implications for behavioral change and, as a consequence, relational transformations and individual outcomes (Collins, 1995; see also Holmbeck et al., 1995). In a related study, Holmbeck and O'Donnell (1991) provided longitudinal evidence that discrepancies between parents and adolescents regarding their perceptions of who makes decisions in the home and how much autonomy the adolescent deserves are related to subsequent changes in mother–adolescent conflict and the level of family cohesiveness (see Paikoff, 1991).

Smetana

Smetana (1988a, 1988b, 1989, 1995) found that the manner in which adolescents reason about important family issues changes during early adolescence. That is, the apparent increase in parent–adolescent conflicts over mundane, everyday issues may be related to realignments in the parent–adolescent relationship, especially insofar as the boundaries of legitimate parental authority are renegotiated during adolescence. More specifically, Smetana (1988b) interviewed 5th through 12th graders (10 to 17 years old) and their parents concerning their justifications regarding the legitimacy of parental authority across moral, conventional, and personal domains. Young adolescents increasingly come to treat conflictive issues as matters of personal jurisdiction, whereas parents tend to reason about the same issues from a social-conventional perspective. Thus, Smetana's findings suggest that, with increasing maturity, incongruities in perceptions of jurisdiction emerge between parents and adolescents. Even though parents and adolescents are aware of their differing viewpoints, these incongruities may become the antecedents of increases in parent–adolescent conflict.

Steinberg

Steinberg (1989) discussed processes that bring about parent–adolescent conflict from a sociobiological perspective. Parent–adolescent conflict is assumed to be, directly or indirectly, a response to adolescent biological change. He maintained that parent–adolescent conflict may have an evolved basis in the sense that it facilitates the home-leaving process and ensures that adolescents will procreate outside of the home. In support of this evolutionary perspective, Steinberg (1988, 1989) presented findings that support the notion that the relationship between puberty and family relationships is bidirectional, concluding that some distance in the parent–adolescent relationship may facilitate physical maturation (at least for girls). Steinberg speculated that such relational distance as well as the accompanying advanced physical maturity may facilitate the seeking of mates outside the immediate family environment.

Holmbeck and Hill

Holmbeck and Hill (1991) asked why increased levels of conflict and emotional distance appear to be characteristic of families shortly after the onset of pubertal change. Although some argue that "conflict is a situation that is best avoided" (Ellis, 1986, p. 156), Holmbeck and Hill (1991) posited that parent–adolescent conflict can serve an adaptive function insofar as conflict is "an essential impetus to change, adaptation, and development" (Shantz, 1987, p. 284; see also Brooks-Gunn & Zahaykevich, 1989; Collins & Laursen, 1992; Cooper, 1988; Hill & Holmbeck, 1987; Smetana, 1995; Steinberg, 1990). They speculated that interpersonal/extrapsychic as well as intrapsychic processes operate (Papini, Micka, & Barnett, 1989); these processes allow conflict to play an adaptive role and make moderate levels of conflict normative in healthy families.

With regard to the interpersonal/extrapsychic processes, conflict may play an information-providing role within the parent–adolescent relationship (Holmbeck & Hill, 1991; Kidwell, Fischer, Dunham, & Baranowski, 1983). Conflicts may inform parents that the adolescents' needs and expectations have changed and that some sort of recalibration of the parent–child relationship is necessary (Collins, 1995; Smetana, 1995). In the case of the intrapsychic processes, conflict may play a role in facilitating the individuation process that is triggered by reactions of the child and parents to developmental change (Holmbeck & Hill, 1991). The process of differentiation is believed to be particularly stressful for the mother–daughter dyad (Brooks-Gunn & Zahaykevich, 1989; Chodorow, 1978; Deutsch, 1944)—however, a similar process appears to occur in other parent–adolescent dyads as well (Josselson, 1980; Kaplan, 1984). The bond that often exists between parent and child prior to adolescence may have to undergo some degree of change in order for the child to develop close relationships outside of the family. A psychoanalytic perspective posits that adolescents come to experience themselves as overattached and undifferentiated and must, at some point, confront their "entanglement in family relationships" (Chodorow, 1978, p. 135). The point here is not that children must sever their relationship with their parents (Gilligan, Lyons, & Hanmer, 1990), but rather, that parent–adolescent relationships must be renegotiated in such a way that the children are able to maintain close relationships with both parents and peers. The conflicts that occur during this renegotiation stage may underlie and facilitate this individuation process.

Conclusions

The theoretical positions reviewed in this section have provided differing perspectives on the types of conflictive processes that may bring about transformations in parent–child relationships during adolescence. Unfortunately, these lines of work have not been integrated in such a way as to be helpful to investigators desiring to do more comprehensive process-level investigations. The purpose of the next section is to provide an organizing framework that brings together many of the speculations already advanced as well as the suggestions for future research reviewed earlier.

A MODEL OF RELATIONAL TRANSFORMATIONS: PARENT–ADOLESCENT CONFLICT AND THE TRANSITION TO ADOLESCENCE

The model that is proposed here (see Fig. 7.1) is based not only on an integration of the theoretical work and recommendations for future research discussed earlier, but it also builds on a model proposed by Paikoff and Brooks-Gunn (1991) in two ways. First, their model is expanded to take into account theorizing by other reviewers. That is, interpersonal and intrapsychic processes, moderating variables, and adaptive and maladaptive outcomes are specified and differentiated. The importance of moderator (as opposed to mediator) variables is emphasized. Second,

178

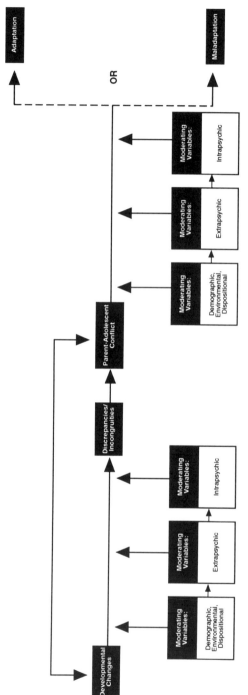

FIG. 7.1. General model of parent–adolescent conflict (antecedents and consequences).

the model presented here focuses specifically on one aspect of the relationship between parent and adolescent—parent–adolescent conflict—and its role in relational transformations during the transition to adolescence (Collins, 1995; Collins & Laursen, 1992; Smetana, 1995). Such specificity is necessary given that the nature of the transformation is likely to vary depending on the relationship dimension under consideration (e.g., conflict, affect, cognitions, control; Collins, 1990; Kelley et al., 1983) and because different types of transformations probably occur at different rates and are driven by different processes.

More generally, conflict was chosen as the focus in this chapter because: (a) conflict is a natural component of any close relationship (Collins & Laursen, 1992; Kelley et al., 1983; Laursen & Collins, 1994), (b) parent–adolescent conflict has been subjected to considerable empirical and theoretical inquiry (e.g., Collins & Laursen, 1992), (c) parent–adolescent conflict has clinical significance insofar as distressed families typically evidence more intense and higher levels of conflict than nondistressed families, and, perhaps most importantly, (d) "adolescence is a period in which conflict becomes . . . more intricately embedded in social bonds that support development toward adult relationships and competencies" (Collins & Laursen, 1992, p. 236).

The general model is presented in Fig. 7.1 and a more complete version of the model is presented in two parts, in Figs. 7.2 and 7.3. Figure 7.2 depicts the antecedents of parent–adolescent conflict and Fig. 7.3 depicts the consequences of parent–adolescent conflict. The purpose of this model is to describe several potential antecedents and consequences of parent–adolescent conflict in such a way as to describe the role that conflict may play in transforming family relationships during the transition to adolescence. In the same way that stress may be linked with adverse outcomes only when certain maladaptive coping strategies are employed (Aldwin, 1994), developmental change during adolescence may be linked with increased levels of parent–adolescent conflict only when certain conditions are present. Regardless of the final verdict on whether or not strong direct associations between developmental change and changes in family relationships exist (Laursen & Collins, 1994), it is likely that high levels of parent–adolescent conflict emerge anew in some dyads as a consequence of developmental change. In families where there is an exacerbation in the level of conflict, such increases may have a detrimental impact on parent–child relationships in some families whereas such increases may result in adaptive outcomes in other families. The main argument here is not that high levels of conflict are inevitable during the adolescent transition nor that conflict is inherently adaptive or maladaptive. Rather, the purpose of the model is to begin to identify those conditions that exacerbate or lessen the level of conflict and those conditions that deter-

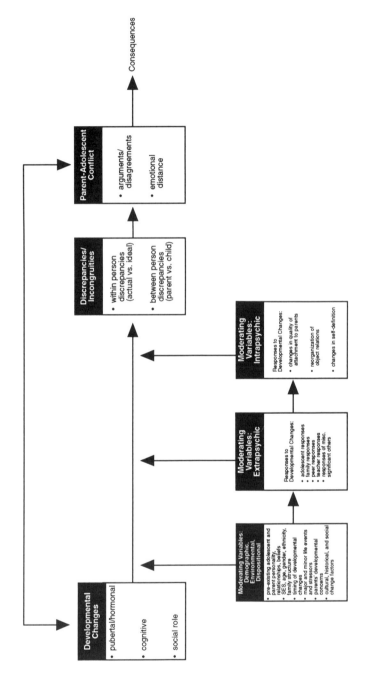

FIG. 7.2. Complete model of parent–adolescent conflict, part I: Antecedents.

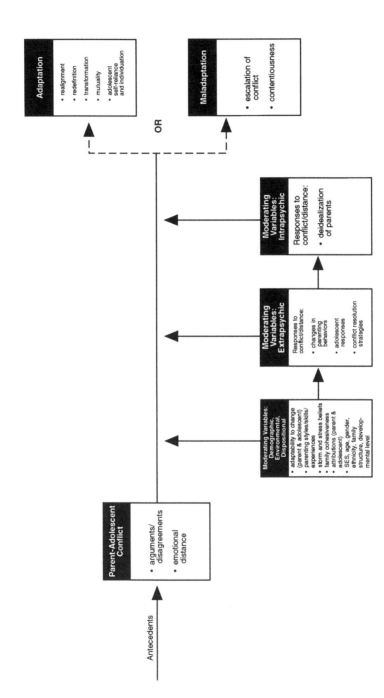

FIG. 7.3. Complete model of parent–adolescent conflict, part II: Consequences.

181

mine whether an increase in conflict results in adaptive or maladaptive outcomes (Barber, 1994; Steinberg, 1990).

Stated differently, this model is an example of how developmental and contextual processes may be integrated within the same framework (Lerner, Hess, & Nitz, 1991; Maccoby, 1984). Although *context* may be defined in relation to intraindividual contextual differences (e.g., the conflict behavior of an individual varies across different family and peer contexts; Laursen & Collins, 1994), context is defined here as an individual differences variable (e.g., parental responses to pubertal change vary considerably across families, associations between developmental change and parent–adolescent conflict vary as a function of cultural background). In the present instance, the contextual factors moderate associations between developmental change and conflict as well as associations between conflict and outcome.

According to the model, discrepancies between parent and adolescent perceptions and expectations of each other are viewed as emerging during the period of early adolescence—a period of considerable intraindividual change (Collins, 1990; Holmbeck & O'Donnell, 1991; Holmbeck et al., 1995). The degree to which discrepancies emerge is moderated by a host of interrelated demographic, environmental, dispositional, extrapsychic, and intrapsychic factors. It is also expected that discrepancies and incongruities within the parent–adolescent relationship will produce conflict. Whether the conflict yields adaptive or maladaptive outcomes is again determined by a host of moderator variables.

It may be helpful to provide an example of how this model might work as applied to an individual adolescent. Suppose a young adolescent begins to develop physically. Such biological changes may produce discrepancies between how the child views himself or herself (e.g., the child may begin to feel entitled to privacy, dating privileges, more decision-making privileges) and how the parent perceives the child (e.g., parents may not alter their parenting and feel that no changes are necessary). The degree to which these discrepancies follow from advances in physical maturity may be impacted by factors such as the gender of the child, the preadolescent parent–child relationship, and the parents' own developmental concerns (Holmbeck et al., 1995). Other influential factors may include, for example, peer responses to the child's pubertal changes and the degree to which the nature of the attachment to parents is altered during the transition to adolescence. Conflict is expected to ensue as a consequence of the discrepant perceptions and expectations. The degree to which a parent and an adolescent are responsive to each other and flexible during the conflicts as well as the nature of the attributions that each have for the behavior of the other is expected to impact on whether the conflicts yield adaptive (e.g., individuation, transformation of family interaction, adolescent feelings of self-reliance) or maladaptive outcomes (e.g., an escalation of conflict).

Definitional Issues and Assumptions

For the purposes of this discussion, a conflict is assumed to occur "when (the) behavior by one member of a dyad is incongruent with the goals, expectations, or desires of the other member, resulting in *mutual opposition*" (Collins & Laursen, 1992, p. 219; Holmbeck & Hill, 1991; Peterson, 1983). A given conflict is also expected to have a number of components, including intensity, initiation, content, resolution, and outcome (Collins & Laursen, 1992; Laursen & Collins, 1994; Shantz, 1987).

It is assumed that this model depicts a conflict cycle that occurs on a day-to-day basis between parents and adolescents and that such cycles occur repeatedly throughout the second decade of life (Holmbeck & O'Donnell, 1991). Given that the moderating variables in the model often constitute responses to developmental changes or responses to parent–adolescent conflict, this model is assumed to be unidirectional. One exception to this is the bidirectional (and direct) relationship between developmental change (e.g., pubertal and cognitive changes) and conflict (indicated in the model by a bidirectional arrow; Brooks-Gunn et al., 1994; Collins & Laursen, 1992; Steinberg, 1988). Also indicated in the model is a causal relationship between extrapsychic and intrapsychic responses to developmental change (e.g., it is expected that an adolescent's responses to his or her own developmental changes will impact on the adolescent's concept of self). It is also acknowledged that within a component of the model (e.g., extrapsychic responses to developmental change), the responses of different individuals (e.g., parents, peers, the adolescents themselves) are expected to have causal effects on each other. Some components of the model may also impact on later components of the model. For example, changes in adolescents' cognitive reasoning skills may exert a direct influence on the adolescents' responses to parent–adolescent conflicts and their ability to participate in negotiated resolutions of conflict (Collins & Laursen, 1992). As can be seen in the figures, these two components (i.e., cognitive change and adolescent responses to parent–adolescent conflict) are not contiguous in the model.

Distinguishing Between Mediating and Moderating Variables

Although use of the terms *mediating* and *moderating* (Baron & Kenny, 1986; Fuhrman & Holmbeck, 1995; Holmbeck, 1995) has become relatively commonplace, their frequent misuse suggests that a review of the differences between mediating and moderating variables would be useful.

Examples of misuse abound and have occurred across a number of literatures, including the stress and coping (e.g., Pearlin, Mullan, Semple, &
Skaff, 1990), child-clinical (e.g., Thompson, Gil, Burbach, Keith, & Kinney,
1993), and marital conflict (Cummings, Davies, & Simpson, 1994; Grych &
Fincham, 1990, 1993) literatures. Confusion over these terms is also evident
in the literature on associations between developmental change and
changes in individual and family behavior during adolescence (e.g.,
Brooks-Gunn et al., 1994; Paikoff & Brooks-Gunn, 1991; Petersen, 1987;
Petersen & Taylor, 1980).

In a useful discussion on the topic, Baron and Kenny (1986; see also
Fuhrman & Holmbeck, 1995; Holmbeck, 1995; Shadish & Sweeney, 1991)
defined a moderator variable as "a qualitative (e.g., sex, race, class) or
quantitative . . . variable that affects the direction and/or strength of a
relation between an independent or predictor variable and a dependent or
criterion variable . . . a basic moderator effect can be represented as an
interaction between a focal independent variable and a factor (the moderator) that specifies the appropriate conditions for its operation" (p. 1174). In
other words, a moderator variable is one that impacts on a relationship
between two variables. Moderators interact with an antecedent variable in
such a way as to have an impact on the level of the consequent variable. A
mediator variable, on the other hand, is the "generative mechanism
through which the focal independent variable is able to influence the
dependent variable of interest" (Baron & Kenny, 1986, p. 1173). Simply put,
"the independent variable causes the mediator which then causes the
outcome" (Shadish & Sweeney, 1991, p. 883). The mediator, unlike the
moderator, falls in the causal pathway between two variables. For example,
if A causes B and B causes C, B is the mediating variable between A and C.
On the other hand, if A is expected to be related to C, but only under certain
conditions of B (or if A is related to C in different ways depending on the
level of B), then B is a moderator variable.

Many of the variables included in the model discussed in this chapter
were designated as moderating based on their possible interactional role
in the model. Moreover, given that associations between developmental
change and parent–adolescent conflict have yielded small effect sizes in
past research (Laursen & Ferreira, 1994; Paikoff & Brooks-Gunn, 1991), a
model based on moderator effects is more likely to be supported by future
research given that strong associations would be needed in order for one
to search for mediational effects (Baron & Kenny, 1986). That is, in order
to isolate a mediating variable, there must first be a strong significant
predictor-criterion effect to mediate. Such a significant effect is not a
requirement of a moderated effect.

Indeed, it is possible that there could be a significant interaction between a variable (e.g., developmental level) and a moderator (e.g., par-

ents' responses to developmental change) in predicting an outcome (e.g., conflict), even though there is little or no effect between the independent variable and the outcome (Baron & Kenny, 1986). In fact, when a perfectly "crossed interaction" is found between two predictors, there are no main effects of either predictor on the outcome of interest. It is possible, for example, that pubertal change may be positively associated with conflict in families where parents respond maladaptively to pubertal changes (e.g., parents dramatically increase the number of rules regarding curfew and dating) and negatively associated with conflict in families where parents respond adaptively (e.g., parents who systematically regulate the number of rules in response to increases in biological or psychosocial maturity). In such a data set, we may find that puberty is nonsignificantly associated with conflict as a main effect. On the other hand, puberty may be highly associated with conflict (albeit in opposite directions) within subsets of the sample in the form of an interaction effect (i.e., a puberty × moderator interaction effect).

The differences between moderation and mediation are discussed in some detail because a misuse of these terms has serious implications for how we design our studies and conduct our data analyses. Whereas mediated effects are confirmed by computing a series of correlations and partial correlations between the variables in the model, moderated effects are tested with interaction terms (Baron & Kenny, 1986). In the puberty–family literature, variables such as gender and responses to puberty have often been designated as *mediating* factors; in the present case, such variables are designated as *moderators* of the relationship between developmental change and parent–adolescent conflict.

Intraindividual Developmental Change

Included at the beginning of the model (see Fig. 7.2) are adolescent biological (e.g., hormonal changes, changes in pubertal status), cognitive (e.g., changes in perceptions, formal operations, social cognitive development), and social role changes (e.g., increases in adult responsibilities). The nature of these changes has been reviewed elsewhere (e.g., Adelson, 1980; Feldman & Elliott, 1990; Hill, 1980b; Holmbeck et al., 1995; Petersen, 1988; Van Hasselt & Hersen, 1987). As indicated in the model, developmental changes can have both direct and moderated effects on parent–adolescent conflict. With regard to the direct effects, Steinberg (1989; see earlier discussion) suggested that there is an evolved basis for the direct effects of puberty, which are expected to occur so as to ensure that the adolescent will emigrate from the home during late adolescence (also see Buchanan, Eccles, & Becker, 1992, and Paikoff & Brooks-Gunn, 1990, 1991, for a discussion of links between hormone levels and adolescent behavior). This direct relationship between pubertal change and conflict also appears to be bidirectional (e.g., Steinberg, 1988). With respect to the moderated effects, the impact of developmental change on parent–adolescent conflict is expected to be moderated by several demographic, environmental, dispositional, extrapsychic, and intrapsychic factors, all of which are themselves expected to be interrelated (see Figs. 7.1 and 7.2).

Moderating Variables: Factors That Moderate the Effects of Developmental Change

Three interconnected types of moderated variables are discussed: (a) Demographic, environmental, and dispositional moderators are assumed to impact on the (b) extrapsychic moderators (responses of the adolescent and significant others to developmental change), which are assumed to impact on the (c) intrapsychic moderators.

Developmental, Environmental, and Dispositional Moderators. It is likely that pre-existing personality characteristics and beliefs of adolescents and parents can interact with developmental changes to influence responses to these changes (e.g., Goodnow & Collins, 1990), although little research has been conducted on these issues. For example, the experience of menarche by girls is highly correlated with premenarcheal expectations (Brooks-Gunn & Ruble, 1982). It is also likely that expectations on the part of parents about what it means to have an adolescent in the home may also have an impact on their parenting behaviors (Collins, 1990, 1992). For example, if parents endorse extreme storm and stress beliefs about adolescence (Buchanan et al., 1990; Holmbeck & Hill, 1988), they may be more likely to "put the brakes on" when their child becomes pubertal, due to anticipatory fears of rebelliousness and conflict.

Level of maternal and paternal psychopathology (e.g., maternal depression; Dodge, 1990; Hauser & Bowlds, 1990; Rutter, 1990), marital conflict (Grych & Fincham, 1990), family structure (Amato & Keith, 1991), as well as major and minor life events and stressors (e.g., school transitions; Simmons & Blyth, 1987) have been found to impact on parent–child interaction and adolescent adjustment. They could also impact on adolescents' and parents' responses to developmental change. Again, however, little research has been conducted to examine these associations. The amount of experience that parents have had with children achieving adolescent status as well as the parents' own parenting skills, parenting style, and developmental concerns may also play an interactive role. Although demographic differences between adolescents are frequently discussed as potential moderator variables for the impact of developmental change, only gender has received intensive study (although family structure was employed as a moderating variable in one study; Anderson,

Hetherington, & Clingempeel, 1989). Finally, it is likely that the pre-existing parent–child relationship will have an impact on responses to developmental change (Paikoff & Brooks-Gunn, 1991; Steinberg, 1990).

Extrapsychic Moderators. Demographic, environmental, and dispositional factors will impact on how adolescents, parents, and significant others respond to developmental change. Extrapsychic responses include interpersonal responses of significant others (parents, peers, teachers, etc.) to developmental change as well as adolescents' responses to their own changes. These responses are assumed to occur because of the social stimulus value of the developmental changes. Regarding parental responses to cognitive and social-cognitive developmental changes, parents of adolescents are more likely to infer intentionality in the behavior of their offspring than are parents of preadolescents (Dix, Ruble, Grusec, & Nixon, 1986; see Collins, 1992; Goodnow & Collins, 1990). Regarding responses to pubertal changes, more physically mature adolescents are expected to assume leadership roles, to perform better in school, to perform more difficult and more socially mature tasks, and to behave like adults (see Brooks-Gunn & Paikoff, 1992; Brooks-Gunn & Zahaykevich, 1989). Similarly, among peers, physical maturity is often highly valued. Finally, menarche in girls is associated with increases in social maturity, peer prestige, and self-esteem (Garwood & Allen, 1979).

In addition to the positive impact of pubertal change, physical changes may also elicit embarrassment or discomfort in adolescents and their parents. Some adolescents may find it difficult to discuss the changes with their parents (e.g., daughters often have difficulty talking about these issues with their fathers). In fact, it has been suggested that girls discuss symptoms of biological change with their parents but discuss their feelings about these changes with their friends (Brooks-Gunn & Warren, 1988). Moreover, parents may deny the importance of the events either because of their own discomfort with their children's physical changes or because of their increasing concerns about their own sexual attractiveness (Brooks-Gunn & Zahaykevich, 1989; Hill, 1988). There is also some evidence that gender-differential socialization may become more common during early adolescence (Galambos, Almeida, & Petersen, 1990; Gilligan et al., 1990; Hill & Lynch, 1983). Although physical maturity in girls may prompt some parents to permit dating and allow more freedom, such maturity is also associated with an increase in parental chaperonage and vigilance, perhaps due to concerns about sexuality and pregnancy (Brooks-Gunn & Zahaykevich, 1989; Hill & Lynch, 1983).

Intrapsychic Moderators. The manner in which adolescents and their significant others respond to developmental change is expected to impact on the intrapsychic functioning of the adolescent. The intrapsychic factors involve changes in the organization of the individual's object relations and/or a reorganization of the individual's concept of self. As a result of developmental changes (e.g., sexual maturity) and responses to developmental change, adolescents may experience changes in their unconscious dynamics—changes that may differ depending on the gender of the parent and the gender of the child (e.g., mother–daughter vs. mother–son; Chodorow, 1978; Holmbeck & Hill, 1991; Rich, 1990). Adolescents at this stage of development appear to seek increased psychological distance from their parents, thus facilitating the individuation process (Steinberg & Silverberg, 1986). Although a discussion of the specifics of these changes is beyond the scope of this chapter (see Blos, 1962, 1979; Brooks-Gunn & Zahaykevich, 1989; Josselson, 1980; Kaplan, 1984; Lerner, 1987), suffice it to say that adolescents do appear to experience differentiation in their relationships with their parents during the transition to early adolescence.

Discrepancies and Incongruities in Parent–Adolescent Perceptions and Expectations

Extrapsychic and intrapsychic responses of adolescents and their significant others to developmental change are likely to alter the perceptions that parents and adolescents have of themselves and each other as well as the expectations that adolescents have for the behaviors of their parents. Based on findings reviewed in the last section, it appears that developmental changes may elicit at least two types of responses in the adolescent: (a) feelings of agency and/or self-esteem, which are presumably empowering experiences (although negative responses are common as well, particularly for those who develop off-time), and (b) a need for distance in the parent–adolescent relationship, either due to intrapsychic changes or to increasing levels of discomfort between parent and adolescent around issues such as pubertal change and sexuality. Parents may respond in a variety of ways, some of which are contradictory. There may be: (a) increases in parents' expectations for adult behavior in the adolescent, (b) denial of the adolescent's increasing maturity level, or (c) an increase in parental control due to anxieties associated with increasing sexual maturity or pre-existing storm and stress beliefs.

Given that such responses may be typical of parents and adolescents during the transition to adolescence, it is likely that incongruities in the perceptions and expectations that adolescents and parents have for each other will emerge (see Figs. 7.1 and 7.2; Collins, 1990, 1992, 1995; Holmbeck & O'Donnell, 1991). Incongruities can exist in many forms (see Holmbeck & O'Donnell, 1991; Holmbeck et al., 1995, for reviews): (a) incongruities between adolescents and parents with respect to perception (e.g., an adolescent feels that he or she is in charge of deciding when it is bedtime vs. a mother who feels that she is in charge of the decision), (b) incongruities between adolescents and parents with respect to expectations (e.g., an adolescent expects that he or she will gain increasing autonomy in deciding when to come home at night vs. a mother who expects to be making this decision until her child is a late adolescent), (c) discrepancies within the adolescent between perceptions and expectations (e.g., many adolescents come to see that the privileges that they currently have [i.e., perceptions of "what is"] are discrepant with the privileges that they feel that they ought to have [i.e., expectations of "what should be"]), and (d) discrepancies within the parent between perceptions and expectations (e.g., some mothers may feel that their adolescents are beginning to demand more privileges [i.e., perceptions] but may not expect to have to make changes in their parenting for several more years [i.e., expectations]).

Regardless of the underlying reasons for the incongruities, the discrepancies that seem to emerge after the onset of developmental change set the stage for differences of opinion on a variety of important family issues. Recent empirical evidence supports this notion. For example, Smetana's (1988a, 1988b, 1989, 1995) work in this area indicates that discrepancies in how parents and adolescents understand family issues increase during early adolescence—discrepancies that may be related to subsequent increases in conflict (Holmbeck & O'Donnell, 1991). In this way, discrepancies between parent and adolescent viewpoints mediate associations between developmental change and parent–adolescent conflict.

Parent–Adolescent Conflict and Emotional Distance

As discussed earlier, past research suggests that temporary perturbations in parent–adolescent relationships occur shortly after the onset of developmental change. It is probably also the case, however, that such relational alterations are more dramatic in some families than in others. In general, the processes underlying these differences across families have not been well understood (Barber, 1994). It has been argued here that developmental changes in combination with certain moderator variables can make it more likely (in certain families) that incongruities will develop in the perceptions and expectations of adolescents and their parents. Such incongruities may lead to conflicts between parents and adolescents as well as an increase in the emotional distance between them (Holmbeck & O'Donnell, 1991; Holmbeck et al., 1995). The outcomes of such conflict and distance will also vary across families. The next section details moderator variables that impact on associations between conflict and subsequent outcomes of conflict.

Moderating Variables: Factors That Moderate the Effects
of Parent–Adolescent Conflict

As was the case with the previous set of moderators, three sets of moderators are again discussed: (a) Demographic, environmental, and dispositional moderators are assumed to impact on the (b) extrapsychic moderators (responses of the adolescent and parents to parent–adolescent conflict), which are assumed to impact on the (c) intrapsychic moderators.

Demographic, Environmental, and Dispositional Moderators. Parents who are more responsive to change in their offspring (e.g., those who are more "ego resilient"; Block & Block, 1980; Lewin, 1951) are probably more likely to respond adaptively to increases in the level of conflictive engagement. Parents can demonstrate such adaptability to their adolescents by: (a) altering their parenting behaviors (e.g., changing the rules in the home, allowing the adolescent to have more decision-making responsibilities; Fuligni & Eccles, 1993; Holmbeck et al., 1995), (b) allowing their adolescents more opportunities to express their points of view (Cooper et al., 1983), and/or (c) providing more explanations for their demands, which serve to legitimize their authority and acknowledge to the adolescent that they are aware of the adolescent's changing cognitive capacities (Hill, 1987). As yet, however, parental adaptability has received little empirical attention (Eccles et al., 1993; Fuligni & Eccles, 1993; Holmbeck & Hill, 1991; Holmbeck et al., 1995).

Parenting styles (e.g., authoritarian, authoritative, indulgent, or uninvolved; Steinberg, 1990), parenting experiences, parenting skills, and parents' beliefs and attributions about why the conflicts are occurring (e.g., Dix et al., 1986) will also impact on the manner in which parents respond to conflicts (Holmbeck et al., 1995). Endorsement of storm and stress beliefs may actually have self-fulfilling prophecy effects; parents who expect their adolescents to be rebellious may become increasingly authoritarian in response to conflicts, thus producing additional, more disruptive conflicts. Moreover, as suggested by Robin and Foster (1989), the degree to which the family has adequate problem-solving and communication skills and lacks faulty belief systems and problematic structural patterns will also determine the nature of the family's reaction to parent–adolescent conflict.

Demographic variables, such as socioeconomic status (SES), gender, family structure, ethnicity, age, and developmental level, are expected to interact with parent–adolescent conflict to determine responses to conflict. Based on past research findings, one would expect that lower SES parents would be more likely than those from higher SES families to respond to parent–adolescent conflict with authoritarian parenting behaviors (Hill,

1985, 1987). Moreover, in families with adolescent boys, one might expect that responses to conflict may involve shifts in the power hierarchy of the family (Steinberg, 1981), whereas in families of girls, gender-role expectations may be intensified and passivity may be rewarded (Hill, 1988). Finally, family cohesiveness is an additional moderating variable that may play a role in determining whether certain responses to conflict yield adaptive or maladaptive outcomes. For example, the granting of autonomy to an adolescent by a parent following repeated conflicts over autonomy-related issues could yield adaptive *or* maladaptive outcomes depending on whether or not such autonomy is granted in a context of connectedness and cohesiveness (Allen, Hauser, Bell, & O'Connor, 1994). Such continuity of family cohesiveness presumably facilitates adaptation during periods of discontinuity (Steinberg, 1990).

Extrapsychic Moderators. Whether or not relational conflicts serve an adaptive function in the life of the family probably depends in large part on how the individuals involved interpret and respond to the conflicts (Cooper, 1988; Grych & Fincham, 1990; Hill & Holmbeck, 1987; Holmbeck & Hill, 1991; Powers, Welsh, & Wright, 1994; Steinberg, 1990; see also Figs. 7.1 and 7.3). Regarding the extrapsychic responses, parents may respond to conflicts in numerous ways. There may be (a) a lack of responsiveness to the conflict, (b) recognition of the conflict followed by an inappropriate or maladaptive response, or (c) recognition of the conflict followed by an appropriate or adaptive response.

The first two types of responses would be expected to produce an escalation in the level of conflict (Peterson, 1983; Robin & Foster, 1989), interrupt the conflict resolution process (Smetana, Yau, & Hanson, 1991), and be more likely to occur in families that experience a deterioration in parent–child relationships during the transition to adolescence. Parents who respond to parent–adolescent conflict by employing a more severe authoritarian parenting style or by making no adjustments in their parenting style are probably responding in such a way as to exacerbate the level of dysfunction in the family system. Similarly, with respect to adolescents' responses to parent–adolescent conflict, coercive responses to conflict (particularly on the part of boys) may also be associated with maladaptive outcomes, such as the inability of parents and adolescents to reach a compromise during an argument (Smetana, Yau, & Hanson, 1991).

On the other hand, conflicts may serve an adaptive function when parents and adolescents not only reflect on the "information" that the conflicts are providing (e.g., that there are incongruities in perceptions and expectations between adolescents and parents), but when they also make appropriate adjustments to their interactions (Holmbeck & Hill, 1991; Smetana, 1995). When incongruities between the adolescents' perceptions of "what is" and their expectations of "what could be" are present, the adolescents' parents may not even be aware that such discrepancies exist until conflicts ensue. Particularly in these types of situations, conflict may serve to inform parents that the incongruities exist.

Intrapsychic Moderators. In some families, contentiousness between adolescents and parents may facilitate the process by which parents are deidealized by their offspring during the transition to adolescence (Fuhrman & Holmbeck, 1995; Lamborn & Steinberg, 1993; Ryan & Lynch, 1989; Steinberg & Silverberg, 1986). Due to increases in the sophistication of their cognitive skills, adolescents may gradually become more adept at engaging in successful conflicts with their parents, and in the process of such engagement, they may observe flaws in the logic of their parents' arguments. In short, parents may appear fallible during conflicts, thus forcing adolescents to re-evaluate the idealized views they have of their parents (Steinberg, 1990). Reconsideration of these views may allow adolescents to develop more egalitarian relationships with their parents. The degree to which parents are deidealized may have an impact on associations between parent–adolescent conflict and whether the outcomes of conflict are adaptive. Adaptive outcomes may be most likely when deidealization has occurred, but not at extreme levels.

Outcomes of Parent–Adolescent Conflict

It is assumed that the nature of parents' and adolescents' responses to conflict determines the nature of the outcomes (adaptive vs. maladaptive; see Figs. 7.1 and 7.3). The adaptive nature of conflict has been supported by research findings. For example, Cooper et al. (1983) found that disagreements in family interaction during adolescence are associated with adolescent identity exploration (see also Hauser, 1991; Hauser et al., 1984). These researchers went on to argue that adaptive relational outcomes, such as a realignment of the parent–adolescent relationship in the direction of cooperation and mutuality, will be more likely to occur when adolescents are provided with opportunities to express how their opinions differ from others in the family, and particularly when they are allowed to do so in a context of familial connectedness (see also Collins & Laursen, 1992; Cooper, 1988; Hauser et al., 1984). Finally, it is also possible that there will be some beneficial adaptive outcomes for the adolescent as a result of the conflicts. Conflicts with parents may aid the adolescent in learning and practicing conflict resolution skills (Smetana, Yau, & Hanson, 1991), conflict expression, and assertive behaviors, as well as assisting in the development of role-taking skills (e.g., Cooper et al., 1983; Hetherington & Anderson, 1988).

CONCLUSION

Significant gains in our knowledge of relational transformations during the second decade of life will be achieved by employing a process-oriented approach to the study of intraindividual change and parent–adolescent relationships. It would be useful for investigators to move beyond tests of main effects (e.g., perturbations, increased conflict) and descriptive-level analyses by considering the processes that underlie the observed transformations (Collins, 1990, 1995; Holmbeck & O'Donnell, 1991; Smetana, 1995). Studies of contextual (i.e., individual differences) variables that moderate the effects of developmental change on family relationships as well as studies of conflict from an adaptational perspective would be particularly helpful in elucidating both the processes outlined in this chapter and the role that conflict plays in relational transformations during the transition to adolescence.

ACKNOWLEDGMENTS

Completion of this chapter was facilitated by a Social and Behavioral Sciences Research Grant (No. 12-FY93-0621) from the March of Dimes Birth Defects Foundation and a grant from the National Institute of Mental Health (R01-MH50423). I wish to thank Roberta Paikoff, Maryse Richards, Mary Jo Rogers, and the editors for their comments on an earlier draft of this chapter.

REFERENCES

Adelson, J. (Ed.). (1980). *Handbook of adolescent psychology*. New York: Wiley.

Aldwin, C. M. (1994). *Stress, coping, and development*. New York: Guilford.

Allen, J. P., Hauser, S. T., Bell, K. L., & O'Connor, T. G. (1994). Longitudinal assessment of autonomy and relatedness in adolescent–family interactions as predictors of adolescent ego development and self-esteem. *Child Development, 65*, 179–194.

Amato, P. R., & Keith, B. (1991). Parental divorce and the well-being of children: A meta-analysis. *Psychological Bulletin, 110*, 26–46.

Anderson, E. R., Hetherington, E. M., & Clingempeel, W. G. (1989). Transformations of family relations at puberty: Effects of family context. *Journal of Early Adolescence, 9*, 310–334.

Barber, B. K. (1994). Cultural, family, and personal contexts of parent–adolescent conflict. *Journal of Marriage and the Family, 56*, 375–386.

Baron, R. M., & Kenny, D. A. (1986). The moderator-mediator variable distinction in social psychological research: Conceptual, strategic, and statistical considerations. *Journal of Personality and Social Psychology, 51*, 1173–1182.

Block, J. H., & Block, J. (1980). The role of ego-control and ego-resiliency in the organization of behavior. In A. Pick (Ed.), *14th Minnesota symposium on child psychology* (pp. 39–101). Minneapolis: University of Minnesota Press.

Blos, P. (1962). *On adolescence: A psychoanalytic interpretation.* New York: The Free Press.

Blos, P. (1979). *The adolescent passage.* New York: International Universities Press.

Brooks-Gunn, J., Graber, J., & Paikoff, R. L. (1994). Studying links between hormones and negative affect: Models and measures. *Journal of Research on Adolescence, 4,* 469–486.

Brooks-Gunn, J., & Paikoff, R. L. (1992). Changes in self-feelings during the transition towards adolescence. In H. McGurk (Ed.), *Childhood social development: Contemporary issues* (pp. 63–97). Hillsdale, NJ: Lawrence Erlbaum Associates.

Brooks-Gunn, J., & Ruble, D. N. (1982). The development of menstrual-related beliefs and behaviors during early adolescence. *Child Development, 53,* 1567–1577.

Brooks-Gunn, J., & Warren, M. P. (1988). The psychological significance of secondary sexual characteristics in nine- to eleven-year-old girls. *Child Development, 59,* 1061–1069.

Brooks-Gunn, J., & Zahaykevich, M. (1989). Parent–daughter relationships in early adolescence: A developmental perspective. In K. Kreppner & R. M. Lerner (Eds.), *Family systems and life-span development* (pp. 223–246). Hillsdale, NJ: Lawrence Erlbaum Associates.

Buchanan, C. M., Eccles, J. S., & Becker, J. B. (1992). Are adolescents the victims of raging hormones: Evidence for activational effects of hormones on moods and behavior at adolescence. *Psychological Bulletin, 111,* 62–107.

Buchanan, C. M., Eccles, J. S., Flanagan, C., Midgley, C., Feldlaufer, H., & Harold, R. (1990). Parents' and teachers' beliefs about adolescence: Effects of sex and experience. *Journal of Youth and Adolescence, 19,* 363–394.

Chodorow, N. (1978). *The reproduction of mothering: Psychoanalysis and the sociology of gender.* Berkeley: University of California Press.

Collins, W. A. (1990). Parent–child relationships in the transition to adolescence: Continuity and change in interaction, affect, and cognition. In R. Montemayor, G. Adams, & T. Gullotta (Eds.), *Advances in adolescent development: From childhood to adolescence: A transitional period?* (Vol. 2, pp. 85–106). Beverly Hills, CA: Sage.

Collins, W. A. (1992). Parents' cognitions and developmental changes in relationships during adolescence. In I. Sigel, A. McGillicuddy-deLisi, & J. J. Goodnow (Eds.), *Parental belief systems* (2nd ed., pp. 175–199). Hillsdale, NJ: Lawrence Erlbaum Associates.

Collins, W. A. (1995). Relationships and development: Family adaptation to individual change. In S. Shulman (Ed.), *Close relationships and socioemotional development* (pp. 128–154). Norwood, NJ: Ablex.

Collins, W. A., & Laursen, B. (1992). Conflict and relationships during adolescence. In C. U. Shantz & W. W. Hartup (Eds.), *Conflict in child and adolescent development* (pp. 216–241). New York: Cambridge University Press.

Collins, W. A., & Russell, G. (1991). Mother–child and father–child relationships in middle childhood and adolescence: A developmental analysis. *Developmental Review, 11,* 99–136.

Cooper, C. R. (1988). Commentary: The role of conflict in adolescent–parent relationships. In M. R. Gunnar & W. A. Collins (Eds.), *21st Minnesota symposium on child psychology* (pp. 181–187). Hillsdale, NJ: Lawrence Erlbaum Associates.

Cooper, C. R., Grotevant, H. D., & Condon, S. M. (1983). Individuality and connectedness in the family as a context for adolescent identity formation and role-taking skill. In H. D. Grotevant & C. R. Cooper (Eds.), *Adolescent development in the family: New directions for child development* (No. 22, pp. 43–59). San Francisco: Jossey-Bass.

Cummings, E. M., Davies, P. T., & Simpson, K. S. (1994). Marital conflict, gender, and children's appraisals and coping efficacy as mediators of child adjustment. *Journal of Family Psychology, 8,* 141–149.

Deutsch, H. (1944). *The psychology of women.* New York: Grune & Stratton.

Dix, T., Ruble, D., Grusec, J., & Nixon, S. (1986). Social cognition in parents: Inferential and affective reactions to children of three age levels. *Child Development, 57,* 879–894.

Dodge, K. A. (1990). Developmental psychopathology in children of depressed mothers. *Developmental Psychology, 26,* 3–6.

Eccles, J. S., Midgley, C., Wigfield, A., Buchanan, C. M., Reuman, D., Flanagan, C., & MacIver, D. (1993). Development during adolescence: The impact of stage–environment fit in young adolescents' experiences in schools and in families. *American Psychologist, 48,* 90–101.

Ellis, G. J. (1986). Societal and parental predictors of parent–adolescent conflict. In G. K. Leigh & G. W. Peterson (Eds.), *Adolescents in families* (pp. 155–178). Cincinnati, OH: South-Western Publishing.

Feldman, S. S., & Elliott, G. R. (Eds.). (1990). *At the threshold: The developing adolescent.* Cambridge, MA: Harvard University Press.

Freud, A. (1958). Adolescence. *Psychoanalytic Study of the Child, 13,* 231–258.

Fuhrman, T., & Holmbeck, G. N. (1995). A contextual-moderator analysis of emotional autonomy and adjustment in adolescence. *Child Development, 66,* 793–811.

Fuligni, A. J., & Eccles, J. S. (1993). Perceived parent–child relationships and early adolescents' orientation toward peers. *Developmental Psychology, 29,* 622–632.

Galambos, N. L., Almeida, D. M., & Petersen, A. C. (1990). Masculinity, femininity, and sex role attitudes in early adolescence: Exploring gender intensification. *Child Development, 61,* 1905–1914.

Garwood, S. G., & Allen, L. (1979). Self-concept and identified problem differences between pre- and post-menarcheal adolescents. *Journal of Clinical Psychology, 35,* 528–537.

Gilligan, C., Lyons, N. P., Hanmer, T. J. (Eds.). (1990). *Making connections: The relational worlds of adolescent girls at Emma Willard School.* Cambridge, MA: Harvard University Press.

Goodnow, J. J., & Collins, W. A. (1990). *Development according to parents: The nature, sources, and consequences of parents' ideas.* Hillsdale, NJ: Lawrence Erlbaum Associates.

Graber, J. A., Brooks-Gunn, J., & Warren, M. P. (1995). The antecedents of menarcheal age: Heredity, family environment, and stressful life events. *Child Development, 66,* 346–359.

Grych, J. H., & Fincham, F. D. (1990). Marital conflict and children's adjustment: A cognitive-contextual framework. *Psychological Bulletin, 108,* 267–290.

Grych, J. H., & Fincham, F. D. (1993). Children's appraisals of marital conflict: Initial investigations of the cognitive-contextual framework. *Child Development, 64,* 215–230.

Hauser, S. T. (1991). *Adolescents and their families: Paths of ego development.* New York: The Free Press.

Hauser, S. T., & Bowlds, M. K. (1990). Stress, coping, and adaptation. In S. S. Feldman & G. L. Elliott (Eds.), *At the threshold: The developing adolescent* (pp. 388–413). Cambridge, MA: Harvard University Press.

Hauser, S. T., & Greene, W. M. (1991). Passages from late adolescence to early adulthood. In S. I. Greenspan & G. H. Pollock (Eds.), *The course of life: Vol. IV. Adolescence* (pp. 377–405). Madison, WI: International Universities Press.

Hauser, S. T., Powers, S. I., Noam, G. G., Jacobson, A. M., Weiss, B., & Follansbee, D. J. (1984). Familial contexts of adolescent ego development. *Child Development, 55,* 195–213.

Hetherington, E. M., & Anderson, E. R. (1988). The effects of divorce and remarriage on early adolescents and their families. In M. D. Levine & E. R. McAnarney (Eds.), *Early adolescent transitions* (pp. 49–67). Lexington, MA: Lexington Books.

Hill, J. P. (1980a). The family. In M. Johnson (Ed.), *Toward adolescence: The middle school years. The seventy-ninth yearbook of the National Society for the Study of Education* (pp. 32–55). Chicago: University of Chicago Press.

Hill, J. P. (1980b). *Understanding early adolescence: A framework.* Chapel Hill, NC: Center for Early Adolescence.

Hill, J. P. (1985). Family relations in adolescence: Myths, realities, and new directions. *Genetic, Social, and General Psychology Monographs, 111,* 233–248.

Hill, J. P. (1987). Research on adolescents and their families: Past and prospect. In C. E. Irwin (Ed.), *Adolescent social behavior and health: New directions for child development* (No. 37, pp. 13–31). San Francisco, CA: Jossey-Bass.

Hill, J. P. (1988). Adapting to menarche: Familial control and conflict. In M. R. Gunnar & W. A. Collins (Eds.), *21st Minnesota Symposium on child psychology* (pp. 43–77). Hillsdale, NJ: Lawrence Erlbaum Associates.

Hill, J. P., & Holmbeck, G. N. (1986). Attachment and autonomy during adolescence. In G. J. Whitehurst (Ed.), *Annals of child development* (Vol. 3, pp. 145–189). Greenwich, CT: JAI.

Hill, J. P., & Holmbeck, G. N. (1987). Familial adaptation to biological change during adolescence. In R. M. Lerner & T. T. Foch (Eds.), *Biological-psychosocial interactions in early adolescence: A life-span perspective* (pp. 207–223). Hillsdale, NJ: Lawrence Erlbaum Associates.

Hill, J. P., & Lynch, M. E. (1983). The intensification of gender-related role expectations during early adolescence. In J. Brooks-Gunn & A. C. Petersen (Eds.), *Girls at puberty: Biological and psychosocial perspectives* (pp. 201–228). New York: Plenum.

Holmbeck, G. N. (1995). *Conceptual and statistical confusion in the study of mediators and moderators: Examples from the child-clinical and pediatric psychology literatures.* Manuscript under review.

Holmbeck, G. N., & Hill, J. P. (1988). Storm and stress beliefs about adolescence: Prevalence, self-reported antecedents, and effects of an undergraduate course. *Journal of Youth and Adolescence, 17,* 285–306.

Holmbeck, G. N., & Hill, J. P. (1991). Conflictive engagement, positive affect, and menarche in families with seventh-grade girls. *Child Development, 62,* 1030–1048.

Holmbeck, G. N., & O'Donnell, K. (1991). Discrepancies between perceptions of decision-making and behavioral autonomy. In R. L. Paikoff (Ed.), *Shared views in the family during adolescence: New directions for development* (No. 51, pp. 51–69). San Francisco: Jossey-Bass.

Holmbeck, G. N., Paikoff, R. L., & Brooks-Gunn, J. (1995). Parenting adolescents. In M. Bornstein (Ed.), *Handbook of parenting: Vol. 1. Children and parenting* (pp. 91–118). Mahwah, NJ: Lawrence Erlbaum Associates.

Josselson, R. (1980). Ego development in adolescence. In J. Adelson (Ed.), *Handbook of adolescent psychology* (pp. 188–210). New York: Wiley.

Kaplan, L. (1984). *Adolescence: The farewell to childhood.* New York: Simon & Schuster.

Kelley, H. H., Berscheid, E., Christensen, A., Harvey, J. H., Huston, T. L., Levinger, G., McClintock, E., Peplau, L. A., & Peterson, D. R. (1983). *Close relationships.* New York: Freeman.

Kidwell, J., Fischer, J. L., Dunham, R. M., & Baranowski, M. (1983). Parents and adolescents: Push and pull of change. In H. I. McCubbin & C. R. Figley (Eds.), *Stress and the family: Vol. I. Coping with normative transitions* (pp. 74–89). New York: Brunner/Mazel.

Lamborn, S. D., & Steinberg, L. (1993). Emotional autonomy redux: Revisiting Ryan and Lynch. *Child Development, 64,* 483–499.

Larson, R. W., Richards, M. H., Moneta, G., Holmbeck, G. N., & Duckett, E. (in press). Changes in adolescents' daily interactions with their families from ages 10 to 18: Disengagement and transformation. *Developmental Psychology.*

Laursen, B., & Collins, W. A. (1994). Interpersonal conflict during adolescence. *Psychological Bulletin, 115,* 197–209.

Laursen, B., & Ferreira, M. (1994, February). Does parent–child conflict peak at mid-adolescence? In B. Laursen & W. A. Collins (Chairs), *Relationship transformations in adolescence: Processes of parent–child adaptation.* Symposium paper presented at the meetings of the Society for Research on Adolescence, San Diego, CA.

Leigh, G. K., & Peterson, G. W. (Eds.). (1986). *Adolescents in families.* Cincinnati, OH: South-Western Publishing.

Lerner, H. (1987). Psychodynamic models. In V. B. Van Hasselt & M. Hersen (Eds.), *Handbook of adolescent psychology* (pp. 53–76). New York: Pergamon.

Lerner, R. M., Hess, L. E., & Nitz, K. (1991). Toward the integration of human development and therapeutic change. In P. R. Martin (Ed.), *Handbook of behavior therapy and psychological science: An integrative approach* (pp. 13–34). New York: Pergamon.

Lewin, K. (1951). *Field theory in social science.* New York: Harper.

Maccoby, E. E. (1984). Socialization and developmental change. *Child Development, 55,* 317–328.

Maccoby, E., & Martin, J. (1983). Socialization in the context of the family: Parent–child interaction. In P. H. Mussen (Series Ed.) & E. M. Hetherington (Vol. Ed.), *Handbook of child psychology: Vol. 4. Socialization, personality, and social development* (4th ed., pp. 1–101). New York: Wiley.

McAdoo, H. P. (Ed.). (1988). *Black families* (2nd ed.). Newbury Park, CA: Sage.

McAdoo, H. P., & McAdoo, J. L. (Eds.). (1985). *Black children: Social, educational, and parental environments.* Newbury Park, CA: Sage.

Montemayor, R. (1982). The relationship between parent–adolescent conflict and the amount of time adolescents spend alone and with parents and peers. *Child Development, 53,* 1512–1519.

Montemayor, R. (1983). Parents and adolescents in conflict: All families some of the time and some families most of the time. *Journal of Early Adolescence, 3,* 83–103.

Montemayor, R. (1986). Family variation in parent–adolescent storm and stress. *Journal of Adolescent Research, 1,* 15–31.

Paikoff, R. L. (Ed.). (1991). *Shared views in the family during adolescence: New directions for child development* (No. 51). San Francisco, CA: Jossey-Bass.

Paikoff, R. L., & Brooks-Gunn, J. (1990). Physiological processes: What role do they play during the transition to adolescence? In R. Montemayor, G. Adams, & T. Gullotta (Eds.), *Advances in adolescent development: From childhood to adolescence: A transitional period?* (Vol. 2, pp. 63–81). Beverly Hills, CA: Sage.

Paikoff, R. L., & Brooks-Gunn, J. (1991). Do parent–child relationships change during puberty? *Psychological Bulletin, 110,* 47–66.

Papini, D. R., Micka, J., & Barnett, J. (1989). Perceptions of intrapsychic and extrapsychic functioning as bases of adolescent ego identity statuses. *Journal of Adolescent Research, 4,* 460–480.

Pearlin, L. I., Mullan, J. T., Semple, S. J., & Skaff, M. M. (1990). Caregiving and the stress process: An overview of concepts and their measures. *The Gerontologist, 30,* 583–594.

Petersen, A. C. (1985). Pubertal development as a cause of disturbance: Myths, realities, and unanswered questions. *Genetic, Social, and General Psychology Monographs, 111,* 205–232.

Petersen, A. C. (1987). The nature of biological psychosocial interactions: The sample case of early adolescence. In R. M. Lerner & T. T. Foch (Eds.), *Biological-psychosocial interactions in early adolescence: A life-span perspective* (pp. 35–61). Hillsdale, NJ: Lawrence Erlbaum Associates.

Petersen, A. C. (1988). Adolescent development. *Annual Review of Psychology, 39,* 583–607.

Petersen, A. C., & Taylor, B. (1980). The biological approach to adolescence: Biological change and psychological adaptation. In J. Adelson (Ed.), *Handbook of adolescent psychology* (pp. 117–155). New York: Wiley.

Peterson, D. R. (1983). Conflict. In H. H. Kelley, E. Berscheid, A. Christensen, J. H. Harvey, T. L. Huston, G. Levinger, E. McClintock, L. A. Peplau, & D. R. Peterson (Eds.), *Close relationships* (pp. 360–396). New York: Freeman.

Powers, S. I., Hauser, S. T., & Kilner, L. A. (1989). Adolescent mental health. *American Psychologist, 44,* 200–208.

Powers, S. I., Welsh, D. P., & Wright, V. (1994). Adolescents' affective experience of family behaviors: The role of subjective understanding. *Journal of Research on Adolescence, 4,* 585–600.

Rich, S. (1990). Daughters' views of their relationships with their mothers. In C. Gilligan, N. P. Lyons, & T. J. Hanmer (Eds.), *Making connections: The relational worlds of adolescent girls at Emma Willard School* (pp. 258–273). Cambridge, MA: Harvard University Press.

Robin, A. L., & Foster, S. L. (1989). *Negotiating parent–adolescent conflict: A behavioral-family systems approach.* New York: Guilford.

Rutter, M. (1990). Commentary: Some focus and process considerations regarding effects of parental depression on children. *Developmental Psychology, 26,* 60–67.

Rutter, M., Graham, P., Chadwick, O. F. D., & Yule, W. (1976). Adolescent turmoil: Fact or fiction? *Journal of Child Psychology and Psychiatry, 17,* 35–56.

Ryan, R., & Lynch, J. (1989). Emotional autonomy versus detachment: Revisiting the vicissitudes of adolescence and young adulthood. *Child Development, 60,* 340–356.

Sessa, F. M., & Steinberg, L. (1991). Family structure and the development of autonomy during adolescence. *Journal of Early Adolescence, 11,* 38–55.

Shadish, W. R., & Sweeney, R. B. (1991). Mediators and moderators in meta-analysis: There's a reason we don't let dodo birds tell us which psychotherapies should have prizes. *Journal of Consulting and Clinical Psychology, 59,* 883–893.

Shantz, C. U. (1987). Conflicts between children. *Child Development, 58,* 283–305.

Silverberg, S. B., & Steinberg, L. (1987). Adolescent autonomy, parent–adolescent conflict, and parental well-being. *Journal of Youth and Adolescence, 16,* 293–312.

Simmons, R. G., & Blyth, D. A. (1987). *Moving into adolescence: The impact of pubertal change and school context.* New York: Aldine de Gruyter.

Smetana, J. G. (1988a). Adolescents' and parents' conceptions of parental authority. *Child Development, 59,* 321–335.

Smetana, J. G. (1988b). Concepts of self and social convention: Adolescents' and parents' reasoning about hypothetical and actual family conflicts. In M. R. Gunnar & W. A. Collins (Eds.), *21st Minnesota Symposium on child psychology* (pp. 79–122). Hillsdale, NJ: Lawrence Erlbaum Associates.

Smetana, J. G. (1989). Adolescents' and parents' reasoning about actual family conflict. *Child Development, 60,* 1052–1067.

Smetana, J. G. (1995). Conflict and coordination in adolescent–parent relationships. In S. Shulman (Ed.), *Close relationships and socioemotional development* (pp. 155–184). Norwood, NJ: Ablex.

Smetana, J. G., Yau, J., & Hanson, S. (1991). Conflict resolution in families with adolescents. *Journal of Research on Adolescence, 1,* 189–206.

Smetana, J. G., Yau, J., Restrepo, A., & Braeges, J. L. (1991). Adolescent–parent conflict in married and divorced families. *Developmental Psychology, 27,* 1000–1010.

Spencer, M. B., & Dornbusch, S. M. (1990). Challenges in studying minority youth. In S. S. Feldman & G. L. Elliott (Eds.), *At the threshold: The developing adolescent* (pp. 123–146). Cambridge, MA: Harvard University Press.

Spencer, M. B., & McLoyd, V. C. (Eds.). (1990). Special issue on minority children. *Child Development, 61,* 263–589.

Steinberg, L. (1981). Transformations in family relations at puberty. *Developmental Psychology, 17,* 833–840.

Steinberg, L. (1987). Recent research on the family at adolescence: The extent and nature of sex differences. *Journal of Youth and Adolescence, 16,* 191–197.

Steinberg, L. (1988). Reciprocal relation between parent–child distance and pubertal maturation. *Developmental Psychology, 24,* 122–128.

Steinberg, L. (1989). Pubertal maturation and family relations: Evidence for the distancing hypothesis. In G. Adams, R. Montemayor, & T. Gullotta (Eds.), *Advances in adolescent development* (Vol. 1, pp. 71–92). Beverly Hills, CA: Sage.

Steinberg, L. (1990). Interdependence in the family: Autonomy, conflict, and harmony in the parent–adolescent relationship. In S. S. Feldman & G. L. Elliott (Eds.), *At the threshold: The developing adolescent* (pp. 255–276). Cambridge, MA: Harvard University Press.

Steinberg, L., & Silverberg, S. (1986). The vicissitudes of autonomy in early adolescence. *Child Development, 57,* 841–851.

Thompson, R. J., Gil, K. M., Burbach, D. J., Keith, B. R., & Kinney, T. R. (1993). Role of child and maternal processes in the psychological adjustment of children with sickle cell disease. *Journal of Consulting and Clinical Psychology, 61,* 468–474.

Van Hasselt, V. B., & Hersen, M. (Eds.). (1987). *Handbook of adolescent psychology.* New York: Pergamon.

Vuchinich, S., Emery, R. E., & Cassidy, J. (1988). Family members as third parties in dyadic family conflict: Strategies, alliances, and outcomes. *Child Development, 59,* 1293–1302.

White, K. M., Speisman, J. C., & Costos, D. (1983). Young adults and their parents: Individuation to mutuality. In H. D. Grotevant & C. R. Cooper (Eds.), *Adolescent development in the family: New directions for child development* (No. 22, pp. 61–76). San Francisco: Jossey-Bass.

Youniss, J., & Smollar, J. (1985). *Adolescent relations with mothers, fathers, and friends.* Chicago: University of Chicago Press.

8

Adolescent Parenthood and the Transition to Adulthood

Bertram J. Cohler
The University of Chicago

Judith S. Musick
The Erikson Institute

This chapter considers the psychosocial consequences of becoming a parent across the adolescent decade within contemporary society. This chapter focuses on issues of timing of the advent of parenthood within the course of life, the sequence of this transition to parenthood in terms of other expectable adult role changes, and the interplay of social timing, sequence, and motivational factors in the experience of this transition, particularly among young women of color living within circumstances characterized by economic privation and social disorganization. This discussion is founded on the concept of a social timetable that places particular individual attainments across the course of life within the context of socially defined entrances and exits from particular roles.

Ironically, although early off time from a larger social perspective, experiences of adolescent girls living in the poverty of the nation's inner cities provides both the anticipatory socialization and convoy of social support that makes this transition on time in ways similar to the advent of first-time parents among more socially advantaged counterparts nearly a decade later in the course of life. Emergence of adolescent parenthood as a reality among young women living in the midst of social disorganization and poverty points to the limitations in present conceptions of social timing as universal within particular societies.

Although early off time from the perspective of the larger social order, the very different expectations for both timing and sequence of role changes within underclass communities suggest the need for a more complex consideration of the interplay of timing and sequence in determining both present morale and subsequent life attainments. The off-time nature of this transition to parenthood among families living in poverty may lead to problems in managing life within the larger society. However, within the underclass community where there is support for this early off-time role transition and a convoy of role colleagues who are also mothers early in the course of life as defined by the larger society makes possible certain advantages within this community that are less often appreciated both by the larger society and those studying lives over time.

In general, more advantaged families view the advent of first-time parenthood across the years of adolescence as problematic because it may compromise the young person's academic and vocational success, and interferes with an expected developmental progression. At least to some extent, these limitations may be less significant for young women growing up in the midst of poverty. Forced by difficult circumstances to resolve developmental issues and accompanying role transitions in contexts where normal options, opportunities, and models to help them do so are scarce— and pressures to engage in unprotected sex are plentiful—these young women are more likely than their advantaged counterparts to bear children in their adolescent years and to derive certain benefits within the community that accrue to those who are parents. Adolescents growing up in the midst of the poverty of our inner cities may look forward to raising their children, which both provides access into the status of an adult within their community, and also provides comfort and solace in an alien world. Teenage parenthood provides important sources of satisfaction and esteem that make this a particularly positive option for more than a third of all young women living in poverty.

PARENTHOOD AS A SOCIAL ROLE

Parenthood is perhaps the most central and complex of adult social roles in contemporary society (LeMasters, 1970). Essential for continuation of social life, this role is also significant for definition of self and place in the context of generations and the larger society. Active participation in parenting may reorganize memories of a lifetime and change perspectives regarding past and future. As Benedek (1973) observed, once one has become a parent, one remains a parent as long as there is memory. However, in contrast with other roles such as work and marriage, neither anticipation nor rehearsal of parenthood prepares either husband or wife for the reality of providing complete care for another (Entwisle & Doering, 1981; Leifer, 1980). It is difficult for prospective parents to imagine the time and effort required to raise children, or the extent to which work and leisure are affected by such care.

More significantly, as Gutmann (1977) observed, there is sense of continuous concern and responsibility involved in becoming a parent. Not only is parenthood the one adult role for which there can be little preparation, but it is also a role uniquely capable of reorganizing adult personal commitments. Although fundamentally disagreeing regarding the consequences, Gutmann (1977, 1987) and Chodorow (1977) do agree that the advent of parenthood in our society leads to a sense of crisis and imperative unlike any other adult role transition.

Roles constitute the building blocks of the social encounter. These shared understandings, obligations, expectable rewards, and satisfactions serve to guide a person's actions in particular situations (Goffman, 1961). More or less deliberately transmitted across generations, among persons sharing a common situation, roles comprise a shorthand set of expectations regarding a person's actions toward specific categories of others. Although these expectations may change over time and vary as a function of the shared understandings of the larger culture, within a particular culture, at a particular time, there is general agreement regarding expectations for performing particular roles. Further, these become essential in one's definition of self and identity (Goffman, 1961; McCall & Simmons, 1978). The cluster of roles is hierarchically organized, with those most central encompassing those most salient in the hierarchy (Burke & Tully, 1977; McCall & Simmons, 1978).

Over the course of preadult socialization, from earliest childhood through adolescence, children gradually learn expectable adult roles. Indeed, the infant's relationship with the mother constitutes the earliest learned role, which is then generalized to father, siblings, and others within the family and community. The number of and interrelationship among roles increases in complexity across childhood and adolescence, as the child accumulates an ever-expanding "portfolio" of roles, including those as student, friend, club member and, somewhat later in adolescence, worker, partner, and, particularly among females, caretaker or "kinkeeper" for other family members.

Roles are not discrete and separate; each new role acquired changes the hierarchy of urgency with which other roles need to be performed. For example, becoming a mother may change the salience of other roles such as worker or daughter in one's own parental family. Both the order of entrance into a role and the sequence in which it is attained in relation to other adult roles alter perceptions about the manner in which that role will be enacted. Adolescent parenthood presents problems for our society because of the manner in which the role of parenthood interacts with the roles of student and worker, affecting both the sequence and timing of assumption of these other characteristic adult roles.

Hagestad (1974) referred to role colleagues as those others who share similar roles, such as other mothers; there is some evidence that shared time and discussion with role colleagues alleviates strain for persons performing particular roles. Role strain refers to extent of effort required to perform a particular role, with increased strain leading to increased feelings of burden. Role strain differs from role conflict in that the latter refers more explicitly to problems encountered in trying to simultaneously fulfill legitimate expectations of two roles, for example, parent and worker. If balancing these two roles is challenging for adults, it is often daunting for adolescents. Role overload is a consequence of both strain and conflict within and across major adult roles. For example, demands within a role, such as the shifting day, evening, and night schedules required in some jobs, and demands across roles, such as those felt by middle-aged women who care for both children and elderly parents (Brody, 1985), each contribute to the sense of role overload. Continuous role overload can adversely affect physical and mental health, impairing the capacity to perform other expected adult roles.

Social Roles and the Timing of Role Transitions

The realization of social roles is critically intertwined with timing. Across cultures, the course of life, indeed the very concept of time itself, is markedly variable (Geertz, 1966). Consensus regarding the expectable course of life provides the basis of age stratification in society (Burton, 1990; Elder, 1975, 1979; Elder & Rockwell, 1979; Linton, 1942; Neugarten & Moore, 1968; Neugarten, Moore, & Lowe, 1965; Neugarten & Peterson, 1957; Ragan & Wales, 1980; Riley, 1971, 1976). Age functions to differentially allocate scarce resources and rewards, including prestige, honor, and remuneration based on occupational attainment. This ageism must be differentiated from age categorization, understood as consensual understanding of regularized and expectable actions that endure over time and are characteristic of particular ages within particular cohorts of persons.

Within our own society, the life course is understood as a progression through a series of *life stations* (Hagestad & Neugarten, 1985; Neugarten & Hagestad, 1976; Riley, Johnson, & Foner, 1972), or socially defined tasks, stages, or strata, each of which is accompanied by a particular set of expectations regarding performance and sanctions for nonperformance. The assumption of most social roles is viewed within a temporal framework, and generally characterized as being on time, in terms of the expectable course of life in our society, or as early or late relative to others. Chronological age may be less important in understanding changes within lives over time than present meanings attributed to be a particular ages and particular life changes. As Neugarten and Moore (1968) and Neugarten, Moore, and Lowe (1965) noted, there is consensus regarding not only the very duration of life itself, but also regarding the age at which particular role transitions or life events may be anticipated (Hagestad & Neugarten, 1976; Hagestad & Neugarten, 1985). Children learn this timetable for the course of life during the preschool years (Farnham-Diggory, 1966), and are well socialized into such expectations by adolescence. It is precisely this social definition of the course of life that transforms study of the life span or life cycle into study of the life course.

Although there may be consensus among persons regarding the expectable course of life, this timetable shifts across cohorts, reflecting sociohistorical change (Rossi, 1972, 1987). Nevertheless, there is consensus within particular cohorts regarding the timetable for specific role transitions such as leaving school, marriage, birth of first child, grandparenthood, death of own parents, retirement, widowhood, and so on (Neugarten et al., 1965). As Roth (1963) noted:

> Each individual uses the timetable norms of the group as a yardstick to measure his own progress. From a comparison of his own rate of progress with the norm he can determine whether he is behind, on, or ahead of schedule. In order to know what norms to apply as a yardstick, the individual must have a model group with which he identifies—a group with which he believes he closely shares relevant career characteristics and experiences, and from whose members he may obtain information about future expectations in his timetable. (p. 116)

Life changes taking place too early or late in terms of when they are expected, have important implications for psychological well-being or morale. Commonly, those life events taking place early off time—for example, early widowhood—have greater negative impact than those taking place late off time. Life changes occurring off time early are generally marked by their unexpected, adverse quality, providing little opportunity for preparation, but in addition there is a lack of role colleagues (Hagestad, 1974) or a social convoy (Antonucci & Akiyama, 1987; Kahn, 1979; Kahn & Antonucci, 1980; Rowe & Kahn, 1987).

Much of the discussion regarding the advent of first-time parenthood assumes that men and women become parents first during the mid- to late 20s (Entwisle & Doering, 1981; Hill & Rodgers, 1964; Hill & Mattessich, 1979; Miller & Sollie, 1980). This discussion assumes that the advent of parenthood first during the teen years must be off time not only because of presumed absence of anticipatory socialization through encounters with other women who have become parents first during the teen years, but also because it is assumed that there are few role colleagues with whom to share this early off-time role transition. However, whereas this role transition may be "early" off time from a larger social perspective, within particular communities it may be perceived as less off time (Gershenson, 1983).

Indeed, the issue of timing of significant developmental milestones may vary to a greater extent within ethnic groups in our present multicultural society than has been represented in much of the social science literature (Rindfuss, Morgan, & Swicegood, 1984). There has been little study of adolescent parenthood from the perspective of social timing; observation of life within the underclass family of the inner city suggests that these adolescents may be able to find consociates who have become parents during the teen years and who are able to assist in socialization of the prospective teen mother into the parental role. It is also easier to become friends and to share the lives of other teens who also have young children; as many as one third of inner-city adolescent women have a first child before the age of 18 (Musick, 1993b).

At the same time, teenage childbearing may have a negative effect both on the teen mother's health and on the intellectual and social problems experienced by young mothers and their offspring. These problems reflect the interplay of the insensitivity of the larger society to the reality that within some minority groups teen parenthood may be more normative and require increased resources, together with the reality that these teen mothers may be more likely to be poor, to have realized little formal education or cognitive attainment, and to live either in dangerous urban neighborhoods or in isolated rural areas, both of which also have inadequate schools (Klerman, 1993). Lack of services for these adolescent parents compounds the problems posed for these families and leads to further isolation from the larger society, which may play a role in perpetuating adolescent parenthood across generations.

Conflict and Strain in the Parental Role

The significance attached to successful realization of the parental role in contemporary U.S. society, closely tied to successful offspring educational and occupational attainment, is closely tied to issues of parental self-esteem (Bane & Ellwood, 1983). Because parental hopes and aspirations are strongly bound up in their children's attainments, failure of offspring to realize later success has a negative effect on parental self-definition. Precisely because of its centrality for self-definition, parenthood lays claim to priority in terms of personal time and energy. Even among adults for whom advent of first-time parenthood takes place normatively on time, and with the support of family and friends, role conflict, strain, and overload are all characteristic of not only the first birth but also successive births, and to particular feelings of burden and strain while caring for children across the preschool years (Callan, 1987; Cohler, 1984; LeMasters, 1970; Pearlin, 1975).

In few other societies does becoming a parent lead to such concern and risk for personal distress as within contemporary industrialized societies (Minturn & Lambert, 1964). Gutmann (1977, 1987) characterized parenthood as a "chronic emergency" in the lives of both mother and father. Although Rossi (1968), Neugarten (1979), and Osofsky and Osofsky (1984) protested the use of the concept of "crisis" to describe adult role transitions, as initially portrayed by Erikson (1963) or Benedek (1959), the study of parenthood and the life course provides evidence that supports a view of the transition to parenthood as a crisis in the lives of both mothers and fathers of infants and young children (Galatzer-Levy & Cohler, 1993).

Most prospective parents are largely unprepared for the responsibility and care engendered by the birth of the first baby; prebirth education classes cannot completely help parents to prepare for the reality of this event (Dyer, 1963; Entwisle & Doering, 1981; Hobbs, 1965, 1968; Jacoby, 1969; McKim, 1987; Meyerowitz & Feldman, 1966; Rossi, 1975; Shereshefsky & Yarrow, 1973). In addition, introduction of a third person into the husband–wife dyad may disrupt the existing marital relationship (Goldberg, Michaels, & Lamb, 1985). In view of these findings regarding the burdens characteristically experienced in our society accompanying the transition to parenthood, it is not surprising that parents in our own society are well above the median in terms of hostility expressed toward childrearing, as shown by the classic cross-cultural report of Minturn and Lambert (1964).

In part, this sense of crisis or role strain is a reflection of the geographic isolation of the nuclear and modified-extended family in U.S. society (Belsky & Isabella, 1985). Even though there may be much continuing contact and companionship among generations within the modified-extended family, generally, mainstream young adult parents and their own parents both believe that the generations should live in separate households and that, after the first postpartum weeks, it is inappropriate for young parents to receive regular, expectable help from their parents in raising their children (Cohler & Grunebaum, 1981). Indeed, controversy regarding this issue is a major concern within contemporary society (Cohler, 1987–1988). Having completed their own active parenting, today's grandparents do not believe that their adult offspring should depend on them for regular assistance and support, although it is permissible to expect some babysitting help.

Reviewing findings regarding this issue of transition to parenthood as crisis, Hill (1978) and his colleagues (Hill & Mattessich, 1979; Hill & Rodgers, 1964) proposed an alternative model, the development-crisis approach, that recognizes both the continuing impact of parenthood across the adult life course and also the unique impact of parenthood on persons' understanding of self and others. Studies of the transition to parenthood reflect this sense of crisis represented by the experience of enduring role strain and overload in the lives of each parent extending for periods of more than a year after the birth of the first child (Aneshensel, Fredrichs, & Clark, 1981; Grossman, Eichler, Winickoff, & Associates, 1980; McLanahan & Adams, 1987). Survey findings by Hobbs and Cole (1976) and Weissman and her associates (Weissman & Klerman, 1977; Weissman & Myers, 1978a, 1978b; Weissman, Myers, & Thompson, 1981) regarding the mental health of women in a U.S. community show that more than one third of women with young children report marked loss of morale and cross-sectional national survey findings of Campbell, Converse, and Rodgers (1976) show a precipitous drop in morale after the birth of the first child, gradually increasing over time until all offspring have become adults and left the home.

Continuing role strain across the first postpartum year and beyond may also be due to the impact of incredible responsibility for the care of another and totally dependent being (Entwisle & Doering, 1981; Gordon & Gordon, 1958, 1965; Rossi, 1968). This experience of strain, overload, and conflict following the transition to parenthood may be enhanced by lack of continuing support with grandparents or other family members characteristic of the life of the young couple after the first few weeks postpartum.

Up to this point we have been primarily concerned with the transition to parenthood for married adults; that is, as a life event normatively occurring in the mid- to late 20s and early 30s for most couples in contemporary U.S. society (Hogan, 1980, 1987). There has been some discussion of off-time late parenthood, with couples having children in their late 30s—and, increasingly, in their 40s—reporting less role conflict and strain than those making this transition on time (Daniels & Weingarten, 1982; Nydegger, 1981a, 1981b). Certainly, they are a good deal farther along in terms of educational attainment and career than those making this transition during their adolescent years.

THE TRANSITION TO PARENTHOOD
AND THE ADOLESCENT PARENT

First-time parenthood is a turning point in the course of life that reflects both new responsibilities and new challenges (Bibring, Dwyer, Huntington, & Valenstein, 1961; Erikson, 1963). Normatively, within contemporary urban society, expectation that parents will care for offspring apart from shared responsibility for child care with other relatives and that the quality of offspring adjustment is a function of child care enhances the sense of isolation, responsibility, and sometimes crisis, reported among first-time parents in our society. These stresses are repeated in caring for offspring across the years of childhood and adolescence (Shanok, 1990).

Although the transition to parenthood has interested scholars for many years, since LeMasters' (1957) landmark study of "parenthood as crisis," most of this interest has focused on adults—usually, married, middle-class, White adults.

Transition to parenthood made by very young parents or those from other ethnic, social, and economic groups raises a separate set of issues (Burton, 1990; Goldberg, 1988). For example, prior study has shown that the quality of the marital (or couple) relationship may be the critical factor in adjustment to new parenthood for middle-class families. Yet in ethnic groups such as those of Hispanic background (primarily Mexican and Puerto Rican families) where living with the extended family is typical for young single mothers, an adolescent's relationship with her child's father may be much less important to her adjustment than the supportive relationships she has with other family members, at least for the earliest years of childrearing.

Any new mother, no matter what her age, reorients and reorganizes herself as she adapts to her new role. Still, because the central tasks of adolescent psychological development are so closely connected to identity issues, and because the new role of parent represents a change in identity, we should not be surprised to find an adolescent element in the young mother's response to this new role and its functions (Caldwell, 1980). That is, when the transition to parenthood takes place during the transitional phase of adolescence it is likely to have a characteristically adolescent quality. Indeed, in assuming the role of parent, a girl may use this particular transition to resolve the developmental tasks around identity that confront her during these years.

Development and Adolescent Childbearing

No matter where the adolescent lives, no matter what her social class or ethnic group, she struggles with issues of identity and personal coherence (Cohler, 1993; Erikson, 1968). For many years scholars representing a broad range of perspectives have discussed and debated the development of identity (e.g., Erikson, 1959, 1968; Freud, 1965; Gilligan, 1982; Gilligan, Lyons, & Hanmer, 1990; Harter, 1988, 1990; Hauser & Follansbee, 1984; Marcia, 1966, 1980; Waterman, 1985). Despite diversity in their methods and their conclusions, all see identity themes as playing important roles in directing a person's life trajectory, and most are concerned with adolescence in this regard. Although concern with issues of identity formation is a continuous process throughout the life cycle, it is particularly salient across the adolescent decade. According to Erikson (1980), "Identity formation neither begins nor ends with adolescence: it is a lifelong development" (p. 122). At the same time, although identity themes continue to resurface throughout adulthood (Shanok, 1990), they do have heightened salience during adolescence, and individuals may be more strongly affected by them at this time because of their relative lack of maturity. Shaped by the past, and shaping the future, identity themes are compelling motivational forces more generally in adolescence, and particularly in adolescent childbearing.

Identity is not something bestowed on the individual by society, nor is it simply a product of maturation that suddenly appears at the right time. Rather, identity is acquired through sustained personal effort requiring time and opportunities, for the adolescent to broaden her experience and increase her exposure to diverse aspects of life, to explore alternatives, and to experiment with the various roles to which she is drawn. Ideally she will fashion a unique sense of who she is by integrating those values, beliefs, goals, and roles that feel most personally expressive and appropriate. Whereas this may be the ideal mode for the negotiation of identity in our society, the reality is often quite different among disadvantaged girls, many of whom commit to a role without exploring alternatives, either because there are few (or no) viable alternatives, or because of family and social pressures to assume particular adult roles.

Applying Marcia's (1966, 1980, 1988) extension of Erikson's concept of identity to adolescent childbearing, one could view the resolution of identity issues through early parenthood as a case of "identity foreclosure," rather than identity achievement. According to Marcia, the foreclosure adolescent is one who has already made commitments without having experienced an identity crisis. These commitments, however, are not the result of personal searching and exploration, but are instead handed to the young person already made by others. In the case of adolescent mothers, there are often many such "others" who play this part, if not always directly, then simply through the example of their own lives.

Identity formation is located both in the self and in the core of one's communal culture, and adolescents are exquisitely sensitive to their communal culture. Viewed from this perspective, a girl becomes a mother because the maternal role fits with her sense of who she is and what she can do; her externally based knowledge of what is available, and what others expect of her. She "chooses" motherhood because the interweaving of these internal and external forces makes the emotional costs of doing otherwise far too high. When an adolescent girl fails to make use of options other than motherhood, it is not solely because there are so few other options (and for poor girls there are indeed few), but also, it is because were she to do so, she might become estranged from the emotionally significant people in her life. With decreasing employment possibilities and increasing social problems such as substance abuse, those who confer and validate her sense of identity are less and less likely to model and lead girls toward the world of work.

Even when alternatives to early motherhood are objectively available, for certain adolescent girls, they may not be subjectively so. If a girl has been socialized from early in her life to view motherhood as the principal arena in which she can expect to satisfy her basic needs, she may be unwilling or unable to seriously consider other opportunities, even when these are objectively available. This socialization pattern may be exceedingly significant if the girl's mother began childbearing at an early age, because in such a family seeking gratification through early motherhood is modeled by the adolescent's primary attachment figure (Michaels, 1988). The presence of many other women of both the girl's own generation and that of her mother and grandmother increases the possibility of electing adolescent parenthood as an option, much less acceptable within middle-class culture, which views the psychological costs of this alternate route to adulthood as much too great and a journey much too lonely (Musick, 1993a). For many adolescents, to choose actively not to have a child is more prudent and consistent with prevailing norms—these young women recognize problems associated with little material, educational/vocational, or emotional support for electing adolescent parenthood.

Motivational Factors Associated With Adolescent Parenthood

Although socioeconomic factors such as a limited opportunity structure, low income, and unemployment may act as barriers to seeking other forms of need satisfaction, these factors may not fully account for the motivation for early parenthood. Nor do socioeconomic factors explain the difficulties many teens have internalizing and deploying newly gained knowledge and skills to move ahead in their lives. Such difficulties underlie the striking variation in capacity for positive change sometimes observed among groups of disadvantaged adolescents, and are important in understanding variation in the effectiveness of particular intervention strategies. It is not simply a matter of variation in personal competence and resilience but also motivation to employ personal competence in overcoming barriers that may be a consequence of early off-time parenthood viewed from the perspective of the larger society.

Reporting on their study of psychological as well as demographic barriers to seeking alternative need satisfaction outside of parenthood, Michaels and Brown (1987) commented:

> Quite early in life cultural and demographic factors set lifelong limits on available sources of need gratification. Then, within this overall context,

such socialization experiences as having an identification figure who became a parent at an early age herself may more directly influence the
adolescent to look to having children for primary need gratification. Finally,
the adolescent's individual level of social maturity may limit her ability to
attain the alternative need satisfactions that her culture and socialization
experiences have made available to her. During adolescence, gratification
of psychological needs through having children may seem to be easier to
attain than long-range sources of need gratification. (cited in Michaels, 1988,
p. 45)

Adolescents who decide against parenthood at a time defined by the
larger society as early off time, in spite of growing up in circumstances
in which this option is more acceptable, generally have more than skills,
strengths, and talent associated with the decision not to elect adolescent
parenthood; they usually have extraordinary families. Such families do
more than nurture, they also buffer, educate, guide, mentor, and model
(Clark, 1983; Comer, 1988; Hans, Jagers, & Musick, 1994; Musick, 1993b).
Sadly, even these families cannot always keep their daughters from becoming mothers too soon in the course of life. It is powerful testimony
to the strength of the forces promoting early childbearing that some very
bright and promising girls from loving families also have babies in their
teens. When these forces interact with the developmentally normal adolescent desire to be a "woman" and fulfill an adult role, and with a social
milieu that encourages or at least does not condemn teenage parenthood
(Anderson, 1989; Dash, 1989), we must ask what is currently available to
the disadvantaged young woman that is as emotionally satisfying as the
idea (if not always the reality) of motherhood. What is worth the struggle
and risks entailed in trying to be something else? What other pathways
lead so directly to achievement, identity, and intimacy?

The psychological rewards of early pregnancy and parenthood arise
from gratification of important needs that are particularly salient during a
developmental period that reverberates with issues of change, separation,
and potential loss. The psychological forces that promote and perpetuate
adolescent parenthood are further strengthened through interaction with
the special set of social and economic circumstances that characterize the
lives of poor young women, reducing their chances of eventual marriage;
blocking alternative routes to the achievement of intimacy, identity, and
competence; and depriving them of social, educational, and vocational
experiences and opportunities available to mainstream girls.

At a time in the girl's life when she feels as though everything is up in
the air, motherhood promises to reduce emotional conflict and to resolve
issues that seem to be unresolvable. The desire for motherhood grows out
of and is intimately connected to the adolescent's sense of herself and where
she fits into the world. At the developmental crossroads of adolescence,

within an environment that offers little chance to explore other options, and with few alternative models, motherhood promises the girl a path to personhood—a path to her own place in the world. Having a baby means she need no longer wonder who she is—she knows—she is a mother. This new identity may indeed be successful in providing at least a temporary increased sense of self-esteem and social significance.

Within the set of complex motivational factors accounting for adolescent childbearing there is some pattern and order, yet striking individual diversity as well. Developmental tasks differ for each of the subphases of adolescence, and individual life experiences vary among adolescents, leading to variation in perceived psychological benefits of teenage motherhood (Musick, 1993). For example, through pregnancy and parenthood, an adolescent girl can recreate a close mother–child bond to heal the pain provoked by conflict with her own parents (Brazelton & Cramer, 1990). She may take on adult status but avoid the potentially fragmenting experience of individuating and becoming too psychologically separate from her mother (Musick, 1987); obtain the emotional sustenance she believed she never received as a child and be able to extend her dependent bond with her mother through identification with her baby (Osofsky, Osofsky, & Diamond, 1988).

Further, the adolescent mother may hope that her mother will love and care for both her and her baby in ways not before realized. At the same time, the adolescent mother seeks opportunities for competence in a new and highly valued role around which she can reorganize herself (Burton, 1990; Hamburg, 1986), developing a new identity through the process of becoming a parent (Benedek, 1970b; Bibring et al., 1961; Shanok, 1990). Finally, she hopes that she might be able to fulfill her mother's spoken or unspoken desire for the "second chance" provided by grandparenthood (Burton, 1990; Ladner & Gourdine, 1984). As a result of providing for her child those emotional resources that she believes were denied to her as a child, the adolescent mother seeks to obtain what she did not get as a child. In this manner, the adolescent mother hopes she will be able to make up for past deprivation, master the pain of this deprivation, and reduce the hold of an unfulfilled childhood over her present life. Now she will have someone of her own, someone whose childhood she will make happier than hers was, and someone who will return her love.

These are only a few of the psychological benefits that can accrue to an adolescent mother, in addition to the comforting feeling of being like her mother or her sisters and friends, many of whom are already pregnant or raising young children. Further, by bearing at least one child, an adolescent girl can avoid the considerable risks of change. She can escape the psychological penalties of attempting to be different (i.e., better) than most of the emotionally significant people in her life. In a milieu where adolescent childbearing is ubiquitous, and other avenues for self-enhancement are absent, questions of whether and when to have children represent developmental and psychological moments of truth. From a psychological perspective, having a baby can be viewed both as a reaction to fears of ego-threatening change and as a concrete means of gaining a respite (if only a temporary one) from the psychic pain of these fears. Bearing a child can be the adolescent's way of saying she wants to remain as she is, at least for the time being.

Balancing Roles

For many poor adolescent girls, early motherhood promises to resolve salient developmental issues of identity, intimacy, and achievement. In the absence of other pathways to proficiency, childbearing represents a tangible achievement providing a new opportunity for mastery, and a new arena for experiencing oneself as competent. Some adolescents actually do succeed in realizing the goals that first led them to become parents. Among these young women, motherhood seems to serve as a psychological catalyst for these adolescents, a way to stop them from really destroying their lives—a sort of self-administered slap in the face. As one adolescent mother observed, "That's how I straightened myself out, by getting pregnant. After all the places that tried to help me, I ended up doing it myself . . . I've never went back to my old ways."

For these young women, who are able to profit psychologically from the transition to parenthood across the years of adolescence, the transition to adulthood (or quasi-adulthood) can be managed without the emotional risks of leaving the family behind. The young woman is spared the ordeal of uprooting herself from her family and its history, as might be the case were she to choose to live in a manner radically different from her female kin. Therefore, a central task of adolescence—moving toward adulthood—can be accomplished by identifying with the mother and her way of life, a separation without psychological amputation and loss. The adolescent now views herself (and others now view her) as a changed, more adultlike person, yet one who nonetheless remains a vital limb on her family's tree.

Concurrent with such events, the advent of parenthood obliges the girl to assume new responsibilities that require distinctive skills and increased maturity. Successful accomplishment of this maternal role (assuming that others such as the grandmother have not completely taken over the care of the child) can provide a sense of proficiency that is highly rewarding, a sense of personal worth rarely experienced before. The concept of "required helpfulness" sheds light on the self-enhancing aspects of adolescent mothering. As Rachman (1979) observed, "Under the incentive of high social demands, helpers often act more effectively and more persistently than at other times. The execution of required helpfulness may lead to enduring changes in the helper himself" (p. 4).

Again what is important is the complex interplay between individual (psychological and developmental) forces and broader socioenvironmental forces. Describing the experiences of adolescents from impoverished families, Elder (1974) depicted a downward extension of "adult-like experience" (p. 80). Reviewing the lives of children growing up during the Great Depression, Elder's observations have particular relevance for disadvantaged young people within contemporary society. Secular or structural changes such as those brought about through deindustrialization (Bowman, 1988) and radical demographic shifts in urban communities (Wilson, 1987) have resulted in major changes in role performance and functioning in the family (see also Steinberg, 1991).

This may involve premature assumption of the role of primary, sometimes even sole caretaker, beginning in the early middle school years (and in some cases even earlier). Many firstborn (or oldest female) preteen and teenage girls spend most of their out-of-school time caring for younger siblings. If they are especially mature or responsible, they may also function in a caretaking role vis-à-vis their own immature or poorly functioning parents. Research on girls dropping out of high school suggests that poor preadolescent and adolescent girls living in poverty provide inordinate amounts of caretaking for their families and lose out on school as a consequence. Fine (1990) saw these young women as surviving at the public–private boundary, "while their schools erect a partition between these ostensibly separable worlds, asking young women to make a choice. And so they do. They choose kin and relationships, and sacrifice their academic lives in the process." Similarly Ianni (1989) found that from about 14 years of age:

> Urban minority girls exhibited the least satisfaction with their schooling . . . the feminine conflict of family versus career had already begun to demand some resolution in terms of a future orientation to one or the other, or required some balancing to avoid decentralizing identity. This suggests another possible dimension of teenage pregnancy, as an acceptance of which way the future is likely to go and an early decision to escape role confusion. (p. 246)

Although the consequences of these role reversals are complex and varied, the heightened sense of competence accompanying such required helpfulness should not be underestimated. Making a psychological virtue out of the particular necessities of her life, a girl may derive a sense of mastery from her role as caretaker. A young woman in these circumstances might well say to herself, "I'm taking care of my mother's kids; why not have my own?" or, "I can do a better job as a parent than my own mother and I'll prove it." In such instances, adolescent parenthood provides the adolescent with the means to leave her mother's house, at least symbolically, and gratifies her need to see and to present herself as an independent person. This type of independence is illusory though: By doing as her mother has done before her, the girl remains psychologically connected. Hamburg (1986) noted that African American adolescent mothers "use their first years of parenthood to consolidate their own growth and solidify their networks . . . (For some young mothers) early childbearing is a strategy that promotes personal and social development and cultural survival given their socio-environmental contingencies" (p. 122).

Ladner and Gourdine (1984) and Burton (1990) arrived at similar conclusions. Among these young women, assumption of the parental role during early to midadolescence provides an opportunity for membership and increased participation in adult society. Adolescent parenthood assists these young women in preparing to manage their own household once they are ready to work. Hamburg (1986) suggested that early parenthood may serve an adaptive function among some disadvantaged young women, particularly those poor, urban, Black, older adolescents who are more mature and less emotionally troubled. Musick (1993a) also found evidence of this same phenomenon in her samples among Hispanic and White adolescent mothers living in rural areas and small towns. For these adolescents, the role of mother confers a distinct and highly valued identity, serving as a catalyst for psychological reorganization, and in its wake, self-advancement.

Based on clinical and anecdotal evidence (Musick, 1993a, 1993b, 1994) we suspect that this is most likely to be the case where an adolescent's motives for motherhood also include the need to be like emotionally significant females in her life—or, more specifically, not to be different from them. Gilligan and her associates (Belenky, Clinchy, Goldberger, & Tarule, 1986; Gilligan, 1982; Gilligan, Lyons, & Hanmer, 1990) reported that women may be more sensitive than men to others' emotional needs— perceived as well as real—and thus are more likely to feel pressured to meet these needs. The symbolic value of the role itself may be enough to enable the young woman to move ahead once she has attained it. Having "achieved" the role of motherhood, a girl with potential may be psychologically freed to realize that potential in other domains. By first choosing motherhood, she is symbolically telling those who are close to her, "I am like you in the ways that matter most; I am not trying to set myself apart." To herself, she may say that having gotten the role of parent out of the way, she can now go on with her life and find her own path. Now, no matter how distant she becomes in terms of occupation, and, eventually, of lifestyle; no matter how far she goes beyond where her family and friends have gone, something special will always be shared—the role and identity of motherhood.

Among more psychologically resilient teen mothers, assumption of the parental role during adolescence may ultimately lead to a positive outcome. At worst, it diverts or sidetracks the young woman for some time, facilitating a temporary regression in the service of the ego (Freud, 1966). If she is fortunate enough to have substantial emotional and practical support from her family (and often participation in a good intervention program as well) and if she has the opportunity to prepare herself educationally or vocationally, she may eventually succeed. Under such optimal circumstances, her role as a parent will not be in serious conflict with her other roles as student or worker, girlfriend or wife. In addition, her personal success will not be at the expense of her child. If it can be said that any child of an adolescent is fortunate, it can be said of the child of a mother such as this. Many children of adolescent mothers are raised by young women struggling to balance three fundamental and often conflicting roles: parenthood, partnerhood, and work (or education as preparation for work, or education and work). These conflicting role demands in the context of timing for this life change that is defined by the larger society as early off time, provide particularly daunting obstacles for later adult accomplishment.

An increasing number of middle-class mothers today find themselves balancing maternal and economic roles, some by choice, some by necessity. In general, however, they are not obliged to juggle these two roles when they are still very young and inexperienced. It is likely that, in addition to her greater social, material, and child-care resources, the more advantaged mother (married, unmarried, or suddenly single) has already acquired her education and at least some occupational expertise by the time she assumes her maternal role. If she is divorced or widowed, she can realistically conceive of remarriage and the possibility of some relief from unceasing role strain. Such a possibility is far more remote for the average adolescent mother. Roxanne, the 17-year-old mother of a 2-year-old, commented after her car broke down for one last time:

> I decided to just save the rest of my money and try and buy me something cheap and to get me around. Because there was no way that I could get a ride to both jobs everyday plus take CeeCee to the babysitters. When I got off work I went to get CeeCee and I found out that she had been real sick all day. I just cry(ed) because I feel bad because I couldn't be there with her when she needed me . . . I have to be a lot but I know that I can make it. I am going to (college) and make it better for CeeCee and me. I just got to keep on my self about getting that GED and going to college.

Eighteen-year-old Lou, an unhappily married mother of a 1-year-old, 7 months pregnant with her second child, day-care provider for another child, and part-time worker, commented that, "I get so tired. I have a 1-year-old and a 2-year-old all day plus try to cook and clean, school at night and selling Mary Kay."

Adolescent mothers seek to fulfill roles other than parenthood, for both developmental and practical reasons. It is in her best interest to realize her own personal goals no matter what her maternal role obliges her to do. However, success in realizing these goals entails psychological tasks involving relationships (especially her relationship with her own mother, or mother figure) and role-related tasks involving school, preparation for work, and a social life including boyfriends. Conflict is unavoidable because the adolescent process is essentially an egocentric one, focused on developing and consolidating the girl's own intellectual and interpersonal skills. On the other hand, the other-directed parenting process is focused on nurturing and fostering the development of another person.

Adolescence is to a large extent a self-oriented process, whereas parenting is other oriented—selfless, as opposed to being preoccupied with self and making sense of futurity (Greene, 1986, 1990; Greene & Wheatley, 1992). Assumption of the parental role requires an abundance of precisely those emotional resources that the normal, self-centered tasks of adolescence are likely to deplete. Hetherington (1984) observed that "the needs of children and parents are not always the same . . . a solution that contributes to the well-being of one may have disastrous outcomes for the other" (p. 12). Although Hetherington was concerned primarily with the consequences of divorce (and by implication, adult parents), her point is doubly relevant to the conflicting needs of adolescent mothers and their children.

Because so much of the adolescent developmental agenda is centered on concern for self, solutions that contribute to the adolescent's well-being and ultimate success are apt to be developmentally costly for her children. This is one important way in which adolescents may be at a disadvantage in comparison to adult mothers. Although, as noted earlier, female adolescents are very much other directed in the sense of wanting to please and be close to significant others (Belenky et al., 1986; Gilligan, 1982; Gilligan et al., 1990), such motives stem from the more self-oriented adolescent need to take emotional care of one's self, rather than the more mature adult desire to take care of another person.

Concern with the impact of child care on parents has increased over the past two decades, with wide-scale reconsideration of the role of women in society. Although there may have been some change in the direction of increased involvement by men in the care of their young children, there has been relatively little change in the amount of time or interest expected of women as their children's primary caretaker. In spite of hopes expressed by feminist scholars such as Chodorow (1977) and others, that the feminist movement would ease the burden of this role transition for women, it is still generally true that the transition to parenthood is actually the transition to motherhood. Although most studies show that husbands are also adversely impacted by this transition, the burden of care falls inequitably on the wife and mother (Cohler, 1984) among married adult couples. If it is true that married women cannot look to their partners for substantial assistance in raising their children, it is even truer for unwed mothers; and, increasingly, adolescent mothers are single mothers.

Trends over the past several decades for women to spend at least part of their time at work, even during the time when they have preschool children at home, means additional role conflict as these women struggle with conflicting demands of work and family. It is possible, from the perspective of career sequence (Hogan, 1978, 1980, 1981), that it may be more advantageous for some women to complete childbearing before taking up a career than to disrupt a career in process, especially if their chances for eventual marriage are slim, as is especially the case for poor minority women. Further, Geronimus (1992) hypothesized that the health status of Black women, especially poor women, may begin to deteriorate in young adulthood, and suggested that they may benefit from bearing children while older family members are still healthy and able to help them with the care of their young children. Geronimus (1987) also found that for Whites, neonatal mortality rates were lower among infants born to women in their 20s. On the other hand, neonatal mortality for Blacks was higher for infants born to women age 20 to 29 years than to women age 15 to 19 years. Geronimus suggested that postponing pregnancy might have adverse effects with this group of women living in poverty.

Considering Different Outcomes of Adolescent Parenthood

There is a common assumption that women who become mothers as teens never build up sufficient "human capital" in terms of education and early work experience to enable them to become economically self-sufficient. However, as the Baltimore longitudinal study of adolescent parenthood (Furstenberg, Brooks-Gunn, & Morgan, 1987) shows, women leaving school during high school often do return to complete their education. Although early off-time or off-sequence parenthood does have certain short-term costs for adolescent mothers, many complete so much of active parenthood by their mid- to late 20s that they are able to return to school or to the labor force as full-time employees at about the same time that their counterparts who become parents at a more expected time are at home caring for children (Furstenberg, 1976; Furstenberg, Morgan,

& Allison, 1987). The sense of well-being of these early off-time adolescent parents increases as their children become independent and free parental time and energy to return to work. Fifteen years after the birth of the first child, nearly 90% of these adolescent mothers had returned to work. At the same time, it should be noted that these women continue to struggle, lacking family and social supports more readily available to their on-time and on-sequence counterparts. Furstenberg, Brooks-Gunn, and Morgan (1987) concluded:

> Many teenage parents seem to stage a recovery of sorts in later life. Most do not fit the popular image of the poorly educated, unemployed woman with a large number of children living on public assistance. Nonetheless, early childbearing extracts a price for many women. Premature parenthood diminishes the chance of economic mobility, in part by restricting educational and occupational opportunities, but also in large measure because it decreases the likelihood of marriage and marital stability. A strong implication of these findings is that teenage child-bearers do worse because they are much more likely in later life to become female heads of households, primarily or exclusively dependent on their own earning ability. (p. 131)

The problems posed by the advent of off-time and out-of-sequence parenthood prior to marriage may be mitigated to some extent by family supports available to women in the Baltimore study as they negotiated the tasks of parenthood. This group of African American adolescent mothers are particularly likely to live with extended family, and to receive greater support than their White counterparts (Waite & Moore, 1978). Nearly two thirds of these teenaged parents in the Baltimore study were still living with their own parents 2 years after a first birth, with nearly half (46%) continuing to live with parents 5 years after a first teenage birth. In the Baltimore study, most women maintained good relations with their family; movement out of the household most often occurs when there is conflict between generations. Even when the young mothers established a separate residence, their parental family continued to provide assistance and emotional support.

Findings to date regarding the transition to parenthood among adolescent women leave many questions unanswered. In the first place, Furstenberg and his colleagues recognized that the social changes of the past several decades mean that many of the findings of their study might not be replicated with subsequent cohorts of adolescent parents. For example, far fewer adolescent mothers of all ethnic groups elect to get married than within past cohorts (Furstenberg, Levine, & Brooks-Gunn, 1990). Further, such significant family and community problems as violence and substance abuse have dramatically increased across the past quarter-century, at the same time that unemployment, poverty, and social isolation have posed far greater problems than at the time of their study nearly 25 years ago (Bane & Ellwood, 1983; Wilson, 1989).

Although the Baltimore study provides evidence of some later "catch-up" in terms of expected adult roles, off-time and off-sequence role transitions frequently do interfere with such later outcomes as financial self-sufficiency (Quint, Musick, & Ladner, 1993), advancement at work (Hogan, 1981), or realization of such family goals as effective socialization of offspring (Musick, 1993b; Osofsky, Osofsky, & Diamond, 1988). Whereas for some girls, pregnancy and parenthood serve as catalysts for positive change and "enhancement of the maturational process," others "find that their action has not made their conflicts disappear" (Osofsky et al., 1988, pp. 227–228). In addition, if adolescents become parents in order to resolve core developmental or psychological issues, not all will succeed in doing so.

Adolescent mothers are a highly diverse group of women; it is not surprising that there is such marked diversity across individual life paths. Although it would not be difficult to maintain that early childbearing places numerous risks and obstacles in a young mother's way, with time it is possible to overcome a good many of these and go on to succeed as a parent, partner, worker, and member of society. Research following teenage mothers for 20 years indicates that roughly two thirds of them have completed school, gotten and stayed off welfare, and noticeably improved their employment status (Furstenberg, Brooks-Gunn, & Morgan, 1987; Furstenberg, Levine, & Brooks-Gunn, 1990; Horwitz, Klerman, Kuo, & Jekel, 1991; Klerman, 1993). Not surprisingly, the adolescent mothers most likely to succeed are those who are at grade level when they become pregnant, or who are able to finish high school within 5 years after the babies' birth. These are also the young mothers who have few siblings, and whose own parents are not on public assistance, and have more than a 10th-grade education themselves (Chase-Landsdale, Brooks-Gunn, & Paikoff, 1991).

Although many young mothers eventually do succeed within the larger community, their children appear to be at a developmental disadvantage when contrasted with children of women who delay childbearing until they are in their 20s. The children of women who first gave birth in their teens do have more school-related and behavioral problems, especially when they reach late childhood and early adolescence (Brooks-Gunn & Furstenberg, 1987; Card & Wise, 1981; Klerman, 1993; Mott & Marsiglio, 1985), and are more likely to become adolescent parents themselves. This is especially true among those adolescents whose mothers have experienced recent periods of time on welfare.

Furstenberg, Hughes, and Brooks-Gunn (1992) remarked that women who are persistently on welfare may have less education and fewer marketable skills. They may have larger families, live within more crowded households, and also report lowered morale and life satisfaction. These women may also live in more distressed neighborhoods and send their children to poorer schools. At the same time, as a group—like their mothers—they too demonstrate considerable diversity. Many of these women are able to do quite well in terms of school, work, and fertility control. Furstenberg et al. (1990) reported that about two thirds of the daughters of adolescent mothers in the groups they studied had postponed childbearing beyond their teenage years. It is important to understand differences between those young women able to postpone parenthood and those who become parents across the adolescent decade and to understand the determinants of resilience among the larger number of adolescent women who are able to remain on time in terms of expected adult role transitions.

Variability in adolescent mothers' lives over time is also reflected in the greater variability in their children's outcomes. As the years pass, these children do better if their mothers' lives improve, especially if these improvements involve welfare and marital status (Chase-Landsdale et al., 1991). Furstenberg et al. (1992) observed that this relationship of welfare and poverty is not a simple one. A former teenage mother who improves her socioeconomic status through work and/or marriage is able to provide her children with increased educational opportunity and with higher quality housing and neighborhood. In addition, she also provides for her children and their friends a model of personal initiative, high self-standards, and competence.

However, there may also be significant costs for children associated with their mother's economic success; an upwardly mobile young mother may well have to expend so much effort to get (and stay) ahead in her own life that she has little time or energy left for her children. Children within these families characterized by increased upward mobility may realize material benefits. At the same time, parental preoccupation with their own lives may have an impact on the child's own adjustment so that it is difficult to take advantage of the psychological and social benefits as a consequence of their mother's own success.

CONCLUSION

Parenthood is among the most salient roles across the course of life and one that remains as long as the parent has memory (Benedek, 1973). Functionally essential for the reproduction of society itself, parenthood represents a major source of effort and satisfaction for both mothers and fathers (LeMasters, 1970; Rapoport, Rapoport, Strelitz, & Kew, 1977;

Russell, 1974). At the same time, both because of the lack of prior preparation for this role within contemporary society, and also the extent to
which enactment of this role impacts such other major roles as marriage
and work, it often becomes a source of conflict and strain (Pearlin, 1975).
Becoming a parent has the capacity to elicit unresolved problems and
concerns among parents stemming from their own life experiences as
children within their own parental families (Fraiberg, Adelson, & Shapiro,
1975; Main & Hesse, 1990). For all these reasons, it is not surprising that
the transition to parenthood is one that is inherently a source of distress
in our society. Although findings vary according to the group studied
and the questions asked, most studies show that the transition to parenthood is a source of at least moderate personal crisis.

Variation in this sense of crisis is a function both of the timing of the
advent of parenthood in the life course and the sequence of this transition
in terms of other adult transitions. Variations must be understood in
terms of broader historical and social factors that affect the meaning of
parenthood and the desire for children (Bram, 1978; Kaltreider & Margolis, 1977; Modell, Furstenberg, & Strong, 1976; Veevers, 1973, 1979).
Early parenthood during the teenage years poses dual problems, due
both to timing of this event, and to the sequence of the transition to
parenthood in the portfolio of expectable adult roles. Timing issues are
particularly important in terms of their influence on school completion,
work, and marriage. Whereas issues of expectable sequence and social
support manifest themselves differently across ethnic groups, intertwined
sequence and timing are issues for all adolescents.

Most studies of teenage mothers have been based on cross-sectional
study. In those few reports that have followed up teen parents over time,
findings suggest that it is possible for teenage parents to at least partly
"catch up" with counterparts who have not given birth as teens. Such
findings raise questions about whether linear models are the most appropriate for the study of lives over time. Maintenance of a short-term
perspective in which early parenthood is viewed as an off-time transition
that causes a range of social problems makes it difficult to study this
phenomenon in a life-course perspective. As is often the case in the study
of lives over time, adoption of a life-course perspective demonstrates that
under certain circumstances, certain individuals will be able to move
beyond early dislocations and difficulties, realizing later success after
initial adversity.

A next step in research on the transition to adolescent parenthood
might be to separate the issues of sequence of entrance into expected
adult roles from the time of role transitions, and to concentrate more
explicitly on the means by which some teenage parents are able to attain
success as adults despite earlier diversion from the expectable course of

life. It is particularly important to understand differences between that group of girls permanently derailed by the early advent of parenthood and those able to catch up in expectable life attainments with their on-time counterparts. A recent follow-up study of young, unwed mothers addresses this issue (Quint et al., 1993), but much more study is clearly required. If the life course is intrinsically less ordered, and the past less likely to predict the future than has been assumed in much life-course social science to date (Gergen, 1977; Kagan, 1980; Neugarten, 1969), future study must include cross-sequential designs encompassing cohort, sequence, and timing in the transition to parenthood and their sequelae over the adult life course.

REFERENCES

Anderson, E. (1989). Sex codes and family life among poor inner-city youths. *Annals, AAPSS, 501,* 59–78.

Aneshensel, C., Fredrichs, R., & Clark, V. (1981). Family roles and sex differences in depression. *Journal of Health and Social Behavior, 22,* 379–393.

Antonucci, T., & Akiyama, H. (1987). Social networks in adult life and a preliminary examination of the convoy model. *Journal of Gerontology, 42,* 519–527.

Bane, M. J., & Ellwood, D. (1983). *The dynamics of dependence: The routes to self-sufficiency.* Cambridge, MA: Urban Systems Research and Engineering, Inc.

Belenky, M., Clinchy, B., Goldberger, N., & Tarule, J. (1986). *Women's ways of knowing: The development of self, voice, and mind.* New York: Basic Books.

Belsky, J., & Isabella, R. (1985). Marital and parent–child relationships in family of origins and marital change following the birth of a baby: A retrospective analysis. *Child Development, 56,* 342–349.

Benedek, T. (1959). Parenthood as a developmental phase: A contribution to libido theory. *Journal of the American Psychoanalytic Association, 7,* 389–417.

Benedek, T. (1970a). Motherhood and nurturing. In E. J. Anthony & T. Benedek (Eds.), *Parenthood: Its psychology and psychopathology* (pp. 153–166). Boston: Little, Brown.

Benedek, T. (1970b). Parenthood during the life cycle. In E. J. Anthony & T. Benedek (Eds.), *Parenthood: Its psychology and psychopathology* (pp. 185–206). Boston: Little, Brown.

Benedek, T. (1973). Discussion of parenthood as a developmental phase. In T. Benedek (Ed.), *Psychoanalytic investigations: Selected papers* (pp. 401–407). New York: Quadrangle Press.

Bibring, G., Dwyer, T., Huntington, D., & Valenstein, A. (1961). A study of the psychological processes in pregnancy and of the earliest mother–child relationship. *Psychoanalytic Study of the Child, 16,* 9–72.

Bowman, P. (1988). Post-industrial displacement and family role strains. In P. Voydanoff & L. Majka (Eds.), *Families and economic distress* (pp. 75–96). Beverly Hills, CA: Sage.

Bram, S. (1978). Through the looking glass: Voluntary childlessness as a mirror of contemporary changes in the meaning of parenthood. In W. B. Miller & L. F. Newman (Eds.), *The first child and family formation* (pp. 368–391). Chapel Hill, NC: Carolina Population Center.

Brazelton, T. B., & Cramer, B. (1990). *The earliest relationship: Parents, infants, and the drama of early attachment.* Reading, MA: Addison-Wesley.

Brody, E. (1985). Parent care as a normative family stress. *The Gerontologist, 25,* 19–29.

Brooks-Gunn, J., & Chase-Landsdale, L. (1991). Children having children: Effects on the family system. *Pediatric Annals, 20*(9), 467–481.

Brooks-Gunn, J., & Furstenberg, F. (1987). Continuity and change in the context of poverty: Adolescent mothers and their children. In J. Gallagher & C. Ramey (Eds.), *The malleability of children* (pp. 171–188). Baltimore: Brookes Publishing.

Burke, P., & Tully, J. (1977). The measurement of role identity. *Social Forces, 55,* 881–897.

Burton, L. (1990). Teenage childbearing as an alternative life-course strategy in multigeneration black families. *Human Nature, 1*(2), 123–143.

Caldwell, S. (1980). Life-course perspectives on adolescent parent research. *The Journal of Social Issues, 36,* 130–144.

Callan, V. (1987). The personal and marital adjustment of mothers and of voluntarily and involuntarily childless wives. *Journal of Marriage and the Family, 49,* 847–856.

Campbell, A., Converse, P., & Rodgers, W. (1976). *The quality of American life: Perceptions, evaluations, and satisfactions.* New York: Russell Sage.

Card, J., & Wise, L. (1981). Teenage mothers and teenage fathers: The impact of early childbearing on the parents' personal and professional lives. In F. Furstenberg, R. Lincoln, & J. Menken (Eds.), *Teenage sexuality, pregnancy, and childbearing* (pp. 211–222). Philadelphia: University of Pennsylvania Press.

Chase-Landsdale, P. L., Brooks-Gunn, J., & Paikoff, R. (1991). Research programs for adolescent mothers: Missing links and future promises. *Family Relations, 40,* 396–404.

Chodorow, N. (1977). *The reproduction of mothering.* Berkeley: The University of California Press.

Clark, R. (1983). *Family life and school achievement: Why poor Black children succeed or fail.* Chicago: The University of Chicago Press.

Cohler, B. (1984). Parenthood, psychopathology, and child-care. In R. Cohen, B. Cohler, & S. Weissman (Eds.), *Parenthood: A psychodynamic perspective* (pp. 119–148). New York: Guilford.

Cohler, B. (1987–1988). The adult daughter–mother relationship: Perspective from life-course family study and psychoanalysis. *Journal of Geriatric Psychiatry, 21,* 51–72.

Cohler, B. (1993). Aging, morale, and meaning: The nexus of narrative. In T. Cole, W. A. Achenbaum, P. Jakobi, & R. Kastenbaum (Eds.), *Voices and visions of aging: Toward a critical gerontology* (pp. 107–113). New York: Springer.

Cohler, B., & Grunebaum, H. (1981). *Mothers, grandmothers, and daughters: Personality and child-care in three generation families.* New York: Wiley.

Comer, J. (1988). *Maggie's American dream: The life and times of a Black family.* New York: New American Library.

Daniels, P., & Weingarten, K. (1982). *Sooner or later: The timing of parenthood in adult lives.* New York: Norton.

Dash, L. (1989). *When children want children: The urban crisis of teenage childbearing.* New York: Morrow.

Dyer, E. (1963). Parenthood as crisis: A restudy. *Journal of Marriage and Family Living, 25,* 196–201.

Elder, G. (1974). *Children of the great depression.* Chicago: The University of Chicago Press.

Elder, G. (1975). Age differentiation and the life course. *Annual Review of Sociology, 1,* 165–190.

Elder, G. (1979). Historical change in life patterns and personality. In P. Baltes & O. G. Brim, Jr. (Eds.), *Life-span development and behavior* (Vol. 2, pp. 117–159). New York: Academic Press.

Elder, G., & Rockwell, R. (1979). The life-course and human development: An ecological perspective. *International Journal of Behavioral Development, 2,* 1–21.

Entwisle, D., & Doering, S. (1981). *The first birth: A family turning point.* Baltimore, MD: Johns Hopkins University Press.

Erikson, E. (1959). Identity and the life cycle: Selected papers. *Psychological Issues, 1*(1), 18–164.

Erikson, E. (1963). *Childhood and society* (2nd ed.). New York: Norton.

Erikson, E. (1968). *Identity, youth and crisis.* New York: Norton.

Erikson, E. (1980). *Identity and the life cycle.* New York: Norton.

Farnham-Diggory, S. (1966). Self, future, and time: A developmental study of the concepts of psychotic, brain injured and normal children. *Monographs of the Society for Research in Child Development, 33* (Whole No. 103).

Field, T., Widmayer, S., Stringer, S., & Ignatoff, E. (1980). Teenage lower class mothers and their preterm infants: An intervention and follow-up. *Child Development, 51,* 426–436.

Fine, M. (1990, Fall–Winter). Creating space. *Women and Foundations Newsletter.*

Fraiberg, S., Adelson, E., & Shapiro, V. (1975). Ghosts in the nursery: A psychoanalytic approach to the problems of impaired mother–infant relationships. *Journal of the American Academy of Child Psychiatry, 14,* 387–422.

Freud, A. (1965). *Normality and pathology in childhood.* New York: International Universities Press.

Freud, A. (1966). Instinctual anxiety during puberty. In *The writings of Anna Freud: Vol. 2. The ego and the mechanisms of defense* (2nd ed.). New York: International Universities Press.

Furstenberg, F. (1976). *Unplanned parenthood: The social consequences of teenage childbearing.* New York: The Free Press.

Furstenberg, F., Brooks-Gunn, J., & Morgan, S. P. (1987). *Adolescent mothers in later life.* New York: Cambridge University Press.

Furstenberg, F., Hughes, M., & Brooks-Gunn, J. (1992). The next generation: Children of teenage mothers grow up. In M. Rosenheim & M. Testa (Eds.), *Early parenthood and the coming of age in the 1990s* (pp. 113–135). New Brunswick, NJ: Rutgers University Press.

Furstenberg, F., Levine, J., & Brooks-Gunn, J. (1990). The children of teenage mothers: Patterns of early childbearing in two generations. *Family Planning Perspectives, 22*(2), 54–61.

Furstenberg, F., Morgan, S., & Allison, P. (1987). Paternal participation and children's well-being after marital dissolution. *American Sociological Review, 52,* 695–701.

Galatzer-Levy, R., & Cohler, B. (1993). *The essential other.* New York: Basic Books.

Geertz, C. (1966). Person, time, and conduct in Bali. In C. Geertz (Ed.), *The interpretation of cultures* (pp. 360–412). New York: Basic Books.

Gergen, J. (1977). Stability, change, and chance in understanding human development. In N. Datan & H. Reese (Eds.), *Life-span developmental psychology: Dialectical perspectives on experimental research* (pp. 32–65). New York: Academic Press.

Geronimus, A. (1987). On teenage childbearing and neonatal mortality in the United States. *Population Development Review, 13,* 245–279.

Geronimus, A. (1992). The weathering hypothesis and the health of African-American women and infants. Evidence and speculations. *Ethnicity and Disease, 2,* 207–221.

Gershenson, H. (1983). *The ecology of childrearing in white families with adolescent mothers.* Unpublished doctoral dissertation, The University Of Chicago, Chicago.

Gilligan, C. (1982). *In a different voice: Psychological theory and women's development.* Cambridge, MA: Harvard University Press.

Gilligan, C., Lyons, N., & Hanmer, T. (Eds.). (1990). *Making connections: The relational worlds of adolescent girls at Emma Willard School.* Cambridge, MA: Harvard University Press.

Goffman, E. (1961). *Relations in public: Microstudies of the public order.* New York: Basic Books.

Goldberg, W. (1988). Introduction: Perspectives on the transition to parenthood. In G. Michaels & W. Goldberg (Eds.), *The transition to parenthood: Current theory and research* (pp. 1–20). Cambridge, UK: Cambridge University Press.

Goldberg, W., Michaels, G., & Lamb, M. (1985). Husbands' and wives' adjustment to pregnancy and first parenthood. *Journal of Family Issues, 6*, 483–503.

Gordon, K., Eli, E., & Gordon, K. (1965). Factors in post-partum emotional adjustment. *Obstetrics and Gynecology, 25*, 158–166.

Gordon, K., & Gordon, K. (1958). Psychiatric problems of a rapidly growing suburb. *Archives of Neurology and Psychiatry, 79*, 543–548.

Greene, A. L. (1986). Future time perspective in adolescence: The present of things future revisited. *Journal of Youth and Adolescence, 15*, 99–113.

Greene, A. L. (1990). Great expectations: Constructions of the life-course during adolescence. *Journal of Youth and Adolescence, 19*, 289–306.

Greene, A. L., & Wheatley, S. (1992). "I've got a lot to do and I don't think I'll have the time": Gender differences in late adolescents' narratives of the future. *Journal of Youth and Adolescence, 21*, 667–686.

Grossman, F. K., Eichler, L., Winickoff, S., & Associates. (1980). *Pregnancy, birth, and parenthood.* San Francisco: Jossey-Bass.

Gutmann, D. (1977). Parenthood: A key to the comparative psychology of the life-cycle. In N. Datan & L. Ginsberg (Eds.), *Life-span developmental psychology: Normative life crises* (pp. 167–184). New York: Academic Press.

Gutmann, D. (1987). *Reclaimed powers: Towards a psychology of men and women in later life.* New York: Basic Books.

Hagestad, G. (1974). *Middle aged women and their children: Exploring changes in a role relationship.* Unpublished doctoral dissertation, The University Of Minnesota, Minneapolis.

Hagestad, G., & Neugarten, B. (1985). Age and the life-course. In R. Binstock & E. Shas (Eds.), *Handbook of aging and society* (2nd ed., pp. 35–61). New York: Van Nostrand-Reinhold.

Hamburg, B. (1986). Subsets of adolescent mothers: Developmental, biomedical and psychosocial issues. In J. B. Lancester & B. Hamburg (Eds.), *School age pregnancy and parenthood* (pp. 115–146). New York: Aldine De Gruyter.

Hans, S., Jagers, R., & Musick, J. (1995). *Giving children what they need: Discussions with poor parents who raise competent children.* Manuscript submitted for publication.

Harter, S. (1988). The construction and conservation of the self: James and Cooley revisited. In D. Lapsley & F. Power (Eds.), *Self, ego, and identity: Integrative approaches* (pp. 43–70). New York: Springer-Verlag.

Harter, S. (1990). Self and identity development. In S. Feldman & G. Elliott (Eds.), *At the threshold: The developing adolescent* (pp. 352–387). Cambridge, MA: Harvard University Press.

Hauser, S., & Follansbee, D. (1984). Developing identity: Ego growth and change during adolescence. In H. Fitzgerald, B. Lester, & M. Yogman (Eds.), *Theory and research in behavioral pediatrics* (Vol. 2, pp. 207–268). New York: Plenum.

Hetherington, E. M. (1984). Stress and coping in children and families. In A.-B. Doyle, D. Gold, & D. Moskowitz (Eds.), *Children in families under stress* (New directions in child development, Vol. 24, pp. 7–33). San Francisco: Jossey-Bass.

Hill, R. (1978). Psychological consequences of the first birth: A discussion. In W. B. Miller & L. F. Newman (Eds.), *The first child and family formation* (pp. 392–401). Chapel Hill, NC: Carolina Population Center.

Hill, R., & Mattessich, P. (1979). Family development theory and life-span development. In P. Baltes & O. G. Brim, Jr. (Eds.), *Life-span development and behavior* (Vol. 2, pp. 161–204). New York: Academic Press.

Hill, R., & Rodgers, R. (1964). The developmental approach. In H. Christensen (Ed.), *Handbook of marriage and the family* (pp. 171–211). Chicago: Rand-McNally.

Hobbs, D. (1965). Parenthood as crisis: A third study. *Marriage and Family Living, 27*, 367–372.

Hobbs, D. (1968). Transition to parenthood: A replication and extension. *Journal of Marriage and the Family, 30,* 413–417.

Hobbs, D., & Cole, S. P. (1976). Transition to parenthood: A decade of replication. *Journal of Marriage and the Family, 38,* 723–731.

Hoffreth, S., & Moore, K. (1979). Early childbearing and later economic well being. *American Sociological Review, 44,* 784–815.

Hogan, D. (1978). The variable order of events in the life-course. *American Sociological Review, 43,* 573–586.

Hogan, D. (1980). The transition to adulthood as a career contingency. *American Sociological Review, 45,* 261–276.

Hogan, D. (1981). *Transitions and social change: The early lives of American men.* New York: Academic Press.

Hogan, D. (1987). Demographic trends in human fertility, and parenting across the life-span. In J. B. Lancaster, J. Altman, A. Rossi, & L. Sherrod (Eds.), *Parenting across the life-span: Biosocial dimensions* (pp. 315–350). New York: Aldine De Gruyter.

Horwitz, S., Klerman, L., Kuo, S., & Jekel, J. (1991). School-age mothers: Predictors of long-term educational and economic outcomes. *Pediatrics, 87*(6), 862–868.

Ianni, F. (1989). *The search for structure: A report on American youth today.* New York: The Free Press.

Jacoby, A. (1969). Transition to parenthood: A reassessment. *Journal of Marriage and the Family, 31,* 720–727.

Kahn, R. (1979). Aging and social support. In M. Riley (Ed.), *Aging from birth to death* (pp. 77–91). Boulder, CO: Westview Press.

Kahn, R., & Antonucci, T. (1980). Convoys over the life course: Attachment, roles, and social support. In P. Baltes & O. G. Brim, Jr. (Eds.), *Life-span development and behavior* (Vol. 3, pp. 353–386). New York: Academic Press.

Kagan, J. (1980). Perspectives on continuity. In J. Kagan & O. G. Brim, Jr. (Eds.), *Constancy and change in human development* (pp. 26–74). Cambridge, MA: Harvard University Press.

Kaltreider, N., & Margolis, A. (1977). Childless by choice: A clinical study. *American Journal of Psychiatry, 134,* 179–182.

Klerman, L. (1993). Adolescent pregnancy and parenting: Controversies of the past and lessons for the future. *Journal of Adolescent Health, 14,* 553–561.

Ladner, J., & Gourdine, R. (1984). Intergenerational teenage motherhood: Some preliminary findings. *SAGE: A Scholarly Journal on Black Women, 1*(2), 22–24.

Leifer, M. (1980). *Psychological effects of motherhood: A study of first pregnancy.* New York: Praeger.

LeMasters, E. E. (1957). Parenthood as crisis. *Marriage and Family Living, 19,* 352–355.

LeMasters, E. E. (1970). *Parents in modern America.* Homewood, IL: Dorsey Press.

Linton, R. (1942). Age and sex categories. *American Sociological Review, 7,* 589–603.

Main, M., & Hesse, E. (1990). Parents' unresolved traumatic experiences are related to infant disorganized attachment status: Is frightened or frightening parental behavior the linking mechanism? In M. Greenberg, D. Cicchetti, & M. Cummings (Eds.), *Attachment in the preschool years* (pp. 161–182). Chicago: University of Chicago Press.

Marcia, J. (1966). Development and validation of ego-identity status. *Journal of Personality and Social Psychology, 3,* 551–558.

Marcia, J. (1980). Identity in adolescence. In J. Adelson (Ed.), *Handbook of adolescent psychology* (pp. 159–177). New York: Wiley.

Marcia, J. (1988). Common processes underlying ego identity, cognitive/normal development, and individuation. In D. Lapsley & F. Power (Eds.), *Self, ego, and identity: Integrative approaches* (pp. 111–125). New York: Springer-Verlag.

McCall, G., & Simmons, J. (1978). *Identities and interactions* (Rev. ed.). New York: The Free Press.

McKim, M. (1987). Transition to what? New parents' problems in the first year. *Family Relations, 36*, 22–25.

McLanahan, S., & Adams, J. (1987). Parenthood and psychological well-being. *Annual Review of Sociology, 5*, 237–257.

Meyerowitz, J., & Feldman, H. (1966). Transition to parenthood. *Psychiatric Research Reports, 20*, 78–84.

Michaels, G. (1988). Motivational factors in the decision and timing of pregnancy. In G. Michaels & W. Goldberg (Eds.), *The transition to parenthood: Current theory and research* (pp. 23–61). Cambridge, UK: Cambridge University Press.

Michaels, G., & Brown, R. (1987). *Values of children in adolescent mothers.* Unpublished manuscript, Northwestern University Medical School, Evanston, IL.

Miller, B., & Sollie, D. (1980). Normal stresses during the transition to parenthood. *Family Relations, 29*, 459–465.

Minturn, L., & Lambert, W. (1964). *Mothers of six cultures: Antecedents of childrearing.* New York: Wiley.

Modell, J., Furstenberg, F., & Strong, D. (1976). Social change and transitions to adulthood in historical perspective. *Journal of Family History, 1*, 7–32.

Modell, J., Furstenberg, F., Jr., & Strong, D. (1978). The timing of marriage in the transition to adulthood: Continuity and change, 1860–1975. *American Journal of Sociology, 84*, S120–S150.

Mott, F., & Marsiglio, W. (1985). Early childbearing and completion of high school. *Family Planning Perspectives, 17*(3), 118–124.

Musick, J. (1987). *The psychological and developmental dimensions of adolescent pregnancy and parenting: An interventionist's perspective.* Paper prepared for the Rockefeller Foundation.

Musick, J. (1993a). Children and families in poverty: Two profiles. In J. Chafel (Ed.), *Childhood poverty: Trends, issues and public policy.* Washington, DC: The Urban Institute.

Musick, J. (1993b). *Young poor and pregnant: The psychology of teenage motherhood.* New Haven, CT: Yale University Press.

Musick, J. (1994). The special role of parenting in the context of poverty: The case of adolescent motherhood. In C. A. Nelson (Ed.), *Threats to optimal development: Integrating biological, psychological, and social risk factors* (Minnesota Symposium on Child Psychology, Vol. 27). Hillsdale, NJ: Lawrence Erlbaum Associates.

Neugarten, B. (1969). Continuities and discontinuities of psychological issues into adult life. *Vita Humana (Human Development), 12*, 121–230.

Neugarten, B. (1973). Personality change in late life: A developmental perspective. In C. Eisorfer & M. P. Lawton (Eds.), *The psychology of adult development* (pp. 311–338). Washington, DC: The American Psychological Association.

Neugarten, B. (1979). Time, age, and the life-cycle. *American Journal of Psychiatry, 136*, 887–894.

Neugarten, B., & Hagestad, G. (1976). Age and the life-course. In R. Binstock & E. Shas (Eds.), *Handbook of aging and the social sciences* (pp. 35–55). New York: Van Nostrand-Reinhold.

Neugarten, B., & Moore, J. (1968). The changing age-status system. In B. Neugarten (Ed.), *Middle-age and aging: A reader in social psychology* (pp. 5–20). Chicago: The University of Chicago Press.

Neugarten, B., Moore, J., & Lowe, J. (1965). Age norms, age constraints, and adult socialization. *The American Journal of Sociology, 70*, 710–717.

Neugarten, B., & Peterson, W. (1957). A study of the American age-grade system. *Proceedings of the Fourth Congress of the International Association of Gerontology, 3*, 497–502.

Nydegger, C. (1981a). On being caught up in time. *Human Development, 24*, 1–12.

Nydegger, C. (1981b, November). *The ripple effect of parental timing.* Paper presented at Annual Meetings, The Gerontological Society, Toronto.

Osofsky, J., & Osofsky, H. (1984). Psychological and developmental perspectives on expectant and new parenthood. *Review of child development research: Vol. 7. The family* (pp. 372–397). Chicago: The University of Chicago Press.

Osofsky, J., Osofsky, H., & Diamond, M. (1988). The transition to parenthood: Special tasks and risk factors for adolescent parents. In G. Michaels & W. Goldberg (Eds.), *The transitions to parenthood: Current theory and research* (pp. 209–232). Cambridge, UK: Cambridge University Press.

Pearlin, L. (1975). Sex roles and depression. In N. Datan & L. Ginsberg (Eds.), *Life-span developmental psychology: Normative life crises* (pp. 191–207). New York: Academic Press.

Quint, J., Musick, J., & Ladner, J. (1993). *Lives of promise, lives of loss.* New York: Manpower Demonstration Research Corporation.

Rachman, S. (1979). The concept of required helpfulness. *Behavior Research and Therapy, 17,* 1–6.

Ragan, P., & Wales, J. (1980). Age stratification and the life course. In J. Birren & R. B. Sloane (Eds.), *Handbook of mental health and aging* (pp. 591–615). Englewood Cliffs, NJ: Prentice-Hall.

Rapoport, R., Rapoport, R., Strelitz, Z., & Kew, S. (1977). *Fathers, mothers, and society: Toward new alliances.* New York: Basic Books.

Riley, M. (1971). Social gerontology and the age stratification of society. *The Gerontologist, 11,* 79–87.

Riley, M. (1976). Age strata in social systems. In R. Binstock & E. Shanas (Eds.), *Handbook of aging and the social sciences* (pp. 189–217). New York: VanNostrand-Reinhold.

Riley, M., Johnson, M., & Foner, A. (Eds.). (1972). *Aging and society: Vol. III. A sociology of age stratification* (pp. 198–235). New York: Russell Sage.

Rindfuss, R., Morgan, S. P., & Swicegood, C. G. (1984). The transition to motherhood: The intersection of structural and temporal dimensions. *American Sociological Review, 49,* 359–372.

Rossi, A. (1968). Transition to parenthood. *Journal of Marriage and the Family, 30,* 26–39.

Rossi, A. (1972). Family development in a changing world. *American Journal of Psychiatry, 128,* 1057–1066.

Rossi, A. (1987). Parenthood in transition: From lineage to child to self-orientation. In J. B. Lancaster, J. Altman, A. Rossi, & L. Sherrod (Eds.), *Parenting across the life-span: Biosocial dimensions* (pp. 31–84). New York: Aldine De Gruyter.

Roth, J. (1963). *Timetables: Structuring the passage of time in hospital treatment and other careers.* Indianapolis, IN: Bobbs-Merrill.

Rowe, J., & Kahn, R. (1987, July 10). Human aging: Usual and successful. *Science, 237,* 143–149.

Russell, C. (1974). Transition to parenthood: Problems and gratifications. *Journal of Marriage and the Family, 36,* 294–302.

Russell, C. (1980). Unscheduled parenthood: Transition to 'parent' for the teenager. *The Journal of Social Issues, 36,* 45–63.

Shanok, R. (1990). Parenthood: A process marking identity and intimacy capacities. *Zero-to-Three, 11*(2), 1–9.

Shereshefsky, P., & Yarrow, L. (Eds.). (1973). *Psychological aspects of a first pregnancy and early postnatal adaptation.* New York: Raven.

Steinberg, L. (1991). The logic of adolescence. In P. Edelman & J. Ladner (Eds.), *Adolescence and poverty: Challenge for the 1990s* (pp. 19–36). Washington, DC: Center for National Policy Press.

Veevers, J. (1973). The social meanings of parenthood. *Psychiatry, 36,* 291–310.

Veevers, J. (1979). Voluntary childlessness: A review of issues and evidence. *Marriage and Family Review, 2,* 1–26.

Waite, L., & Moore, K. (1978). The impact of an early first birth on young women's educational attainment. *Social Forces, 56,* 845–865.

Waterman, A. S. (1985). Identity in the context of adolescent psychology. *New Directions for Child Development, 30,* 5–24.

Weissman, M., & Klerman, G. (1977). Sex differences in the epidemiology of depression. *Archives of General Psychiatry, 34,* 98–111.

Weissman, M., & Meyers, J. (1978a). Affective disorders in a U.S. urban community: The use of Research Diagnostic Criteria in an epidemiological survey. *Archives of General Psychiatry, 35,* 1304–1311.

Weissman, M., & Meyers, J. (1978b). Rates and risks of depressive symptoms in a United States urban community. *Acta Psychiatrica Scandinavica, 57,* 219–231.

Weissman, M., Meyers, J., & Thompson, D. (1981). Depression and its treatment in a U.S. urban community 1975–1976. *Archives of General Psychiatry, 38,* 417–421.

Wilson, W. (1987). *The truly disadvantaged: The inner city, the underclass and public policy.* Chicago: The University of Chicago Press.

Wilson, W. (1989, January). The underclass: Issues, perspectives and public policy. *Annals, AAPSS, 501,* 182–192.

9

Early Parenting and Intergenerational Family Relationships Within African American Families

Cynthia Merriwether-de Vries
Linda M. Burton
LaShawnda Eggeletion
The Pennsylvania State University

Despite growing national attention from policymakers and social service providers to the prevention of adolescent pregnancy, demographic trends indicate little reduction in the number of births to unmarried teenagers. Recently released figures from the National Center for Health Statistics (NCHS) indicate that adolescent fertility is continuing a tenacious pattern of increase. The decade of the 1980s reflected an increase in the nonmarital birth rate of between 4% and 8% annually (NCHS, 1993). According to NCHS, figures for the 5-year period from 1986 to 1991 show an increase in the birth rate for females ages 15 to 17 ranging from 3% to 8% annually (NCHS, 1993). The fertility rate for older adolescent females is also rising. The birth rate for females ages 18 to 19 years old has increased between 5% and 7% annually in the 4-year period from 1988 to 1991 (NCHS, 1993). The magnitude of these increases challenges the view that the transition to parenthood in adolescence is aberrant and pathological (Burton, 1990b; Caldas, 1994; Geronimous, 1987; Geronimous & Korenman, 1992; Gibbs, 1992; Hamburg & Dixon, 1992; Himes, 1992; Hogan, Astone, & Kitagwa, 1985).

The birth trends for African American adolescents conform to and exceed the national pattern. In 1990 the birth rate for unmarried African American adolescents was 66.5% (De Jong, Cornwall, & Wilmouth, 1993). Although this figure resulted from a slower annual increase, approximately 2 to 3%, it represents a greater total fertility rate of 229.1 births per 1,000 unmarried African American teens, as compared to a rate of 96.1

births per 1,000 to European American teens (NCHS, 1993). Scrutiny of these demographic trends illustrates the necessity to expand rather than curtail investigations of adolescent pregnancy among African Americans.

Statistical profiles provide information on the rate of change in the reported incidence of pregnancy. The enumeration strategy belies the pervasive impact of the pregnancy on the adolescent parent's family members. The impact of adolescent pregnancy is not restricted to the young mother and father, nor is it limited to coresident members of the young parent's household. Longitudinal assessments of unmarried African American adolescent mothers indicate that members of the mother's family of origin continue to bear an inordinate amount of the financial and emotional burden beyond the pregnancy and well into the child's early years (Burton, 1985, 1990a, 1992; Conner, 1988; Furstenburg, 1976; Furstenburg, Brooks-Gunn, & Morgan, 1987; Willard-Williams, 1991). Grandparents, especially grandmothers, but often grandfathers, great-grandmothers, and great-grandfathers, have been identified in numerous studies as critical actors in the successful negotiation of the transition to parenthood for African American adolescent mothers. The negotiation of this transition is not without cost to the caregiver, but the maintenance of family solidarity is perceived as a greater objective (Apfel & Seitz, 1991; Burton, 1985, 1990b; Burton & Stack, 1989; Cherlin & Furstenburg, 1986; Elder, Caspi, & Burton, 1987; Flaherty, Facteau, & Garver, 1991; Kivett, 1991, 1993).

This chapter applies a life-course perspective (Clausen, 1986) to develop a conceptual framework that aids our understanding of how intergenerational relationships in African American families influence the successful negotiation of the transition into adolescent parenthood. The availability and provision of parental support for an adolescent parent implies that the adults providing that support have successfully negotiated the transition from the role of parent to grandparent. We explore two contexts that impact these transitions. The first is the temporal context, relating to the impact of sequencing on the transition into new family roles (Burton, 1985; Burton, Dilworth-Anderson, & Merriwether-de Vries, 1995; Burton & Sorensen, 1992; Elder, 1987; Elder, Caspi, & Burton, 1987; Giocorsica, 1972). The second is the developmental context relating to the transition through the life stages and roles that results from early parenting and grandparenting. The negotiation of these two contexts is irrefutably associated with the successful transition into parenthood (Burton & Bengeston, 1985; Burton & Dilworth-Anderson, 1991; Hagestad & Lang, 1986; Hamburg & Dixon, 1992; Hansen & Jacob, 1992; Pearson, Hunter, Ensminger, & Kellam, 1990). Our perspective is that attention must now be focused on the successful negotiation of the transition to grandparenthood if we hope to elucidate the nature of the contexts and circumstances in which adolescents begin their parenting careers.

We believe that for African Americans, the experience of adolescent pregnancy exerts a ubiquitous influence on the experience of role transitions for all family members. Historically the experience of many African American families has incorporated multigenerational family systems and households to counter the deleterious effects of financial hardship and economic and racial oppression. Adolescent parents rarely embark on their new role without any form of support from their family of origin (Hamburg & Dixon, 1992; Himes, 1992; Pearson et al., 1990). More often, the transition to parenthood for adolescents is characterized by increasing dependence on the family of origin for economic, emotional, and instrumental support. The addition of risk factors such as limited economic opportunities, dangerous neighborhood contexts, and single-parent households may increase the reliance on multigeneration childrearing strategies and lead to increased distribution of the impact of the role transition among family members (Burton & Dilworth-Anderson, 1991; Caldas, 1994; Furstenburg, 1976; Furstenburg et al., 1987; Pearson et al., 1990; Willard-Williams, 1991; Wilson, 1987).

Essentially, an adolescent's successful transition to parenthood implies that parents possess, and can communicate, a basic knowledge of what the role of parent entails. In addition, these new grandparents have also begun to negotiate the transition to grandparenthood. The consequence of an effective mutual progression is that the parental resources for emotional support are more likely to be available for both the adolescent parent and their offspring (Burton, 1985, 1990b; Harrison, Wilson, Pine, Chan, & Buriel, 1990; Kivett, 1991; Pearson et al., 1990; Rossi, 1980). Delineating the contextual parameters that influence the availability of parental resources requires the development of a framework that incorporates our knowledge of the heterogeneity of the African American experience pertaining to the transition to grandparenthood.

ESTABLISHING A RELEVANT FRAME OF REFERENCE

Historically the empirical and theoretical writings pertaining to African Americans have been predicated on models of disorganization and deficit (Dodson, 1988; McRoy, 1990; Moynihan, 1965). These deficit models characterized the African American family culture as a monolithic entity comprised of broken, illegitimate families and unstable households, tacitly ignoring the pervasive socioeconomic factors that contributed to the manifestation of disorganized family patterns. Additionally, these theories ignored the adaptive structures of the extended multigenerational family (Bernstein, 1991; Billingsley, 1968, 1990; Burton & Dilworth-Anderson, 1991; Hill, 1972; Stack, 1974).

Scholars in the mid-1970s began to challenge deficit models from diverse theoretical perspectives. These studies generally focused on the resiliency of the African American family system and its ability to persevere in the face of untenable odds (Allen, 1978; Boulin-Johnson, 1988; Dodson, 1988; Hale-Benson, 1986; Hill, 1972; Peters, 1988). Unfortunately, many of these models did not satisfactorily answer questions about the sources of the negative patterns observed and the maintenance of these negative patterns. The legacy of this paradigm shift has been a renewed emphasis on developing culturally relevant and sensitive models of family life among African Americans (Allen, 1978; Billingsley, 1990; Dilworth-Anderson, Burton, & Boulin-Johnson, 1993; Franklin, 1992; Hill, 1989; McAdoo, 1988; Washington & McLoyd, 1982).

New conceptual models have emanated as scholars are increasingly focusing attention on the intergenerational structure of African American familial relations (Bengston & Robertson, 1985; Burton & Bengston, 1985; Burton & Dilworth-Anderson, 1991; Hill, 1989; Hill & Shackelford, 1987; Hofferth, 1987; Kivett, 1993; Pearson et al., 1990). Intergenerational models have provided great insight into the experience of role transitions for African American adolescents, and the members of their extended family network. The transition to parenthood has traditionally been discussed in terms of the heterosexual marital dyad. Nonetheless, the introduction of a newborn into the family affects relationships within the immediate family and extended family in addition to the lives of the biological parents (Gibbs, 1992; Hansen & Jacob, 1992; Stevenson-Hinde, 1988).

Radke-Yarrow, Richters, and Wilson (1988) posited that researchers in the field of human development need to explore relationships occurring in domains beyond the traditional dyadic sphere. Their rationale is that the proposed expansion could more fully elucidate the nature of family interaction. Although these authors presented conceptual and empirical material gleaned from traditional two-parent, European American families, the lessons are equally applicable to researchers of African American families. Unfortunately, much research related to African American families replicates traditional models of dyadic relationships.

Finally, it is imperative that researchers acknowledge that much of the research on "early parenting" and "off-time grandparenting" are in fact studies of early mothering and grandmothering (Furstenburg et al., 1987; Gibbs, 1988; Hofferth, 1987; Kivett, 1991; Willard-Williams, 1991; Wilson, 1987). The nature of the transition to parenthood and grandparenthood as negotiated by African American males represents the most substantial lacuna in the existing literature. Although the body of work relating to the transitions of young mothers and grandmothers may have relevance to the transitions of young fathers and grandfathers, researchers must not assume that their experiences are identical (Gibbs, 1992; Klinman,

Sander, Rosa, Longo, & Martinez, 1985; Robinson, 1988; Sander & Rosen, 1987; Sullivan, 1990). Gender serves as a powerful mediator of all experience in the United States, and nothing inherent in the experience of early parenting and grandparenting reduces this influence.

APPLICABLE CONTEXTS FOR THE EXPLORATION OF FAMILY TRANSITIONS

Extending the model proposed by Burton, Dilworth-Anderson, and Merriwether-de Vries (1995), we begin with a conceptual discussion of the temporal context. We define the temporal context as a focus on the timing of entry to a new role and the specific sequencing and synchronization of assumption of the parental and grandparental roles relative to age, peer reactions, and other social roles (Bengeston & Allen, 1993; Elder, 1987; Rossi, 1980). Turkewitz and Devenny (1993) illustrated the complexity of identifying the temporal influence on developmental outcome. The probabalistic nature of developmental transitions is widely accepted, yet many theorists continue to structure assessments of developmental transitions within a deterministic framework. This tendency is often manifested in investigations of mediating events such as family support or personal history as monolithic entities with unidirectional effects. The result of this trend is that the variation in life-course patterns of African Americans is obscured (Billingsley, 1990).

The sequencing and synchronization of major life role transitions such as parenthood and grandparenthood is germane to any exploration of the temporal context (Burton & Sorensen, 1992; Hagestad, 1990; Hagestad & Lang, 1986). The timing of these role transitions is gauged in our society by specific social timetables. Social timetables are shared ideas of when key life changes should happen. These timing norms serve as implicit guides to individuals about the appropriate or inappropriate times to enter and exit specific roles over the course of the life span (Hogan, 1978; Neugarten, Moore, & Lowe, 1965; Wood, 1971).

Current research suggests that an inappropriate or "off-time entry" to certain roles may be associated with a greater number of negative family events due to role overload of family members charged with the role of providing support (Brim & Ryff, 1980; Burton, 1990b; Burton & Bengeston, 1985; Burton & Sorenson, 1992; Elder & Rockwell, 1976; Furstenburg, 1993; Furstenburg et al., 1987; Giorsca, 1972; Seltzer, 1976; Sullivan, 1990). Neugarten (1970) commented:

> It is the unanticipated, not the anticipated which is likely to represent the traumatic event. Major stresses are caused by events that upset the sequence

and rhythm of the expected life cycle, as when the death of a parent comes in adolescence rather than in middle age; when the birth of a child is too early or too late; when occupational achievement is delayed; when the empty nest grandparenthood, retirement, major illness, or widowhood occur off time. (p. 86)

Although the event of adolescent pregnancy occurs among African American families from a variety of sociocultural settings and socioeconomic contexts, empirical studies focusing on the intergenerational impact of teen pregnancy identify common stressors that impinge on the successful negotiation of the associated role transitions. Burton's (1985) study of young great-grandmothers who assumed primary care for the offspring of their adolescent grandchildren reported that respondents experienced considerable stress associated with the overload of role demands emanating from their "later life" childrearing responsibilities. Burton and deVries (1992), in an analysis of the challenges and rewards of surrogate parenting among 101 African American grandparents and great-grandparents, identified four sources of stress related to the off-time assumption of the role of primary parent. Grandparents who assumed this role of primary parent either off time, or as a function of nonnormative family life events consistently experienced four circumstances. First was an intensified perception of, and expectation for, the young grandparent to assume the instrumental responsibilities related to the daily maintenance of the household. Second was an increasing level of difficulty experienced by the young grandparent in attempting to meet the expectations for the academic, social, and physical activities of their grandchildren. Third, financial hardships were incurred. Fourth, there was insufficient time for young grandparents to meet their personal social and emotional needs.

Despite these challenges, the grandparents studied indicated that parenting the offspring of their adolescents was a rewarding endeavor. There were three perceived rewards that emerged. First, there was an opportunity to have another chance to "raise a child right," thus overcoming the presumed shortcomings that may have contributed to the pregnancy of their own adolescent. Second was the ability to nurture family legacies and traditions through the lives of their grandchildren. Finally, there was the receipt of the unconditional love and supportive companionship of a child.

An additional aspect of temporal context that is important for understanding the role of grandparents in the provision of a supportive environment for teenage parents is the concept of peer time (Burton & Sorenson, 1992). *Peer time* is the temporal spacing of role acquisitions among agemates, friends, or colleagues. The relationship between peer time and grandparenthood is hypothesized as follows: Individuals who assume primary responsibility for the child of an adolescent parent at the same time as a group of agemates, friends, or colleagues are more likely to view their roles more positively than individuals who do not have access to peer support. Peers who are experiencing off -time transitions together have access to group solidarity, and peer support because of their common life experience.

The transition of adolescents to the role of parent involves similar concerns related to the domains of social support and peer interaction. Negotiation of individuation tasks is often related to the availability of peer support and the formation of peer groups. Embarking on the role of parent limits an adolescent's access to the social world of nonparents because economic and instrumental responsibilities for their offspring frequently preclude the expenditure of precious resources on leisure activities (Burton, 1990b; Flaherty, 1988; Gibbs, 1988; Hofferth, 1987; Willard-Williams, 1991). Although the issue of temporal context is assumed to be salient for adolescent parents, it is important to recognize and explore the similarity of experience for grandparents.

Burton and Sorenson's (1993) ethnographic study of the caregiving responsibilities of African American grandparents indicate that respondents who did not have peers engaged in similar life tasks reported feeling isolated and "out of sync" with respect to the roles of their agemates. In contrast, those grandparents with peers engaged, to varying degrees, in augmenting the parenting efforts of their adolescents reported a stronger sense of social support. In the words of one respondent the perception that "her friends were dealing with the same frustrations and joys as she was" provided a sense of affinity with her peers. Access to social support has been identified as a crucial component in the successful transition through off-time grandparenting (Flaherty et al., 1991; Logan, Freeman, & McRoy, 1990). Thus, when off-time or early transitions into grandparenthood occur in a context of peer support, the process may evoke less disruption.

DEVELOPMENTAL CONTEXT

Developmental context is the second domain of interest. It is focused on (a) the process of initiating parental and grandparental roles and whether the process hinders or facilitates individual development among adolescent parents and young grandparents, and (b) how individual factors such as the compatibility of the developmental stages that the young grandparent and their grandchildren experience are negotiated (Burton & Sorenson, 1992). The developmental context is evaluated from the theoretical perspective of the life course, and is also informed by the literature of developmental psychology (Bengeston & Allen, 1993; Bronfenbrenner, 1986; Clausen, 1986).

Authors from the developmental perspective discuss notions of "the normal expectable life"—a set of seasons with characteristic preoccupations, changes, challenges, and rewards (Levinson, 1978). Psychodynamic approaches to the lifetimes of individuals emphasize how developmental changes and social context act in concert to present individuals with a series of developmental tasks (Erickson, 1982; Havinghurst, 1972). Erickson (1963, 1980), for example, described late adolescence and young adulthood as a period in which personal identity and intimacy must be achieved. Middle age is identified as the phase of life in which a sense of generativity is achieved. Havinghurst (1972) described the developmental tasks of young adulthood as involving differentiation from one's family of origin and the establishment of a new and independent family. In contrast, the developmental tasks of late life involve attaining integrity (Erickson, 1980), adjusting to the limitations created by diminished physical strength, shrinking social networks, and reduced income (Havinghurst, 1972). Inherent in each of these developmental tasks is the process of negotiating and resolving psychosocial tensions at each stage of life.

The life-course perspective is characterized by an emphasis on the examination of role transitions that occur at specific developmental stages. Role transitions occur within a socially recognized temporal context. Individual development within this social context facilitates the creation of shared expectations about the trajectory of adulthood. Events occurring outside of the presumed trajectory represent violations of shared expectations and may, in turn, be perceived as crises. Thus, timing of entry into the grandparent role has implications for the psychosocial development of the young grandparent, adolescent parent, and grandchild. For example, the timing of assuming primary responsibility for care of a grandchild may in some cases interfere with, and in others, facilitate the immediate developmental tasks individuals face at different life stages.

Consider the potential for conflict that ensues when a young grandparent is focused on adjusting to reduced social networks and the provision of child care. The assumption of primary child care is often aimed at facilitating adolescent autonomy and further reduces the grandparent's potential access to peer contact and support. This type of sacrifice may not be recognized by the adolescent parent and may contribute to the sense of limited reciprocity. Ethnographic studies of early grandparenting reveal that this conflict can have long-term repercussions for all involved (Apfel & Seitz, 1991; Baranowski, 1982; Burton, 1985, 1990b, 1992; Burton & Bengeston, 1985; Burton & Stack, 1989; Conner, 1988; Flaherty et al., 1991).

The process of negotiating developmental tasks is also affected by the individual's involvement with other people, with institutions, and with society at large (Kivnick, 1985). The assumption of off-time parenting responsibilities by grandparents can conflict with some of these involvements and thereby hinder the achievement of developmental tasks. For example, the main task of young adulthood involves establishing an identity, differentiating from family, and achieving intimacy. The transition to parenthood in adolescence is associated with higher levels of dependency on the family of origin for economic and instrumental assistance with childrearing. The grandparent's provision of primary economic support and child care is in conflict with the manifestation of independence for the adolescent and with the grandparent's development of roles beyond those associated primarily with family functions.

Burton (1992), in a study of early grandparents (age 27–36) who assumed the role of principal care provider for their grandchildren, reported that the majority of respondents expressed that they had insufficient time in their own lives without the additional responsibility of childrearing. Childrearing in this population is perceived as a constant pressure to push the child to grow up, do what other people their ages were doing, truly learn about who they were as individuals, and make decisions about what they wanted in life (Burton, 1992). This may impact the quality of parenting provided by grandmothers (Chase-Landsdale, Brooks-Gunn, & Zamsky, 1994).

The second aspect of developmental context we explore is the compatibility of developmental stages between the young grandparent and their grandchildren. Kivnick (1985) argued that grandparenting represents an "age appropriate involvement through which the grandparent may reface issues directly related to parenting (Generativity versus Stagnation), and perhaps less directly related to such other tensions as Identity versus Identity confusion; Industry versus Inferiority; Autonomy versus Shame and doubt" (p. 157). Thus grandparenthood may give individuals the opportunity to renew earlier psychosocial balances. Particularly in the case of compressed generations the process of embarking on the grandparent trajectory may allow the demonstration of successful childrearing strategies not developed during the parenting life stage (Burton, 1990b). Reciprocally, grandchildren as they move through developmental stages may have an opportunity to "pre-face" the tensions they will experience in later life through interacting with their grandparents.

Compatibility of developmental stage may also impinge on the process of parental value transmission from the young grandparent to the adolescent parent. Parental expectations for their adolescent's involvement in an intimate, committed male–female relationship are often violated as a result of early pregnancy (Burton, 1985, 1990b; Burton & de Vries, 1992; Furstenburg et al., 1987; Gibbs, 1988; Spencer, 1990). The perception of foreclosed opportunities for their adolescent's future marriage may encourage young grandparents to inculcate values that downplay the need for male–female mutuality and cooperation. This perception may be a contributing factor in the continued focus on the need to promote male responsibility for economic assistance to the exclusion of other forms of support (Conner, 1988; Robinson, 1988; Sander & Rosen, 1987; Sullivan, 1990; Stack, 1991). Unfortunately, this may result in setting the stage for continued male–female conflict, especially when adolescent fathers do not have access to the financial resources to comply with the provision of resources.

In a recently completed ethnographic study, Eggeletion (1994) explored the expectations of young African American grandmothers and their pregnant or parenting daughters pursuant to male–female relationships. The findings are consistent with numerous studies, in that they demonstrate that respondents focus on the provision of resources as a salient factor in the assessment of relationship satisfaction (Gibbs, 1988; Robinson, 1988; Sullivan, 1990). Both adolescent and adult respondents reported that assuming responsibility for the economic and instrumental needs of both mother and child is essential to maintenance of the male–female relationship. Adult mothers expressed the importance of having a man with a job, who could take care of them, regardless of the woman's ability or willingness to share her own financial earnings with her male partner. Teen mothers also reported a preference for mutual material and financial exchange with their partners. This exchange of resources resembled the "swapping" process detailed by Stack (1974). Although the male–female relationships among adolescent parents were not initiated to alleviate the impact of poverty, economic exchange represents an essential component to the maintenance of these relationships.

The partners of the adolescent mothers in this sample provide a much-needed financial resource when unexpected expenses arise. In addition, these young men potentially provide a source to fulfilling the financial "wants" that are not available from the young mother's household. Although financial exchange is important when discussing the expectations young mothers have within their relationships, it does not tell the whole story. Performance of instrumental tasks, including child care, honesty, communication, and emotional support were also described as important expectations for males (Eggeletion, 1994). Conflicts may emerge when expectation of appropriate role performance differ across generations (Burton, 1990b; Gibbs, 1988; Logan et al., 1990; Robinson, 1988; Sanders & Rosen, 1987; Stack, 1991; Wilson, 1986).

Current research suggests that from a developmental perspective, the connectedness between grandparents and their grandchildren is particularly beneficial for adolescents (Dellman-Jenkins, Papalia, & Lopez, 1987; Matthews & Sprey, 1985). Other research indicates that the supportive effects of parental involvement are only present for younger mothers who coreside with their mothers. The data suggest that the patterns for older adolescent mothers may be quite different (Chase-Landsdale et al., 1994). Baranowski (1982) suggested that close relationships between teens and their grandparents may be beneficial to the successful resolution of adolescent identity issues. Little is known about the impact of adolescent pregnancy on those relationships. Further research is needed to explore the process of the transition to great-grandparenthood and its influence on young grandparents' development.

The research cited concerning the benefits of synchrony between the developmental stages of grandparents and grandchildren principally explores the relationship among White middle-class families where grandparents do not necessarily assume the surrogate or coparent role. Consequently, a number of questions emerge with respect to developmental synchrony in the situations of young parents and grandparents. Is the developmental life course similar for children whose grandparents are actively engaged in parenting compared to those who are reared exclusively by adolescent parents? What are the developmental rewards and liabilities for young parents and grandparents who engage in coparenting? What are the long-term consequences for the intergenerational family relationship in coparenting and surrogate parenting relationships?

The sociohistorical literature on the life course of extended Black families suggests that many Black grandparents have served as either coparents or surrogate parents to their grandchildren (Burton & Sorenson, 1992; Huling, 1978; Lensoff-Caravaglia, 1982; Scott, 1991; White, 1985). Often grandparents assume these roles in response to cultural precedence, historical events, and the needs of extended kin (Hill & Shackelford, 1987; Jackson, 1971; F. C. Jones, 1973; J. Jones, 1985). This pattern is likely to continue as the demographic trends indicating increases in adolescent fertility are maintained. The adaptive strategies that promote success in the short run may establish circumstances that continue the cycle of early childbearing. Rather than "blaming the victim," recognition of the long-term impact of coping strategies may portend a shift in the patterns of adolescent fertility.

DIRECTIONS FOR FUTURE RESEARCH

The objective of this chapter was to suggest ways for social scientists to begin conceptualizing investigations of the contexts in which the transition to parenthood and grandparenthood occur. Clearly there are additional contexts beyond the developmental and temporal contexts to be explored. Additional investigations must expand to include the role of gender, socioeconomic, and neighborhood contexts on these transitions. Future studies of grandparenting among young African Americans must expand the current knowledge base by acknowledging the heterogeneity of the transition experience. Research must examine these transitions not only in highly dependent, at-risk intergenerational family networks, but also in families whose structure and composition offer alternative options for grandparental behavior.

It is our hope that the ideas presented in this chapter stimulate the formation of research questions pertaining to the transition to parenthood for adolescent African Americans rather than answer questions about the transition. We contend that a rigorous research, policy, and education agenda will occur when these issues are pursued.

REFERENCES

Allen, W. R. (1978). The search for applicable theories of Black family life. *Journal of Marriage and the Family, 40*, 117–129.

Apfel, M. D., & Seitz, V. (1991). Four models of adolescent mother–grandmother relationships in Black inner city families. *Family Relations, 40*, 421–429.

Baranowski, M. D. (1982). Grandparent–adolescent relations: Beyond the nuclear family. *Adolescence, 17*, 575–584.

Bengeston, V., & Allen, K. R. (1993). Life course perspectives applied to the family. In P. G. Boss, W. Dougherty, R. La Rossa, W. Schuman, & S. K. Steinmetz (Eds.), *Sourcebook of family theories and methods: A contextual approach* (pp. 469–498). New York: Plenum.

Bengston, V. L., & Robertson, J. F. (1985). *Grandparenthood: Research and policy perspectives.* Beverly Hills, CA: Sage.

Bernstein, B. (1991). Since the Moynihan report. In R. Staples (Ed.), *The Black family: Essays and studies* (pp. 23–27). Belmont, CA: Wadsworth.

Billingsley, A. (1968). *Black families in White America.* Englewood Cliffs, NJ: Prentice-Hall.

Billingsley, A. (1990). Understanding African-American family diversity. In J. Dewart (Ed.), *The state of Black America 1990* (pp. 85–105). New York: National Urban League.

Boulin-Johnson, L. (1988). Perspectives on Black family empirical research: 1965–1978. In H. P. McAdoo (Ed.), *Black families* (2nd ed., pp. 91–106). Newbury Park, CA: Sage.

Brim, O. G., & Ryff, C. D. (1980). On the properties of life events. In P. B. Baltes & O. G. Brim (Eds.), *Life span development and behavior* (Vol. 3, pp. 386–388). New York: Academic Press.

Bronfenbrenner, U. (1986). Ecology of the family as a context for human development: Research perspectives. *Developmental Psychology, 22*, 723–742.

Brooks-Gunn, J., & Chase-Landsdale, L. P. (1994). *Adolescent parenthood.* Unpublished manuscript, Virginia & Leonard Marx Center for Children and Families, Teachers College, Columbia University, New York.

Burton, L. M. (1985). *Early and on-time grandparenthood in multi-generation Black families.* Unpublished doctoral dissertation, The University of Southern California, Los Angeles.

Burton L. M. (1990a, November). *Grandparents as parents in drug-addicted families.* Paper presented at the annual meeting of the Gerontological Association of America, Boston, MA.

Burton L. M. (1990b). Teenaged childbearing as an alternative life-course strategy in multigeneration Black families. *Human Nature, 1*(2), 123–143.

Burton, L. M. (1992). Black grandparents rearing children of drug addicted parents: Stressors outcomes and social service needs. *The Gerontologist, 32*, 744–751.

Burton, L. M., & Bengeston, V. L. (1985). Black grandmothers: Issues of timing and meaning in roles. In V. L. Bengeston & J. Robertson (Eds.), *Grandparenthood: Research and policy perspectives* (pp. 61–77). Beverly Hills, CA: Sage.

Burton, L. M., & de Vries, C. A. (1992). Challenges and rewards: African-American grandparents as surrogate parents. *Generations, 17,* 51–54.

Burton, L. M., & Dilworth-Anderson, P. (1991). The intergenerational family roles of aged Black Americans. *Marriage & Family Review, 16,* 311–330.

Burton, L. M., Dilworth-Anderson, P., & Merriwether-de Vries, C. (1995). Context and surrogate parenting among contemporary grandparents. *Marriage & Family Review, 20,* 349–366.

Burton, L. M., & Sorenson, S. (1993). Temporal context and the caregiver role: Perspectives from ethnographic studies of multigeneration African-American families. In S. H. Zarit, L. I. Pearlin, & K. W. Schaie (Eds.), *Caregiving systems: Informal and formal helpers* (pp. 47–66). Hillsdale, NJ: Lawrence Erlbaum Associates.

Burton, L. M., & Stack, C. B. (1989, April). *Kinscripts and adolescent childbearing.* Paper presented at the conference Interdisciplinary Perspectives on Adolescent Pregnancy, Stanford, CA.

Caldas, S. J. (1994, January). Teen pregnancy: Why it remains a serious social, economic and educational problem in the U.S. *Phi Delta Kappan,* pp. 402–406.

Chase-Lansdale, P. L., Brooks-Gunn, J., & Zamsky, E. S. (1994). Young African-American families in poverty: Quality of mothering and grandmothering. *Child Development, 65,* 373–393.

Cherlin, A. J., & Furstenburg, F. F. (1986). *The new American grandparent.* New York: Basic Books.

Clausen, J. A. (1986). *The life course.* Englewood Cliffs, NJ: Prentice-Hall.

Conner, M. E. (1988). Teenage fatherhood: Issues confronting young Black males. In J. T. Gibbs (Ed.), *Young Black and male in America: An endangered species* (pp. 188–218). New York: Auburn House.

DeJong, G. F., Cornwall, G. T., & Wilmouth, J. M. (1993). *The well-being of children and youth in Pennsylvania demographic trends.* Harrisburg, PA: The Population Research Institute, The Pennsylvania State University, and The Pennsylvania State Data Center.

Dellmann-Jenkins, M., Papalia, P., & Lopez, M. (1987). Teenagers recorded interactions with grandparents: Exploring the extent of alienation. *Lifestyles: A Journal of Changing Patterns, 3–4,* 35–46.

Dilworth-Anderson, P., Burton, L. M., & Boulin-Johnson, L. (1993). Reframing theories for understanding race, ethnicity and families. In P. G. Boss, W. J. Dougherty, R. LaRossa, W. R. Schumm, & S. K. Steinmetz (Eds.), *Sourcebook of family theories and methods: A contextual approach* (pp. 627–646). New York: Plenum.

Dodson, J. (1988). Conceptualizations of Black families. In H. P. McAdoo (Ed.), *Black families* (2nd ed., pp. 77–90). Newbury Park, CA: Sage.

Eggeletion, L. E. (1994). *Stereotypes and expectations in African-American relationships: A qualitative and quantitative analysis of pregnant adolescents and their mothers.* Unpublished master's thesis, The Pennsylvania State University, University Park.

Elder, G. H., Jr. (1987). Families and lives, some developments in lifecourse studies. *Journal of Family History, 12,* 179–199.

Elder, G. H., Caspi, A., & Burton, L. M. (1987). Adolescent transition in development perspective: Sociological and historical insights. In M. Gunnar (Ed.), *Minnesota symposium on child development* (Vol. 21, pp. 121–143). Hillsdale, NJ: Lawrence Erlbaum Associates.

Elder, G. H., & Rockwell, R. (1976). Marital timing and women's life patterns. *Journal of Family History, 4,* 34–53.

Erickson, E. H. (1963). *Childhood and society* (2nd ed.). New York: Norton.

Erickson, E. H. (1980). On generational cycle: An address. *International Journal of Psycho-analysis, 61*, 213–233.

Erickson, E. H. (1982). *The life cycle completed.* New York: Norton.

Flaherty, M. J. (1988). Seven caring functions of Black grandmothers in adolescent mothering. *Maternal-Child Nursing Journal, 17*, 191–207.

Flaherty, M. J., Facteau, L., & Garver, P. (1991). Grandmother functions in multigenerational families: An exploratory study of Black adolescent mothers and their infants. In R. Staples (Ed.), *The Black family: Essays and studies* (4th ed., pp. 193–200). Belmont, CA: Wadsworth.

Franklin, D. L. (1992). Early childbearing patterns among African-Americans: A socio-historical perspective. In M. K. Rosenheim & M. F. Testa (Eds.), *Early parenthood and coming of age in the 1990's* (pp. 55–70). New Brunswick, NJ: Rutgers University Press.

Furstenburg, F. F. (1976). *Unplanned pregnancy: The social consequences of teenaged childbearing.* New York: The Free Press.

Furstenburg, F. F., Brooks-Gunn, J., & Morgan, S. P. (1987). *Adolescent pregnancy in later life.* New York: Cambridge University Press.

Geronimous, A. T. (1987). On teenage childbearing and neonatal mortality in the United States. *Population and Development Review, 13*, 245–279.

Geronimous, A. T., & Korenman, S. (1992). The socioeconomic consequences of teen childbearing reconsidered. *Quarterly Journal of Economics, 107*, 1187–1214.

Giorsca, V. (1972). On social time. In H. Yanker (Ed.), *The future of time* (pp. 10–37). Garden City, NY: Anchor Books.

Gibbs, J. T. (1988). *Young, Black and male in America: An endangered species.* Dover, MA: Auburn House.

Gibbs, J. T. (1992). The social context of teenage pregnancy and parenting in the Black community: Implications for public policy. In M. K. Rosenheim & M. F. Testa (Eds.), *Early parenthood and coming of age in the 1990's* (pp. 71–89). New Brunswick, NJ: Rutgers University Press.

Hagestad, G. O. (1990). Social perspectives on the life course. In R. Binstock & L. George (Eds.), *Handbook of aging and the social sciences* (3rd ed., pp. 35–61). New York: Van Nostrand & Reinhold.

Hagestad, G. O., & Lang, M. E. (1986). The transition to grandparenthood: Unexplored issues. *Journal of Family Issues, 7*, 115–130.

Hale-Benson, J. E. (1986). *Black children: Their roots, culture, and learning styles.* Baltimore, MD: Johns Hopkins University Press.

Hamburg, B. A., & Dixon, S. L. (1992). Adolescent pregnancy and parenthood. In M. K. Rosenheim & M. F. Testa (Eds.), *Early parenthood and coming of age in the 1990's* (pp. 17–33). New Brunswick, NJ: Rutgers University Press.

Hansen, L. B., & Jacob, E. (1992). Intergenerational support during the transition to parenthood: Issues for new parents and grandparents. *Families in Society: The Journal of Contemporary Human Services, 73*(8), 471–481.

Harrison, A. O., Wilson, M. N., Pine, C. J., Chan, S. Q., & Buriel, R. (1990). Family ecologies of ethnic minority children. *Child Development, 61*, 347–362.

Havinghurst, R. J. (1972). *Developmental tasks and education* (3rd ed.). New York: D. McKay.

Hill, R. B. (1989). Critical issues for Black families in the year 2000. In J. Dewart (Ed.), *The state of Black America 1989.* New York: National Urban League.

Hill, R. B. (1972). *The strength of Black families.* New York: Emerson Hall.

Hill, R., & Shackelford, L. (1987). The Black extended family revisited. *The Urban League Review, 1*, 18–24.

Himes, C. L. (1992). Social demography of contemporary families and aging. *Generations, 17*, 13–16.

Hofferth, S. L. (1987). The children of teen childbearers. In S. L. Hofferth & C. D. Hayes (Eds.), *Risking the future: Adolescent sexuality, pregnancy, and childbearing* (pp. 174–206). Washington, DC: National Academy Press.

Hogan, D. P. (1978). The demography of life-span transitions: Temporal and gender comparisons. In A. Rossi (Ed.), *Gender and the life course* (pp. 65–78). New York: Aldine.

Hogan, D. P., Astone, N. M., & Kitagwa, E. M. (1985). Social and environmental factors influencing contraceptive use among Black adolescents. *Family Planning Perspectives, 17,* 167–169.

Huling, W. P. (1978). Evolving family roles for the Black elderly. *Aging, 27,* 21–27.

Jackson, J. J. (1971). Sex and social class variation in Black aged parent–adult child relationships. *Aging and Human Development, 2,* 96–107.

Jones, F. C. (1973). The lofty role of the Black grandmother. *Crisis, 89.*

Jones, J. (1985). *Labor of love, labor of sorrow: Black women, work and the family from slavery to the present.* New York: Basic Books.

Kivett, V. R. (1991). The grandparent–grandchild connection. *Marriage and Family Review, 16*(3–4), 267–290.

Kivett, V. R. (1993). Racial comparisons of the grandmother role: Implications for strengthening the family support system of older Black women. *Family Relations, 42,* 165–172.

Kivnick, H. Q. (1985, August). *Grandparenthood and life cycle.* Paper presented at the annual meeting of the American Psychological Association, Toronto, Ontario.

Klinman, D. G., Sander, J. H., Rosa, J. L., Longo, K. R., & Martinez, L. P. (1985). *Reaching and servicing the teenage father.* New York: Bank Street College of Education.

Lensoff-Caravaglia, G. (1982). The Black granny and the Soviet babushka: Commonalities and contrasts. In R. C. Manuel (Ed.), *Minority aging: Social and psychological issues.* Westport, CT: Greenwood.

Levinson, D. J. (1978). *The seasons of a man's life.* New York: Ballantine Books.

Logan, S. M. L., Freeman, E., & McRoy, R. G. (1990). Treatment considerations for working with pregnant Black adolescents, their families, and their partners. In M. L. Logan, E. M. Freeman, & R. G. McRoy (Eds.), *Social work practice with Black families: A culturally specific perspective* (pp. 148–169). Reading, MA: Addison-Wesley.

Matthews, S. H., & Sprey, J. (1985). Adolescents' relationships with grandparents: An empirical contribution to conceptual clarification. *Journal of Gerontology, 40,* 621–626.

McAdoo, H. P. (1988). Transgenerational patterns of upward mobility in African-American families. In H. P. McAdoo (Ed.), *Black families* (2nd ed., pp. 148–168). Newbury Park, CA: Sage.

McRoy, R. G. (1990). A historical overview of Black families. In M. L. Logan, E. M. Freeman, & R. G. McRoy (Eds.), *Social work practice with Black families: A culturally specific perspective* (pp. 3–17). Reading, MA: Addison-Wesley.

Moynihan, D. P. (1965). *The Negro family: A case for national action.* Washington, DC: Office of Policy Planning and Research, U.S. Department of Labor.

National Center for Health Statistics. (1993). Advance report of final natality statistics 1991. *Monthly Vital Statistics Report, 42.*

Neugarten, B. (1970). Dynamics of transition of middle to old age: Adaptation in the life cycle. *Journal of Geriatric Psychology, 4,* 71–87.

Neugarten, B. L., Moore, J. W., & Lowe, J. C. (1965). Age norms, age constraints, and adult socialization. *American Journal of Sociology, 70,* 710–717.

Pearson, L. L., Hunter, A. G., Ensminger, M. E., & Kellam, S. (1990). Black grandmothers in multigenerational households: Diversity in family structure and parenting involvement in the Woodlawn community. *Child Development, 61,* 434–442.

Peters, M. F. (1988). Parenting in Black families with young children: A historical perspective. In H. P. McAdoo (Ed.), *Black families* (2nd ed., pp. 228–241). Newbury Park, CA: Sage.

Radke-Yarrow, M., Richters, J., & Wilson, W. E. (1988). Child development in a network of relationships. In R. A. Hinde & J. Stevenson-Hinde (Eds.), *Relationships within families: Mutual influences* (pp. 48–68). New York: Oxford University Press.

Robinson, B. (1988). *Teenage fathers*. Lexington, MA: Lexington Books

Rossi, A. (1980). Life-span theories and women's lives. *Signs: Journal of Women in Culture and Society, 6,* 4–32.

Sanders, J. H., & Rosen, J. L. (1987). Teenage fathers: Working with the neglected partner in adolescent childbearing. *Family Planning Perspectives, 19,* 107–110.

Scott, Y. K. (1991). *The habit of surviving.* New York: Ballantine Books.

Seltzer, M. (1976). Suggestions for the examination of time-disordered relationships. In J. F. Gubrium (Ed.), *Time, roles, and self in old age.* New York: Human Sciences Press.

Spencer, M. B. (1990). Parental value transmission: Implications for the development of African-American children. In H. E. Cheatham & J. B. Stewart (Eds.), *Black families: Interdisciplinary perspectives* (pp. 111–130). New Brunswick, NJ: Transaction.

Stack, C. B. (1974). *All our kin: Strategies for survival in a Black community.* New York: Harper & Row.

Stack, C. B. (1991). Sex roles and survival strategies in an urban Black community. In R. Staples (Ed.), *The Black family: Essays and studies* (pp. 106–116). Belmont, CA: Wadsworth.

Stevenson-Hinde, J. (1988). Individuals in relationships. In R. A. Hinde & J. Stevenson-Hinde (Eds.), *Relationships within families: Mutual influences* (pp. 68–82). New York: Oxford University Press.

Sullivan, M. L. (1990). *The male role in teenage pregnancy and parenting: New directions for public policy.* New York: Vera Institute of Justice.

Turkewitz, G., & Devenny, D. A. (1993). *Developmental time and timing.* Hillsdale, NJ: Lawrence Erlbaum Associates.

Washington, E. D., & McLoyd, V. L. (1982). The external validity of research involving American minorities. *Human Development, 25,* 324–339.

White, D. G. (1985). *Arn't I a woman? Female slaves in the plantation south.* New York: Norton.

Willard-Williams, C. (1991). *Black teenage mothers: Pregnancy and childrearing from their perspective.* Lexington, MA: Lexington Books.

Wilson, M. N. (1986). The Black extended family: An analytical consideration. *Developmental Psychology, 22,* 246–258.

Wilson, W. J. (1987). *The truly disadvantaged: The inner city, the underclass and public policy.* Chicago: University of Chicago Press.

Wood, V. (1971). Age-appropriate behavior for older persons. *The Gerontologist, 11*(3), 74–78.

IV

SCHOOL AND WORK TRANSITIONS

10

School Transitions in Early Adolescence: What Are We Doing to Our Young People?

Jacquelynne S. Eccles
Sarah Lord
University of Michigan

Christy Miller Buchanan
Wake Forest University

There has been growing concern with adolescence as a time of risk. By whatever criteria one uses, a substantial portion of U.S. adolescents are not succeeding: Between 15% and 30% (depending on ethnic group) drop out of school before completing high school, adolescents have the highest arrest rate of any age group, and increasing numbers of adolescents consume alcohol and other drugs on a regular basis (Office of Educational Research and Improvement, 1988). In addition, the prevalence of several types of clinical dysfunctions increases at this time (Kazdin, 1993). For example, there is an increase in the prevalence of depression and eating disorders, particularly among females. Perhaps most serious, the incidence of attempted and completed suicides increases dramatically with the onset of adolescence.

Many of these problems appear to begin during the early adolescent years (Carnegie Council on Adolescent Development, 1989). Why? Several investigators have suggested that the transition to junior high school may contribute to the emergence of these problems (Eccles et al., 1993; Simmons & Blyth, 1987). This transition occurs at a time when most young adolescents are also experiencing the physical, psychological, and social changes associated with adolescence, including the new role demands presented by parents, peers, and teachers. Moreover, the environments of traditional junior high schools are usually quite different from those of elementary schools. Several investigators have argued that these differences undermine healthy development for many youth (e.g., Eccles et al., 1993; Simmons & Blyth, 1987). The first part of this chapter focuses on this hypothesis.

Difficulties with this transition, however, are by no means universal. Hirsch and Rapkin (1987), for example, found no change in self-esteem in students making the transition from sixth grade into a junior high school. These authors did report, however, an increase in depressive symptomatology in girls making the transition as compared to boys. Other studies have also found no change in the self-esteem of children making the transition (e.g., Fenzel & Blyth, 1986; Hawkins & Berndt, 1985; Nottelmann, 1987). Although some of these differences undoubtedly reflect variations across studies in populations, school environments, and varying methodological techniques, it is likely that individual differences in young adolescents' responses to the transition to junior high school also play a role. In support of this hypothesis, several studies have found negative changes for some youth and not for others. For example, Simmons and Blyth (1987) found that girls already involved in dating and showing the most advanced pubertal development were most at risk for negative changes in their self-esteem in conjunction with the transition to junior high school. Similarly, Midgley, Feldlaufer, and Eccles (1988a, 1989) found more extreme negative effects of the junior high school transition on low-achieving students. Thus, it is probable that some adolescents adapt well to the transition, whereas others find the transition more difficult. What factors influence individual differences in the response to the junior high school transition? The second part of this chapter focuses on this question.

GENERAL DEVELOPMENTAL CHANGES
IN ADOLESCENTS' SCHOOL MOTIVATION
AND SELF-CONFIDENCE

The Possible Effects of Stage–Environment Match

Several investigators have reported mean level declines at early adolescence in such motivational constructs as interest in school (Epstein & McPartland, 1976), intrinsic motivation (Harter, 1981), theories about the nature of ability (Stipek & Mac Iver, 1989), and self-concepts (Eccles, Midgley, & Adler, 1984; Eccles et al., 1989; Simmons & Blyth, 1987; Wigfield, Eccles, MacIver, & Reuman, 1991). Furthermore, these declines appear to be associated with the junior high school transition. For example, Simmons and Blyth (1987) found a marked decline in some young adolescents' school grades as they move into junior high school. Furthermore, the magnitude of this decline was predictive of subsequent school failure and drop out. Simmons and Blyth (1987) also reported declines in self-esteem among girls making the junior high school transition. There are also reports of similarly timed developmental increases in such negative motivational and behavioral characteristics as focus on self-evaluation rather than task mastery (Maehr & Anderman, 1993; Midgley, Anderman, & Hicks, 1995; Nicholls, 1980; Roeser, Midgley, & Maehr, 1994), and both truancy and school drop out (Rosenbaum, 1976; see Eccles et al., 1984, for a full review). Although these changes are not extreme for most adolescents, there is sufficient evidence of gradual decline in various indicators of academic motivation, behavior, and self-perception over the early adolescent years to make one wonder what is happening (see Eccles & Midgley, 1989, for a review).

A variety of explanations have been offered to explain these "negative" changes. Some have suggested that these declines result from the intrapsychic upheaval assumed to be associated with early adolescent development (e.g., Freud, 1969; Hamburg, 1974). Others have suggested that it is the coincidence of the timing of multiple life changes. For example, Simmons and her colleagues have demonstrated that the coincidence of the junior high school transition with pubertal development accounts for the declines in the school-related measures and self-esteem (e.g., Blyth, Simmons, & Carlton-Ford, 1983; Simmons & Blyth, 1987; see also Crockett, Petersen, Graber, Schulenberg, & Ebata, 1989). Drawing on cumulative stress theory, these theorists suggested that declines in motivation result from the fact that adolescents making the transition to junior high school at the end of Grade 6 must cope with two major transitions: pubertal change and school change. Because coping with multiple transitions is more difficult than coping with only one, these adolescents are at greater risk of negative outcomes than adolescents who only have to cope with pubertal change during this developmental period. To test this hypothesis, Simmons and her colleagues have compared the pattern of changes on young adolescents' school-related outcomes for children who move from sixth to seventh grade in a K–8, 9–12 system with the pattern of change for children who make the same grade transition in a K–6, 7–9, 10–12 school system. This work unconfounds the conjoint effects of age and transition operating in most developmental studies of this age period. These researchers find clear evidence, especially among girls, of greater negative change among children making the junior high school transition than among children remaining in the same school setting. The fact that the junior high school transition effects are especially marked for girls provides additional support for the cumulative stress theory, because girls are more likely than boys to be undergoing both a school transition and pubertal change at this age.

We have obtained similar findings using the data from the National Educational Longitudinal Study. We compared eighth graders in a K–8 school system with eighth graders in either a K–6, 7–9 system or a K–5, 6–8 system. The eighth-grade students in the K–8 systems looked better on several motivational indicators such as self-esteem, preparedness, and attendance than the students in either of the other two types of school systems (Eccles, Lord, & Midgley, 1991). In addition, the eighth-grade teachers in the K–8 system reported fewer student problems, less truancy, and more student engagement than the teachers in either of the other two types of school systems. Clearly both the young adolescents and their teachers seem to be faring better in K–8 school systems than those in the more prevalent junior high school and middle school systems. Why?

Several investigators have suggested that the changing nature of the educational environments experienced by many young adolescents may also explain both these types of school system differences and the mean level declines in the school-related measures associated with the junior high school transition (e.g., Eccles, 1993; Eccles & Midgley, 1989; Eccles et al., 1984; Simmons & Blyth, 1987). Drawing on person–environment fit theory (see Hunt, 1975), Eccles and Midgley (1989) proposed that these motivational and behavioral declines could result from the fact that junior high schools are not providing appropriate educational environments for many young adolescents. According to person–environment theory, behavior, motivation, and mental health are influenced by the fit between the characteristics individuals bring to their social environments and the characteristics of these social environments. Individuals are not likely to do very well, or be very motivated, if they are in social environments that do not fit their psychological needs. If the social environments in the typical junior high school do not fit very well with the psychological needs of adolescents, then person–environment fit theory predicts a decline in the adolescents' motivation, interest, performance, and behavior as they move into this environment. Furthermore, Eccles and Midgley (1989) argued that this effect should be even more marked if the children experience a fundamental change in their school environment when they move into a junior high school or middle school; that is, if the school environment of the junior high school or middle school fits less well with their psychological needs than the school environment of the elementary school.

Is there any evidence that such a negative change in the school environment occurs with the transition to junior high school? Yes, and it occurs at both the macro and micro levels. For example, Simmons and Blyth (1987) enumerated the following types of macro changes: increased school size, increased bureaucratic organization, increased departmentalization, and decreased teacher–student individual contact and opportunity to have a close relationship with a particular teacher. Simmons and Blyth (1987) suggested that such changes put young adolescents at risk in several ways. Because early adolescence is a period of exploration, youth in this developmental period are likely to try out various types of behaviors and identities. Although such experimentation is both healthy and normal, it can also be quite risky. Successful passage through this period of experimentation requires a tight safety net carefully monitored by caring adults—adults who provide opportunities for experimentation without letting the youth seriously mortgage their futures in the process. Clearly the large, bureaucratic structure of the typical junior high and middle school is ill suited to such a task. In addition, Higgins and Parsons (1983) suggested that the increased size results in the disruption of one's peer network at a time when peer relations are especially important. Each of these characteristics of the junior high school transition could have detrimental effects on young adolescents, especially those already somewhat at risk due to psychological, social, or academic problems.

Although remarkably few empirical studies have been done on more microlevel changes in the classroom environment, there is some evidence of negative changes at this level. Looking across the various relevant studies, the following five patterns seem especially important for this discussion. First, junior high school classrooms, as compared to elementary school classrooms, are characterized by a greater emphasis on teacher control and discipline and fewer opportunities for student decision making, choice, and self-management (e.g., Brophy & Evertson, 1976; Midgley & Feldlaufer, 1987; Midgley, Feldlaufer, & Eccles, 1988b; Moos, 1979). For example, in our own work with the Michigan Study of Adolescent Life Transitions (MSALT), sixth-grade elementary school teachers in 12 different school districts reported less concern with controlling and disciplining their students than these same students' seventh-grade junior high school math teachers reported 1 year later (Midgley et al., 1988b). Similar differences emerged on our indicators of student opportunity to participate in decision making regarding their own learning (see also Ward et al., 1982).

Such differences in the opportunity for participation in decision making and self-control are likely to be especially problematic for young adolescents. This is a time in development when youth begin to think of themselves as young adults. It is also a time when they increase their exploration of possible identities. They believe they are becoming more responsible and, consequently, deserving of greater adult respect. Presumably, the adults responsible for their socialization would also like to encourage them to become more responsible for themselves as they move toward adulthood. In fact, this is what typically happens across the elementary school grades (see Eccles & Midgley, 1989). Unfortunately, the evidence suggests this developmentally appropriate progression is disrupted with the transition to junior high school. Advocates of the stage–environment fit theory would predict that such a developmentally disruptive and perhaps regressive change in the school environment is likely to undermine the motivation and engagement of the young adolescents experiencing the change.

Second, junior high school classrooms, as compared to elementary school classrooms, are characterized by less personal and positive teacher–student relationships (see Eccles & Midgley, 1989). For example, in the MSALT study, both students and observers rated junior high school math teachers as less friendly, less supportive, and less caring than the teachers these students had 1 year earlier in the last year of elementary school (Feldlaufer, Midgley, & Eccles, 1988). In addition, the seventh-grade teachers in this study also reported that they trusted the students less than did these students' sixth-grade teachers (Midgley et al., 1988b). Such a shift in the quality of student–teacher relationships is likely to be especially detrimental at this stage of development. Adolescence is a time when children are trying to find their own identity. This process often involves questioning the values and expectations of one's parents. In more traditional cultures, children have the opportunity to do this questioning with supportive nonparental adults such as religious counselors, neighbors, and relatives. In our highly mobile, complex society, such opportunities are not as readily available. Teachers are the one stable source of nonparental adults left for many U.S. youth. Unfortunately, the sheer size and bureaucratic nature of most junior high schools, coupled with the stereotypes we hold regarding the negative characteristics of adolescents, lead teachers to distrust their students and to withdraw emotionally from them (see Eccles et al., 1993; Miller et al., 1990). Consequently, these students have little choice but to turn to peers as nonparental guides in their exploration of alternative identities. Evidence from a variety of sources suggests that this can be a very risky solution for many youth. The demise of the close relationship between students and teachers has another unfortunate consequence for children at this age: It decreases the likelihood that teachers will be able to identify students on the verge of getting themselves into serious trouble and to get these students the help they need. In this way, the holes in the safety net may become too big to prevent unnecessary "failures."

Third, the shift to junior high school is associated with an increase in practices such as whole-class task organization, between classroom ability grouping, and public evaluation of the correctness of work (see Eccles & Midgley, 1989). For example, in the Junior High School Transition Study (Rounds & Osaki, 1982), whole-group instruction was the norm in the seventh grade, small-group instruction was rare and individualized instruction was not observed at all. In contrast, the sixth-grade teachers mixed whole- and small-group instruction within and across subject areas (Rounds & Osaki, 1982). Similar shifts toward increased whole-class instruction with most students working on the same assignments at the same time, using the same textbooks, and the same homework assignments were evident in the MSALT (Feldlaufer et al., 1988). In addition, several reports have documented the increased use of between-class ability grouping beginning at junior high school (e.g., Oakes, 1981). Changes such as these are likely to increase social comparison, concerns about evaluation, and competitiveness (see Eccles et al., 1984). Such changes may also increase the likelihood that teachers will use normative grading criteria and more public forms of evaluation, both of which have been shown to impact negatively on many young adolescents' self-perceptions and motivations. These changes may also make aptitude differences more salient to both teachers and students, leading to increased teacher expectancy effects and decreased feelings of efficacy among teachers.

Fourth, junior high school teachers feel less effective as teachers, especially for low-ability students. This was one of the largest differences we found between sixth- and seventh-grade teachers in the MSALT study. Seventh-grade teachers in traditional junior high schools reported much less confidence in their teaching efficacy than sixth-grade elementary school teachers in the same school districts (Midgley et al., 1988b). This decline in teachers' sense of efficacy for teaching the less competent students could help explain why it is precisely these students that appear to give up on themselves following the junior high school transition.

Finally, junior high school teachers appear to use a more competitive standard in judging students' competence and in grading their performance than do elementary school teachers (see Eccles & Midgley, 1989). There is no stronger predictor of students' self-confidence and sense of personal efficacy for schoolwork than the grades they receive. If grades change, then we would expect to see a concomitant shift in the adolescents' self-perceptions and academic motivation. In fact, it appears that junior high school teachers do use stricter and more social comparison-based standards than elementary school teachers to assess student competency and to evaluate student performance, leading to a drop in grades for many young adolescents as they make the junior high school transition. For example, Simmons and Blyth (1987) found a greater drop in grades between sixth and seventh grade for adolescents making the junior high school transition at this point than for adolescents enrolled in K–8 schools. Interestingly, this decline in grades is not matched by a decline in the adolescents' scores on standardized achievement tests, suggesting that the decline reflects a change in grading practices rather than a change in the rate of the students' learning (Kavrell & Petersen, 1984). Imagine what this decline in grades might do to young adolescents' self-confidence, especially in light of the fact that the material they are being tested on is not likely to be more intellectually challenging.

Changes such as these are likely to have a negative effect on many children's motivational orientations toward school at any grade level. However, Eccles and Midgley (1989) argued that these types of changes are particularly harmful at early adolescence given what is known about psychological development during this stage of life. Evidence from a variety of sources suggests that early adolescent development is characterized by increases in desire for autonomy, peer orientation, self-focus and self-consciousness, salience of identity issues, concern over heterosexual relationships, and capacity for abstract cognitive activity (see Simmons & Blyth, 1987). Simmons and Blyth (1987) argued that adolescents need a reasonably safe, as well as an intellectually challenging, environment to adapt to these shifts—an environment that provides a "zone of comfort" as well as challenging new opportunities for growth. In light of these needs, the environmental changes often associated with the transition to junior high school seem especially harmful in that they disrupt the possibility for close personal relationships between youth and nonfamilial adults at a time when youth have increased need for this type of social support; they emphasize competition, social comparison, and ability self-assessment at a time of heightened self-focus; they decrease decision making and choice at a time when the desire for self-control and adult respect is growing; and they disrupt peer social networks at a time when adolescents are especially concerned with peer relationships and social acceptance. We believe the nature of these environmental changes, coupled with the normal course of individual development, is likely to result in a developmental mismatch so that the "fit" between the early adolescent and the classroom environment is particularly poor, increasing the risk of negative motivational outcomes, especially for adolescents who are already having difficulty succeeding in school academically.

IMPACT OF ENVIRONMENTAL CHANGES
ON YOUNG ADOLESCENTS' MOTIVATION

To test these predictions, we conducted a large-scale longitudinal study of the impact of changes in the school and classroom environment on adolescents' achievement-related beliefs, motives, values, self-evaluations, affective reactions, and behaviors. The first 2 years of this study focused intensively on the junior high school transition. Although all of the children made the junior high school transition between Grades 6 and 7 and all districts had a K–6, 7–9, 10–12 grade structure at the time of this study, we purposely selected 12 school districts in Southeastern Michigan that differed in nature of the junior high school environment. The data summarized in this chapter come from the first 2 years of this study (the MSALT). Approximately 1,500 young adolescents participated at all four waves of the first 2 years of this study. The median family income for these students was approximately $30,000 per year in 1983. Most families would be classified as working or middle class based on their occupation, education, and family income and most lived in the working- and middle-class communities surrounding Detroit. Seventy-five percent of the mothers reported being married, 8% reported being remarried, and 13% reported being separated or divorced. Eighty-five percent of the sample were White; 8% were African American. Questionnaires were administered at school during the fall and spring terms of the two consecutive school years. In this chapter we summarize the results for changes in teacher efficacy, teacher support and warmth, and opportunities for involvement in autonomous decision making.

Teacher Efficacy

As noted earlier, one of the largest differences between the sixth- and seventh-grade teachers is in their confidence in their teaching efficacy. Consistent with other studies, the seventh-grade teachers in the MSALT study reported less confidence in their ability to teach all children in their classes than the sixth-grade teachers. Do these differences in teachers' sense of efficacy before and after the transition to junior high school contribute to the decline in young adolescents' beliefs about their academic competency and potential? To answer this question, we divided our sample into four groups based on median splits of their math teachers' ratings of their personal teaching efficacy (see Midgley et al., 1989, for a full description of this study). The largest group (559 out of the 1,329 included in these analyses) moved from a high-efficacy sixth-grade math teacher to a low-efficacy seventh-grade math teacher. Another 474 adolescents had low-efficacy teachers both years, 117 moved from low- to high-efficacy teachers, and 179 had high-efficacy teachers both years. Thus, fully 78% of our sample of children moved to a low teacher efficacy math classroom in the seventh grade. As predicted, the adolescents who had moved from high-efficacy to low-efficacy teachers during the transition (the most common pattern) ended their first year in junior high school with lower expectancies for themselves in math, lower perceptions of their performance in math, and higher perceptions of the difficulty of math than the adolescents who had experienced no change in teacher efficacy or who had moved from low- to high-efficacy teachers. Also as we had predicted, teacher efficacy beliefs had a stronger impact on the low-achieving adolescents' beliefs than on the high-achieving adolescents' beliefs. By the end of the junior high school year, the confidence of those low-achieving adolescents who had moved from high- to low-efficacy teachers had declined dramatically. It is important to note, however, that the decline in self-confidence and efficacy for learning math was not characteristic of either the low- or high-achieving adolescents who moved into a high teacher efficacy classroom at the seventh grade, suggesting that the decline is not a general feature of early adolescent development but rather a consequence of the fact that so many young adolescents experience a debilitating shift in their classroom environments as they make the junior high school transition.

Teacher–Student Relationships

Negative change in the affective relationship between students and teachers is also one of the characteristic changes associated with the junior high school transition. Consistent with this pattern, we found that student–teacher relationships deteriorated after the transition to junior high school in the MSALT sample. Using a strategy similar to that described for teacher efficacy, we divided the sample of students into four groups based on the pattern of change they experienced in teacher support and warmth as they made the junior high school transition. As predicted, the young adolescents who moved from elementary teachers they perceived to be high in support to teachers they perceived to be low in support showed a decline in the value they attached to math; in contrast, the young adolescents who moved from teachers they perceived to be low in support to junior high school teachers they perceived to be high in support showed an increase in the value they attached to math. Again we found evidence that low-achieving students are particularly at risk when they move to less facilitative classroom environments after the transition (Midgley et al., 1988a).

Both of these analyses show that the declines in adolescents' school motivation and self-concepts often reported in studies of young adolescents' development are not inevitable. Instead these declines are associated with specific types of changes in the nature of the classroom environment experienced by many young adolescents as they make the junior high school transition. A transition into more facilitative types of classrooms can induce positive changes in young adolescents' motivation and self-perceptions. Unfortunately, for all adolescents, but especially for low-achieving adolescents, the findings from MSALT also indicate that most adolescents experience a negative change in their classroom experiences as they make the junior high school transition.

Stage–Environment Fit in Classroom Decision Making

Neither of these analyses, however, directly tested our stage–environment fit hypothesis. To do this one must directly assess person–environment fit and relate this fit to changes in adolescents' self-perceptions and motivation. Both the adolescents and the teachers in this study were asked to rate whether students were allowed to have input into classroom decisions regarding where to sit, classwork, homework, class rules, and what to do next and whether students ought to have input into each of these decisions (items were developed by Lee, Statuto, & Kedar-Voivodas, 1983). These questions can be used in the following ways: (a) to plot the developmental changes in adolescents' preferences for decision making opportunities in the classroom, (b) to determine changes in the opportunity for them to participate in decision making, and (c) to determine the extent of match or mismatch between their preferences and the opportunities actually afforded them in the school environment. If developmental changes in this match are related to developmental changes in the adolescents' self-perceptions and school-related motivation then we would have support for our stage–environment fit hypothesis.

As noted earlier, both the young adolescents and their teachers reported that there was less opportunity for participation in classroom decision making in the seventh grade than in the sixth grade. In contrast, the young adolescents' desire for more participation in classroom decision making increased over the transition. As a consequence of these two divergent patterns, the congruence between young adolescents' desire for the opportunity to participate in classroom decision making and their perception of the extent to which such opportunities were available to them was lower when the adolescents were in the seventh grade than when they were in the sixth grade (Midgley & Feldlaufer, 1987).

How might the widening mismatch between the students' desire for autonomy and their perceptions of their opportunity for autonomy affect motivation? Person–environment fit theories suggest that a mismatch between one's needs and the environmental affordances will lead to declines in motivation and engagement. Mac Iver, Klingel, and Reuman (1986) tested this prediction with the sixth-grade students by relating perceived congruence versus perceived incongruence to student motivation and behavior. Congruent children differed from incongruent children in several ways: They rated math as more useful and interesting, they liked the teacher and their school better, they had higher expectations for their own performance in math, and they engaged in less misbehavior according to their own and their teachers' reports. Therefore, it seems likely that this decline in the opportunity for decision making and this increase in the misfit between students' desire for autonomy and their perceptions of the opportunities for autonomy in their seventh-grade math classrooms could contribute to the decline we find in their motivation to study math.

However, more specifically, given the general developmental progression toward increased desire for independence and autonomy during the early adolescent period, Eccles and Midgley (1989) predicted that adolescents who experience decreased opportunities for participation in classroom decision making along with increased desires for greater participation in such decisions (i.e., a "can't but should be able to" mismatch) should be most at risk for negative motivational outcomes. In a longitudinal analysis, Mac Iver and Reuman (1988) provided some support for this prediction. They compared the changes in intrinsic interest in math for adolescents reporting different types of changes in their responses to the actual and preferred decision-making items across the four waves of data. Consistent with the Eccles and Midgley (1989) prediction, the adolescents who perceived their seventh-grade math classrooms as putting greater constraints on their preferred level of participation in classroom decision making than their sixth-grade math classrooms showed the largest and most consistent declines in their intrinsic interest in math as they moved from the sixth grade into the seventh grade. These are the students who are experiencing the type of developmental mismatch Eccles and Midgley (1989) predicted would be most detrimental to positive growth.

Summary

Thus far, a theoretical rationale has been outlined for the average level declines in motivation and self-evaluation associated with the junior high school transition. The results of a longitudinal study designed to provide an in-depth description of the classroom environment changes experienced by most children as they make the transition from elementary school into junior high schools have been summarized. In general, evidence of the following types of predicted changes was reported: an increase in teacher control of students and a decrease in teacher's feelings of efficacy and in the quality of teacher–student relations. We have also begun to assess the impact of these changes on student motivation using a quasi-experimental approach. These results confirm the negative consequences of these types of changes and provide evidence that a different type of change would produce positive motivational changes at this developmental period. Together these two outcomes support our suggestion that declines in motivation often assumed to be characteristic of the early adolescent period are less a consequence of the students' developmental stage than of the mismatch between the students' needs and the opportunities afforded them in the traditional junior high school environment.

The MSALT results also suggest that there are individual differences in adolescents' response to the junior high school transition. In both the study on the impact of changes in teacher efficacy and the study on the impact of changes in student–teacher relationships, low-achieving students were more negatively affected by the change than high-achieving students. In the two studies of person–environment fit, students varied in their desire for autonomy and only those students who perceived a mismatch between their desire for autonomy and the opportunities for autonomous behavior showed the negative changes in motivation and self-concept often associated with the junior high school transition.

INDIVIDUAL DIFFERENCES IN THE ADJUSTMENT TO SCHOOL TRANSITIONS DURING EARLY ADOLESCENCE

In the next sections, we explore individual differences in the response to school transition more thoroughly. First, we summarize our work on pubertal development. Then we summarize our findings regarding the moderating influence of a set of psychological and familial protective and risk factors on adaptation to the junior high school transition.

Differences Related to Pubertal Timing

In their now classic study, Simmons and Blyth (1987) found that girls were more at risk for showing negative changes in response to the junior high school transition than boys. As they explored gender differences in more depth, a particular subset of girls were most at risk—White girls who were advanced in both their physical and social pubertal development. These girls had already begun dating and were well advanced in their physical development. Simmons and Blyth (1987) interpreted this effect in terms of the cumulative negative effects of multiple transitions on individual development (see also Petersen & Crockett, 1985, for studies with a similar theoretical perspective). People who experience more than one transition simultaneously are more at risk for the negative effects of the stress associated with transitions than people who experience only one major transition (Garmezy, 1983).

The person–environment fit perspective outlined earlier provides another way to look at this individual difference in response to the junior high school transition. It is quite possible that variations in pubertal development are associated with variations in the adolescents' desire for autonomy and adult respect. If so, the types of regressive changes in the authority relationships between students and teachers associated with the junior high school transition would create a particularly salient mismatch for the most pubertally advanced students—who at this age are most likely to be females. To test this hypothesis with the MSALT data, we related an indicator of maturational level to the female adolescents' desire for input into classroom decisions on the Lee et al. (1983) items collected at one wave. As we expected, the more physically mature female adolescents expressed a greater desire for input into classroom decision making than their less developmentally mature female classmates (Miller, 1986). Unfortunately, the more physically mature females did not perceive greater opportunities for participation in classroom decision making (see Fig. 10.1). Although the females with varying degrees of pubertal development were in the same classrooms, the more physically mature females (i.e., the early developers) reported fewer opportunities for participation in classroom decision making than did their less mature female peers (i.e., the on-time and late developers).

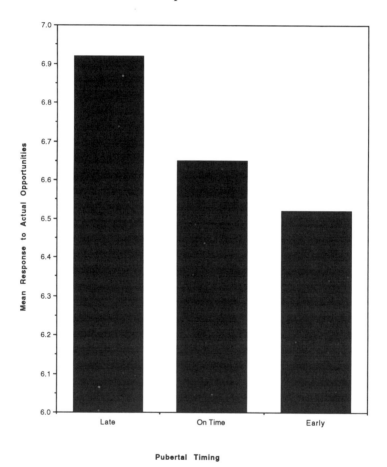

FIG. 10.1. Young adolescent females' perceptions of decision-making opportunities in their classroom in the spring of their sixth-grade year. Score represents the sum of the young woman's response to five items. A no response was coded 1 and a yes response was coded 2.

These maturational differences were even more striking when we looked at the within-year changes in these female adolescents' perceptions of the opportunities they have to participate in classroom decision making. We calculated the mean change in these females' perceptions of opportunities from the fall to the spring evaluation. We then looked at this change as a function of pubertal status. The early-maturing females showed a negative change (a decline) over the course of the school year in the extent to which they could participate in classroom decision making. In contrast, the late-maturing females in these same classrooms showed a positive change (an increase) over the course of the school year (Miller, 1986). How can this be, given that these adolescents were in the same classrooms? Did the teachers actually treat these adolescent females differently (i.e., did the teachers respond to earlier physical maturity with more controlling behavior)? Or did the adolescents perceive a similar environment differently (i.e., did the early-maturing adolescents perceive the same level of adult control as providing less opportunity for self-control than did the later maturing adolescents)? Evidence from educational psychology, developmental psychology, and general psychology suggests that either or both of these explanations could be accurate: Teachers do respond differently to various children in the same classroom depending on a variety of characteristics (Brophy & Evertson, 1976), and people do perceive similar environments differently depending on their cognitive and/or motivational orientation (see Baron & Graziano, 1991). In addition, Paikoff and Brooks-Gunn (1991) reviewed evidence that parents respond differently to young adolescents depending on their physical maturity. More detailed classroom observations are needed to determine the exact nature of the relation between teachers' behavior and adolescents' perceptions.

More importantly, however, for the issues central to this discussion, the pubertal maturity of the female adolescents was associated with the degree of mismatch between the adolescents' desires for input and their perceptions of these opportunities in their classroom environment; that is, there was a greater degree of mismatch among the more physically mature female adolescents than among the less mature. As can be seen in Fig. 10.2, over the course of the school year, all girls reported greater frequency of "can't but should" situations. These are situations in which the student reports that she should be able to have a say in a particular decision (like where to sit) but is not allowed to have a say by the teacher. Both the frequency of this type of mismatch and the degree of change over the school year are greater for the early-maturing girls in this sample. In fact, by the end of the school year, almost twice as many early-maturing females reported experiencing the "can't but should" type of mismatch (e.g., Answering "no" to the question "Do you get to help decide what math you work on during math class?" but "yes" to the question "Should

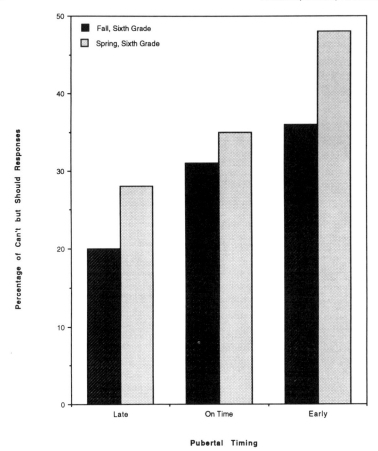

FIG. 10.2. Frequency of "can't but should" mismatches in decision-making opportunities in the fall and spring of the sixth-grade year. For each pair of items, the type of match was recorded. A can't but should mismatch occurs when the young woman responds yes to the question regarding whether they should have the particular decision-making opportunity and a no to the question regarding whether they actually do have this opportunity.

you have a say about this?") as did their less physically mature classmates. As a result, the change in the congruence between the young women's desire for opportunities for decision making and the existence of such opportunities in their classrooms was greatest for the early-maturing females (see Fig. 10.3). For these young women only, the perceived congruence had substantially declined over the course of the school year.

We find these results especially interesting in light of the findings of Simmons and her colleagues (e.g., Simmons & Blyth, 1987) linking the pubertal status of female adolescents at the time of the junior high school

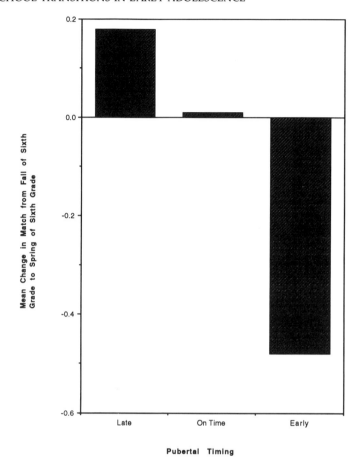

Pubertal Timing

FIG. 10.3. Mean change in match in decision-making opportunities from the fall until the spring of the sixth-grade year. For each pair of items, the type of match was recorded. A match occurs when the young woman answers yes to both the can and should question for a particular decision-making opportunity.

transition to changes in the females' self-esteem and to the females' reports of truancy and school misconduct. In particular, the more physically mature females in their study reported the highest amount of truancy and school misconduct after they made the junior high school transition. Simmons and Blyth (1987) suggested that experiencing both school and pubertal transitions simultaneously puts these girls at risk for negative outcomes. It is also possible that it is the mismatch between their desire for a less controlling adult environment and their perceptions of the actual opportunities for participation that puts these females at additional risk for negative motivational outcomes.

Individual Differences Related to Protective and Risk Factors

Both Simmons and Blyth (1987) and Fenzel (1991) analyzed the transition to junior high school in terms of stress and coping. From this perspective, transitions are considered stressful events in that they tap the individual's resources for adaptation. Within the stress and coping literature (e.g., Garmezy, 1983; Rutter, 1981), differences in individuals' responses to stressful life events are assumed to result from the balance between the protective and the risk factors they have at their disposal. Protective factors buffer against the adverse effects of transitions, whereas risk factors tend to exacerbate such effects.

We have now completed a set of analyses of the MSALT data based on this perspective (Lord, Eccles, & McCarthy, 1994). We investigated both psychological and general family environment factors as potential moderators of our adolescents' response to the junior high school transition. The psychological factors included adolescents' ability self-concepts, worries, and self-consciousness. The family environmental factors included decision-making opportunities and developmental attunement to the adolescent. The rationale for each of these sets of moderating constructs is summarized in the following sections, followed by a summary of our findings.

Psychological Protective and Risk Factors

In thinking about the psychological protective and risk factors most likely to affect adjustment to the junior high school transition, we decided to focus on a set of constructs directly related to the school setting. In terms of protective factors, several investigators have suggested that personal coping resources are key influences on individuals' adjustment to stressful situations such as school transitions. Personal coping resources are typically conceptualized as a set of relatively stable personality, attitudinal, and cognitive dispositions that promote effective adaptation, thereby reducing the potentially harmful effects of stress (Fenzel, 1991). Personal coping resources that seem most likely to buffer against the detrimental effects of stressful school transition at adolescence include a sense of autonomy, a sense of personal efficacy, and confidence in one's competence (Bandura, 1986; Compas, 1987; Garmezy, 1983; Harter, 1990).

Perceptions of one's competencies and efficacy are especially relevant for an understanding of the changes in self-esteem associated with the junior high school transition. Several studies support a connection between these self-relevant beliefs. For example, Bohrnstedt and Felson (1983) showed that perceived academic and athletic competence are positively predictive of self-esteem among adolescents. Similarly, Harter (1990) showed that perceived competence in academic, social, athletic, and physical appearance domains are positively related to self-esteem, with confidence in one's physical appearance and social competence having the strongest relations. Other studies have focused on the protective role that actual abilities may play as one makes the junior high transition. This work has demonstrated that success in academic and social domains in the sixth grade is positively related to increases in self-esteem following the junior high school transition (e.g., Hirsch & Rapkin, 1987; Simmons & Blyth, 1987). These studies suggest that both ability self-concepts and actual achievement levels are related to the children's overall self-esteem as well as to their adjustment to the junior high school transition.

In terms of risk factors, achievement-related worries and self-consciousness seem the most likely candidates for undermining the school transition adjustment process. For example, Elkind and Bowen (1979) showed that self-consciousness is negatively related to self-esteem. Similarly, several studies indicate that anxiety about one's performance in the academic and social domains is negatively related to children's school performance (e.g., Payne, Smith, & Payne, 1983; Willig, Harnish, Hill, & Maehr, 1983). Eccles and her colleagues have suggested that both anxiety and self-consciousness may be particularly detrimental as the early adolescent is forced to adjust to a new school environment characterized by increased rigor in grading, less variety in evaluation techniques, and an increase in social comparison among students (Eccles & Midgley, 1989; Feldlaufer et al., 1988). These detrimental effects are likely to be especially salient during early adolescence, as this developmental period is characterized by increased self-focus and self-consciousness (e.g., Eccles & Midgley, 1989; Eccles et al., 1984; Elkind & Bowen, 1979).

Family Protective and Risk Factors

In thinking about the possible impact of the family environment on adolescents' adaptation to the junior high school transition, it is useful to consider the salient developmental tasks confronting adolescents during this time. A central task of adolescence is to develop a sense of oneself as an autonomous individual (Blos, 1979; Eccles et al., 1993; Steinberg, 1990). The drive for such autonomy derives from the internal, biological processes marking the transition to a more adult role, such as puberty and increasing cognitive maturity, as well as from the social changes and expectations that accompany these physiological changes. As Eccles et al. (1993) noted, social changes in the worlds of adolescents increase the opportunity for them to experience independence outside of the home.

This increased out-of-home independence is often in the form of unsupervised peer contact, providing the adolescent with the opportunity to spend a great deal of time in relationships that are likely to be more mutual in terms of interpersonal power and authority (Eccles et al., 1993; Higgins & Parsons, 1983).

In keeping with our stage–environment fit perspective, we have focused on the fit between an early adolescent's family environment in terms of support of autonomous decision making and his or her developmental needs as the framework for studying the relation of adolescents' developing need for autonomy to adolescents' adjustment to the junior high transition (e.g., Eccles et al., 1993; see also Hunt, 1975). Similar to our earlier discussion regarding the importance of fit in the school environment, person–environment fit theory suggests that the fit between the individual's need for autonomy and the amount of control parents continue to exert on the adolescent's decision making should affect the individual's motivation and sense of satisfaction. Adopting a developmental framework (i.e., a developmental stage–environment fit perspective), we assume that the "fit" between desire for self-control and opportunities for self-control is likely to change as the individual develops unless the environment changes at the same rate and in the appropriate direction. As children mature, they are likely to desire more control and opportunities for decision making. When they enter early adolescence, the rate of increase in this desire for control over one's own life likely accelerates, increasing the need for the family to renegotiate the power balance between parent and child (Collins, 1990; Eccles et al., 1993; J. P. Hill, 1988; Montemayor, 1986; Steinberg, 1990). It seems plausible that those parents who are able to adjust to the adolescent's changing needs with relatively little conflict will provide a better match between the early adolescent and his or her family environment. This better match should then serve a positive role in the adolescent's developmental trajectory.

In support of this hypothesis, research has shown that family environments that provide opportunities for personal autonomy and encourage the adolescent's role in family decision making are associated with such positive outcomes as higher self-esteem, greater self-reliance, greater satisfaction with school and student–teacher relations, more positive school adjustment, more advanced moral reasoning, and a mastery orientation toward problem solving in the classroom (e.g., Epstein & McPartland, 1977; Flanagan, 1985, 1986, 1989; Yee, 1986, 1987; Yee & Flanagan, 1985). Conversely, a parenting style that is coercive, authoritarian, and not attuned to the adolescents' need for more decision-making opportunities is associated with greater self-consciousness, lower confidence in the self, and greater self-image disparity (Leahy, 1981; Ryan & Lynch, 1989; Yee & Flanagan, 1985). In a study that addressed the fit between early adolescent needs and family decision-making opportunities using the MSALT data, Flanagan (1986) found that young adolescents' perceptions of fit between how much say they should have in decisions and how much they do have is positively correlated with their perceptions of autonomy and negatively correlated with their perceptions of parent–child conflict and high parent control.

Consistent with this perspective, the period of early adolescence has been acknowledged by developmentalists (e.g., Collins, 1990; Eccles et al., 1993; J. P. Hill, 1988; Paikoff & Brooks-Gunn, 1991; Steinberg, 1990), family sociologists (e.g., Aldous, 1977), and clinicians (e.g., Blos, 1979) as a time of transition that requires a renegotiation of family rules and roles for successful adaptation. Research and clinical evidence suggests that the family's ability to adapt to the changing needs of its early adolescent has implications for the process of identity formation (Grotevant, 1983), for the development of psychopathology such as eating disorders (Minuchin, Rosman, & Baker, 1978) and possibly, for how the early adolescent negotiates the transition to junior high school (Eccles et al., 1993).

It is reasonable to postulate that family environments that are responsive and developmentally sensitive to the early adolescent may serve as protective factors for the transition to junior high school. These family environments may provide enough psychological support and scaffolding for the young adolescent so that the transition is less stressful and disruptive. A developmentally responsive environment may also help the adolescent develop certain competencies that can serve as protective factors for the transition such as autonomy, maturity, and high self-esteem. For example, Leahy (1981) found that when parents encourage children to express their opinions and listen to and consider the opinions of other family members, their adolescent children develop a more internally elaborated system for moral judgments and a more positive sense of self-esteem. When parents emphasize unilateral respect for authority and inhibit opportunities for debate and questioning, lower self-esteem can result (e.g., Leahy, 1981).

Lord et al. (1994) examined adolescents' perceptions of the family environment with regard to two general dimensions: parent–adolescent mismatch and provision of decision-making opportunities. Parent–adolescent mismatch refers to the degree to which the adolescent feels his or her parents do not communicate reasons for rules and inhibit the adolescent's pursuit of autonomous behavior. This construct reflects a lack of attunement of the parents to the developmental needs of their child. Provision of decision-making opportunities refers to the degree to which the parents provide their adolescent with opportunities to be involved in making decisions that would affect the adolescent. Both of these dimensions are considered relevant because the premise of stage-environment fit theory suggests that optimal positive growth occurs in the context of a family environment that is developmentally sensitive and that offers the kinds of stimulation that will propel continued growth toward maturity. Such an environment conveys to the adolescent a sense of acknowledgment and appreciation of the adolescent as an individual. Meaningful autonomy should then facilitate the young adolescent's transition to a new school setting and may compensate for the lack of support for autonomy in this new context.

Findings of the Lord, Eccles, and McCarthy Study

Lord, Eccles, and McCarthy (1994) assessed the association of the following psychological, achievement, and family constructs to adolescents' adjustment to the junior high school transition: sixth-grade school achievement level, perceptions of one's own abilities, worries about one's abilities and self-consciousness, and perceptions of the family environment. They tested the following general hypotheses: (a) actual levels of competence, and perceptions of both one's own competence and of the support of autonomy and involvement in decision making at home at Grade 6 will be positively related to adolescents' adjustment to the junior high school transition; and (b) worries about one's competence, self-consciousness, and perceptions of parent–adolescent mismatch, or lack of attunement, at Grade 6 will be negatively related to this adjustment.

Analyses were conducted using preplanned hierarchical multiple regression techniques. These analyses were run for outcomes at both Wave 3 and Wave 4, representing adjustment at the beginning (Wave 3) and end of seventh grade (Wave 4). Self-esteem assessed at Wave 2 was entered into the regression equation first based on the hypothesis that posttransition self-esteem would be most affected by students' self-esteem prior to the transition and based on the desire to test the impact of the other predictors on change in self-esteem from Wave 2 to Waves 3 and 4. Academic competence (ability) was entered second. By controlling for self-esteem and academic ability at Wave 2, these models test the extent to which the other predictor variables are associated with a gain or loss in self-esteem between the end of the sixth grade and the beginning (or end) of the seventh-grade year, controlling for prior achievement level.

The other predictors were entered as sets of conceptually related constructs (i.e., all ability self-concept scales were entered at one step, all worries and self-consciousness scales were entered at the next step, etc.). Gender (coded as −1 = male and +1 = female) was added at the last step in order to determine if gender contributed additional variance once the psychological predictors (on which there are gender differences) were taken into account.

Although several indicators of adjustment were used, only the results for changes in self-esteem are summarized here. These results are illustrated in Table 10.1. The table presents the summary results of each step of the hierarchical multiple regression analyses (columns 2–4 and 6–8), as well as the unstandardized regression coefficients for each predictor in the final model (columns 5 and 9). Steps 1 and 2 represent the change in explained variance in self-esteem with the addition of Wave 2 self-esteem and ability, respectively. Step 3 presents the change in explained variance when the first set of predictors (specific self-concepts) was added to the equation. Step 4 presents the change in explained variance when the second set of predictors (worries and self-consciousness) was added. Step 5 presents the change in explained variance when perceived family characteristics were added and Step 6 represents the change when gender was added.

Psychological Protective and Risk Factors. As expected, both self-esteem in Grade 6 and academic performance in Grade 6 were related to self-esteem. However, sixth-grade academic ability was not a significant predictor of self-esteem change in the final full model at either Wave 3 or 4 (see columns 5 and 9). In contrast, self-esteem at the end of Grade 6 was the strongest predictor by a very wide margin of self-esteem at both Waves 3 and 4, suggesting considerable stability in self-esteem across these time periods.

Also as predicted, over and above Wave 2 self-esteem and academic ability, the psychological protective factors—positive self-concepts of one's ability in both academic and nonacademic domains—were associated with positive change in self-esteem. As a set, students' ratings of their abilities in academic, athletic, and peer social domains and of their physical attractiveness all predicted gains in self-esteem at both waves. In competition with each other as predictors, ratings of one's physical attractiveness, one's math ability, and one's peer-social ability yielded significant coefficients in the final, full model at Wave 3; and ratings of one's math ability and one's peer-social ability yielded significant coefficients in the final, full model at Wave 4.

Again as hypothesized, the psychological risk factors—worries and self-consciousness related to math, school deadlines, and social acceptance—were associated, as a set of predictors with declines in self-esteem over the junior high school transition. However, in competition with the other predictors, only social self-consciousness and academic self-consciousness yielded significant negative coefficients.

Taken as a whole, these results support the hypotheses that protective factors in both academic and nonacademic self-perceptions facilitate positive gains in self-esteem, and that psychological risk factors are linked to

TABLE 10.1

Change in Total Variance Explained in Posttransition Self-Esteem

Step	Self-Esteem Wave 3				Self-Esteem Wave 4			
	Change R^2	Change F	F model	B model	Change R^2	Change F	F model	B model
Step 1								
Self-Esteem 2	.257	631.9***	631.9***	.338***	0.249	621.6***	621.6***	.339***
Step 2								
Ability	.01	25.1***	332.7***	n.s.	0.011	26.7***	328.4	n.s.
Step 3: Self-Concepts	.034	18.0***	112.3***		0.025	13.2***	106.3***	
Appearance				.042***				n.s.
English				n.s.				n.s.
Sports				n.s.				n.s.
Math				.063***				.051***
Friends				.032*				.041**
Step 4: Worries	.02	9.05***	66.3**		0.022	9.72***	63.3***	
Self-conscious: social				-.059***				-.048
Self-conscious: academic				-.041*				-.053
Non-Worried: social				n.s.				n.s.
Non-Worried: academic				n.s.				n.s.
Nervous: english				n.s.				n.s.
Nervous: math				n.s.				n.s.
Step 5: Family environment	.02	25.6***	62.4***		0.017	22.7***	59.2***	
Parent-adolescent mismatch				-.105***				-.078***
Democratic decision-making				.069**				.099***
Step 6: Gender	n.s.	n.s.	—	n.s.	0.001	4.24*	55.8***	-.027*
	Total R^2 = .34				Total R^2 = .33			

Note. Column 1 shows variables entered at each step of the multiple regression model. Columns 2 and 3 indicate the changes in R^2 and the F value and the significance for each step. Column 4 is the F value for the whole model with each additional step. Column 5 indicates the unstandardized regression coefficient for each variable with all variables in the model.

declines in self-esteem across the transition to junior high school. More specifically, greater confidence in one's academic, social, and athletic abilities in the sixth grade is associated with gains in one's self-esteem following the transition to junior high. In contrast, worries and self-consciousness were associated with declines in self-esteem across the transition to junior high school.

That confidence in one's peer-related social skills and one's physical attractiveness emerged as such salient contributors to adolescents' adjustment to junior high school probably reflects the impact of changing pressures on adolescents at this particular period of life. Several investigators have suggested that there is an increased emphasis at this time, from both peers and families, on physical appearance, social presentation, and popularity with the opposite sex (Higgins & Parsons, 1983; Hill & Lynch, 1983). Coupled with the new and much larger social environment of the junior high setting, confidence in one's competence in peer social relationships and one's physical attractiveness may be particularly important protective factors.

The salience of physical appearance for self-esteem across the transition to junior high also raises concern, however. The implications of a focus on physical attractiveness may have a negative effect on some adolescents, particularly females. Given that physical appearance is in large part biologically determined and out of the individual's control, the implications of a focus on physical attractiveness for a person who is not, or does not feel, attractive relative to her peers may propel a young adolescent toward extreme efforts to try to change her natural endowment in order to meet both real and perceived peer and societal standards. It follows that girls at this age who have a negative perception of their appearance may be at risk for developing symptoms that reflect their diminished self-esteem, such as eating disorders. Excessive concern with physical attractiveness could also explain the recently reported increase in interest among adolescents for plastic surgery. We were also struck by the number of young adolescents in our ongoing study of development during middle childhood and adolescence who report that, if given $1 million, they would use this money for plastic surgery or liposuction.

Family Protective and Risk Factors. The two indicators of family protective and risk factors—the adolescent's Wave 2 perception of his or her family environment—were simultaneously entered at Step 4. Again as predicted, these two indicators were related to changes in self-esteem at both waves. As expected, the perception that one's parent is not attuned to one's needs was associated with declines in self-esteem, whereas the perception that one's family uses a democratic decision-making style was associated with increases in self-esteem.

The results also support the hypothesis that adolescents' perceptions of their family environments influence their adjustment to the junior high transition. As predicted, the perception that one's parents are not developmentally attuned to one's needs was associated with declines in self-esteem following this school transition. In addition, adolescents' perceptions of a democratic family environment were associated with increases in self-esteem throughout the seventh grade. Together with the results of other studies, these findings are consistent with the hypothesis that family environments that support the adolescents' need for autonomy are more facilitative of positive adjustment during early adolescence than family environments in which the adolescents' autonomy is suppressed (e.g., Eccles et al., 1993; Epstein & McPartland, 1977; Flanagan, 1989; Yee, 1987; Yee & Flanagan, 1985).

Female Gender as a Risk Factor. Even though student gender was weakly related in a predictable pattern to several of the predictor variables as well as to self-esteem, student gender added little to the predictive power of the regression equation when it was added at the final step of the regression model. Although gender added nothing significant at Wave 3, at Wave 4, it had a negative relation with self-esteem, indicating that males' self-esteem at Wave 4 is still higher than that of females at Wave 4 even after all the other variables are controlled. Consistent with the findings of Simmons and Blyth (1987), this result suggests that being a female is predictive of decreasing self-esteem over time even after the other predictors of self-esteem change are controlled.

CONCLUSION

In this chapter, we reviewed evidence of a decline in school motivation and attachment during early adolescence. We outlined a theoretical perspective—the stage–environment fit perspective—for understanding how changes in school context might contribute to this decline. Stage–environment fit theory suggests that the fit between the individual's psychological needs and the opportunities provided by the school (as well as other contexts) to meet these needs influences the individual's motivation and attachment to the school. We focused on two specific psychological needs: (a) the increasing need for autonomy and participation in decisions regarding one's experiences, and (b) the continuing need for strong social supports and close, trusting relationships with adults. For example, we argued that the match between an adolescent's need for autonomy and the amount of control adults continue to exert on the adolescent's decision making either at home or at school should affect the individual's motivation and sense of satisfaction (Eccles et al., 1993; Eccles, Miller Buchanan, et al., 1991). From a developmental framework, the perceived match between the adolescents' increasing desire for self-control and the opportunities for self-control is likely to decrease if the opportunities for self-control do not increase at the same rate as the young adolescents' desire for autonomy and more democratic participation in decision making. Also, to the extent that the perceived match is not good at school, young adolescents are likely to develop a more negative view of the school context and of themselves as students. Similarly, to the extent that the social relationship with teachers deteriorates as young adolescents move into junior high school, the match between their social needs and the opportunity for positive, healthy relationships with teachers will decrease and the young adolescents will turn away from the adults in the school as a source of emotional support.

We also summarized our findings regarding these hypotheses. In particular, we provided evidence of the negative effects of the decrease in personal and positive relationships with teachers after the transition to junior high school. We also noted the increase in ability grouping and comparative and public evaluation at a time when young adolescents have a heightened concern about their status in relation to their peers. Finally, we provided evidence of the negative consequences of these kinds of developmentally inappropriate environmental changes on early adolescents' school motivation, academic self-concepts, and mental health. We also discussed the role of opportunity for self-determination and participation in rule making. As children enter and move through adolescence, they reported an increasing desire for opportunities for self-control and participatory decision making. It should be noted, however, that, although the adolescents wanted more freedom from adult control than children, they did not want total freedom and they did not want to be emotionally detached from their parents. Instead they reported a gradual increase in the opportunity for self-determination and participation in decision making and rule making. Adolescents who reported having less opportunity to express their own desires and opinions at school than they thought they were entitled to, and adolescents who perceived a lack of attunement between themselves and their parents, adjusted more poorly to the transition into junior high school than did adolescents who had more opportunities for participation in decision making at home and school and who felt their parents and teachers were attuned to them. These findings suggest that family and school environments that are responsive and developmentally sensitive to these changes in young adolescents' needs and desires may serve as protective factors for the transition to junior high school. Those adults who are able to adjust to their adolescent's changing needs for autonomy provide a better match for the adolescent and serve a positive role in the adolescent's developmental trajectory. These family and school environments may provide enough psychological support for the young adolescent so that the transition is less stressful and disruptive.

Unfortunately, our research also suggests that many early adolescents do not have these experiences in either the school or family setting. After the transition to junior high school, in particular, early adolescents are often confronted with a regressive environmental change; that is, many early adolescents experience a decrease in the opportunity to participate in classroom decision making when they move into junior high school. Not surprisingly, there is also a decrease in intrinsic motivation and an increase in school misbehavior associated with this transition, as well as a decline in indicators of mental health. These changes are most apparent among the adolescents who report experiencing the greatest mismatch between their needs and their opportunities to participate in classroom decision making. Clearly, these results point out the importance of creating educational and family environments for early adolescents that provide a better match to their developing needs and desires. How could the creation of such developing appropriate environments be accomplished?

Turning Points (Carnegie Council on Adolescent Development, 1989) outlines a variety of changes in the structure of middle-grades educational institutions that would make it easier for teachers to maintain a high sense of self-efficacy, and for students and teachers alike to have a stronger sense of shared community with each other. In turn, these changes could make it easier for teachers to provide a more positive learning environment for early adolescents. One potential strategy for remediating the impersonal quality of traditional junior high schools involves within-school reorganization based on the middle school teaching philosophy. Some characteristics of the middle school philosophy that have been identified as potentially helpful are small house programs, team teaching, and advisory sessions (see Eccles & Midgley, 1989).

Field studies of the more successful middle and junior high schools provide numerous examples of classrooms and schools that have more positive and developmentally appropriate learning environments—for example, higher teacher efficacy, greater opportunity for meaningful student participation in both school and classroom decision making, an academic culture that stresses task mastery and improvement, and more positive student–teacher relationships (see Bryk, Lee, & Smith, 1989; Carnegie Council on Adolescent Development, 1989; Dryfoos, 1990; Eccles & Midgley, 1989). Young adolescents in these schools do not evidence the same declines in intrinsic motivation and school attachment stereotypically associated with students in junior high schools; they also do not engage in the same amount of school misbehavior as students in more traditional junior high schools. Unfortunately, many junior high schools do not provide such a developmentally appropriate environment (see Eccles & Midgley, 1989). Clearly, future research is needed to determine the beneficial impact of these restructuring strategies on adolescent adjustment.

In addition to the structural changes that would facilitate a more community-oriented environment in schools, there are other changes that schools can implement to foster a more positive, developmentally responsive environment. One such change is the promotion of greater parent involvement in schools. The evidence is fairly strong that parent involvement in their child's schools is linked to better academic performance and overall psychological competence in the children (e.g., Epstein & McPartland, 1977). A school governance that provides a more integral role for parents in policy and curriculum decision making can result in parents feeling more efficacious for influencing their child's education, which, in turn, can be reflected in the adolescent's own improved competence, both academically and psychologically. For example, teachers could encourage parent involvement by assigning tasks in which parents and their adolescents work together on tasks or issues that are relevant to the adolescents—such as occupational exploration or delineation of one's family lineage tree. Tasks such as these encourage parents to be a resource for the adolescents' own self-development.

The promotion of increased parent involvement in school can also be the gateway to greater parent–teacher communication about the child. Such communication can be used to facilitate the integration of the home and school lives of adolescents in order to get a more complete picture of what adolescents' lives are like. This integration of contexts would help foster the type of safety zone Simmons and Blyth (1987) advocated as necessary for healthy development during this period—a zone in which adolescents can experiment but where the adults are available to catch the adolescent if he or she starts to get into trouble. Again, such communication should not be intended as a venue for strict monitoring of adolescents, but rather as a means by which teachers and parents can better understand and be attuned to the experiences of their adolescents.

Better efforts could also be made in school environments to increase the degree to which teachers are attuned to the psychological needs of adolescents. For example, focus groups in which adolescents are given a forum to openly discuss the issues most relevant to them could provide an excellent arena from which teachers, and parents for that matter, can learn about what is happening in the lives of adolescents and about what their concerns are. It is likely that both policy and practice could be greatly informed if we as adults listen to what adolescents themselves are saying about their lives and their social environments.

Overall, each of these reform efforts may serve to increase the degree to which teachers and parents are attuned to the psychological needs of adolescents. For example, creating smaller groups with more consistent contact between teachers and specific students would increase the opportunity for teachers to get know students in the same way elementary school teachers get to know their students. In addition, facilitated parent involvement in schools and parent–teacher communication could increase the amount of important information shared concerning the progress and wellness of each adolescent in his or her home and school settings. Furthermore, more individualized techniques such as focus groups in which adolescents are given a forum to openly discuss the issues most relevant to them could provide a superb arena within which the significant adults in young adolescents' lives can learn about adolescents' lives. Finally, increased opportunities for adolescents to become involved in their community would not only model prosocial ways in which young people can be responsible, but could also help young people feel like they belong and are valued members of their community.

ACKNOWLEDGMENTS

Funding for this project was provided by grants from NICHD, NSF, Spencer Foundation, W. T. Grant Foundation, and the MacArthur Foundation Research Network on Successful Adolescent Development among Youth in High Risk Settings to the first author. We wish to thank the following people for their help throughout data collection and analysis: Janis Jacobs, Harriet Feldlaufer, Dave Klingel, Douglas Mac Iver, Karen McCarthy, Carol Midgley, David Reuman, Allan Wigfield, and Doris Yee. We would also like to thank all of the school districts, teachers, and students who participated in these studies.

REFERENCES

Aldous, J. (1977). Family interaction patterns. *Annual Review of Sociology, 3*, 105–135.
Bandura, A. (1986). The explanatory and predictive scope of self-efficacy theory [Special Issue: Self-efficacy theory in contemporary psychology]. *Journal of Social and Clinical Psychology, 4*(3), 359–373.
Baron, R. M., & Graziano, W. G. (1991). *Social psychology.* Chicago: Holt, Rinehart, & Winston.
Blos, P. (1979). Modifications in the classical psychoanalytic model of adolescence. *Adolescent Psychiatry, 7*, 6–25.
Blyth, D. A., Simmons, R. G., & Carlton-Ford, S. (1983). The adjustment of early adolescents to school transitions. *Journal of Early Adolescence, 3*, 105–120.
Bohrnstedt, G., & Felson, R. (1983). Explaining the relations among children's actual and perceived performances and self-esteem: A comparison of several causal models. *Journal of Personality and Social Psychology, 45*(1), 43–56.
Brophy, J. E., & Evertson, C. M. (1976). *Learning from teaching: A developmental perspective.* Boston: Allyn & Bacon.

Bryk, A. S., Lee, V. E., & Smith, J. B. (1989, May). *High school organization and its effects on teachers and students: An interpretative summary of the research.* Paper presented at the invitational conference on "Choice and Control in American Education," Robert M. La Follette Institute of Public Affairs, University of Wisconsin, Madison.

Carnegie Council on Adolescent Development. (1989). *Turning points: Preparing American youth for the 21st century.* New York: Carnegie Corporation.

Collins, W. A. (1990). Parent–child relationships in the transition to adolescence: Continuity and change in interaction, affect, and cognition. In R. Montemayor, G. Adams, & T. Gullotta (Eds.), *Advances in adolescent development: Vol. 2. From childhood to adolescence: A transitional period?* (pp. 85–106). Newbury Park, CA: Sage.

Compas, B. E. (1987). Coping with stress in childhood and adolescence. *Psychological Bulletin, 101*, 393–403.

Crockett, L. J., Petersen, A. C., Graber, J. A., Schulenberg, J. E., & Ebata, A. (1989). School transitions and adjustment during early adolescence. *Journal of Early Adolescence, 9*, 181–210.

Dryfoos, J. G. (1990). *Adolescents at risk: Prevalence and prevention.* Oxford, UK: Oxford University Press.

Eccles, J. S. (1993). School and family effects on the ontogeny of children's interests, self-perceptions, and activity choice. In J. Jacobs (Ed.), *Nebraska Symposium on Motivation, 1992: Developmental perspectives on motivation* (pp. 145–208). Lincoln: University of Nebraska Press.

Eccles, J. S., Lord, S., & Midgley, C. M. (1991). What are we doing to adolescents? The impact of educational contexts on early adolescents. *American Journal of Education, 99*, 521–542.

Eccles, J. S., & Midgley, C. (1989). Stage/environment fit: Developmentally appropriate classrooms for early adolescents. In R. E. Ames & C. Ames (Eds.), *Research on motivation in education* (Vol. 3, pp. 139–186). New York: Academic Press.

Eccles, J., Midgley, C., & Adler, T. (1984). Grade-related changes in the school environment: Effects on achievement motivation. In J. G. Nicholls (Ed.), *The development of achievement motivation* (pp. 283–331). Greenwich, CT: JAI.

Eccles, J. S., Midgley, C., Buchanan, C. M., Wigfield, A., Reuman, D., & Mac Iver, D. (1993). Development during adolescence: The impact of stage/environment fit. *American Psychologist, 48*, 90–101.

Eccles, J. S., Miller Buchanan, C., Flanagan, C., Fuligni, A., Midgley, C., & Yee, D. (1991). Control versus autonomy during adolescence. *Journal of Social Issues, 47*(4), 53–68.

Eccles, J. S., Wigfield, A., Flanagan, C. A., Miller, C., Reuman, D. A., & Yee, D. (1989). Self-concepts, domain values, and self-esteem: Relations and changes at early adolescence. *Journal of Personality, 57*(2), 283–309.

Elkind, D., & Bowen, R. (1979). Imaginary audience behavior in children and adolescents. *Developmental Psychology, 15*, 38–44.

Epstein, J. L., & McPartland, J. M. (1976). The concept and measurement of the quality of school life. *American Educational Research Journal, 13*, 15–30.

Epstein, J. L., & McPartland, J. M. (1977). *Family and school interactions and main effects on affective outcomes* (Report No. 235). Baltimore, MD: Johns Hopkins University, Center for Social Organization of Schools.

Feldlaufer, H., Midgley, C., & Eccles, J. S. (1988). Student, teacher, and observer perceptions of the classroom environment before and after the transition to junior high school. *Journal of Early Adolescence, 8*, 133–156.

Fenzel, L. M. (1991, April). *A prospective study of the relationships among role strain, self-esteem, competence, and social support in early adolescence.* Paper presented at the Biennial Meeting of the Society for Research in Child Development, Seattle, WA.

Fenzel, L. M., & Blyth, D. A. (1986). Individual adjustment to school transitions: An exploration of the role of supportive peer relations. *Journal of Early Adolescence, 6,* 315–329.

Flanagan, C. (1985, April). *The relationship of family environments in early adolescence and intrinsic motivation in the classroom.* Paper presented at the meeting of the American Educational Research Association, Chicago.

Flanagan, C. (1986, April). *Early adolescent needs and family decision-making environments: A study of person–environment fit.* Paper presented at the meeting of the American Educational Research Association, San Francisco.

Flanagan, C. (1989, April). *Adolescents' autonomy at home: Effects on self-consciousness and intrinsic motivation at school.* Paper presented at the meeting of the American Educational Research Association, Montreal.

Freud, A. (1969). Adolescence as a developmental disturbance. In G. Kaplan & S. Lebovici (Eds.), *Adolescence: Psychosocial perspectives* (pp. 5–10). New York: Basic Books.

Garmezy, N. (1983). Stressors of childhood. In N. Garmezy & M. Rutter (Eds.), *Stress, coping and development in children* (pp. 43–84). New York: McGraw-Hill.

Grotevant, H. D. (1983). The contribution of the family to the facilitation of identity formation in early adolescence. *Journal of Early Adolescence, 3*(3), 225–237.

Hamburg, B. A. (1974). Early adolescence: A specific and stressful stage of the life cycle. In G. V. Coelho, B. A. Hamburg, & J. E. Adams (Eds.), *Coping and adaptation* (pp. 101–124). New York: Basic Books.

Harter, S. (1981). A new self-report scale of intrinsic versus extrinsic orientation in the classroom: Motivational and informational components. *Developmental Psychology, 17,* 300–312.

Harter, S. (1990). Developmental differences in the nature of self-representations: Implications for the understanding, assessment, and treatment of maladaptive behavior. *Cognitive Therapy and Research, 14,* 113–142.

Hawkins, J. A., & Berndt, T. J. (1985, April). *Adjustment following the transition to junior high school.* Paper presented at the Biennial Meeting of the Society for Research in Child Development, Toronto, Canada.

Higgins, E. T., & Parsons, J. E. (1983). Social cognition and the social life of the child: Stages as subcultures. In E. T. Higgins, D. W. Ruble, & W. W. Hartup (Eds.), *Social cognition and social behavior: Developmental issues* (pp. 15–62). New York: Cambridge University Press.

Hill, J. P. (1988). Adapting to menarche: Familial control and conflict. In M. Gunnar & W. A. Collins (Eds.), *Minnesota Symposia on child development* (Vol. 21, pp. 43–77). Hillsdale, NJ: Lawrence Erlbaum Associates.

Hill, J. P., & Lynch, M. E. (1983). The intensification of gender-related role expectations during early adolescence. In J. Brooks-Gunn & A. C. Petersen (Eds.), *Girls at puberty: Biological and psychosocial perspectives* (pp. 201–228). New York: Plenum.

Hirsch, B., & Rapkin, B. (1987). The transition to junior high school: A longitudinal study of self-esteem, psychological symptomatology, school life, and social support. *Child Development, 58,* 1235–1243.

Hunt, D. E. (1975). Person–environment interaction: A challenge found wanting before it was tried. *Review of Educational Research, 45,* 209–230.

Kavrell, S. M., & Petersen, A. C. (1984). Patterns of achievement in early adolescence. In M. L. Maehr (Ed.), *Advances in motivation and achievement* (pp. 1–35). Greenwich, CT: JAI.

Kazdin, A. E. (1993). Adolescent mental health: Prevention and treatment programs. *American Psychologist, 48,* 127–141.

Leahy, R. L. (1981). Parental practices and the development of moral judgment and self-image disparity during adolescence. *Developmental Psychology, 17*(5), 580–594.

Lee, P., Statuto, C., & Kedar-Voivodas, G. (1983). Elementary school children's perceptions of their actual and ideal school experience: A developmental study. *Journal of Educational Psychology, 75,* 838–847.

Lord, S., Eccles, J. S., & McCarthy, K. (1994). Risk and protective factors in the transition to junior high school. *Journal of Early Adolescence, 14*, 162–199.

Mac Iver, D., Klingel, D. M., & Reuman, D. A. (1986, April). *Students' decision-making congruence in mathematics classrooms: A person–environment fit analysis.* Paper presented at the meeting of the American Educational Research Association, San Francisco.

Mac Iver, D., & Reuman, D. A. (1988, April). *Decision-making in the classroom and early adolescents' valuing of mathematics.* Paper presented at the annual meeting of the American Educational Research Association, New Orleans, LA.

Maehr, M. L., & Anderman, E. M. (1993). Reinventing schools for early adolescents: Emphasizing task goals. *The Elementary School Journal, 93*, 593–610.

Midgley, C., Anderman, E., & Hicks, L. (1995). Differences between elementary and middle school teachers and students: A goal theory approach. *Journal of Early Adolescence, 15*, 90–113.

Midgley, C., & Feldlaufer, H. (1987). Students' and teachers' decision-making fit before and after the transition to junior high school. *Journal of Early Adolescence, 7*, 225–241.

Midgley, C., Feldlaufer, H., & Eccles, J. S. (1988a). Student/teacher relations and attitudes toward mathematics before and after the transition to junior high school. *Child Development, 60*, 375–395.

Midgley, C., Feldlaufer, H., & Eccles, J. S. (1988b). The transition to junior high school: Beliefs of pre- and post-transition teachers. *Journal of Youth and Adolescence, 17*, 543–562.

Midgley, C., Feldlaufer, H., & Eccles, J. S. (1989). Change in teacher efficacy and student self- and task-related beliefs during the transition to junior high school. *Journal of Educational Psychology, 81*, 247–258.

Miller, C. L. (1986, April). *Puberty and person–environment fit in the classroom.* Paper presented at the meeting of the American Educational Research Association, San Francisco.

Miller, C. L., Eccles, J. S., Flanagan, C., Midgley, C., Feldlaufer, H., & Harold, R. D. (1990). Parents' and teachers' beliefs about adolescents: Effects of sex and experience. *Journal of Youth and Adolescence, 19*, 363–394.

Minuchin, S., Rosman, B. L., & Baker, L. (1978). *Psychosomatic families: Anorexia nervosa in context.* Cambridge, MA: Harvard University Press.

Montemayor, R. (1986). Family variation in parent–adolescent storm and stress. *Journal of Adolescent Research, 1*, 15–31.

Moos, R. H. (1979). *Evaluating educational environments.* San Francisco, CA: Jossey-Bass.

Nicholls, J. G. (1980, June). *Striving to develop and demonstrate ability: An intentional theory of achievement motivation.* Paper presented at Conference on Attributional Approaches to Human Motivation, Center for Interdisciplinary Studies, University of Bielefeld, West Germany.

Nottelmann, E. D. (1987). Competence and self-esteem during the transition from childhood to adolescence. *Developmental Psychology, 23*, 441–450.

Oakes, J. (1981). Tracking policies and practices: School by school summaries. A study of schooling (Tech. Rep. No. 25). Los Angeles: University of California Graduate School of Education.

Office of Educational Research and Improvement. (1988). *Youth indicators 1988.* Washington, DC: U.S. Government Printing Office.

Paikoff, R. L., & Brooks-Gunn, J. (1991). Do parent–child relationships change during puberty? *Psychological Bulletin, 110*, 47–66.

Payne, B. D., Smith, J. E., & Payne, D. A. (1983). Grade, sex, and race differences in test anxiety. *Psychological Reports, 53*(1), 291–294.

Petersen, A. C., & Crockett, L. (1985). Pubertal timing and grade effects on adjustment [Special Issue: Time of maturation and psychosocial functioning in adolescence]. *Journal of Youth and Adolescence, 14*(3), 191–206.

Roeser, R. W., Midgley, C. M., & Maehr, M. L. (1994, February). *Unfolding and enfolding youth: A developmental study of school culture and student well-being.* Paper presented at the Society for Research on Adolescence, San Diego, CA.

Rosenbaum, J. E. (1976). *Making inequality: The hidden curriculum of high school tracking.* New York: Wiley.

Rounds, T. S., & Osaki, S. Y. (1982). *The social organization of classrooms: An analysis of sixth- and seventh-grade activity structures* (Rep. EPSSP-82-5). San Francisco: Far West Laboratory.

Rutter, M. (1981). Stress, coping, and development: Some issues and some questions. *Journal of Child Psychology and Psychiatry, 22,* 323–356.

Ryan, R. M., & Lynch, J. H. (1989). Emotional autonomy versus detachment: Revisiting the vicissitudes of adolescence and young adulthood. *Child Development, 60,* 340–356.

Simmons, R. G., & Blyth, D. A. (1987). *Moving into adolescence: The impact of pubertal change and school context.* Hawthorne, NY: Aldine de Gruyter.

Steinberg, L. (1990). Interdependence in the family: Autonomy, conflict, and harmony in the parent–adolescent relationship. In S. S. Feldman & G. R. Elliott (Eds.), *At the threshold: The developing adolescent* (pp. 255–276). Cambridge, MA: Harvard University Press.

Stipek, D., & Mac Iver, D. (1989). Developmental changes in children's assessment of intellectual competence. *Child Development, 60,* 521–538.

Ward, B. A., Mergendoller, J. R., Tikunoff, W. J., Rounds, T. S., Dadey, G. J., & Mitman, A. L. (1982). *Junior high school transition study: Executive summary.* San Francisco, CA: Far West Laboratory.

Wigfield, A., Eccles, J. S., MacIver, D., & Reuman, D. A. (1991). Transitions during early adolescence: Changes in children's domain-specific self-perceptions and general self-esteem across the transition to junior high school. *Developmental Psychology, 27*(4), 552–565.

Willig, A. C., Harnish, D. L., Hill, K. T., & Maehr, M. L. (1983). Sociocultural and educational correlates of success-failure attributions and evaluation anxiety in the school setting for Black, Hispanic, and Anglo Children. *American Educational Research Journal, 20*(3), 385–410.

Yee, D. K. (1986, April). *Family decision-making, classroom decision-making, and student self- and achievement-related attitudes.* Paper presented at the meeting of the American Educational Research Association, San Francisco.

Yee, D. K. (1987, April). *Participation in family decision-making: Parent and child perspectives.* Paper presented at the meeting of the Society for Research in Child Development, Baltimore, MD.

Yee, D. K., & Flanagan, C. (1985). Family environments and self-consciousness in early adolescence. *Journal of Early Adolescence, 5,* 59–68.

11

Dropping Out

Francis A. J. Ianni
Institute for Social Research

Margaret Terry Orr
Teachers College, Columbia University

Youth, what they do and where and why they do it, what they think and say about themselves, their peers, and the adults and social institutions in their lives hold a compelling interest for all of us. We view this period of the life cycle as a very special one, more accountable than childhood, but still a time of growth and development, one of preparation and promise for the adult roles we cast for our children. Some of our concerns seem remarkably similar from place to place and from generation to generation. Will they grow and develop into proper adults and have a happy and productive life? What can we do as parents or adult caretakers to help them along in this? Yet at the present time, and, especially in particular communities, we have come to see adolescence as a time of trouble and uncertainty, a period that presents adolescents and us with some very special and increasingly ominous problems—dropping out of school and chronic unemployment, drug and alcohol abuse, sexual laxity leading to early parenthood and HIV infection, and aggressive and sometimes violent behavior to others and to themselves—we have come to associate with youth. Each of these problems has its own social drama and deficits and its own solutions and public demands for prevention and remediation, yet these share the same disturbing portrait of youth rejecting or rebelling against what we project as appropriate roles and behavior and in many cases dropping out of the life-cycle script we have projected for them.

Each of these problems and their attendant risk factors can be injurious to adolescent development and destructive to social competence and an integrated and rewarding identity achievement. However, the evidence is clear that, at least for those most likely to be affected, the risk factors and social and behavioral abuses that grow out of them are often interconnected, combining and reinforcing each other with devastating effects on the life course (Benson, 1990; Dryfoos, 1990; Ianni, 1989). Substance abuse and school failure, for example, can be interconnected and can be followed by lives on the fringes of employability and legitimate behavior. Daily media accounts of gang violence, drug-related crime, and the wastage of young lives when youngsters flee or are pushed out onto the streets project a vivid portrait of the devastating effects on young lives and on communities. Yet dropping out of school, although it lacks the immediate intensity and stark tragedy of teenage suicide, juvenile delinquency, or violent behavior, holds a special concern and is viewed as a continuing crisis for youth, their communities, and society at large.

A number of assumptions underwrite the special importance assigned to dropping out of school. One is that dropping out prior to high school graduation is believed to be directly associated with youth unemployment. As the national economy and consequently the job market have placed increasing emphasis on literacy and skills learning, the school-to-workplace transition has become even more a focus of national and local attention. A related aspect of the school-to-work connection is the widespread and deep belief that if youth are not in school learning, they should be doing something productive (working) or they will get into trouble, or, at the very least, remain on the fringes of society, socially and economically. The current emphasis on schooling as preparation for work has come to mean that unemployment among youth is directly linked to the social failure of high schools in the public perception.

The U.S. high school is also perceived as the principle and preferred source of prevention and remediation for a wide variety of social and individual ills that beset children and youth. This model is as clear as it is simplistic. If we experience problems with student discipline and violence, a new course or a special program is added to a high school's curriculum; if drug abuse reaches endemic proportions, a new course or program on drug abuse is added; and the accumulation continues with each new or intensified social problem. This pattern is experienced in every type of community. Schools now offer an astounding (and sometimes confounding) array of programs aimed at youth problems such as adolescent pregnancy, AIDS, drug and alcohol abuse, and the need for conflict resolution, and peer mediation. Usually supported by federal or other external funds, the programs often intrude on class time and sometimes seem to be as controversial as the problems they hope to resolve (Farrar & Hampel, 1987).

At issue, then, are a series of questions about dropping out that center around the relationships between and among students, schools, the structure of a community's institutions, particularly families, business sectors, social service institutions, churches, the criminal justice system, and larger domains such as the economy and the labor force. Questions such as the relative responsibility of the learner, the school, or the family for personal investment in or disengagement from schooling have an almost obsessive quality to them whenever dropping out is examined or explained. Is dropping out of school indeed a special event in the life course or simply one more event in the cycle of rebellion, alienation, and withdrawal from society? Or, is it simply correct "market" behavior for youth who feel ill served by their schools and seek alternatives instead? Finally, to what degree do the solutions exist in single add-on programs or in more substantive restructuring of schools and the role of the broader community institutions? Answers to these questions are of more than academic or clinical interest, and should involve more than a search for who or what is at fault.

There is an extensive literature on dropouts that has identified a number of contributory aspects of a young person's life and lifestyle both in and out of school to this occurrence. Some studies find the problems to be inherent in the youngsters themselves; some physical or intellectual impairment or some character deficit: low self-esteem, poor motivation, impaired intellectual ability, some problem in the developmental self-image, a sense of powerlessness, or a lack of commitment or attachment to the school (Barber, 1984; Orr, 1987). A second area of study sees the problem in a consumer-market framework, indicating the lack of congruence between the school and the world of work, poor school performance, and the distinct possibility that students are making appropriate choices in leaving an educational system that is not serving their future interests (Orr, 1987; Steinberg, Blinde, & Chan, 1984).

A third area of study is related more to the failures of the institutions, primarily schools, that serve youth (see Natriello, McDill, & Pallas, 1990; Wehlage, Rutter, Smith, Lesko, & Fernandez, 1989). Other studies point to problems inherent in the social structure such as poverty or racial and ethnic discrimination, the changing character of the labor market or periods of economic decline and, more recently, to ecological factors such as the diminishing of parental and other social controls and the opportunities for association with delinquent and nonschool peers, which result from a lack of integration among institutional sectors (Cardenas & First, 1985; Hahn, Danzberger, & Lefkowitz, 1987; Ianni, 1989; Rumberger, 1983).

Ever since "the dropout problem" became a major concern of national educational policy in the mid-1980s, attempts at prevention and remediation have taken a number of different directions as a result of changing assumptions and experience. The early strategies were based on the view that dropping out was not unlike drug addiction or teen pregnancy, treating each adolescent as an individual at risk because of some handicapping or predisposing problem, and using a clinical approach to intervention. Early programs of prevention and remediation targeted particular students through special programs usually as part of the school day (U.S. General Accounting Office, 1987). As the focus on dropout prevention shifted from the view of the dropout as an individual victim to an indictment of school practices and then out to reconsider the broader structure and role of communities, the institutions, the labor market, and society itself, there was a developing consensus that improving schools through a more generalized school reform or restructuring was needed to prevent dropping out (Orr, 1987).

Our own view, and the premise of the argument of this chapter, is that the decision to drop out is neither a willful individual act nor is it the result of irresistible pressure from social forces. Rather, it takes place somewhere in the interaction between the inner and outer worlds of each student. We are aware, for example, that this problem varies among communities in its size, density, and distribution. As a result, we have concluded, therefore, that the greater the breadth and severity of the problem within a community, the more likely are the broader external forces contributing to the causes of dropping out, thereby creating a need for institutional responses. However, the consequences are experienced individually and regardless of the density of the dropout problem among various communities, some targeted interventions are necessary.

In all cases, the role of "learner" as presented by the school, the family, peers, and other social forces and perceived and experienced by the individual (through a conflict of expectations, roles, and culture) may not be congruent with a dropout's own developing identity, and so the feeling results that "school is not for me" (William T. Grant Foundation, 1988). Thus, although the focus of inquiry should be on early school leaving as a marker event, the search for causative and contributory factors needs to reach beyond the school into the community and the larger society to look at their effects on all students as well as back into the socialization, enculturation, and developmental history of individual learners. It follows that some prevention programs must establish that identity relationship early in individual learners' social, cultural, and educational experiences and that intervention programs must find ways to reinforce or reconnect student identities and the learning process when alienation occurs. In other cases, or in conjunction with these more individual approaches, districts and their communities must examine the strength and contribution of their efforts to support high-risk youth in staying in school and succeeding, including reducing the possible culture conflict in expectations, reducing structural barriers to continued school attendance, and making schooling more relevant and germane to each student's future success.

DEFINITIONS AND DIMENSIONS
OF DROPPING OUT

Defining who is and who is not a dropout is complicated by the lack of common agreement even among educators and other youth professionals about what constitutes dropping out. District and state definitions of and procedures for counting dropouts differ widely. In one study, it was found that various school districts throughout the country may or may not record a student as a dropout if he or she leaves school to be married, have a baby, take a job, enter the armed services, enroll in college prior to graduation, transfer to another school district, be expelled, or go to jail (Ianni, 1989). Some localities only recognize students as dropouts if they are over 16 (the legal age for leaving school); younger students who have withdrawn or been long-term absentees are not considered dropouts and are given other enumeration classifications such as "status unknown." Some districts never verify whether students who apply for transfers actually enroll elsewhere or never follow up students who complete one school year but do not re-enroll the following year. In addition, many districts and states only track the number of students who have dropped out annually, rather than follow the cumulative dropout rate for a cohort of students. As a result of the disparity in these policies and practices, many school districts and states have historically undercounted the number of dropouts in their jurisdictions, a practice that serves to mask the true dimensions of this problem. At the same time, given the variety of behaviors that have been used to decide who is and who is not a dropout, it is difficult to assess the patterns of behavior, such as infrequent attendance or not re-enrolling after the summer break, that may be precursors to dropping out, without better enumeration systems.

In recent years, the National Center for Educational Statistics has worked with states and local districts to adopt a standard dropout definition. According to this definition, a dropout is a student who was enrolled during the prior school year, has not re-enrolled at the start of the current school year, has not graduated from high school or enrolled in another state- or district-approved program (e.g., as might be offered in prisons), has not enrolled in another school district or state-approved program, is not absent for illness or suspension, and is not dead (National Center for Education Statistics, 1994). A clear definition of who is a dropout, however, is just a starting point for tracking this problem.

There is variability in how students go about dropping out of school. Whereas some students formally withdraw from school at one point, many students leave through a gradual process, as evidenced by their increasingly infrequent attendance and frequent suspensions and expulsions. Some students may also "skip" a semester, withdrawing for one semester, only to return the next, dropping out of and back into school on a cyclical basis as they struggle to remain in school and balance other competing demands or interests. Thus, becoming a dropout is actually more of an evolutionary process for most high-risk students rather than a momentary act of withdrawal.

Current national estimates of the demography of dropping out give some estimation of the dimensions of this problem. Nationwide, it is estimated that there are 39.7 million individuals 18 years of age or older who never completed high school, although about 55% did complete at least some high school (National Center for Education Statistics, 1993). In 1992, 11% of youth ages 16 to 24 were dropouts, representing 3.4 million youth nationally. Selected subgroups of youth are more likely than others to include dropouts, with the greatest differences existing by race or ethnicity and family income status. Hispanic and African American youth are much more likely than White youth to be dropouts (29% and 14% in contrast to 8%). Yet, 49% of all dropouts are White. Youth from low-income families are more than twice as likely as youth from middle-income and substantially more likely than those from high-income families to be dropouts (25% in contrast to 10% and 2%, respectively). Despite these differences, 52% of the dropouts are from middle-income families.

Since the 1970s, there has been a very slight decrease in the status dropout rate—the proportion of individuals in any given year who have not completed high school and are not currently enrolled. This includes a substantial decrease in the status dropout rate for African American youth, accompanied by a simultaneous increase in the number of Hispanic youth with a consistently large dropout rate. Combined, these trends have kept the overall status dropout rate up (National Center for Education Statistics, 1993).

The severity of the dropout rate must be considered within broader demographic changes projected for the near future. It has been estimated that between 1988 and 2020, the U.S. children and youth population will increase by 4%, but will include a decline of 27% among White children and a dramatic increase in the number of Hispanic children. Altogether, the number of minority children will increase from 30% of the school-aged population in 1988 to 51% in 2000. This trend implies a substantial increase in the size of the educationally disadvantaged population and the number of children who are in poverty, because these are so highly correlated with minority status. Also associated with this trend is an increase in the number of children not living with both parents and for whom English is not the primary language, both of which are also highly correlated with being educationally disadvantaged (Natriello et al., 1990). The long-term projects negative consequences for our national economic growth and prosperity, because business and industry will become increasingly dependent on workers who have been educationally disadvantaged and thus likely to lack the necessary skills and competence (National Center on Education and the Economy, 1990).

Although dropping out of school is perceived to be primarily an urban education problem, youth from central cities are only somewhat more likely than suburban and rural youth to drop out (13% in contrast to 10% and 11%) and only 39% of all dropouts are from central cities. Within urban high schools, as much as 50% or more of the ninth-grade cohort drops out, whereas in many suburban and rural high schools, less than 5% of the ninth-grade cohort may drop out. Thus the dropout problem varies in density among different communities, reflecting the mix of causes, the local capacity to redress this problem, and possibly the strategies used.

Certain student performance and other characteristics are highly correlated with dropping out. In particular, grade retention is highly related to subsequent dropping out. Those who repeat more than one grade are substantially more likely to later drop out, particularly if they are held back at the middle school level (National Center for Education Statistics, 1993). In addition, as pointed out by the Panel on High Risks of the National Research Council (1993):

> Studies of the characteristics of dropouts have found that they are more likely to come from poor families, living in single-parent households, have parents who do not participate in decision making for adolescent problems, and live in urban areas. Dropping out is also associated with having a handicapping condition, engaging in delinquent behaviors, being retained in grade, being truant from school, being pregnant or a parent, having poor grades, and working more than 15 hours per week. (p. 116)

There is strong evidence that dropping out, or at least its behavioral precursors, begins before high school and identification of potential dropouts can come as early as elementary school or even preschool (Zigler & Berman, 1983). Yet, finding the characteristics that are highly predictive of the future risk of dropping out at an early age is challenging. Many characteristics that are highly correlated with dropping out are not constant circumstances throughout each child's educational career. Second, there is a danger that some students may be labeled at an early age, establishing a harmful identity that may have negative consequences. Third, the most predictive characteristics may be effective only with some types of potential dropouts, overlooking the needs of other children and youth who are also at risk of dropping out.

Some retrospective studies of dropouts and graduates have isolated characteristics that can correctly identify 60% to 70% of future dropouts among third-grade students. These are being older for the grade, being from families with lower occupational and educational levels, being from families with several siblings, being from a single-parent household, having lower course marks and standardized test scores, and having been retained by the third grade (Lloyd, 1978). Barrington and Hendricks (1989) found school performance measures that were equally predictive as of the third grade of future dropouts. These measures were having six or more absences per year, a low composite achievement test score (of less than 55 on the Iowa Basic Skills Test), a low achievement to intelligence ratio, as indicated by a measure of underperformance in comparison to their potential (of less than .55 for the Iowa Achievement Test/Otis–Lennon IQ test), and negative teacher comments. Like Lloyd, Barrington and Hendricks could predict 70% of the potential dropouts by the third grade.

Dropping out of school is not always a complete step, either. Within 4 years of initially leaving high school, about 40% of the dropouts eventually return to school or another program to try to complete their education. About 30% of the dropouts eventually graduate or earn a GED. Predictably, those with better prior educational performance and personal and social supports are more likely to return and complete their high school education or an equivalency diploma (Pallas, 1986).

Not completing high school has severe consequences, particularly as reflected in subsequent employment and earnings. Dropouts are much more likely to be unemployed than are their graduate counterparts. For example, in 1992, dropouts aged 20 to 24 years were almost twice as likely as high school graduates and three times as likely as college graduates to be unemployed (22%, 13%, and 7%, respectively; National Center for Education Statistics, 1993). Osterman (1989) called the employment phase following high school a *moratorium period*, as youth transition from primarily youth jobs in the secondary labor market to the more stable adult labor market. This moratorium period is longer (and appears to be increasingly so) for youth dropouts than for youth graduates, which has long-term implications for their eventual stable employment. According to Berlin and Sum (1986), by the time young men, for example, are 25 to 29, most (66% in 1986) are employed in full-time year-round jobs. Those who have completed high school and college, however, are much more likely to be settled into stable employment (68% and 78%, respectively) than the dropouts (51%) are.

In addition to delayed employment consequences, there are other individual and social costs for dropouts, including substantially lower annual and lifetime earnings and dissatisfaction with available jobs (Catterall, 1985; Owings & Kolstad, 1985). In addition, obtaining a high school diploma decreases the likelihood of being arrested by over 90% and of having an out-of-wedlock birth by over 50% for youth aged 19 to 23 years (Berlin & Sum, 1986). The increased likelihood of being arrested, having out-of-wedlock births, and being unemployed translates into substantial societal costs for the criminal justice, welfare, and health care systems (Catterall, 1985). Thus, the individual and societal savings from improving the employability of youth dropouts and reducing the incidence of these other problems far outweighs the costs of dropout prevention and intervention programs and services.

WHY YOUTH DROP OUT OF SCHOOL

Much of what is known about why youth drop out of school comes from national surveys of youth dropouts within 2 years of leaving school. As we have seen, youth may leave school for a variety of reasons, and these national surveys reflect how youth respond when asked why they left school.

The National Educational Longitudinal Survey conducted by the National Center for Education Statistics tracked the number of dropouts from an eighth-grade cohort in 1988 throughout a 4-year period. Follow-up survey results showed that 12% of the cohort dropped out by the time they should have been in the 12th grade, with about half leaving between 8th and 10th grades. In the surveys, the youth dropouts revealed why they left. They gave several reasons, most commonly that they left for school-related reasons (43% did not like school, 39% were failing school, 30% could not keep up with the schoolwork, 24% reported that they did not feel that they belonged, and 21% could not get along with the teachers). A substantial percentage of the young women left for parenting reasons (27% were pregnant and 21% were parents). Many, particularly young men, left for employment reasons (29% had a job and 11% had to support their family). In contrast to another national survey of youth, High School and Beyond (also conducted by the National Center for Education Statistics) conducted 10 years earlier, the currently surveyed youth dropouts were much more likely to drop out for school-related reasons, whereas the percentage of young women who drop out because of pregnancy has remained fairly consistent (National Center for Education Statistics, 1993).

Although these survey results tell us what young people say when asked why they left school and provide some insight into the personal and school-related factors involved, these do not reveal the degree to which each reason contributed to their school leaving or what combination of reasons may have been dynamically involved in their decision or behavior; nor do these tell us anything about the inner feelings, the presence or absence of discussion about the decision with peers or adult caretakers, or how they made the decision (if it were consciously made). Neither do the results provide insight into what affects the availability (or lack) of other educational alternatives or an evaluation of what existing programs and resources might have contributed to their action. What they do demonstrate is that both personal and educational-environmental circumstances are critical to whether a student remains in school or drops out, and that these circumstances have been somewhat consistent over time.

Thus, school dropouts do not constitute a singular, homogeneous group. Rather, students drop out for a variety of reasons and under different circumstances. Orr (1987), in her study of dropout prevention and retrieval programs, classified potential and actual youth dropouts based on their circumstances and need for services. She divided them into four groups:

- Marginally at-risk—Students who are still in school but are marginally at risk of dropping out because they are in the lower academic quartile of their cohort, are not involved actively in extracurricular activities, and lack clear direction and purpose.
- Having barriers to education—Students who are at risk of dropping out as evidenced by their lack of credit accumulation and school attendance, their poor academic performance, their frequency of school disciplinary referrals and their general lack of interest in school and school-related activities.
- At high risk—Students who are interested in staying in school but cannot because of personal circumstances (such as health problems, mobility, lack of housing, and abuse).
- Actual dropouts—Students who have already left school, but need services to complete their education and find quality employment.

School districts traditionally recognize the third group as their potential dropouts, rarely targeting services for the other three groups. Instead, districts tend to concentrate their resources on a small number of very high-risk youth who are usually on the verge of leaving school for good. Limited district resources are allocated as preventive intervention for more marginally at-risk youth or to help those experiencing difficulties cope so they can remain in school. Finally, school districts almost never target out-of-school youth for programs and services. Unfortunately, out-of-school youth have few other social service systems that take responsibility for their academic and employment preparation, leaving the youth most in need without significant alternatives.

Quite apart from these national survey results, there are other posited answers as to why youth drop out of school. Some are research based and others are more speculative. Although, as we indicated earlier, no one of these risk factors can fully explain why youth leave school early and it is clear that often more than one reason or cause is involved in

TABLE 11.1
Theoretical Constructs on Reasons for Dropping Out

Adolescent Development Within an Institutional Context
Psychological development
Social identification
Social Role Behavior
Consumer behavior
Role conflict
Culture Conflict
Adolescents' culture conflict
Institutional culture conflict
Structural Domains
School structure
Interagency structure

the process of dropping out, there are a number of explanatory approaches that draw on one or more of the risk factors already described. The underlying theoretical assumptions of various educational researchers and policymakers have in turn become the basis for program planning and design, yielding, in recent years, a wide range of approaches to dropout prevention. In the following, we discuss the variety of theoretical explanations for the reasons youth drop out and conclude with a partial integration of these differing explanations as a basis for policy and program development. As an organizing approach, we have divided these differing explanations into four primary categories—theories about adolescent psychological and social development, social behavior, cultural differences for adolescents and schools, and structural facets within and between schools and other institutions (as shown in Table 11.1).

Adolescent Development Within an Institutional Context

Some theories and research on dropping out have focused on developmental causes, particularly the formation of a sense of self and how schooling experiences and institutional factors can thwart this for some youth. As the examination of the process rather than the event of dropping out focuses more systematically on the developmental process leading to the decision to leave school, the question of how psychosocial needs are involved and what assets or deficits contribute to the presence or absence of risk factors becomes central. To some extent, development involves the emergence or unfolding of biological changes at various stages in life. Both the external and the internal changes impact on the achievement of the sense of self or identity, but these do not come evenly or on equal schedules for all young people. This variability in growth rates and development can produce considerable anxiety and frustration for early-

or late-maturing youth with important implications for self-image and esteem. The development of these two psychological qualities in particular is often viewed as influential on subsequent positive and negative behavior, such as dropping out.

Psychological Development. Most theories of the development of self-identities are based on some form of reciprocity between the self-concept and the social structure (Kohut, 1971; Turner, 1968). It follows that how a student is viewed by peers and adult caretakers in his or her educational life is of considerable importance as to how he or she comes to identify the self as a successful learner. One element of such a positive self-image is the need for a sense of personal competence, capability, and efficacy.

One explanatory model of dropping out centers on the developing identity of the individual dropout and the paucity of stimulation for and integration of personal efficacy and self-esteem allowing for a self-identification as a learner. Exponents of this model inevitably look back into the early childhood and later psychological development of the dropout.

Finn (1989) identified this theoretical approach as a "frustration-self esteem model," which "identifies school failure as the starting point in a cycle that may culminate in the student's rejecting, or being rejected by, the school" (p. 117). According to Finn, the sequence begins with actual or anticipated school failure; not attaining academic goals in turn leads to frustration and withdrawal. The reflective, evaluative aspect of the self-concept and its associated sense of self-esteem develop awkwardly in this social milieu. Early and continued experiences of failure cumulatively contribute to a self-identification as a nonlearner, a view often exacerbated by parents, peers, and even teachers. This negative identification is self-reinforcing and a cycle of self-doubt, declining success, self-blame, and withdrawal can result. Frustrated at school, a student may seek other arenas for success, eventually leaving school altogether (Gold & Mann, 1984).

Our own qualitative research has shown the existence of this pattern of reinforced sense of failure and frustration, and the consequential dropping out. In one study of dropouts in a southern city, for example, Ianni and Reuss-Ianni (1992) were struck by the number of comments from teachers and administrators that "we have known since the second grade" that a particular student would eventually drop out. A study of school records for a sample of middle school and high school dropouts showed that of those who eventually dropped out, most had a progressive and cumulative pattern of school failure and behavioral problems. First a student lost or in some cases never seemed to acquire any interest in schoolwork; the consequence was lowered grades and often retention in grade. Frustrated and now "left behind" neighborhood and school peers, a student began to skip classes and soon came into conflict with school authorities, in some cases exhibiting disruptive behavior against peers as well as in the classroom. Increasingly, teacher comments and even counseling or psychological reports described the student as feeling isolated and powerless. Then, at some point, all of these accumulating deficits and frustration reinforced some incident, some crisis, or even some "bad day" and the reluctant student stopped coming to school.

According to Finn (1989), as one's self-view is consistently thwarted by repeated failure, the youth's frustration and withdrawal increases, "resulting in a search for alternative activities that may be less sanctioned socially but through which the youngster can experience some success" (p. 120). Exponents of this view speculate that dropouts, by leaving school, may be taking a positive action to remove the source of frustration—the school—or form positive peer-group relationships with other similar youth. Yet, whereas the research on the correlation of self-concept and self-esteem measures and school performance and problem behavior are correlated, the relationship between self-esteem and dropping out is less conclusive.

Social Identification. Another theoretical approach identified by Finn (1993) is a "participation-identification model," which focuses on how students are involved in schooling both emotionally and behaviorally. In this model, successful school completers should have "multiple, expanding forms of participation in school-relevant activities" (p. 117). According to Finn, without participation in school activities, students may not develop a sense of identification with school, leading to significant negative consequences. Thus, active participation in school as well as a feeling of commitment or identification with the school are critical to fostering school retention and ultimately completion.

This model, as Finn explained, draws heavily on sociology, particularly delinquency theory, for its explanatory base. Finn specifically saw the school as the locus for the development of a commitment to a pattern of educational and occupational goals and of a belief in the rules and laws of society, thereby becoming engaged in conventional activities. It follows that resistance to or departure from education inhibits or restricts the successful development of the sense of commitment and its associated belief system. The growing current consensus on the importance of student alienation as a prime factor in dropping out and the emphasis on school reform as a vehicle for its prevention are extensions of this model (Hamilton, 1990).

Social Role Behavior

To some degree, potential and actual dropouts act on their role as students and the opportunities and constraints of this role in their deliberate or evolving choice to quit school without graduating. Less research exists on this theoretical perspective, but there is some evidence from national surveys of dropouts and studies of selected subgroups of dropouts to suggest that there are role-related dimensions to the causes of dropping out. This includes two areas; one reflects an active process of choice in remaining a student or dropping out, which we have termed *consumer behavior*. The other reflects the stresses that some students experience from the demands of multiple roles, forcing them to give up on being a student.

Consumer Behavior. One view of dropping out is that a student may be exercising appropriate consumer behavior. If the school is not meeting his or her needs, a student may be taking a positive step (rather than a negative one) by leaving. This may be a reaction to poor teaching, uncaring interest, lack of culturally relevant curriculum, and a poor climate for learning caused by the deficient physical and social environment. This action may be particularly relevant in communities where the promised payoff between schooling and future employment is weak or nonexistent. If schools have failed to demonstrate (or deliver) that obtaining a high school diploma will afford a student a better future, a student may be showing good consumerism by not investing more time in school. Unfortunately, these same youth are most likely not to have viable alternatives, and to be accepting what appears to be a bleak future for themselves, as it exists for others around them.

Generally, there is a need to see some payoff in terms of one's possible futures and the efficacy of one's own control to reach them. Poor employment and career prospects, particularly among minority youth, project bleak futures for many and this reality feature is an important determinant of a student's sense of fate control. Developing and sustaining a commitment to education requires that the student see and accept a direct relationship between what he or she is learning in school and the possibilities of a good job and future well-being. Seeing the relationship between what the school is teaching and what the workplace demands is difficult for many youth and for some who are afflicted by personal, cultural, or social deficits, their reduced sense of efficacy and fate control makes the problem even greater.

There is little research on dropouts to support this theory, although it can be somewhat surmised from the percentage of dropouts who claimed (in the national survey of recent dropouts) that they left because "school is not for me." In addition, differences in employment rates between minority and nonminority youth by their educational status reveals that the payoff of a high school diploma does little for minority youth in contrast to nonminority youth dropouts, although it does improve their opportunities slightly in contrast to minority dropouts.

Role Conflict.   Adolescents have many roles, including being a student. When the demands of these different roles are too great or in conflict with continued schooling, youth often will respond to the greatest demands, which may not be to remain in school. In addition, the draw of continued schooling in part is dependent on each student perceiving himself or herself as a learner. The more this view is in jeopardy and the greater the demands of other roles, the more likely it is a student will drop out. As a result, one approach to the problem of dropping out is to see role overload—having to juggle too many responsibilities with inadequate time and experiential resources—as a major factor.

One externally demanding role is being an employee. In the authors' decade-long field study of adolescents in 10 communities throughout the United States, we found many adolescents combined part-time employment with schooling. Working alone is not enough to stress continued school completion for students. Working long hours (more than 15 to 20 hours per week) is a great strain, however, making school achievement and involvement more difficult and putting students at risk of dropping out. Yet, some youth have to work to help support their families or even themselves. As shown in national survey results of recent dropouts, 23% reported that they left school because they could not go to work and school at the same time and 11% had to support a family (National Center for Education Statistics, 1993). The more youth take on responsibility for the economic well-being of their families, the less likely it will be that they can remain in school. Finally, because it is difficult for youth to work full-time jobs that conform to the school schedule, the choices become even starker.

Some youth have other significant responsibilities at home—caring for younger siblings and a variety of "chores"—and the role of son or daughter, in a family in which education is not valued, may devalue the role of student to the point at which dropping out is seen as responsive to parental wishes (Ianni, 1989). According to a recent national survey, 12% of dropouts left school to care for a family member (National Center for Education Statistics, 1993).

Some adolescents who are parents themselves find it very difficult to continue their high school education with the added responsibility of an infant or young child, particularly given the severe lack of affordable and accessible child care in our country. Even highly motivated young mothers who are willing to leave their children in child care while they are in school are severely challenged by the lack of available resources. In addition, if child care can be found, the added complications of readying themselves and their children, transporting them, and getting to school on time can be overwhelming. Thus, it is not surprising that many adolescent mothers never complete high school (McGee, 1989) and that 21% of female dropouts reported in a national survey that they left school because they were a parent and 27% left because they were pregnant (National Center for Education Statistics, 1993).

Peer group roles can also be in opposition to school roles; where the peer group is economically, ethnically, or racially based, identification with the group may be antagonistic to commitment to school. Finally, sometimes the school itself presents roles for students that are competitive or even antagonistic with the academic role. All schools sort youngsters formally by putting them in tracks or ability groups, and informally into groupings ("jocks," "brains," "freaks") that indicate what is valued and what is condemned in the school. Trying to negotiate the variety of roles in and out of school and focusing the time, energy, and commitment required can be overwhelming and for some students withdrawal from school may seem the most immediate solution at hand.

Culture Conflict

Various researchers and academicians have looked at the dropout experiences of youth as a cultural problem rather than a consequence of individual differences and circumstances, approaching this perspective from two vantage points—the students' and the teachers'.

Adolescents' Culture Conflict. Drawing on the ecological principle that individual behavior is transactional with its cultural environment and so cannot be understood in isolation from it, this model describes dropping out as the result of cultural dissonance or conflict between the school and community worlds of a child. The school, home, and community all contribute to a youth's perception of his or her social identity. To the extent that the school formally or informally uses social, racial, and ethnic identification to sort students' access to educational resources and reinforces culturally biased perspectives and expectations, it can confuse and sometimes confound the consolidation of an authentic identity as a learner, for it is more discriminated against students.

Ethnographers Fordham and Ogbu (1986) argued that one reason Black students seem to do so poorly in school and eventually drop out is the ambivalence and dissonance they experience from "the burden of acting White." Many academically able Black students, they found, do not put forth the necessary effort to succeed academically because they are caught in the bind between a school system that refuses to acknowledge that Black students are capable of academic achievement and a Black community that comes to consider academic striving as "acting White."

Institutional Culture Conflict. The professional culture of a school, as embodied by the teachers and other staff, may be dissonant for some students, undercutting the sense of community and inclusiveness for these students and discouraging their continued school attendance. Wehlage et al. (1989) examined teacher–student interactions and how these affect students' sense of belonging and school membership. They concluded that for teachers to be successful with all students, particularly those at risk of dropping out, they must be respectful of students (and vice versa) and take an initiative "in helping students overcome impediments" (p. 135) to fuller participation in learning and other aspects of school life. They identified four teacher beliefs and values and related behaviors that constitute "a positive teacher culture facilitating membership and engagement of students" (p. 135). These four beliefs are (a) that teachers accept personal accountability for student success, (b) that they believe in and practice an extended teacher role, (c) that teachers accept the need for and are persistent with all students, not just those who are ideal, and (d) that they believe that all students can learn, particularly if building on students' strengths and not weaknesses.

Their research and conclusions come from a study of small alternative schools where these values and practices are most likely to be found. There is little research available, however, on how prevalent these values and practices are among more traditional comprehensive high schools and the degree to which the absence of these contributes to dropping out. Nonetheless, these beliefs and practices represent both an ideal supportive culture to assist all students, particularly potential dropouts, in successfully completing their education and areas for school improvement.

Other educational researchers have broadened this view of school culture to define the school as a community. Bryk and Driscoll (1988), for example, tried to measure the extent of a sense of a school community using the national High School and Beyond survey data. They used various measures, such as teachers having a sense of shared beliefs and values, belief that students can learn, similarity in student course taking, and teacher knowledge of and contact with students beyond the classroom, to form a communal school organization construct. Their construct was found to be significantly correlated with smaller school size and a lack of ethnic diversity. It was also significantly associated with selected teacher and student outcomes, including teacher efficacy, morale, and lower absenteeism; lower student absenteeism, dropping out, and misbehavior; and greater interest in academics and mathematics achievement. Thus, the culture created within the school is significantly related to student success.

Structural Domains

A developing perspective on the causes of dropping out comes from studies of large urban districts with very high dropout rates. In considering their patterns, researchers and policymakers now look beyond the individual student-specific explanations of why students drop out to consider broader structural reasons that make it more difficult to serve all students well and that discourage a substantial percentage from school completion. From this perspective, the focus shifted from just dropouts to improvement of a school's educational performance and accountability for all students or general school reform.

This perspective also includes whether schools can be held accountable for a broad range of social problems that interfere with students' successful schooling, such as the ramifications of poverty and deprivation, the inadequacy of other social institutions, and dramatically increasing social problems such as drug abuse and homelessness. This re-examination has led to efforts to broaden constituency involvement in school governance (through school-based management and increased parental involvement) and stress on collaborative interagency participation in service delivery (Dryfoos, 1994).

School Structure. In her classification of dropout prevention program models, Orr (1987) identified school districtwide intervention and change as one approach. The need for this form of intervention stems from the existence of policies, procedures, curriculum, and school organization that may deter continuous school enrollment for some students. In unpublished research, Orr (1991) found that some urban school districts had policies that actually discouraged some at-risk students from continuous attendance. For example, students who accumulate too many unexcused absences early in a semester would earn an automatic course failure and have no incentive to continue school until the next semester. As another example, some urban districts aggressively used out-of-school suspensions with difficult students, counting this time as unexcused absences. This practice only contributed to course failure and gave many students a clear message from the school and district not to return (Orr, 1991). Other specific policies that may harm the educational achievement of large numbers of children are now being called into question—specifically grade retention and homogeneous grouping. Both have been found to hinder, rather than assist, better achievement among poorly performing students (National Research Council, 1993).

Finally, the existing school system structure has been severely criticized in recent years for its industrial-type organizational approach to education—uniform curriculum and grade structures, batch processing of student learning according to set time parameters, and a focus on lower level basic skills rather than the higher order thinking skills that are required of work in our growth industries (Marshall & Tucker, 1992). Existing organizational structure has been criticized for working best with only a subset of students and being grossly inadequate for the majority of students who do not go on to college but who seek employment directly after high school. Natriello et al. (1990) stressed that disadvantaged students are least well served by the existing structure of public education because it cannot cope well with diversity and the deficiencies that many disadvantaged students have. In addition, their students lack the social and economic resources and support systems that other more advantaged students have. With insufficient resources and strategies for coping, schools are left "to adopt a custodial model of organization in which the goal is simply for the school to survive as an organization" (p. 158).

The same concerns for our economic growth, competitiveness, the related quality of our human capital (in recognition in part that a large and increasing percentage of our children live in poverty and are poorly educated), and the possible crisis in the quality of public school teaching has led to a general call for school reform. The strategies for these most recent school reform efforts have been broadly based as school restructuring—addressing teaching and learning, the conditions of teachers' work, and the governance and incentive structures (Elmore & Associates, 1990). These include increasing the challenges in the curricular content (to develop higher order thinking skills), reducing the irrelevance and fragmentation of curricular content, and making the school day more flexible to allow for innovative instruction. Elmore emphasized, however, that the primary approach has been to redress the relationship between schools and their clients, from becoming more instructionally responsive to generally being held accountable for the success of all students (including potential dropouts).

Interagency Structure. Schools can be instrumental in providing the community and its constituent institutions with a structure through which youth can strive for healthy, happy, and productive lives. However, schools cannot do it alone. We have always known that much of what we need to know in life is learned outside school, and what we learn in these social contexts is particularly important in making a living, making it in the world, and the many other forms of instrumental knowledge that we need. Problems for youth in any of these institutional sectors of the community—the family, the peer group, the workplace, and the criminal justice system—can contribute as much, and sometimes more, than the school to dropping out. Most frequently, it is the interactive effects of these sectors that are implicated.

Natriello et al. (1990) also couched the educational problems of school dropouts more broadly by defining being educationally disadvantaged in terms of insufficient educational experiences in any one of these three domains: the school, family, and community. They stressed that whereas the consequences of these deficiencies may occur in the schools, the causes may be derived from one or more of these areas. Walberg (1984), for example, after reviewing all of the research on student achievement, concluded that environmental factors "hold the best hope for increasing educational productivity" (p. 25). Walberg also asserted that what might be called the "alterable curriculum of the home" is twice as predictive of academic learning as is family socioeconomic status. Bloom (1984) made similar analyses, with similar results, and congruent recommendations for strengthening school and family ties.

The occurrence of deficiencies in these three domains (the family, school, and community), however, is more pronounced in some communities than in others. Increasingly, our poor urban communities in particular are becoming more isolated, socially and economically, yielding fewer social supports and greater concentrations of poverty. Wilson (1987) documented the effects of this ecological and economic isolation on poor urban minorities. He argued that the increase of social problems (including high dropout rates) in the inner city with the "crystallization of underclass culture" may reflect "some very important structural and institutional changes in the inner city that have accompanied the black middle and working class exodus" (p. 56), thereby sharply increasing social dislocation. The exodus negatively affected the basic social institutions—churches, schools, stores, recreational facilities, and social services. Gone also with the middle- and working-class are the mainstream role models that demonstrated the value of education, employment (rather than welfare), and family stability. Without positive role models and a network system of resources, finding productive employment and completing high school, he argued, have different social meaning, because joblessness is more of a way of life. The social and economic isolation influence norms and behaviors that may not be conducive for working—reinforcing tardiness and absenteeism, rather than timeliness and responsibility.

This scenario for highly impoverished inner-city communities represents the interdependence of the family, social institutions (including schools), and the community in shaping the norms, expectations, and even opportunities for its youth and young adults. For poor inner-city communities, this interdependence is quite fragile and the absence of one or more dimensions has had strong negative consequences, particularly for its children.

Optimally, various community institutions—the family, the school, the workplace, the criminal justice system, and social agencies—should work together to provide what Winnicott (1965) described as a *facilitating environment*. The role of such an environment is to provide supports and resources as well as models for the development of personally and socially rewarding behavior and attitudes in the lives of youth. Wynn, Richman, Rubenstein, and Littell (1988) described these as *community supports*, each of which has a distinct function in the developmental process and all of which should be available to all youth in order for them to develop a sense of competence and responsibility. What this suggests is that attempting to reform or restructure schools alone is a necessary but insufficient means of ensuring that students are encouraged to stay the course and not drop out.

RELATIONSHIP AMONG THEORIES
OF DROPPING OUT

What we can discern from looking at the various theories is that the complex and demanding requirements for social and individual development toward an identity as a competent and valued adult challenge youth and society and involve some risks, greater for some than for others. Poverty, for example, compounds and exacerbates the risks that all young people face, and presents some additional problems such as hunger or homelessness. Some youth from racial or ethnic minorities and recent immigrants and refugees often must contend with problems that attend poverty, as well as prejudice, bias, and differential access to opportunity structures increasing their risks of failure in life. For some poor and minority youth, risk factors tend to be multiple in number and have greater impact because of the absence of social supports in their families and communities to mitigate them (Ianni & Reuss-Ianni, 1992; Wilson, 1987).

From our review of the theories and related literature on the reasons and causes for dropping out, and our own research, we have identified four major factors that contribute: an adolescent's own development of self, particularly as a learner; occurrence of role conflict within the school and between the school and other environments; the existence of cultural dissonance for students and staff; and structural deficits and limitations within the school (in particular), families, and communities. None of these factors independently explain why students drop out. Instead they overlap, combining in a variety of somewhat predictable ways to influence whether students drop out.

Structural deficits within the school, family, and community seem to be the most influential of the reasons and causes for dropping out, and are most severe and concentrated in urban and poor rural communities. High-poverty areas, both urban and rural, for example, tend to have the poorest and weakest schools. All of the indicators of school success— various standardized tests, reading levels, rates of grade retention, absenteeism and alienation, and teachers' and students' expressions of satisfaction with their learning—reflect more unfavorably on schools in poor areas. These schools and the streets surrounding them are also less-safe havens for learners and frequently (for poor urban schools) their larger size and greater diversity lead to increased anomie and alienation. In addition, the deficiencies in these schools result in limited curricular and instructional offerings and poor community support. These conditions can yield an unsupportive climate for students, rather than a culture and engagement for positive educational success.

In reporting on over a decade of fieldwork with youth in a variety of communities, we have stressed the importance of community youth charters that consciously construct facilitating and caring environments for development and integrating youth into the life course. We continue to believe that we cannot empower young people and their relationships until we strengthen and enrich their social contexts (Ianni, 1989). Thus, in our study of the dropout problem and the design of solutions, we stress the need to consider the influence of structural deficits on creating role and culture conflict, and the development of poor self-esteem and alienation.

Although the relationship between social institutions and adolescent development is important in every community, it is most critical in the inner city, where social isolation has its own devastating ecological basis and where dropping out is much more prevalent than elsewhere. According to Wilson (1987) the solutions to the social isolation of some inner-city communities, therefore, lie in changing "the structure of constraints and opportunities" (p. 61), particularly the broader economic structure. In our view, dropout prevention in such communities requires even broader structural changes. These types of communities require dropout prevention strategies that are different than those used in other communities, where the structural resources and the cultural imperative that underwrite the attitudes and behaviors to utilize them are more prevalent.

In the absence of pronounced structural deficits (as may be more typical in schools and communities with low dropout rates), the other three contributing factors—adolescent development, social role behavior, and culture conflict—are more likely to explain why some students are dropping out. More individualized approaches to dropout prevention may then be necessary in these cases, to address both the causes and consequential problems for potential dropouts.

PROGRAMS THAT WORK

Given the array of perspectives in interpreting the causes and reasons for students to drop out of school, it is challenging to determine the best strategies and approaches. In considering different approaches, we have identified the linkage between the theoretical explanations and the relevant strategies. These are summarized separately in the following (see also Table 11.2). In our conclusion, we propose a model to integrate the various theoretical explanations and to provide a decision-making process for considering when best to use these various strategies.

TABLE 11.2
Theoretical Constructs and Dropout Prevention Approaches

Theoretical Construct	*Dropout Prevention Approach*
Adolescent Development	
Psychological development	Counseling
	Peer support programs
Social identification	More diverse and relevant curriculum
	Smaller school environments
	Block scheduling
	Expanded sports and recreation
	Aggressive attendance improvement efforts
Social Role Behavior	
Consumer behavior	More relevant program offerings
	Improved school-to-work transition
	Academic alternatives
Role conflict	Assistance for students in meeting competing role demands
	School-based child care
	Flexible schedule for working youth
Culture Conflict	
Adolescents' culture conflict	Multicultural education
	Recognition of diversity
	Mentoring
	Alternative school
	Pull-out programs in alternative settings
	Resocialization program
Institutional culture conflict	School restructuring
	Staff development
	Community involvement
Structural Domains	
School structure	Adaption of the school's organization
	Revision of negatively affecting school policies and practices
	Use of heterogeneous grouping
	Elimination of tracking
	Dropout prevention programs
	Comprehensive school restructuring
	Use of management information in problem solving
	Programs for out-of-school youth
Interagency structure	Comprehensive, integrated services
	Broadened community and business involvement
	Increased parental involvement
	Full-service schools

Adolescent Development

The strategies developed from the assumption that an individual student's own psychological development (such as a poor sense of self-esteem) is the root cause of dropping out tend to be counseling based or experiential. The objective is to give the student a sense of accomplishment and self-worth (thereby raising self-esteem). Counseling-based approaches can be as limited as extending counseling services to high-risk youth, self-esteem workshops, or more broadly considered such as courses that emphasize coping and problem-solving skills (such as is included in the WAVE In Schools curriculum). In addition, community service projects are often used as a strategy for developing students' sense of positive self-worth and responsibility, also providing them with opportunities to contribute to their community.

A similar but somewhat alternative approach is to provide the student with a different peer group, which is structured as a support group for problem solving in school. The Twelve-Together program, started in Detroit, combines 12 high- and low-achieving ninth-grade students for weekly peer-group meetings throughout the school year. The high-achieving students provide positive role models for the low-achieving students. As a peer group, they help each other tackle personal and school-related problems through the guidance of an adult professional volunteer.

The social identification model works from the premise that students who are engaged in school activities (academic and extracurricular) are less likely to drop out. From this perspective, the appropriate interventions for dropout prevention are to increase student interest in and access to school offerings. Many of these interventions are actually structural changes in the school—expanding the relevance of the curriculum, creating smaller within-school environments, such as through block scheduling and house structures, expanding sports and other extracurricular activities, and removing penalties that punish students by not permitting them to participate in extracurricular activities that hold their interest (and thus school enrollment). Combined, they reflect changes that increase the fit between the students' social development needs and continued schooling.

Many traditional approaches to dropout prevention address the consequential behavior of students whose developmental needs have been negatively affected by their educational experiences. These behaviors include poor attendance, disruptiveness, and poor grades and credit accumulation. These approaches have been to reduce the problem behaviors, singularly or in combination. For example, some schools added aggressive attendance improvement strategies to track down students with a high number of absences, provide early-morning calls for frequently absent students, and engage parents in reinforcing good attendance. Because students with a high number of absences often fail their courses, some schools also add special classes just for them to help them catch up academically. These strategies, however, do not resolve the problems or circumstances that may have caused poor attendance or other behaviors in the first place. At best, these may include counseling services to help students develop better coping skills. However, improving students' attendance alone is not sufficient to prevent them from dropping out.

Role Conflict

When students' risk of dropping out of high school stems instead from role conflict, the appropriate solution should be to help alleviate the need for or burden of the multiple roles. The most common burdens are needing to work, being an adolescent parent, and having competing family responsibilities. Dropout prevention interventions for these conditions should be service or resource focused—providing students with the means of balancing or coping with these competing demands. For example, schools could offer students who need to work flexible course schedules, including evening or weekend courses. Several districts, including Los Angeles, offer flexible scheduling as a means of alleviating overcrowding, but it also benefits students who need to work.

Students with child-care and other family responsibilities would benefit most from linkages with and access to appropriate support services such as child care and family assistance, to free up their time to attend school. For example, some high schools, including those in Detroit, have added school-based child care for their adolescent mothers, and others have developed comprehensive programs for adolescent mothers (McGee, 1989; Orr, 1987).

In contrast, to address the consumer marketing problem, schools need to look at their total program offerings generally, as it relates to their dropout problem. If a sizable number of students leave high school without graduating because they find the curriculum and instruction to be irrelevant, particularly for their future successful employability, schools can take several steps to improve the program and course relevance and interest. These strategies include rethinking the inclusiveness and relevance of the curriculum for different student groups as well as its applicability for future employment and educational success. This includes adoption of school-to-work transition strategies, such as integrating academic and vocational skills development, adding career development courses, and offering comprehensive preparation programs such as career academies and youth apprenticeships, which offer work-based training as well as industry-specific academic courses (see, e.g., National Academy Foundation literature and Jobs for the Future, 1990, for more information on these models).

A more traditional approach has been to add small, comprehensive alternative schools (some with a strong employment-preparation focus) for potential dropouts. This strategy offers alternative choices, often with more supportive and relevant program designs for potential dropouts, but has also been used to segregate students within academic and behavioral problems in order to provide intensive academic and support services. Rich's Academy in Atlanta and Project COFFEE in rural Massachusetts are two examples of such approaches (Orr, 1987). They provide academic remediation, counseling, and other support services to help students catch up academically, cope with personal problems that hinder their continued schooling, and gain exposure to employment preparation. Both are isolated programs, physically separate from the regular high school, but formally affiliated.

Cultural Approaches

Narrative psychologists and symbolic anthropologists tell us that when we are concerned with questions of emotion or affect and morals or ethics, stories, legends, myths, cultural artifacts, and symbols are far more powerful than structural mechanisms, scientific reasoning, and quantitative evidence (Bruner, 1986; Geertz, 1973; Howard, 1991; Spence, 1982; Turner, 1968). It is, then, to the cultures of schools and their communities that we should turn if we want to embed shared and valued images of schooling and basic beliefs about the importance of education and its efficacy for developing job-related skills and of the ability of students to achieve. Such cultural enhancement resurfaces in role modeling, mentoring, reward and sanction systems, and the everyday life of the school and its community. This means enriching that culture with new artifacts and legends, culture heroes, and other mechanisms to support that culture with ideological (in the true meaning of the word) notions about the contributions of educational attainment to future roles and successes (Geertz, 1973; Greene, 1988).

Such a conscious approach will be "picked up on" by youth as scripts for their intrapersonal world and scenarios for their interpersonal experiences. It has the added advantage of allowing subcultures to adapt the subjective culture to their own understanding, ignoring or modifying images circumscribed by culture history or the vicissitudes of particular social contexts.

The strategies and program models that develop under the cultural approach reflect attention on the values imparted and the ecological dimensions of the experiences. These strategies can be individualized, such as mentoring, in which adults (often professionals) are paired with adolescents through a series of structured encounters to offer the adolescents opportunities to learn about other avenues to success (than the one they may be on). These strategies can also be structured as an inclusive program, such as an alternative school, which provides youth with a separate, nurturing environment, that reinforce selected values (such as achievement and school completion) while trying to address the social and cultural needs of the students. Finally, these strategies can be extended as a form of school reform, uncovering and revamping the ways in which the values and expectations of teachers and administrators may be negatively affecting some students, discouraging their continued enrollment. This last approach can be broadened further to include strategies that bridge the culture of the school and the broader community, as a means of supporting students and reinforcing their school success.

Mentoring programs have become very widespread and range from continuous and very intense encounters to occasional, sometimes almost superficial arrangements. Many programs, such as Inroads in Chicago, which pairs a minority youngster with a person from the business or corporate sector throughout high school and college, relate mentors to their protégés on a one-to-one basis. Others extend their relationships to include groups of youth who work either with one mentor or a number of them. Yet, although the specific structural arrangements may differ, all mentoring programs are based on a conception of mentoring as an interpersonal relationship that develops out of a bond or exchange between individuals rather than as a process that has any reality outside that relationship.

A more radical form of changing the culture environment as a form of dropout prevention is removing potential and actual dropouts from their community and placing them in new settings with a different and distinctive approach to socialization and enculturation. Such pull-out approaches usually follow one of two different forms to resocialization and re-enculturation. One long-standing approach is typified in the federally financed Job Corps, which is a residential program (with some nonresidential model variations) that attempts to provide comprehensive academic and occupational training as well as health care, housing, food, and clothing for economically disadvantaged youth dropouts. Although criticized for its high service-delivery costs, the 5-month program in construction-related and service occupation training has demonstrated its effectiveness in yielding higher employment and earning rates for participants in contrast to nonparticipants, as well as lower levels of welfare dependency (Natriello et al., 1990).

Another form of resocialization and re-enculturation program, whose advocates if not its critics see its antecedents in the New Deal era Civilian Conservation Corps, is the paramilitary model "boot camps." Increasingly, these are being proposed as an alternative to incarceration when youth enter the criminal justice system, but voluntary programs also exist that are primarily intended to reshape dropouts to increase their employability. The basic philosophy applies military-style discipline to restructure young lives, a philosophy, say its critics, not too different from the days when juvenile judges would "sentence" young offenders to join the military as an alternative to jail time. Although the volunteers are required to wear uniforms, live in barracks, submit to inspection, and are organized into platoons, the remediation programs attempt to deal with the multiple deficits of the youth in the program, and help them to prepare for the GED test. Although such programs now receive significant public approval, there are as yet inconclusive results to evaluate their value (Cronin, 1994).

Conversely, some emerging strategies work within the existing communities to improve the support for educational attainment. One example is found in the Algebra Project, which was actually designed to improve educationally disadvantaged students' achievement in algebra. It combines alternative teaching strategies with community organizing techniques to increase expectations and encouragements for student success (Moses, Kamii, Swap, & Howard, 1989). Although not a dropout program per se, the project is a model for student success in algebra regardless of the students' prior skill development level, by changing the values and expectations of school staff and building up community support for student success. Early emphasis on algebra skill development improves the capacity of students to subsequently enroll in advanced high school math and science courses, improving their access to college and high-skill jobs. The basic intent of the program is to redefine the "culture of achievement" for these youth among teachers, administrators, parents, and the larger community to create a shared culture of values and beliefs that support mathematical and scientific literacy; to improve self-esteem; and to overcome doubts about intellectual capacity. In doing so, the program draws heavily on the traditions established through the civil rights movement to organize community support for access to and promotion of math and science literacy, using community meetings, special events, and other highly symbolic artifacts and activities (Moses et al., 1989).

Structural Approaches

Structural approaches to dropout prevention encompass changes in the delivery of education within the school and district, as well as developing interagency service delivery for high-risk youth.

Structural approaches to dropout prevention can begin with a review of a school's or district's existing policies and procedures that may mask or contribute to the dropout problem. A first step would be to improve documentation of dropouts, to obtain a more accurate and inclusive picture of the pattern and severity of dropping out. This can be coupled with a review of the impact of policies and related practices—such as penalties for poor attendance (e.g., failing students for low attendance) and excessive use of out-of-school suspensions and expulsions—on discouraging student retention.

Other structural approaches have been to re-examine existing organizational practices that may be contributing to rather than resolving student failure and eventual dropping out. The most commonly criticized practices are homogeneous grouping and grade retention. Research has shown that both practices are ineffective in improving the academic performance of low-ability students (National Research Council, 1993). In turn, low achievement and having been retained at least once in school are highly correlated with subsequently dropping out. In addition, some schools are implementing alternative practices to create a positive setting for learning, particularly for low-performing students (National Research Council, 1993). This includes using accelerated classes with extra teaching assistance, interdisciplinary teacher teams to work with students in small groups, peer tutoring, cooperative learning, and more diverse instructional and curricular strategies.

Some traditional approaches to structural changes for serving potential dropouts have been to add a variety of dropout prevention programs and dedicated services, without considering the possible need for broader school change. In addition, we have found, based on our research of dropouts and schools, that these added programs and services rarely are large enough to serve the entire need that may exist within a school or district.

Some policymakers and educational researchers advocate more comprehensive approaches to addressing the needs of high-risk students like potential dropouts. Rather than simply adding programs and strategies to the existing structure, they recommend redesigning public schools. Natriello et al.'s (1990) recommendations for school restructuring are premised on three challenges facing schools: "the diversity of student needs and the resources required to meet them, the diversity of goals for schooling, and the increasing level of performance necessary for success" (p. 159). To meet these challenges, they recommended decentralizing school decision making, making rules and programs more flexible, and increasing local educator discretion and resources. All their strategies are designed to make the existing organizational structure of schools more adaptable to the needs of disadvantaged students at all levels, particularly in the classroom. They recommend that schools be organized into "self-contained teaching/learning teams" such as houses or blocks to serve groups of students in a more holistic and integrated manner, and target extra resources for high-risk youth. The effectiveness of these strategic changes would be monitored through systematic data collection and analysis and feedback.

Not all their recommended changes are at the classroom level. They stressed restructuring of the entire management system of school districts, particularly in the way information is processed and decisions made, to maximize responsiveness, particularly in serving large numbers of disadvantaged students. These structural changes include a more differentiated hierarchy, greater staff and parental involvement in school-based decisions, and organizing staff according to educational problems to better focus resources and expertise. More horizontal or lateral linkages are needed within the hierarchy, again to increase responsiveness to local problem solving, allowing schools greater latitude to meet students' needs, particularly those most disadvantaged.

Part of a structural approach is to identify and serve high-risk youth who are being underserved, particularly those who have already left school without graduating or enrolling elsewhere. Youth dropouts have few viable educational and training alternatives, except for limited adult basic education, GED preparation and job training programs, and these are often for only the economically disadvantaged. Rarely do school districts aggressively recruit youth dropouts to return to school and complete their education, particularly if they leave after age 16. A few states and local districts, however, have developed community-based educational programs specifically for youth dropouts, recognizing that without a high school diploma or equivalency, their employment prospects are limited, putting them at high risk for other social problems, such as welfare dependency and criminal behavior.

The Alternative Schools Network in Chicago, for example, coordinates a series of community-based educational programs, some of which are affiliated with local high schools. These schools afford youth dropouts easy access to alternative schooling for academic instruction toward a high school diploma or GED, social support services, job readiness instruction, and job placement assistance. Their small size (25–200 students each) creates an intimate and supportive atmosphere and their open-entry, open-exit structure provides flexibility for dropouts to complete their education in their own manner (Orr, 1987). California and Washington state have provided separate funding for educational clinics that specifically target youth dropouts and help them to earn a GED or return to their regular high school. The programs are also small, usually community based, and provide individualized academic instruction and some employment orientation (Orr, 1987).

In general, there is a push for comprehensive services for youth in high-risk settings, reflecting an understanding that many adolescents have multiple problem behaviors that can be more effectively served through an integrated delivery model. According to the National Research Council (1993), there are four strategic elements critical to serving high-risk adolescents: (a) having sustained adult support that provides nurturance, safety, and guidance (such as mentors and case managers); (b) engaging in community learning and service to promote positive competencies and achievement; (c) developing emotional strengths and life skills for positive youth development, such as through peer or other group counseling and life-skills training programs; and (d) demonstrating trust and respect for adolescents by giving them greater choice within service delivery (as with drop-in or flexible services) and a role in program decision making. Dryfoos (1990) added the importance of intensive individualized attention and the use of communitywide, multiagency collaborative approaches, engagement of parents, and a link to the world of work.

Structural approaches, however, are not limited to changes in the design, delivery, and scope of just school services. These approaches also extend to joint efforts among schools, families, and the broader community, including social institutions and businesses. Several models have recently been developed that at the least coordinate and at the most integrate services between schools and relevant social institutions and provide meaningful avenues for parental participation and support. These models address the various risk behaviors common to young adolescents, and coordinating services and solutions to reduce their occurrence and their effects, improving the students' chances of successfully completing school.

New York City has recently established just such a model, the Beacon Schools, in over 30 schools in high-risk communities citywide. The Beacons are school-based community centers that operate in collaboration with individual community-based organizations and its own community advisory board. This approach is premised on a social orientation that takes a "youth development rather than a youth deficit orientation" (Cahill, 1993, p. 5). According to Cahill, youth have a need to develop competencies and connections for their own perception of success. Without positive supports and opportunities to develop constructive skills, youth will engage in more risky behavior, such as joining gangs, to develop a sense of competence and belonging. To help youth develop resiliency to survive within high-risk communities and succeed in their future, intervention programs like the Beacon model must be based on five protective factors: opportunities for caring relationships, high expectations and clear standards, opportunities to engage in high-quality activities, opportunities to make a contribution, and continuity of supports (Cahill, 1993).

To provide this positive structure and types of opportunities, the Beacon Schools remain open afternoons, evenings, and weekends to offer students and other community residents (particularly parents) educational, recreational, and other support services, often in conjunction with other city agencies. These activities include drama, sports, music, counseling, leadership development, and community service. Several offer health services and employment programs and a few are linked to local colleges that offer on-site courses. The schools, therefore, become a focal point for community activity and a safe haven for children and youth to have positive outlets for recreation and support. Through its approach, the Beacon Schools build ties among schools, community agencies, public resources, families, and youth.

Finally, interagency efforts to improve student retention and to better educate and prepare all students academically and economically can be orchestrated on a citywide basis. Cities with very high dropout and youth unemployment rates often have inadequate public school systems and limited social service and business sector involvement. Redressing the dropout problem in these severe conditions and coupling it with economic development and improved youth employment opportunities, the Boston Compact represents the most ambitious school and business partnership to contribute resources and develop solutions for these twin problems. Although only modest progress has been made since the Boston Compact was initiated in 1982, the school district and prominent business partners continue to set benchmarks for student achievement and retention and youth employment, and to experiment with viable intervention strategies (Orr, 1987).

CONCLUSION

The literature on dropping out presents a number of perspectives on risk factors and prevention and remediation models that alternatively look to flawed intra- and interpersonal relationships, cultural conflicts, failing schools, depressed economies, and structural problems among community institutions and draw their prevention and remediation strategies from the particular causation context they espouse. As a result, much of what we know about dropping out is conditioned by how we see the problem, at the intra- or interpersonal, institutional, community, or the macrolevels of social, economic, and political forces that form the developmental contexts of young lives. What seems clear, however, is that dropping out is not just another example of irresponsibility among youth, nor is it a problem that can easily be assigned to failing schools or depressed economies and changing job markets, or even one that invariably grows out of an educationally disadvantaged family background. Rather, the multiple risks that lead to dropping out fall somewhere in the untenanted space that develops in the family-to-school-to-work transition when these social contexts are not purposively integrated and coordinated.

Risk factors for dropping out can differ by type of community, family background, type of school attended, enculturation and socialization experiences, age, and even gender. Thus, just as there is no single, identifiable cause for dropping out, so there is no universalistic, national, or even local "silver bullet" program that can keep children in school or ensure a smooth and productive transition from the home to the school to the workplace. New programmatic tinkering at the labor market, school, or even family or individual level has not, and will not alter (much) what is fundamentally a lack of well-defined and well-described, believable, and attainable career and social pathways clearly marked out from early childhood programs through secondary and postsecondary education. If career and social development are a major education goal, then a structured and demonstrable system of job preparation and social development is needed to which all young people have access and that begins in early enculturation and socialization practices and continues throughout education.

As we have seen, the foundations for eduational and career preparation begin at home and are associated with learning how to learn, the valuation of education, and a concept of and commitment to preparation for productive employment as part of the life course. In raising their children, parents may stress the values that reflect their work conditions, in effect restricting career pathways as well as reinforcing and perpetuating the class structure. It could be and has been argued that school is simply responsive to those characteristics that students bring with them from their families. Many of the more successful programs we reviewed earlier, however, are based on the notion of creating a new sense of community among adults and students in the school. Although there are a number of different approaches prescribed, the various programs focus on some common aspects.

The potential dropout usually comes to school lacking the essential preparatory experiences, positive expectations of opportunities, and self-reinforcing motivation that are important ingredients of school success. As a result, the school and the student find it difficult to develop and maintain the attachment that encourages positive social ties and conformity to the school's norms and expectations. Improving the school portion of the transition by targeting resources better, expanding and enriching instructional methods and curricula, and providing programs to accommodate the greater diversity of students and learning styles found in schools today is a necessary beginning for reform. It is, however, also necessary to undertake staff development programs that will invest schools with resources for a better integration of academic and vocational preparation and social development.

Just improving schools, however, cannot be expected to resolve the dropout problem. First, there must be some systematic approach for schools and in families to prepare capable learners. In delineating a theory of educational productivity, Walberg (1984) found in a meta-analysis of the research on student achievement that two sets of factors are commonly required "to increase affective, behavioral and cognitive learning" (p. 20). These are student aptitude, which includes the factors of ability or prior achievement, development, and motivation; and instructional factors, which include the amount of time students engage in learning and the quality of the instructional experience. He concluded that whereas these factors are unquestionably of major importance in learning, they are really only partly alterable by educators and so do not offer the optimal vantage point for educational reform. A third and less frequently considered set of factors are environmental rather than school specific: (a) enduring affection and stimulation from adults in the home; (b) the psychological climate of the classroom social group; (c) the out-of-school peer group and its learning interests, goals, and activities; and (d) the use of out-of-school time, particularly the amount of leisure-time television watching. Walberg saw these environmental influences as significantly more alterable than the in-school influences and he maintained that they hold the best hope not only for educational reform, but for improving the quality and productivity of social and behavioral learning for youngsters as well.

In recent decades there have been continuing debates between human capital versus segmented market theory economists as to whether it is the lack of qualifying characteristics of teenagers or the decline of opportunity in the labor market that explains why so many youth are periodically or permanently unemployed (Ginsberg, 1962; Osterman, 1980, 1989). What seems clear today is that both are at work against many youths' sense of a payoff if they work hard in school. However, just as improving schools is a necessary but insufficient means of keeping youth in school, so school reform will not ensure a productive school-to-work transition without the interactive investment of the educational and labor market resources. Kazis (1993), writing for the American Youth Policy Forum, proposed bringing programs focusing on work and career issues directly into the school curriculum, at the same time establishing programs such as service learning, youth apprenticeship, and school-based enterprises. He also suggested that we look into a system of recovery centers for youth who have dropped out of school, a program already in effect in Sweden.

Although a new vision of the relationship among the primary institutional sectors of the family, the school, and the workplace is the fundamental basis for a new system of engagement with the home-to-school-to-work transition, the resources of all the enculturating and socializing environments of the community—those that work with adults as well as youth-serving agencies—are necessary to sustain such a system. The causes and consequences of dropping out are frequently as much, if not more, attributable to communitywide social forces than to exclusively individual decision making by the student or the failure of the school. Some of the problems dropouts share are just not amenable to educational intervention. Schools, however, as the most omnipresent institutional setting and the one that links and guides development from dependent child to interdependent adult, should have the major responsibility for fostering the transition process. Yet given the massive and diverse responsibilities we assign the school for preparing students for adult life as well as remediating the problems they pick up along the way, and given the limited resources schools have to meet these challenges, we need to look to a communitywide resurgence and reinforcement of educational values. The problem of youngsters getting lost or falling through the net where agencies, families, schools, and other sectors do not have a collaborative, programmatic vision of youth care and the often parochial concerns of professionals in the various institutional sectors require a community-chartered and monitored approach.

However, just recasting and symbolizing or even promulgating values that support and encourage staying in school and the importance of work is not enough to enact and empower the shared assumptions and the belief system that will undergird and sustain them. If the direction of our changing diagnoses and prescriptions for the causes of dropping out have been a trajectory away from the individual to the school and, more recently, from the school to the community and thence to the labor market and society itself, we believe it is necessary to complete the loop back to the individual identity and self-development. We can socialize and enculture for achievement, as do the Japanese (DeVos, 1975) or we can make a shared sense of community our goal, as did the Navaho (Kluckhohn & Leighton, 1974). Actually, we can do both if we view values as a means of empowering and enhancing rather than restricting or controlling human behavior. As a result of differential cultural and subcultural experiences and different traditions, we have different perceptions. Any questions and doubts about means and ends should develop out of disagreement or dissent rather than ascribed ignorance or planned disenfranchisement.

REFERENCES

Barber, L. (1984). *Dropouts, transfers, withdrawn, and removed students*. Bloomington, IN: Phi Delta Kappa, Center for Evaluation, Development and Research.

Barrington, F. L., & Hendricks, B. (1989, August). Differentiating characteristics of high school graduates, dropouts and nongraduates. *Journal of Educational Research, 82*(6), 309–318.

Benson, P. (1990). *The troubled journey: A portrait of 6–12th grade youth*. Minneapolis: Search Institute.

Berlin, G., & Sum, A. (1986). *American standards of living, family welfare, and the basic skills crisis*. New York: Ford Foundation.

Bloom, B. S. (1984, May). The search for methods of group instruction as effective as one-to-one tutoring. *Educational Leadership*, 4–17.

320   IANNI AND ORR

Bruner, J. (1986). *Actual minds, personal worlds*. Cambridge, MA: Harvard University Press.
Bryk, A. S., & Driscoll, M. E. (1988, November). *The high school as community: Contextual influences, and consequences for students and teachers*. Madison, WI: National Center for Effective Secondary Schools.
Cahill, M. (1993, December). *A documentation report on the NYC Beacons Initiative*. New York: Fund for the City of New York.
Cardenas, J., & First, J. (1985, September). Children at risk. *Educational Leadership*, 4–8.
Catterall, J. S. (1985). *On the social costs of dropping out of school*. Palo Alto, CA: Stanford Policy Institute, Stanford University.
Cronin, R. (1994, October). *Boot camp for adult and juvenile offenders: Overview and update*. Washington, DC: National Institute of Justice.
DeVos, G. A. (1975). *Socialization for achievement: Essays in the cultural psychology of the Japanese*. Berkeley: University of California Press.
Dryfoos, J. G. (1990). *Adolescents at risk*. New York: Oxford University Press.
Dryfoos, J. G. (1994). *Full-service schools*. San Francisco: Jossey-Bass.
Elmore, R., & Associates. (1990). *Restructuring schools*. San Francisco: Jossey-Bass.
Farrar, E., & Hampel, R. (1987, December). Social services in American high schools. *Phi Delta Kappan, 69*, 297–303.
Finn, J. D. (1989). Withdrawing from school. *Review of Educational Research, 59*, 465–489.
Fordham, S., & Ogbu, J. U. (1986). Black students school success: Coping with the burden of 'acting white.' *Urban Review, 18*, 176–206.
Geertz, C. (1973). *The interpretation of cultures*. New York: Basic Books.
Ginsberg, E. (1962). *The optimistic tradition and American youth*. New York: Columbia University Press.
Gold, M., & Mann, D. W. (1984). *Expelled to a friendlier place: A study of effective alternative schools*. Ann Arbor: University of Michigan Press.
Greene, M. (1988). Qualitative research and the uses of literature. In R. R. Shermand & R. B. Webb (Eds.), *Qualitative research in education: Focus and methods* (pp. 29–44). Philadelphia: Falmer.
Hahn, A., Danzberger, J. J., & Lefkowitz, B. (1987). *Dropouts in America: Enough is known for action*. Washington, DC: Institute for Educational Leadership.
Hamilton, S. F. (1990). *Apprenticeship for adulthood: Preparing youth for adulthood*. New York: The Free Press.
Howard, G. S. (1991). Culture tales. *American Psychologist, 46*(3), 47–53.
Ianni, F. A. J. (1989). *The search for structure: A report on American youth today*. New York: The Free Press.
Ianni, F., & Reuss-Ianni, E. (1992). The education of mobile populations. In M. C. Alkin (Ed.), *Encyclopedia of educational research* (pp. 852–856). New York: Macmillan.
Jobs for the Future. (1990, December 7). *Youth apprenticeship, American style: A strategy for expanding school and career opportunities*. Cambridge, MA: Author.
Kazis, R. (1993). *Improving the transition from school to work in the United States*. Washington, DC: American Youth Policy Forum, Competitiveness Policy Council, and Jobs for the Future.
Kohut, H. (1971). *The analysis of the self*. New Haven, CT: Yale University Press.
Kluckhohn, C., & Leighton, D. (1974). *The Navaho*. Cambridge, MA: Harvard University Press.
Lloyd, D. N. (1978). Prediction of school failure from the third grade data. *Educational and Psychological Measurement, 38*, 1193–1200.
Marshall, R., & Tucker, M. (1992). *Thinking for a living*. New York: Basic Books.
McGee, E. (1989). *A stitch in time, helping young mothers complete high school*. New York: Academy for Educational Development.

Moses, R. P., Kamii, M., Swap, S. M., & Howard, J. (1989). The Algebra Project: Organizing the spirit of Ella. *Harvard Educational Review, 59*(4), 423–443.

National Center for Education Statistics. (1993). *Digest of education statistics.* Washington, DC: U.S. Government Printing Office.

National Center for Education Statistics. (1994). [Unpublished materials]. Washington, DC: Department of Education.

National Center on Education and the Economy. (1990). *America's choice: High skills or low wages?* Rochester, NY: Author.

National Research Council. (1993). *Losing generations: Adolescents in high risk settings.* Washington, DC: National Academy Press.

Natriello, G., McDill, E. L., & Pallas, A. (1990). *Schooling disadvantaged children.* New York: Teachers College Press.

Orr, M. T. (1987). *Keeping students in school.* San Francisco: Jossey-Bass.

Orr, M. T. (1991). [Unpublished evaluation research]. New York: Academy for Educational Development.

Osterman, P. (1980). *Getting started: The youth labor market.* Cambridge, MA: MIT Press.

Osterman, P. (1989). The job market for adolescents. In D. Stern & D. Eichorn (Eds.), *Adolescents and work: Influences of social structure, labor markets, and culture* (pp. 235–258). Hillsdale, NJ: Lawrence Erlbaum Associates.

Owings, J. A., & Kolstad, A. J. (1985). *High school dropouts two years after scheduled graduation.* Washington, DC: National Center for Education Statistics.

Pallas, A. M. (1986). *School dropouts in the United States.* Washington, DC: National Center for Education Statistics.

Rumberger, R. W. (1983). Dropping out of high school: The influence of race, sex, and family. *American Educational Research Journal, 20*, 199–220.

Spence, D. P. (1982). *Narrative truth and historical truth: Meaning and interpretation in psychoanalysis.* New York: Norton.

Steinberg, L., Blinde, P. L., & Chan, K. S. (1984). Dropping out among language minority youth. *Review of Educational Research, 54*, 113–132.

Turner, R. (1968). The self-conception in social interaction. In C. Gordon & K. Gergen (Eds.), *The self in social interaction.* New York: Wiley.

U.S. General Accounting Office. (1987). *School dropouts: Survey of local programs.* Washington, DC: Author.

Walberg, H. J. (1984). Improving the productivity of America's schools. *Educational Leadership, 41*(8), 19–27.

Wehlage, G. G., Rutter, R. A., Smith, G. A., Lesko, N., & Fernandez, R. R. (1989). *Reducing the risk: Schools as communities of support.* New York: Falmer.

William T. Grant Foundation Commission on Youth and America's Future. (1988). *The forgotten half: Non-college youth in America.* Washington, DC: Commission on Work, Family, and Citizenship.

Wilson, W. J. (1987). *The truly disadvantaged: The inner city, the underclass, and public policy.* Chicago: University of Chicago Press.

Winnicott, D. W. (1965). *The maturational process and the facilitating environment.* New York: International Universities Press.

Wynn, J., Richman, H., Rubenstein, R. A., & Littell, J. (1988). *Communities and adolescents: An exploration of reciprocal supports.* Washington, DC: The William T. Grant Foundation Commission on Work, Family, and Citizenship.

Zigler, E., & Berman, W. (1983). Discerning the future of early childhood intervention. *American Psychologist, 38*, 894–906.

12

Working Poor: Low-Wage Employment in the Lives of Harlem Youth

Katherine S. Newman
Columbia University

A great deal has been written in recent years about soaring rates of persistent poverty. Inner-city ghettos dominated by poor minorities are said to be the breeding ground of the underclass, a group permanently disconnected from U.S. society. Adolescents are seen as particularly harmed by the experience of long-term poverty whose consequences play out in increasing school dropout rates, joblessness, teenage pregnancy, and involvement in the underground economy. Indeed, it is in the period of adolescence that fateful decisions are made that either put individuals on the path toward adult poverty or pull them into the mainstream. Literature on the inner city tells us that to an ever increasing degree, the path to poverty is the road more often taken by minority youth.

This dismal portrait overlooks the fact that vast numbers of minority adolescents and young adults are working in the low-wage labor market, supporting their own living expenses and contributing to the survival of poverty-level households. Even in neighborhoods with high concentrations of poverty and unemployment, working for a living remains the dominant ethos and a characteristic practice. In central Harlem, for example, where official unemployment is nearly 18% and poverty levels are almost 40%, more than two thirds of all households have a minimum of one worker in them (City of New York Department of Urban Planning, 1993). Nonetheless, researchers working in the underclass tradition often overlook the cultural and practical importance of work in inner-city communities, and the importance of this experience in shaping adolescent and early adult life.

In this chapter, I explore the role of paid employment in the lives of African American and Latino youth (16–24) who are working at the very bottom of the service sector in Harlem. Their minimum wage jobs are tiring, stressful, and poorly compensated. Most workers have few prospects for significant internal advancement or higher wages in these industries. Young people must often run a social gauntlet in order to work in the low-wage market, for they are stigmatized as fools who take "chump change."

Nonetheless, as I explain later, young people from high-poverty neighborhoods do indeed run this gauntlet because they believe in being independent and because their wages are essential to the survival of the poor households in which they are embedded. Investment in the "work ethic" is powerful and persistent, even among youth who were raised in households that have relied for long periods of time on welfare. Indeed, more often than not, inner-city youth begin working when they are 13 to 15 years of age at jobs that are "off the books" and pay less than minimum wage. Their familiarity with the labor market exceeds the babysitting experience of their middle-class counterparts to a considerable degree. In short, from a very early age, young people in poor, minority households are incorporated into the wage labor system and from this vantage point they become significant contributors to the household budget.

I argue that a full understanding of adolescent development in high-poverty neighborhoods must take into account the psychological and sociological consequences of joining the workforce. In particular, researchers should not overlook the importance of work as a process of identity formation among inner-city youth, simply because they come from areas where the opposite condition—unemployment—remains a serious problem.

THE RESEARCH SETTING

Harlem, long the cultural capital of African American life, is populated largely by Black families whose ascendant generations migrated to the area from the southeastern seaboard. Washington Heights, a neighborhood northwest of Harlem, is an adjacent community dominated by Latino immigrants from the Dominican Republic, Puerto Rico, and other parts of the Caribbean world. Both communities suffer from high levels of poverty, a rundown and segregated housing stock, and serious problems with street violence. Good jobs, jobs that pay well, are scarce in these neighborhoods and those that exist are likely to be in the public sector where budget pressures are reducing what is left of the "good job" of the past.

Minimum wage jobs are not exactly plentiful either, although they are highly sought after. Employers are able to pick and choose among a large supply of "reserve labor" in order to fill service sector positions that pay no more than the minimum wage—currently $4.25 per hour—provide no benefits, and offer limited prospects for the future. Nonetheless, applicants flock to their doors seeking employment, and the vast majority are turned away. The days when high school dropouts could expect immediate employment in a fast-food restaurant are gone in Harlem and Washington Heights. These days, high school diplomas often distinguish those who hold "McJobs" from those who do not. Very young workers, those aged 16 to 18, are also at a competitive disadvantage because so many older, more experienced people have been "pushed down" into the low-wage market as a result of high unemployment and slow growth.

Because the demand for entry-level employment vastly outstrips the available supply of low-wage jobs, the value of social networks as critical tools for job hunting is very high. Individuals whose friends or relatives are already employed in local workplaces have a considerable advantage over job seekers who are not blessed with these connections. Grannovetter's (1974) classic observation that "weak ties" result in effective job referrals is as true of the low-wage labor market in ghetto neighborhoods as it was for the Boston-based white collar workers he studied long ago.

Nonetheless, thousands of young people do find their way into the low-wage labor market, including the 200 individuals who participated in this study of low-wage workers in the fast-food industry. Conducted between January 1993 and May 1994, this project involved a structured interview on the demographics, human capital characteristics, work and job-hunting experiences, and household/family work and education profiles of all 200 respondents, the universe of individuals working in four fast-food restaurants (three in Harlem and one in Washington Heights). This was followed by 60 tape-recorded life history interviews on a random sample of the workers, stratified by race and "living situation."[1] Finally, a very small sample of the life history interviewees participated in a 9-month period of "shadowing," during which they recorded their daily experiences in personal diaries and kept consistent company with graduate students engaged in participant observation.

Table 12.1 presents a breakdown of the race/ethnicity and age distribution of the workers in the study. It shows that the sample was approximately 54% African American; 24% Dominican; 16% Latino from Puerto Rico, Mexico, and other parts of Latin America; and about 7% from other immigrant groups (including Africa, South Asia, Jamaica, and other parts of the English-speaking Caribbean).

---

[1]A seven-layer variable expressing the sociological role of the individual within the household/family (e.g., single parent, child of a single parent, adult in a nuclear family household, child living with aunt/uncle, member of large coethnic household, etc.).

TABLE 12.1
Age and Ethnic Background of Harlem Fast-Food Workers

Age	African American[a]	Dominican[b]	Other Latino[c]	Other[d]
15–18	25	9	10	1
19–22	25	7	10	8
23–32	39	3	7	2
33–50	9	4	2	3
Total	98	43	29	14
	(53%)	(23%)	(16%)	(8%)

Note. Three of the four restaurants from which these respondents were recruited were in Harlem; one was in Washington Heights.

[a]Includes all respondents who self-identified as African American (including the nonnative born) and 20 individuals who identified themselves as "Black" plus any other ethnicity (e.g., "Black and Puerto Rican," "Black and Asian"). We did not force respondents to choose a single race identifier as the census does because they are often uncomfortable with single categories. The census bureau is now experimenting with multiple check-offs for the same reason.

[b]Includes all respondents who self-identified as Dominican, even if they were born in the United States.

[c]Includes all respondents who self-identified as Latino, Latin American, Puerto Rican (the majority in this category), Mexican, South American, or Central American.

[d]Jamaicans, Africans, Canadians, South Asians.

The discussion that follows is based primarily on the life history and "shadowing" data. I seek to highlight the social consequences of joining the labor force in a low-wage job, in terms of the composition of peer groups and of personal identity. In particular, I seek to show how the stigma attached to "McJobs," coupled with the experience of incorporation into a work setting, combines to shift an individual's reference group out of the neighborhood or school and into the workplace. At the same time, earning a paycheck places minority youths in positions of quasi-adult responsibility in their natal homes. They contribute in a variety of ways to the stability of poverty-level households, shifting their own roles from that of a dependent child to that of a "junior" adult. Such a shift is not always smooth and problem free, but it is a major turning point in the familial hierarchies in which minority youth are embedded.

WHY WORK?

You know, when I was out, when I wasn't working, I used to get into fights. Well, it wasn't really fights, it was like really arguments ... [Now, my friends] ask me, "Why don't we see you anymore?" Like, I can't. I don't have time. But, you know, I don't really wanna hang around my block anymore 'cuz its like, getting real bad. You know, it's a lot of people fighting around there for no reason. And they shooting and stuff like that.

Julie Harris has worked at a fast-food restaurant in the middle of Harlem since she was 17, her first private-sector job following several summers as a city employee in a youth program. During her junior and senior year, Julie commuted 45 minutes each way to school, put in a full day at school, and then donned her work uniform for an 8-hour afternoon/evening shift. Exhausted by the regimen, she took a brief break from work, but returned when she graduated from high school. Now, at the age of 21, she is a veteran fast-food employee with an unbroken work record of about 3 years.

Julie had several motivations for joining the workforce when she was a teenager, principal among them the desire to be independent of her mother and provide for her own material needs. No less important, however, was her desire to escape the pressures of street violence and the fast track to nowhere that was capturing her peers. For in Julie's neighborhood, many a young person never sees the other side of age 20. Her own brother was shot in the chest, a victim of mistaken identity. Julie's mother narrowly escaped a similar fate:

> It had to have been like twelve or one o'clock. My mother was in her room and I was in my room. . . . I sleep on the top bunk. We started hearing gunshots, so first thing I did, I jumped from my bed to the floor. I got up after the gun shots stopped and went into my mother's room. She was on the floor. . . . "Are you alright, are you alright?" she said. "Yeah, yeah."

> The next morning we woke up and it was like a bullet hole in the window in her room. Her bed is like the level of the window. Lucky thing she jumped, I mean went to the floor, because it could have come in through the window.

Incidents of this kind happen every day in Julie's neighborhood, but they never become an acceptable part of the social landscape, something to be shrugged off as "business as usual." Street violence, drive-by shootings, and other sources of terror are obstacles Julie and other working poor people in her community have to navigate around. However, Julie knows that troubles of this kind strike more often among young people who have nothing to do but spend time on the street. Going to work was, for her, a defensive strategy of disengagement from such a future.

Julie had many positive reasons for seeking employment as well. Even as a young teen, Julie wanted to be autonomous and responsible for her own financial needs. In this she typifies minority youth who work in low-wage service-sector jobs in Harlem. They want a sphere of action that they can control, where they are adultlike actors. Earning their own money and being able to decide, for the most part, how it is spent is a common manifestation of this underlying desire for autonomy.

For young teens, fiscal autonomy is desirable because it makes it possible for them to participate in youth culture and its stylistic trends. Many writers have dismissed teenage workers on these grounds, complaining that their sole (read trivial) motivation for working (and neglecting school) is to satisfy infantile desires for gold chains and designer sneakers. Like teenagers everywhere, Julie and her fellow worker friends want to partake of fashion trends. Julie's job made it possible for her to be a member in good standing of her own stylistic community, a youth culture that, like all others, imposes certain dress standards. Unlike her middle-class counterparts, whose parents can afford to support similar teenage desires, Julie's mother is hard pressed just to make ends meet. As such, part of Julie's income does indeed go toward clothing and recreation.

However, most of her wages are spent providing for basic expenses that her mother finds hard to fund. When she was still in high school, Julie paid for her own books, school transportation, lunches, and basic clothing expenses. Now that she has graduated, she has assumed even more of the cost of keeping herself. Her mother takes care of the roof over their heads, but Julie is responsible for the rest, as well as for a consistent contribution toward the expense of running a home with other dependent children in it.

Minimum-wage jobs cannot buy real economic independence; they cannot cover the full cost of living, including rent, food, and the rest of an adult's monthly needs. What Julie can do with her earnings is cover the marginal cost of her presence in the household, leaving something over every week to contribute to the core cost of maintaining the household. Youth workers, particularly those who are parents themselves, generally do turn over part of their pay to the head of the household as a kind of rent, a pattern familiar to anyone who lived through (or has read about) the Great Depression. In this fashion, working poor youth participate in a pooled income strategy that makes it possible for households—as opposed to individuals—to sustain themselves. Without their contributions, this would become increasingly untenable, for as Edin (1994) pointed out, families cannot really survive on a welfare income.

This pattern is even more striking among immigrants and native-born minorities who are not incorporated into the state welfare system. In working poor households with no connection to the state system, survival depends on multiple workers pooling their resources. Pressures build early on for the older children in these communities to take jobs, no matter what the wages, in order to help their parents make ends meet. Mariela Gomez is a case in point. Now 21 years old, Mariela has been working since she was 15. Originally from Central America, Mariela has been in the United States for 18 months now, having followed her parents who migrated a number of years before and presently work in a factory in New Jersey. Mariela completed her education in her home country and went to work in a clerical job. She emigrated at the age of 18, joining two younger brothers and a 12-year-old sister already in New York. Mariela has ambitions for going back to school, but for the moment she works full time in a fast-food restaurant in Harlem, as does her 16-year-old brother. Her little sister is responsible for cooking and caring for their 5-year-old brother, a responsibility Mariela assumes when she is not at work or in her English as a second language class.

The Gomez family is typical of the immigrant households that partici- pate in the low-wage economy of Harlem and Washington Heights, and bears a strong resemblance to the Puerto Rican families studied by Sul- livan (1993) in Brooklyn. Parents work, adolescent children work, and only the youngest of the children are able to invest themselves in U.S. schooling. Indeed, it is often the littlest of them who is deputized to master the English language on behalf of the whole family. Children as young as 5 or 6 years old are often designated as interpreters who negotiate relations between parents and landlords, parents and teachers, parents and the whole English-speaking world lying beyond the barrio.

The social structure of these households is one that relies on the contributions of multiple earners for cash earnings, child care, and house- work. Parents with limited language skills (and often illegal status) are rarely in a position to support their children without substantial contri- butions from the children themselves. Jobs that come their way rarely pay enough to organize a "child-centered" household in which education and leisure are the predominant activities of the youth until the age of 18. Instead, they must rely on their children and, at most, can look forward to the eventual upward mobility of the youngest of their kids who may be able to remain in school long enough to move up to better occupations in the future.

What this means for older children is that from a relatively young age they are expected to pay their own way, to cook and clean, to buy furniture and pay phone bills. Work is not likely to be a source of intrinsic personal satisfaction. Hence many immigrant adolescents working in service-sector jobs hope that in time they will be able to move on to something better. However, their options for investment in their own human capital are often compromised by family demands for their income, ultimately undermin- ing their chances for advancement in the labor market. If this persists into the mid-20s, such a situation can become a flash point of conflict between the generations. Young people begin to see that "McJobs" go nowhere, that further education or vocational training is going to be necessary to break out of the service sector ghetto, and they chafe under domestic needs that keep them within the fold of the natal family.

This is not to say that youth workers are always forced to subsume their own long-term futures. In some families, parents or older relatives do subsidize the cost of training for the future by providing a roof over a child's head long past the age where, in their home country or their own youth, they would have expected young people to become economically independent. The subsidy takes the form of paying for major monthly living expenses—principally rent and food—while permitting a young worker to keep his or her wages and use them to pay for schooling. It is not unusual, in immigrant communities of this kind, to find over-arching "clusters" of households that pool resources in order to make the advancement of young people possible, a favor they are expected to repay by supporting the needs of cluster members (e.g., for professional services, godparenting children, etc.) in the future. This is a pattern familiar to students of the border regions where transnational households are often organized in this cluster fashion (Velez-Ibanez, 1993).

Gerard Albion, a 22-year-old born in Haiti, has lived in the United States since he was in his teens. His mother remains in Haiti, and his father (from whom she is divorced) lives in a dangerous section of the Bronx. Gerard lives with an aunt and uncle in a safer neighborhood on Long Island. During the period of this research, Gerard worked a full day in a fast-food restaurant, and then took the subway to a technical trade school where he put in another 2 to 3 hours studying for a certificate in air conditioning and refrigeration repair. This trade course took nearly 2 years to complete and cost over $4,000, a sum neither his parents nor his aunt and uncle could afford to pay on his behalf. Gerard paid for the training entirely out of his fast-food earnings. After more than 6 months of searching with trade credentials in hand, Gerard now works in his field, at a salary that nearly triples his previous hourly wage.

Gerard is hardly unique in his efforts to use entry-level work to support training or education. Of the 200 people who constitute the "universe" of the Harlem project, over half are still in school. Of these people, half again have high school diplomas and are seeking further education or vocational training. The households from whence these workers come are not able to foot the bills for schooling, but they do make it possible for young people to earn their way to better credentials on their own. This, then, is one of the primary purposes of holding a low-wage job in the first place: to sustain a poor youth's financial aid system.

Such a perspective goes against the grain of much of the current thinking about the impact of early work experience on adolescents and youth. Critics of youth work have argued that going to work during the teen years "scars" young people by removing their attention from school and focusing their efforts (or their time) on dead-end jobs that provide few opportunities for skill enhancement (Bachman & Schulenberg, 1993; Sedlack, Wheeler, Cusick, & Pullin, 1986; Steinberg, Fegley, & Dornbush, 1993). By the time young people "wake up" and realize that these entry-level jobs lead nowhere, it is too late. They lack the human capital to advance in the labor market, both because they have pulled back from school too early and because the jobs they have held give them little to offer employers with better jobs to fill (McNeil, 1984).

My research suggests a different picture, both of the relationship between school and work and of the human capital consequences of low-wage service-sector employment. Although going to work at a young age does introduce competition for one's time, it also creates a track record of value for future employment (Rich, 1993) and provides a structured, focused culture to become part of, one that is surprisingly supportive of continued involvement in education.

Although enrollment per se tells us little about school performance, it does tell us something about educational engagement in a population where dropping out of high school is quite common. According to the 1990 census, nearly 44% of central Harlem residents over the age of 25 had less than a high school education. More than 20% of persons 16 to 19 were not enrolled in school and were not high school graduates, with only 3% listed as employed or in the armed forces (City of New York, Department of Urban Planning, 1993). Given these rather dismal statistics, it is noteworthy that young workers in minimum wage jobs are doing so much better with respect to continued investment in education.

The difference may be partly attributable to the attitudes and practices of Harlem employers. In several of the restaurants where the fieldwork for this project was conducted, employers have taken proactive steps to monitor the school performance of their high school age workers, examining their report cards, paying for books, and cutting back work hours if grades fall. As Tamesha James, who has worked in a chain restaurant since she was 14, explained, the surveillance of her employer motivated her toward greater involvement in school:

> I don't think I could have made it [in school] without a job, because that was my inspiration. If I hadn't had a job I don't think I would have went to school or nothing like that. [The restaurant] really helped me out, because you know if you have one thing going for you, you want another thing going for you. And . . . it's like a chain reaction.
> See, when I first started [working], I didn't like to go to school at all. But see, my manager told me, "I wanna see your report card. If you're not doing this or you're not doing that, we don't want you here." They told me just like that. My first period class, I was failing it because I was late. My manager told me, "Why are you failing this class?" "Cause I don't get

there on time." She said, "Well I think I should cut your hours [at work] 'cause maybe you're not getting enough sleep."

They just pushed me. If I wanted to keep this job, I had to go [to that class]. . . . You know, they really tried hard 'cause they say, "We don't want you to work here forever. We want you to move on."

Although this is not a universal practice, it should be acknowledged that at least some inner-city employers have taken it upon themselves to reinforce the importance of remaining in school. Moreover, our fieldwork suggests, as in Tamesha's example, that for many young workers, employment provides a structured, disciplined universe whose values "spill over" into other realms, including school. The fact that such a high proportion of these young workers continue going to high school at all puts them several steps ahead of their ghetto agemates who have given up on schooling.

Much of the current research pointing to negative outcomes of part-time work compares the experiences of students who are employed versus those who are simply in school (Bachman & Schulenberg, 1993; Greenberger & Steinberg, 1986; Steinberg et al., 1993). However, for the at-risk population of minorities from poor neighborhoods, the more relevant comparison may well be between working students and their agemates who have dropped out of school altogether, because they are more likely to have come from the same socioeconomic background. For when we look at the experience of the working youth in this study, we see a very impressive degree of engagement in school when compared against those they consider their peers in their neighborhoods, many of whom have dropped out and can no longer even find minimum wage employment.

For many of the young people we interviewed, the confrontation with low-wage work made clear in concrete ways what a lifetime of secondary labor market employment would mean—poor wages, few chances for advancement, minimal respect, and declining prospects for independent adult living (because minimum wage jobs cannot support independent households). The experience spurred them on to further training as an avenue of escape from this end of the labor market. Whether that training or further education pays off, enabling a real escape, is a separate story. The point here is simply that aspirations for more valuable credentials often develop as a result of work experience.

RUNNING THE GAUNTLET

American culture has always placed a high premium on work as a source of moral worth (Newman, 1988, 1993). Individual identity is rooted in occupational experience; communities often derive more from workplace social life than residential affiliation. This is no less true for the working poor than it is for the U.S. middle class. In fact, it may be even more important for those who are excluded from much of the consumer culture that is also integral to the U.S. experience.

In this milieu, secondary labor market jobs are barely recognized as "work." Entirely lacking in prestige, with few material rewards, "McJobs" are the butt of jokes in popular culture and on the streets where inner-city youth often feel compelled to hide their fast-food uniforms. Schoolmates, friends from the neighborhood, and even relatives may look down on them for accepting jobs that epitomize the dead end. The stigma has various roots, only one of which involves the low wages they afford. McJobs are also defined as servile, requiring deference, obedience to authority, and uniformity in a subculture that prizes the opposite qualities: independence, autonomy, resistance, and self-determination (Anderson, 1990). Abstractions of this sort are given concrete meaning in daily experiences across the counter of a fast-food restaurant, where employees are given elaborate instructions for avoiding conflict with customers and pleasing them at all cost to their own dignity, where disagreements with management end up as "infractions" that are written up in a semimilitary fashion. Mainstream popular culture and subcultural street norms conspire to denigrate service work of this routinized type, particularly when it is coupled with perpetual deference (Leidner, 1993).

Confronting this stigma is a lesson in the social pain involved in "marching to a different drummer." Harlem youth and their adult co-workers who accept low-wage jobs in the fast-food industry must run a gauntlet of criticism on the street that is basically relentless. They are taunted, shamed, and made to feel that they have capitulated to a social order that somehow they should resist.

In the face of this barrage, youth workers must find a way to either conceal their involvement in the secondary labor market or deflect the stigma that threatens to undermine them. Some in our study took the former route: They commuted for an hour or more on the subways to work in a Harlem restaurant rather than take a similar job in their own neighborhood where they might be seen by friends. Gerard Albion traveled nearly 2 hours from his home to work, at a considerable expense (particularly given his low wages), even though the same restaurant chain was advertising for workers less than a block from his home. For him, the embarrassment of a stigmatized job was sufficiently powerful that it was worth the expense and the exhaustion to commute this long distance.

Most workers lack the time and resources to adopt this "camouflage" solution. Instead, they rely on a status hierarchy that places workers well above people who do not work, as support for the view that they are superior to their critics. The working poor carve out identities as members of the mainstream through the invidious comparison with those who are less fortunate or less willing to pursue the hard road they have themselves taken. Simply to be working is a step above the detritus that crowds the bottom of the social ladder in the ghetto. It generates an identity that they use to stiffen the spine when the ragging begins again.

Harlem's youth workers do not lack for exposure to people who are out of the labor force. The restaurants and shops where they work are surrounded daily by beggars who come around to ask for food, as well as the drifters and troublemakers who have dropped out of school and have little else to do but hang out on the streets nearby. Even the well-heeled drug dealers, who have more money than anyone serving lunch at Kentucky Fried Chicken can ever hope to possess, are condemned as "losers" who will most likely end up "6 feet under." And the youth workers know whereof they speak, for a goodly number of their acquaintances have died or ended up in jail. Tyesha Smith, a 20-year-old African American woman who has worked since she was 14, explained:

> People [in the projects where I live] like to down me, like [this job] wasn't anything, like it was a low job. Like selling drugs was better than working at [fast foods]. But I was like, "nah." I never went that way [toward drugs], so I'm just gonna stick to what I do. Now they *locked up* and I don't think I'm gonna get locked up for selling hamburgers and french fries! Most of my friends that I knew [before I started working] went to jail, or they sit in the house and have, like, four kids, and they don't wanna work; they on welfare.

Tyesha sees herself as a respectable working person and compares herself quite favorably to her acquaintances from the housing project where she lives who are going nowhere.

Kiesha Summers, a 20-year-old African American woman, began working at McDonalds when she was 16 and discovered firsthand how her "friends" would turn on her for taking a low-wage job. Fortunately, she found a good friend at work who steadied her with a piece of advice:

> Say it's a job. You are making money. Right? Don't care what nobody say. You know? If they don't like it, too bad. They sitting on the corner doing what they are doing. You go to work making money. You know? Don't bother what anybody has to say about it.

Her advisor, a workplace veteran who had long since come to terms with the insults of his peers, called on a general status hierarchy that places the working above the nonworking as a bulwark against the slights. His words were echoed by Kiesha's manager in the course of another episode that took place at work:

Kids come in here ... they don't have enough money. I'll be like, "You don't have enough money; you can't get [the food you ordered]." One night this little boy came in there and cursed me out. He [said] "That's why you are working at McD. You can't get a better job. . . ."

I was upset and everything. I started crying. [My manager] was like, "Kiesha, don't bother with him. I'm saying *you got a job*. You know. It is a *job*."

In a ghetto where unemployment is rampant, this is a reasonably effective counter. It cannot shield the victim from the knowledge that in the world of the employed, her job ranks at the bottom, but it makes her feel better by drawing a line in the sand between the worker and the parasite.

Ironically, for all their marginalization, working adolescents converge with mainstream U.S. values that honor the "honest worker" and denigrate the dependent. Indeed, they are one with general cultural norms that place overwhelming weight on work as the source of moral worth and respect. Service workers in minority communities and elsewhere share with the working class the feeling that the work they do is devalued in comparison with better paid jobs in the white collar world.[2] Still, they are part of the great mainstream of the U.S. labor force. For working youth in Harlem, this membership provides some salve for the wounds inflicted by peers.

And, as they get older, turning the corner from adolescence into early adulthood, the years of steady work in fast foods turn from being a social liability to an advantage. For they gain the reputation—unusual among their peers—of having worked continuously, of sticking with something. Kiesha's friend and co-worker, Tamesha James, explained:

People have this image of people who work at [these restaurants]. They think we just have to be poor or something like that to work [here]. But after awhile it gets better, 'cause they started looking at me. They say, "You're still here! That's good. You've hold a job that long and I don't think I could have did it." They start patting me on my back after awhile.

Kiesha agreed that after a time, she too earned respect for being employed:

---

[2]Sennett and Cobb (1973) described what they termed "hidden injuries" of class enduring by blue collar workers who felt devalued in a world that values white collar work to a greater degree. They had hefty paychecks, often more than their white collar counterparts, but lacked the prestige that comes with "mental work." Service workers share the blue collar view of themselves as devalued and lack the remuneration that serves as a bulwark against self-denigration. Unlike the blue collar workers Halle (1984) studied, who could wave large paychecks in the faces of their children's teachers and boost their pride through a consumer culture in which they were full participants, service workers face the denigration without much of a material reward.

Some of my friends, like, [they'd say], "You making money. Go ahead." They respect me [now] more 'cause I was working and going to school and handling everything.

IMMIGRANT YOUTH IN THE SERVICE SECTOR

Nearly half of the workers in this study were immigrants or the children of immigrants who had arrived in New York in the past decade. Dominicans, Puerto Ricans, Jamaicans, and other "island" peoples were well represented in the Harlem labor market, having made significant inroads into the job market in predominantly African American neighborhoods. Their motivations for seeking employment were essentially the same as their Black counterparts: to contribute to their households, both by relieving their parents of the need to support older teens, and through direct contributions to the cash needs of their natal families.

However, the confrontation with the U.S. status system plays out differently for immigrants in the secondary labor market. First, although aware that U.S. society frowns on "McJobs," Latino youth working in Harlem were less likely to be castigated by their friends and family members for taking low-wage work. Indeed, it is considered an important part of an older teenager's responsibilities to help support his or her family by working. These contributions are essential to the maintenance of an adequate household budget and are not as likely to be defined as "personal expense" money, totally at the disposal of the adolescent worker. It is understood that some essentials will be financed in part through the wages brought in by the oldest siblings in a family. This kind of responsibility affords some protection for immigrant adolescents from the "charge" that they are "playing the fool" by taking a minimum wage job.

Second, immigrants—young and old—are less likely than their native-born counterparts to think of minimum wage work as a source of social stigma. Other elements of social capital—family relations, ethnic networks, connections to their native cultures, future ambitions for their descendants—offer alternative bases for an honored sense of self. Work is more likely to be defined as a means to another end, including the gathering of resources that make it possible to sponsor additional family members for immigration.

Finally, as disagreeable as these jobs may appear from the "domestic" perspective, they are often several cuts above the prospects immigrants faced in their home countries. In particular, they may make it possible to amass savings (by combining the earning power of multiple family members) that would have been quite unthinkable in rural El Salvador, urban Haiti, or the poorest parts of the Dominican Republic. Those savings can be parlayed into forms of comfort "back home" that would be very hard to equal in the sending society. In a sense, then, the reference point for establishing social status remains the immigrant family's consumer status in their home country, rather than their occupational rank in the United States.

This "protective" posture does not last forever, of course. Second-generation children of immigrants, born and raised in New York and thoroughly inculcated into the status hierarchies of the receiving society, come to adopt views that are difficult to distinguish from those of the native born whose families have been in the United States forever. They may be somewhat less subject to the vilification of peers, but they are no less anxious than their African American counterparts to find better jobs and rest their social status on a more elevated platform.

The fact that this rarely transpires, that mobility out of the bottom rungs of the service sector is highly constrained, poses a challenge to developmentalists accustomed to thinking of the transition out of adolescence as a process of increasing independence. What are the consequences, for individuals and for families, when the "normal" maturation process is so compromised by the economic necessities of families and the dearth of better opportunities for young adults?

DISENGAGEMENT FROM THE 'HOOD

For a variety of reasons, some negative and some positive, youth workers in inner-city neighborhoods who maintain a long-time connection to the low-wage workplace begin to shift their center of social gravity from the school or neighborhood to the workplace. This transition has a host of critical ramifications for the shape of their social networks and the constitution of their personal lives.

To some extent the metamorphosis is brought about by the simple fact that youth workers have relatively less time to spend in the neighborhoods where they live than those who are not working. Even those who have only part-time jobs end up spending a goodly proportion of their available nonschool hours in the workplace. All by itself this leads to an increasing frequency of interaction with other workers and decreasing contact with acquaintances and friends who are not part of the work world.

However, stigma and the rejection it brings about is also responsible for the change in orientation. Neighborhood kids who give young workers a hard time for taking a "McJob" become unattractive as friends. Made to feel unwelcome or unworthy, Harlem teens who work in fast-food restaurants begin to gravitate toward young people who have followed the same pathway into the working world. A shared community of the fellow stigmatized develops and becomes the raw material of a friendship network that may not have existed before, one that is likely to have a greater geographical range and heterogeneous composition than the networks drawn from neighborhood locales.

As workers begin to spend more and more of their time on the job, the universe from which they draw their friends begins to narrow to the workplace. After hours young workers socialize together, doing the same kinds of things most young people in the community do—dancing at clubs, partying, going to films, forming romantic relationships, and so on. Yet these leisure activities are, to an increasing degree over time, conducted in the company of fellow workers.

The consequences of this narrowing are both cultural and structural. On the cultural side, increased socializing boosts the centrality of work culture and diminishes the importance of street culture. Casual conversation, humor, the food on which friendship feeds revolves around what workers have in common: the events and personalities of the workplace. Discussions of the tensions and conflicts on the job occupy the leisure hours of young workers, who analyze the ethics of their supervisors or the trustworthiness of compatriots from the shop floor.

Deciding how to manage one's finances, take care of necessary expenses, and budget for leisure or luxuries is also an important developmental realm that working youth can master. Tyesha Smith explains how her job makes it possible to be her own boss (even though she lives at home with her infant son):

> I'm independent and I don't have to ask anybody for anything. You know, I can get things on my own, do things on my own, you know. 'Cuz basically when I work all the time, through the heat and all the other stuff, I basically think about my son. I spend my whole paycheck on my son.

This kind of attitude, coupled with the experience of being responsible for one's finances, is an important aspect of cultural capital. It creates a kind of discipline that dependent youth—including those in middle-class households—often lack.

Values that emerge from work experience, then, are absorbed into adolescent culture, becoming part of a developmental trajectory that leads to adulthood. Anything that enhances the draw, the attractiveness, and the normality of working increases the chances that remaining part of the work world will become an integral part of a person's adult expectations.

On the structural side, the increasing density of social ties drawn from the work world makes it more likely that personal relationships develop between workers as opposed to relations borne of the street. In the course of our fieldwork, many pairs emerged as ongoing romantic relationships. Low wages mitigate against the prospect that these relationships result in marriages and independent household formation, but they do none-theless result in the union—for whatever time duration—of two workers. Where out of wedlock children result, they are the children of two workers, with a greater base of support than the children in welfare-dependent families.

Tyesha Smith and her ex-boyfriend Andre met in a fast-food restaurant. Both had worked in the restaurant for 2 years before they started going out together and formed a long-term relationship. In the course of their life as a couple, Tyesha gave birth to a son whom she named after Andre. Tyesha and Andre both live with their mothers and have never lived together, but both are involved in the support and care of the child, even though they are no longer romantically involved. Moreover, their respective female kin are important sources of child care, shelter, and clothing for the child—a phenomenon well described in Stack's (1974) classic work, *All Our Kin*. Tyesha's mother, a long-time welfare recipient, looks after the little boy during the week so that Tyesha can work, a child-care arrangement that would be impossible to manage if Tyesha had to pay for it on the open market. Tyesha provides part of her paycheck to her mother in return.

Andre and his mother often look after the little boy on the weekends, both to maintain contact with him and to give Tyesha and her mother a break from the constant demands of looking after a 2-year-old. Andre contributes financially to the maintenance of his son on a sporadic basis, but regularly enough for him to be defined as a responsible father. He also makes his views about his son's upbringing known, exerting some regular influence.

Both Tyesha and Andre are full-time workers and think of themselves in precisely those terms: young adults in the work world with financial responsibilities. Such an orientation distinguishes them quite sharply from people they used to know in school or in the neighborhood, and in some respects from other members of their own families who are embedded in the welfare system. Prospects for a fairly stable structure of support undergirding their child's world are greatly enhanced by the fact that these parents are both working. Out of wedlock children born to nonworking parents are far less likely to find this financial and social support structure in place.

Hence one of the critical by-products of employment for young people is that it increases the likelihood that they will develop social relationships that are borne of the workplace, with all the benefits that this entails. It is, in any event, an important step beyond the portrait of the transient, exploitative, and ultimately destructive male–female relationships that are often portrayed as typical of adolescents in the ghetto (Anderson, 1990).

I do not mean to suggest that out of wedlock pregnancy is a common phenomenon among working poor youth, for in fact this research suggests that it is far less likely to happen when young women work. Kraft (1989) showed that women with higher wages are far more likely to utilize birth control or abortion services in order to control their fertility than women in low-wage jobs. Yet even workers at the bottom of the occupational hierarchy have something of value to protect—the ability to stay on the job—that militates against giving birth. Personal diaries kept for a 10-month period during this research project show—admittedly on a very small sample—young women getting pregnant and then weighing the "pros" of having a baby against the "cons" of losing time at work and a lifetime obligation to care for a child alone, opting to terminate their pregnancies. As inadequate as their low-wage jobs are, they still represent an enterprise that is valued, that is worth protecting, particularly in the absence of husbands who can support a family.

Policymakers are well aware that rates of illegitimate births have soared over the last decade, particularly among inner-city minorities in poverty. Ethnographic work of this kind leads to the hypothesis that for the working poor the picture may look substantially more encouraging. If this turns out to be the case in studies of national samples, increased investment in youth employment may well be part of the answer to the problem of out of wedlock childbearing. Curing persistent poverty will require more than the creation of millions of low-wage jobs, for this kind of employment simply sustains the same standard of living that welfare provides—a completely inadequate support structure for independent adult living (Edin, 1994). However, to the extent that out of wedlock childbearing by young women contributes to poverty, early and sustained work experience may well be part of the answer to cutting back on teen pregnancy.

CONCLUSION

The literature on transitions from adolescence to early adulthood revolves around the loosening of ties between young people and their families, and the increasing importance of peers or institutions beyond the family's reach in shaping the adolescent's developmental trajectory. Although seen as normal and natural for the most part, these extrafamilial influences are often regarded as the source of serious problems in the adolescent lives of inner-city minorities. Peers, particularly if bound to street culture, often constitute a pernicious influence. Education, although potentially of great positive importance, is frequently a weak actor in adolescent lives or something akin to a holding pen rather than a skill-enhancing, human capital-fostering institution.

Developmentalists who focus on the study of inner-city communities rarely turn their attention to the world of work, except to point out the ways in which adolescent work experience interferes with involvement in school. Beyond this, the problems of welfare dependency, persistent poverty, high unemployment, and the like loom so large that the existence of a hard-core working population is almost completely obscured.

The fact of the matter, however, is that even in some of the poorest parts of New York City, a city with over 1 million people on welfare, adolescents are working in large numbers in low-wage jobs in order to escape the pressures of the streets, assist their parents in supporting the household, take responsibility for their own cash needs, and amass the capital it takes to invest in post-high-school training and educational opportunities. In the course of their work experience, an involvement that typically begins between 13 and 15 years of age, they acquire a set of values that place a high premium on personal responsibility as well as a set of personal contacts that, over time, become central to their social lives.

The secondary labor market is not a cure for the ills of poverty. Indeed, because these jobs rarely provide a stepping stone to better employment, they can easily become a low-wage trap that leads to a lifetime of working poverty. This problem demands policy solutions that are beyond the purview of this chapter. However, leaving the issue of long-term occupational mobility aside, the benefits of engagement with legitimate work opportunities for adolescents are considerable (not to mention the value their labor has for the support of their natal families). Engagement in the work world confers dignity, enhances a sense of independence and personal responsibility, and makes it possible for young people to make meaningful contributions to their households and the well-being of their own children. These are critical aspects of adolescent development in any setting, but deserve special recognition in those communities where the alternatives are often dangerous or debilitating.

The literature on the Great Depression tells us that family conflict rose to new heights as the labor market collapsed and young people could no longer afford to move out when they reached adulthood (Komarovsky, 1940; Lazarsfeld, 1931). Because the Depression was eventually followed by war-related economic recovery, many of these young people were eventually able to leave home on the strength of their own earnings, although some were scarred for life by their rocky entry into the labor market of the 1930s (Elder, 1974).

If the current period of economic restructuring continues to generate little more than low-wage jobs it may well be the case that we are looking at a sea change in the context of adolescent maturation (Freeman, 1992; Harrison & Bluestone, 1986). Young workers, particularly those who have grown up in segregated ghettos where economic opportunities are limited, may find that they lack permanently the wherewithal to become independent adults. They may never be able to leave home (unless they can lay claim to subsidized housing). Researchers need to be aware of the ways in which a deindustrialized economy impacts the transition to adulthood and study its developmental consequences.

ACKNOWLEDGMENTS

This research was supported by generous grants from the Russell Sage Foundation, the Rockefeller Foundation, the Ford Foundation, the Spencer Foundation, and the W. T. Grant Foundation. I should like to thank my colleague and collaborator at U.C. Berkeley, Carol Stack, as well as my graduate student research team—Eric Clemons, Kate Ellis, Travis Jackson, Chauncey Lennon, and Ana Ramos-Zayas—for their work in connection with this project.

REFERENCES

Anderson, E. (1990). *Streetwise*. Chicago: University of Chicago Press.

Bachman, J., & Schulenberg, J. (1993). How part-time work intensity relates to drug use, problem behavior, time use and satisfaction among high school seniors: Are these consequences or merely correlates. *Developmental Psychology, 29*(2), 220–235.

City of New York, Department of Urban Planning. (1993). *Socio-economic profiles: A portrait of New York City's community districts from the 1980 and 1990 censuses of population and housing*. New York: Author.

Edin, K. (1994). *The myths of dependency and self-sufficiency: Women, welfare and low wage work*. Unpublished manuscript, Department of Sociology, Rutgers University, New Brunswick, NJ.

Elder, G., Jr. (1974). *Children of the Great Depression*. Chicago: University of Chicago Press.

Freeman, R. (1992). *Employment and earnings of disadvantaged young men in a labor shortage economy*. Cambridge, MA: National Bureau of Economic Research.

Grannovetter, M. (1974). *Getting a job*. Boston: Little, Brown.

Greenberger, E., & Steinberg, L. (1986). *When teenagers work: The psychological and social costs of adolescent employment*. New York: Basic Books.

Halle, D. (1984). *America's working man*. Chicago: University of Chicago Press.

Harrison, B., & Bluestone, B. (1986). *The great u-turn*. New York: Basic Books.

Komarovsky, M. (1940). *The unemployed man and his family*. New York: Ayer Company.

Kraft, J. (1989). *Work and fertility: An exploration of the relationship between labor force participation and premarital fertility*. Unpublished doctoral dissertation, Department of Sociology, Northwestern University, Evanston, IL.

Lazarsfeld, P. (1933). *Marienthal*.

Leidner, R. (1993). *Fast food, fast talk: Service work and the routinization of everyday life*. Berkeley: University of California Press.

McNeil, L. (1984). *Lowering expectations: The impact of student employment in classroom knowledge*. Madison: Wisconsin Center for Education Research.

Newman, K. (1988). *Falling from grace: The experience of downward mobility in the American middle class*. New York: The Free Press.

Newman, K. (1993). *Declining fortunes: The withering of the American dream*. New York: Basic Books.

Rich, L. (1993). *The long-run impact of early nonemployment: A reexamination.* Unpublished manuscript, Population Studies Center, University of Michigan, Ann Arbor.

Sedlack, M., Wheeler, C., Cusick, P., & Pullin, D. (1986). *Selling students short.* New York: Teachers College Press.

Sennett, R., & Cobb, J. (1973). *The hidden injuries of class.* New York: Vintage Books.

Stack, C. (1974). *All our kin.* New York: Harper & Row.

Steinberg, L., Fegley, S., & Dornbush, S. (1993). Negative impact of part time work on adolescent adjustment: Evidence from a longitudinal study. *Developmental Psychology, 29*(2), 171–180.

Sullivan, M. (1993). Puerto Ricans in Sunset Park, Brooklyn. In J. Moore & R. Pinderhaus (Eds.), *In the barrios: Latinos and the underclass debate* (pp. 1–26). New York: Russell Sage Foundation.

Velez-Ibanez, C. (1993). U.S. Mexicans in the borderland: Being poor without the underclass. In J. Moore & R. Pinderhaus (Eds.), *In the barrios: Latinos and the underclass debate* (pp. 195–210). New York: Russell Sage Foundation.

Family Factors and Young Adult Transitions: Educational Attainment and Occupational Prestige

Kathy L. Bell
Texas Tech University

Joseph P. Allen
University of Virginia

Stuart T. Hauser
Harvard Medical School

Thomas G. O'Connor
University of Virginia

In this chapter we examine the idea that the processes of continuing education beyond high school and launching a career pose challenges for young adults that are related to the processes of achieving autonomy while maintaining relatedness with parents as adolescents. We focus on educational attainment and occupational prestige as two markers of the success of the transition to early adulthood and explore three central questions: (a) Are qualities of parent–adolescent interactions predictive of high school completion? (b) Are qualities of parent–adolescent interactions predictive of later education and occupational success? (c) Are qualities of marital interaction in families with adolescents predictive of any of these outcomes? In the first section of this chapter, we briefly review the literature on the relationship among family background characteristics, educational attainment, and subsequent occupational prestige. We emphasize the family as a primary context for development, focusing on the association between family background and young adult outcomes. The second section discusses links between parenting and young adult academic and career achievements and illustrates these relationships with a sample of adolescents who were first observed with their families at age 14, and then assessed in terms of educational and occupational out-comes 11 years later at age 25. In a third section we focus on parents' marital dynamics in this same sample and examine the longitudinal relationship of marital behavior to the adolescents' subsequent education attainment and occupational prestige.

During early adulthood, many individuals try out their first adult life structure by committing to their first careers (Levinson, Darrow, Klein, Levinson, & McKee, 1978). Educational and occupational decisions, at this juncture, represent major developmental tasks and can be considered extensions of the earlier stage-salient developmental task of adolescence—becoming an autonomous individual. The process of developing auton-omy and achieving identity during adolescence also involves maintaining family relationships (Campbell, Adams, & Dobson, 1984; Collins, 1990; Grotevant & Cooper, 1985; Hauser & Levine, 1993; Hill & Holmbeck, 1986; Steinberg, 1990) and continues into young adulthood with parents exerting influences on the process and its resolution (e.g., Campbell et al., 1984; Grotevant, 1983; Hauser & Greene, 1992; Josselson, 1987).

The quality of parent–teen relations also appears to continue as a major influence on adolescents as they separate from their parents and begin the process of becoming adults (J. A. Hoffman, 1984). Positive family relations have been linked to less loneliness when leaving home, better adjustment to college, higher college grade point averages, and better peer relationships in college (Cutrona, Cole, Colangelo, Assouline, & Russell, 1994; Frank, Pirsch, & Wright, 1990; Hoffman & Weiss, 1987; Kenny, 1987; Kobak & Sceery, 1988; Lapsley, Rice, & Shadid, 1989; Lopez, 1991; Lopez, Campbell, & Watkins, 1988, 1989a, 1989b; Moore, 1987; Rice, Cole, & Lapsley, 1990). Parents also play a significant role in their off-springs' completion of college, in that the behavior they model (e.g., being employed in a profession that requires higher education) seems to have direct effects and is reflected in the values internalized by their children (Bank, Slavings, & Biddle, 1990). We propose, then, that educational attainment and occupational prestige, viewed as measures of young adult development, are longitudinally related to both family characteristics and qualities of family relations.

INTERGENERATIONAL TRANSMISSION OF EDUCATIONAL ATTAINMENT AND OCCUPATIONAL PRESTIGE

Many different conceptual models of adult educational attainment have been explored in which intergenerational factors play a major role in academic success or failure (Hauser & Featherman, 1977; Haveman,

Wolfe, & Spaulding, 1991; Hill & Duncan, 1987; Rumberger, 1983, 1987). It is well documented that students who come from relatively small, intact, middle-class families, where they are expected to succeed, go further in school, and ultimately obtain relatively high-prestige jobs in comparison to their peers. Adults with higher levels of education are more likely to be employed; they also have increased opportunities for professional advancement (Bureau of Labor Statistics [BLS], 1994; National Center for Education Statistics [NCES], 1993a). In 1992, the unemployment rate for adults 25 years old and over who had not completed high school was 11.4%. This was in contrast to 6.8% for persons with 4 years of high school and 3.2% for individuals who had obtained at least a bachelor's degree (NCES, 1993b). The types of employment opportunities available to individuals also vary by educational attainment. In 1992, over 62% of the adults employed in managerial and professional specialties had at least a bachelor's degree, whereas the majority of persons employed in service occupations, precision production, farming, forestry, and fishing had only a high school education (NCES, 1993b). Earnings are also directly affected by education. Between 1980 and 1990 earnings increased 78% for men with 5 or more years of college, but only 30% for those with 1 to 3 years of high school (NCES, 1993b). It is especially important, then, to understand the processes underlying the intergenerational transmission of educational attainment to gain a better understanding of later occupational outcomes.

Educational attainment and intergenerational transmission of income that are closely linked to occupational prestige have been studied from multiple perspectives, including demographics, economics, education, psychology, and sociology (Astone & McLanahan, 1991; Becker, 1981; Hill & Duncan, 1987; Hogan & Astone, 1986). Much of the research on this subject relies on large-scale surveys (e.g., Astone & McLanahan, 1991; Hill & Duncan, 1987; Sewell & Hauser, 1975) so the information gathered in these studies has been largely based on self- and parent reports (see Brooks-Gunn, Brown, Duncan, & Moore, 1994, for the contents of current national surveys issues). Other factors that have been considered include rank in high school class, perceived expectations of significant others (parents and teachers), educational and occupational aspirations, family structure, sources of family income, and parents' education and occupations (Hill & Duncan, 1987; Sewell & Hauser, 1975). Although these studies underscore the relationship between family background characteristics and educational attainment and occupational prestige or earnings later in life, they offer little data on the possible link between family dynamics and educational and occupational outcomes.

Family contextual variables appear to influence young adult outcomes but it is also important to look beyond them to see how the family processes may mediate the effects of family background. Parental socio-economic status (SES), for example, is related to children's educational attainment and prestige and earnings in adulthood. The effects of parental SES on offsprings' actual occupational prestige, however, appear to be largely transmitted via the educational attainment of the younger generation (Blau & Duncan, 1967; Duncan, 1966; Duncan & Hodge, 1963; Eckland, 1965; Hodge, 1966). If the family environment supports educational attainment, the negative effects of low parental SES on occupational outcomes may be diluted. The relationship of SES to educational attainment, in turn, may be more complex than the simple fact that middle- and upper class families have the financial resources to support advanced education. Family economics are related not only to actual income but also to the ways in which resources (time, money, aptitudes) are allocated in the family (L. W. Hoffman, 1984). Middle- and upper class families tend to allocate their resources in ways that promote the advancement of their children (Becker, 1981; Becker & Tomes, 1986; Coleman, 1988), which may be a reflection of parental values.

PARENT–ADOLESCENT RELATIONSHIPS AND EDUCATIONAL ATTAINMENT AND OCCUPATIONAL PRESTIGE

Darling and Steinberg (1993) presented a contextual model of parenting whereby parental goals and values affect both parenting style and parenting practices. In this model, parenting practices are seen as having direct effects on adolescent outcomes; however, these effects are moderated by parenting style and the effects of parenting style on adolescents' openness to socialization from their parents. Parenting style provides a context within which socialization occurs. In this section we first consider parental goals and values, and then discuss qualities of the parent–adolescent relationship as potential influences on young adult educational attainment and occupational prestige. In particular, we consider the parenting context both as a mediator of parental goals and values and as having direct effects on young adult outcomes.

Goals and Values

Parents' goals for their children, which are related to adult outcomes, may be confounded with SES. Economic hardship, for example, may make parents more pessimistic about their children's futures (Galambos & Silbereisen, 1987) and consequently lower their goals for their children. Parental encouragement, which may be difficult for parents who are financially stressed, however, is the variable that has been most frequently related to educational attainment and occupational success in late adolescence and adulthood (e.g., Bordua, 1960; Ihinger-Tallman, 1982; Kahl, 1953; Marjoribanks, 1989; Rehberg & Westby, 1967; Sewell & Shah, 1968). This variable is usually assessed in the form of self-reports (see Ihinger-Tallman, 1982, for an exception) in which the children or adolescents are asked about the educational plans and desires their parents have for them, and about parental pressure to do well in school. By measuring parental encouragement in this fashion, researchers are attempting to directly access parental values. Sewell and Shah (1968) found that parental encouragement added substantially to the variance in educational goals explained by SES. In these models of individuals' plans for college, however, there is still a portion of the variance that is not explained indicating that additional constructs, such as parenting style, could enhance the prediction of expected educational attainment and occupational goals.

Reports of Parenting Context

There may be other dimensions of parenting, besides parental encouragement and expectations that relate to young adult occupational and educational achievements. Specifically, the emotional climate of the family as communicated to the adolescent can effect the adolescent's receptivity to parental values (Darling & Steinberg, 1993). Generally, research in educational achievement supports this position. Parenting style (Dornbusch, Ritter, Leiderman, Roberts, & Fraleigh, 1987), parents' personal adjustment (Forehand, Long, Brody, & Fauber, 1986), and communications between parents and children (Forehand et al., 1986; Masselam, Marcus, & Stunkard, 1990) all influence adolescent behavior and performance in school. Positive communication between parents and adolescents differentiated teens who were successful in the public school system from teens who left the public school system to receive additional help (Masselam et al., 1990). Multiple aspects of parenting style—acceptance, psychological autonomy, and behavioral control—also contribute to high school success (Steinberg, Elmen, & Mounts, 1989). Adolescents from indulgent homes are frequently less engaged in school than adolescents from authoritative homes (Lamborn, Mounts, Steinberg, & Dornbusch, 1991). Additionally, Rumberger, Ghatak, Poulos, Ritter, and Dornbusch (1990) found that, after accounting for family demographics, permissive parenting was associated with dropping out of high school.

In a similar vein, affective qualities of the parent–adolescent relationship have been implicated in the area of career development. Enmeshment in the family system has been linked to adolescents' difficulties in mastering career development tasks (Penick & Jepsen, 1992). Lopez and

Andrews (1987) speculated that overinvolvement on the part of parents may impede college students' career decision making. They see the process of committing to a career as requiring a transformation in family functioning that would simultaneously facilitate adult identity formation and psychological separation from parents. Overinvolvement on the part of parents, according to this formulation (Lopez & Andrews, 1987), may have negative consequences in career development. College students who exhibit the most career maturity and progress in committing to careers, however, report high levels of emotional support and attachment to their parents (Blustein, Walbridge, Friedlander, & Palladino, 1991; Kenny, 1990). Thus, adolescent achievement seems to be best promoted in families in which parents are not overinvolved with their teens (i.e., they allow sufficient autonomy), but nevertheless maintain close supportive relationships with them.

In the literature reviewed thus far, we have shown that family characteristics relate longitudinally to young adult education and career outcomes and that qualities of the parent–teen relationships have significant relationships to concurrent adolescent educational achievements and career development. Nearly all of the studies previously described rely on reports of family behavior. In this study we redress some of the gaps in the literature by observing family interactions during middle adolescence and reporting on the relationship between observed qualities in family interactions and actual young adult career outcomes.

Observations of Parent–Adolescent Interactions

Sample Characteristics. In this study, 77 teenagers and their mothers and fathers participated. The adolescents were either high school freshmen (ninth grade; $N = 38$) or had a nonpsychotic, nonorganic impairment and had been psychiatrically hospitalized at age 14 ($N = 39$; mean age = 14.5 years). Most of the hospitalized adolescents carried diagnoses related to conduct problems or depression. The families in both groups were predominantly upper middle class (mean SES = 2.08, $SD = 1.07$; Hollingshead, 1975) and all subjects were White. Subjects from the high school and psychiatrically hospitalized group did not significantly differ in terms of age, gender, birth order, or number of siblings; the only demographic criterion on which the samples differed was SES (higher for the high school sample). The sampling procedure was used to examine adolescents across a broader range of levels of social functioning than would typically be available in a representative sample. Psychiatric hospitalization at age 14 was thus used as a criterion to obtain a sample likely to be at lower levels of family and individual functioning. (A more complete description of sampling procedures and rationale is provided in Hauser, Powers, & Noam, 1991.)

Adolescents and their families participated in a revealed-differences task (Strodtbeck, 1951). They were paid $30 for their participation in the family session. Family members were first interviewed separately about Kohlberg moral dilemmas and then brought together to discuss issues they disagreed about. Participants were asked to take up to 10 minutes to discuss their first disagreement and, if possible, to resolve it. Families were then presented with a new disagreement to discuss. This procedure continued for 30 minutes, with disagreements presented to alternate which family member was in the minority in a disagreement. The family interaction was then coded using the Autonomy and Relatedness coding system (Allen, Hauser, Borman, & Worrell, 1991), which yields a rating for each family member's overall behavior toward each other family member in the interaction (e.g., separate ratings for adolescents' hostility toward mothers and for mothers' hostility toward adolescents). The coding system is described in greater detail later.

The adolescents were interviewed again as young adults when they were 25. Seventy-three of the adolescents originally in the study provided us with information. One subject was deceased. Seventy-two subjects provided information about educational attainment, 65 provided information on their current jobs, and 71 provided information about their most important job.[1] Occupational success is assessed in terms of occupational prestige rather than current earnings. Many of the subjects were currently in training status where their occupational prestige and job responsibilities were considerable but their earnings had not yet stabilized. Occupational prestige for both current jobs and most important jobs was coded by two raters who assigned prestige scores to the occupations listed by the subjects. The prestige scores were taken from the 1989 General Social Survey update of the NORC scale scores (Nakao, Hodge, & Treas, 1990; Nakao & Treas, 1990). Disagreements between raters were resolved by conferencing. For those subjects who were currently enrolled in full-time, professional degree programs, their current occupations were coded as corresponding to the occupation for which they will qualify when they complete their degree requirements. This approach was chosen because these subjects were already engaging in tasks associated with the completed degree (teaching at an institution of postsecondary education, finishing internships, etc.).

---

[1]One person did not provide educational information, one person did not provide information about the most important job, and one other person said that no job had been important. Eight persons were currently not working—one was disabled, two were enrolled in school and did not specify a degree program, and five were unemployed.

In relating educational attainment and occupational prestige both to demographic and family interaction variables it is important to assure that the effects found were not artifacts of the two-group selection process for the study. To guard against this possibility, adolescents' history of psychiatric hospitalization at age 14 was controlled for in all correlations reported, and always entered as the first term in multiple regression analyses.

As already mentioned, previous research has documented the relationship between SES and educational attainment (e.g., Sewell & Hauser, 1975). In this sample, parental SES[2] was significantly correlated with reported level of young adults' educational attainment ($r = .40$, $p < .001$) and occupational prestige ($r = .44$, $p < .001$) at 25 years of age. Educational attainment and occupational prestige were significantly correlated ($r = .50$, $p < .001$), as expected.

Consistent with other past investigations, birth order was related to educational attainment (Mare & Chen, 1986) with earlier born adolescents (low birth order) achieving higher levels of education ($r = -.26$, $p < .05$). Birth order was not related to occupational prestige of the current job.

Autonomy and Relatedness and Young Adult Outcomes. Several recent reviews have examined transitions in family relationship during adolescence (Collins, 1990; Holmbeck, Paikoff, & Brooks-Gunn, 1995; Paikoff & Brooks-Gunn, 1991; Steinberg, 1990). There is a general consensus that rather than abrupt changes there are gradual transformations in family relationships around issues of autonomy, parent–child conflict, and the manifestation of parent–adolescent harmony (Steinberg, 1990).

The Autonomy and Relatedness coding system (Allen et al., 1991) is particularly sensitive to these issues. It is used to classify interactional behaviors into three primary scales including: (a) exhibiting autonomous-relatedness, which sums ratings of behaviors expressing and discussing reasons behind disagreements, confidence in stating one's positions, validation and agreement with another's position, and attending to the other person's statements; (b) undermining autonomy, which sums ratings of behaviors overpersonalizing a disagreement, recanting a position without appearing to have been persuaded the position is wrong (thus ending the discussion), and pressuring another person to agree other than by making rational arguments; and (c) hostile conflictual behavior, which sums ratings of behaviors undermining relatedness by overtly expressing hostility toward another member, or by rudely interrupting or ignoring a family member. Intraclass correlations for the three scales were .84, .82, and .70 for exhibiting autonomous-relatedness, hostile conflictual behav-

---

[2]Because high SES in this study was represented by low values, the values were reversed to make the presentation of results more logically consistent.

ior, and undermining autonomy, respectively (Allen, Hauser, Bell, & O'Connor, 1994).

Similar constructs have been discussed in terms of late adolescent and young adult transitions. Blustein et al. (1991) proposed that individuals who have difficulty developing autonomous attitudes will have problems committing to career choices, and Lopez and Andrews (1987) speculated about the importance of parental encouragement of autonomy to facilitate individuation. The implication of this is that establishing appropriate autonomy in adolescence has a longitudinal relationship to career development. Attachment to parents and conflictual independence from parents, defined as the absence of guilt, anxiety, anger, and resentment toward parents, is also related to progress in the career commitment process (Blustein et al., 1991), implying that it is beneficial for adolescents to maintain feelings of closeness with and support from their parents. Whereas there are similarities in the early and late adolescent constructs that have predictive validity for achievements, no one has examined how the manifestations of these constructs in middle adolescence relate to educational and occupational outcomes later in life.

It is recognized that the development of autonomy in the parent–adolescent relationship is of major importance, so we posited that there will be long-term developmental consequences if this task is not successfully negotiated during adolescence. Fourteen-year-olds who actively undermine autonomy in relation to their parents show hostility and an inability to maintain their relationship with their parents at age 16 (Allen, Hauser, O'Connor, Bell, & Eickholt, in press). If adolescents learn models of interaction in their families that they might later generalize to the workplace, then this inability to maintain relatedness might impair later educational and career performance. Qualities of autonomy and relatedness in family interactions have also been found to be related to increases over time in adolescents' levels of ego development and self-esteem (Allen et al., 1994). The same types of family behaviors that promote self-esteem may encourage the development of personality characteristics that are important for career success (Block & Robins, 1993). Specifically, we hypothesize that adolescents' success in achieving autonomy while maintaining relatedness with their parents will predict occupational success both directly and via a path through educational attainment.

In this study we found that the way autonomy and relatedness were negotiated in adolescent–parent groupings did relate to long-term educational and occupational outcomes, but parents' SES also was related to family interaction style. Correlations between SES and exhibiting autonomous-relatedness ranged from .23 ($p < .06$) to .38 ($p < .001$) depending on who was involved in the pairing. Members of high-SES families exhibited high levels of autonomous-relatedness toward each other. Adolescents in low-SES families expressed more behaviors that undermined autonomy when speaking with their mothers ($r = -.40$, $p < .001$). Because SES was related to family interaction style it was always entered into our models before the family interaction variables. This way we were able to examine the relationship between the styles of family interaction over the effects of SES.

Eighty-one percent of the current sample completed high school. Consistent with results of prior research (Rumberger, 1983, 1987), in this current sample, there was a trend for the females to show higher rates of high school completion, $t(51.7) = 1.93$, $p < .06$. Of the subjects who did not finish high school, only one subject was from the nonhospitalized group; all others were from the psychiatric group. In the psychiatric group approximately one third of the subjects did not complete high school. Females in the psychiatric group were more likely than the males in this group to complete high school, $t(25) = 2.82$, $p < .01$.

Logistic regressions were used to analyze the data from only those subjects who were in the psychiatric group to see if adolescent–parent interaction variables contributed to the prediction of high school completion after accounting for SES, birth order, and gender. We expected that parental behaviors exhibiting autonomy and relatedness toward the adolescent and the same types of behaviors on the part of the adolescents toward their parents would be related to high school completion (Steinberg et al., 1989) for this group. Table 13.1 shows that exhibiting autonomous-relatedness in family interactions was associated with high school completion in the psychiatric sample for all adolescent–parent dyads except for mothers' behaviors toward the adolescents. Adolescents' behaviors toward their parents were the strongest predictors, perhaps in-

TABLE 13.1
Predictors of High School Completion Among
Psychiatrically Hospitalized Adolescents

	Standardized Estimates for Directional Pairs for Autonomous-Relatedness			
	Adol → Mother	Adol → Father	Mother → Adol	Father → Adol
Predicting High School Completion				
Socioeconomic status	.21	.08	.27	.25
Birth order	−.17	−.19	−.12	−.16
Gender	.49*	.53*	.43	.37
Autonomous-relatedness	.65**	.78**	.21	.57**
$\chi^2(4)$ for improvement over intercept model	14.44***	15.33***	9.25*	13.03**

Note. Standardized estimates were obtained from logistic regression equations.
*$p < .10$. **$p < .05$. ***$p < .01$.

dicating the importance of the adolescents' own feelings of autonomous-relatedness in determining their life-course directions. Similar logistical models were used to analyze parents' behaviors that undermined adolescents' autonomy and behaviors that were hostile and conflictual toward adolescents in the psychiatric sample. Fathers' undermining of adolescents' autonomy and the adolescents' gender were significant positive predictors of high school completion in this group of psychiatrically hospitalized adolescents ($\chi^2(4) = 14.12$, $p < .01$, standardized parameter estimates for gender = .63, $p < .05$ and for undermining autonomy = .67, $p < .05$).

We also examined overall educational attainment at age 25. Multiple regression equations (one for each of the parent–adolescent pairings on each of the autonomy and relatedness scales) were used to predict educational attainment. Psychiatric status, parental SES, and birth order were entered into each of the analyses prior to the measure of autonomous-relatedness. With these constraints, autonomous-relatedness directed toward fathers was the only significant predictor of educational attainment at age 25 (see Table 13.2). Psychiatric status did not significantly interact with the autonomy and relatedness scales. Because females achieved a higher level of educational attainment in this sample, the relationship between adolescents' behaviors exhibiting autonomous-relatedness toward their fathers and educational attainment also was examined for males and females separately. We found substantially similar patterns of results across gender.

In keeping with the literature on educational attainment, we hypothesized that exhibiting autonomous-relatedness in the parent–teen pairs would contribute to occupational success primarily through educational attainment. As noted earlier, educational attainment was correlated with current prestige of young adults' jobs. When the various parent–teen pairings of exhibiting autonomous-relatedness behaviors were entered into these regression equations after educational attainment, they did not

TABLE 13.2
Relationship Between Adolescents' Exhibiting Autonomous-Relatedness Toward Father and Educational Attainment After Accounting for Psychiatric Status, Socioeconomic Status, and Birth Order

Predicting Overall Educational Attainment	β
Psychiatric status	$-.41^{**}$
Socioeconomic status	$.25^{*}$
Birth order	$-.13$
Autonomous-relatedness of adolescent → father	$.22^{*}$
R^2	$.58^{**}$

Note. $^{*}p < .05$. $^{**}p < .001$.

TABLE 13.3
Relationships Between Undermining Autonomy and Occupational
Prestige for Adolescent–Parent Pairs After Accounting for
Psychiatric Status, Socioeconomic Status, Birth Order,
and Educational Attainment

	Current Prestige	
	Interaction with	
	Mother	Father
Undermining autonomy	β	β
Adolescent → Parent	−.31*	−.37**
Parent → Adolescent	−.01	−.27*

Note. Fs for the overall equations are significant at $p < .05$. Educational attainment was a significant predictor at $p < .05$ in these equations; there were no other significant predictors except undermining autonomy in any of the equations in this table.
*$p < .05$. **$p < .01$.

contribute to the prediction of either prestige measure, confirming the expectation that exhibiting autonomous-relatedness is related to occupational outcomes through its relationship to educational attainment.

Next we considered whether there were developmental consequences related to establishing a successful career trajectory as a young adult when individuals had not demonstrated autonomy with respect to their parents during adolescence. After accounting for psychiatric status, parental SES, birth order, and educational attainment, in our regressions we found that the adolescents' behaviors that undermined autonomy in their families of origin during teenage years had a significant relation to later occupational prestige (see Table 13.3). Adolescents' undermining of mothers' and fathers' autonomy was related to lower occupational prestige for young adults. Fathers' undermining of adolescents' autonomy also was associated with lower young adult occupational prestige. In predicting occupational prestige, even though parent and adolescent behaviors exhibiting autonomy and relatedness were mediated by educational attainment, the effects of undermining autonomy in family interactions appear more directly related to this young adult outcome.

Summary

In this section we have explored the issue of parent–adolescent relationships and educational and career outcomes. Parental values, parenting style, and actual qualities of parent–adolescent interactions all relate to offsprings' attainments. Parents who encourage their children to pursue postsecondary education, demonstrating that they value education, generally have children who pursue postsecondary education (e.g., Bordua, 1960; Ihinger-Tallman, 1982; Kahl, 1953; Marjoribanks, 1989; Rehberg & Westby, 1967; Sewell & Shah, 1968). Parenting style, by providing a context to support adolescent development, was also related to achievements in educational and occupational domains. Authoritative parenting is related to adolescent engagement in school (Lamborn et al., 1991). Similarly, college students who feel supported by their parents exhibit career maturity (Blustein et al., 1991; Kenny, 1990). Finally, in moving beyond a generalized parenting context to examine specific interactional behaviors, we found that autonomy and relatedness in parent–adolescent interactions is related to high school completion and overall educational attainment and occupational prestige in young adulthood.

MARITAL DYNAMICS IN FAMILIES OF ADOLESCENTS AND YOUNG ADULT OUTCOMES

There are also a number of ways in which the interaction patterns in the marital dyad might relate to young adult outcomes. Lopez and Andrews (1987) suggested that one of the ways that parents may support individuation in early adulthood is to consolidate their marital relationship. Additionally, if parents' relations with each other contribute to adolescents' models of interpersonal relationships, then it would be expected that teenagers whose parents were supportive of each other and simultaneously encouraging of individual autonomy in their marriages will be better equipped to handle relational issues in the workplace. Conflict in the parents' marital dyad, on the other hand, may also influence their adolescent's subsequent occupational prestige. A large body of literature points to the negative effects of marital conflict on children (Emery, 1982; Feldman & Wentzel, 1990; Hetherington & Martin, 1986; Maccoby & Martin, 1983; Peterson & Zill, 1986). Although some of the effects of marital conflict are related to school performance, most of the negative outcomes are less context specific. Marital conflict is more generally related to poor psychosocial functioning in children. By extension, parents' marital conflict might contribute to lower occupational prestige in young adulthood.

We expected that the qualities of the marital relationship observed by the young adults during adolescence also would be related to their later career success. Table 13.4 shows that in our sample even after accounting for psychiatric status, parental SES, birth order, and educational attainment, marital interaction variables were significant predictors of occupational outcomes of offspring 11 years later. Mothers' behaviors exhibiting

TABLE 13.4
Relationship Between Parents' Marital Behaviors and Young Adult
Occupational Prestige After Accounting for Psychiatric Status,
Socioeconomic Status, Birth Order, and Educational Attainment

	Current Prestige	
	Mother → Father	Father → Mother
	β	β
Psychiatric status	.08	.09
Socioeconomic status	.14	.16
Birth order	.11	.10
Educational attainment	.44***	.46***
Exhibiting autonomous-relatedness	.29**	.16
R^2	.36***	.31***
Psychiatric status	.15	.12
Socioeconomic status	.23	.22
Birth order	.11	.06
Educational attainment	.46***	.44***
Undermining autonomy	.17	−.21*
R^2	.31***	.33***

$*p < .10. **p < .05. ***p < .01.$

autonomous-relatedness toward fathers predicted young adults' current occupational prestige and there was a trend for fathers' behaviors that undermined mothers' autonomy to predict lower prestige of young adults' current positions. Marital hostility when our subjects were adolescents was not related to young adults' current occupational prestige. When predictions for parents' marital dynamics were examined by gender of child, we found little difference in overall patterns.

CONCLUSIONS AND DISCUSSION

We began this chapter by reviewing a large body of evidence showing that family background and parental encouragement are related to each other, and to adolescents' later educational attainment and occupational success. We also examined family interaction styles, and found evidence to support the idea that qualities of family interactions have long-term developmental impact in these realms. Our exploration of this issue focused on the relationship of autonomy and relatedness in family interactions. Using observed family interactions of 14-year-olds and their parents, we found that even after accounting for prior pathology and family SES, not only were adolescents' behaviors exhibiting autonomous-relatedness and undermining autonomy predictive of young adult outcomes, but parents' behaviors both toward the adolescents and with each other also related to young adult outcomes.

Summarizing the detailed analyses already described, we found that for high school completion of the previously hospitalized group and for educational attainment of the entire sample, the autonomy and related-ness between adolescents and their fathers were especially important in predicting educational achievements. In predicting high school comple-tion, both adolescent behaviors toward fathers and fathers' behaviors toward adolescents were important. In predicting educational attainment, adolescents' behaviors toward their fathers had greater predictive power than the correlated behaviors on the part of the father.

Differences in father–adolescent and mother–adolescent interactions are not necessarily large (Collins & Russell, 1991), but the way adolescents interact with each of their parents may have different relationships to long-term educational outcomes. Other research suggests reasons why father–adolescent interaction differs from mother–adolescent interaction in predicting educational and occupational outcomes. Youniss and Smol-lar (1985) reported that adolescent interactions with fathers tend to have a relatively narrow focus—the domains of academic performance and future plans. Although adolescents discuss these issues with both parents, fathers' realms of authority deal more exclusively with these areas where there are objective performance standards. The issues adolescents discuss with their fathers relate to becoming a productive member of adult society (Youniss & Smollar, 1985) so perhaps the way adolescents respond to their fathers is especially important for how they will ultimately function in these domains. It is possible that teens who respond positively to their fathers in a generalized problem-solving task, like the one in this study, are better able to do the same when discussing their own futures with their fathers or with males in positions of authority at work.

Fathers' realms of influence typically deal with being a productive member of society but the strength of their influence is likely augmented by the quality of their relationship with their children. Other researchers have reported that fathers do not generally have very intimate relation-ships with adolescents (LeCroy, 1988; Youniss & Ketterlinus, 1987), but that when they do have such relationships this is important for adolescent functioning. Adolescents report fewer problem behaviors and higher self-esteem when they have intimate relationships with their fathers (Le-Croy, 1988). Adolescents who exhibit autonomous-relatedness toward their fathers in the laboratory may have especially strong relationships. In this study, adolescents whose behaviors exhibit autonomous-related-ness toward their fathers have fathers who show the same types of behaviors toward them. It previously has been shown in this sample that fathers' behaviors exhibiting autonomous-relatedness toward their teenagers is related to adolescents' ego development and self-esteem (Allen et al., 1994) and this could help explain the association between paternal interaction style and educational success.

Parental support and encouragement may be important for career success but, like the effects of parental SES on occupational success (Blau & Duncan, 1967; Duncan, 1966; Duncan & Hodge, 1963; Eckland, 1965; Hodge, 1966), parental support and encouragement may be largely transmitted by the educational attainment of the younger generation. This also was true of adolescent–parent behaviors that exhibit autonomous-relatedness. There are, however, other aspects of family interaction style that are particularly important when trying to predict young adult occupational outcomes and that do not appear to have their effects mediated by educational attainment. Teens who are exposed to marital relationships that promote autonomy and relatedness have the opportunity to learn to create similar types of relationships for themselves, which might enhance their occupational opportunities. It is possible that teenagers learn about relationship maintenance from observing their parents' marital relationships. This is not to suggest that marital relationships affect adolescent development solely by serving as relational models, but modeling may have long-term developmental significance (Bandura, 1977). Alternatively, there may be behavioral continuities between successive generations (Elder, Caspi, & Downey, 1986) and the intergenerational transmission of behavior and attitudes may account for both the positive qualities in the marital dyad and the young adults' occupational outcomes (Benson, Arditti, Reguero de Atiles, & Smith, 1992). It is also possible that children of parents who are able to respect each other's individuality may function better and put less strain on the marital relationship. These easy teens should ultimately be able to obtain better jobs. From our data we cannot determine the underlying mechanism, but teens who come from families in which parents are supportive and simultaneously willing to be independent of each other clearly fare better in their early careers.

We expected that parental marital conflict would negatively affect young adult occupational success; however, in our sample of two-parent families, marital conflict was not predictive of young adult occupational outcomes.

The opportunity to develop autonomy in a family context seems to be key for later career success. When autonomy is undermined in family relationships there are developmental consequences for adolescents, in that they hold less prestigious jobs at age 25 than adolescents' whose families did not undermine autonomy. Although fathers' behaviors that undermine adolescents' autonomy positively related to high school completion in our previously hospitalized sample, adolescents who were unable to establish autonomy vis-à-vis their parents did hold less prestigious jobs as young adults. These psychiatrically disturbed teenagers may have initially benefited from a restriction of autonomy, but may not have been able to achieve the psychological autonomy from their autonomy-inhibiting fathers that would allow them to develop the requisite psychosocial maturity to be successful in the workplace. Fathers who undermined their teenagers' autonomy had children who at age 25 held relatively low-prestige positions. There also was a trend for fathers who undermined their spouses' autonomy to have children who had less successful careers. It is possible that men who undermine their wives' autonomy hold more traditional gender role attitudes and draw their self-esteem from being the breadwinner and head of the household (Hoffman, 1989). These men's attempts to constrain their wives' autonomy may also carry over to their children. How family members deal with autonomy in the family relationships, then, especially when fathers are involved, clearly has a relationship to later occupational success.

In studying occupational outcomes one needs to be particularly aware of cohort effects (Harmon, 1989). The first wave of data for this study was collected during the mid 1970s and the age 25 follow-up began in 1989. It also is important to be aware of the fact that the subjects' career information was collected at a time when the United States was beginning a major recession. In interpreting the results of this study it is important to keep in mind that the data collected on one cohort may not generalize well to future cohorts growing up under different circumstances.

We first proposed that young adults' educational and occupational achievements were related to the adolescent processes of developing autonomy while maintaining relatedness with parents. Using this principle to guide our research, we have shown continuities from the process of establishing autonomy in adolescence to educational and occupational attainment in young adulthood over and above effects of prior pathology and family SES. These relational processes should now be studied with samples drawn from different ethnic and socioeconomic groups to see if our findings generalize to these groups. Further research is also needed to delineate the specific process by which family interactions in adolescence become linked to educational and career achievements over time.

ACKNOWLEDGMENTS

This study was completed with the assistance of grants from the Spencer Foundation, the National Academy of Education, the National Institute of Mental Health (#R03 MH45239-02), and the W. T. Grant Foundation to Joseph Allen, and from the National Institute of Mental Health (#R01 MH44934-03 and #K05-04-7018) and the John D. and Catherine T. Mac-

Arthur Foundation to Stuart Hauser while a Fellow at the Center for Advanced Study in the Behavioral Sciences, Stanford, CA.

We also gratefully acknowledge Charlene Eickholt for her assistance in this study.

REFERENCES

Allen, J. P., Hauser, S. T., Bell, K. L., & O'Connor, T. G. (1994). Longitudinal assessment of autonomy and relatedness in adolescent–family interactions as predictors of adolescent ego development and self-esteem. *Child Development, 65,* 179–194.

Allen, J. P., Hauser, S. T., Borman, E., & Worrell, C. M. (1991). *The autonomy and relatedness coding system: A scoring manual.* Unpublished manuscript, University of Virginia, Charlottesville.

Allen, J. P., Hauser, S. T., O'Connor, T. G., Bell, K. L., & Eickholt, C. M. (in press). The connection of observed hostile family conflict to adolescents' developing autonomy and relatedness with parents. *Development and Psychopathology.*

Astone, N. M., & McLanahan, S. S. (1991). Family structure, parental practices and high school completion. *American Sociological Review, 56,* 309–320.

Bandura, A. (1977). Self-efficacy: Toward a unifying theory of behavioral change. *Psychological Review, 84,* 191–215.

Bank, B. J., Slavings, R. L., & Biddle, B. J. (1990). Effects of peer, faculty, and parental influences on students' persistence. *Sociology of Education, 63,* 208–225.

Becker, G. S. (1981). *A treatise on the family.* Cambridge, MA: Harvard University Press.

Becker, G. S., & Tomes, N. (1986). Human capital and the rise and fall of families. *Journal of Labor Economics, 4,* S1–S39.

Benson, M. J., Arditti, J., Reguero de Atiles, J. T., & Smith, S. (1992). Intergenerational transmission: Attributions in relationships with parents and intimate others. *Journal of Family Issues, 13,* 450–464.

Blau, P. M., & Duncan, O. D. (1967). *The American occupational structure.* New York: Wiley.

Block, J., & Robins, R. W. (1993). A longitudinal study of consistency and change in self-esteem from early adolescence to early adulthood. *Child Development, 64,* 909–923.

Blustein, D. L., Walbridge, M. M., Friedlander, M. L., & Palladino, D. E. (1991). Contributions to psychological separation and parental attachment to the career development process. *Journal of Counseling Psychology, 38,* 39–50.

Bordua, D. J. (1960). Educational aspirations and parental stress on college. *Social Forces, 38,* 262–269.

Brooks-Gunn, J., Brown, B., Duncan, G. J., & Moore, K. A. (1994, April). *Child development in the context of family and community resources: An agenda for national data collections.* Paper presented at Integrating federal statistics on children, organized by the National Research Council's Committee on Nation Statistics and the Board on Children and Families, Washington, DC.

Bureau of Labor Statistics. (1994). *Occupational outlook handbook* (Bulletin 2450). Washington, DC: U. S. Government Printing Office.

Campbell, E., Adams, G. R., & Dobson, W. R. (1984). Familial correlates of identity formation in late adolescence: A study of the predictive utility of connectedness and individuality in family relations. *Journal of Youth and Adolescence, 13,* 509–525.

Coleman, J. S. (1988). Social capital in the creation of human capital. *American Journal of Sociology, 94*(Suppl.), S95–S120.

Collins, W. A. (1990). Parent–child relationships in the transition to adolescence: Continuity and change in interaction, affect, and cognition. In R. Montemayor, G. R. Adams, & T. P. Gullotta (Eds.), *From childhood to adolescence: A transitional period? Advances in adolescent development* (Vol. 2, pp. 85–106). Newbury Park, CA: Sage.

Collins, W. A., & Russell, G. (1991). Mother–child and father–child relationships in middle childhood and adolescence: A developmental analysis. *Developmental Review, 11*, 99–136.

Cutrona, C. E., Cole, V., Colangelo, N., Assouline, S. G., & Russell, D. W. (1994). Perceived parental social support and academic achievement: An attachment theory perspective. *Journal of Personality and Social Psychology, 66*, 369–378.

Darling, N., & Steinberg, L. (1993). Parenting style as context: An integrative model. *Psychological Bulletin, 113*, 487–496.

Dornbusch, S. M., Ritter, P. L., Leiderman, P. H., Roberts, D. F., & Fraleigh, M. J. (1987). The relation of parenting style to adolescent school performance. *Child Development, 58*, 1244–1257.

Duncan, O. D. (1966). Path analysis: Sociological examples. *American Journal of Sociology, 72*, 1–16.

Duncan, O. D., & Hodge, R. W. (1963). Education and occupational mobility: A regression analysis. *American Journal of Sociology, 68*, 629–644.

Eckland, B. K. (1965). Academic ability, higher education, and occupational mobility. *American Sociological Review, 30*, 735–746.

Elder, G. H., Jr., Caspi, A., & Downey, G. (1986). Problem behavior and family relationships: Life course and intergenerational themes. In A. B. Sorensen, F. E. Weinert, & L. R. Sherrod (Eds.), *Human development and the life course: Multidisciplinary perspectives* (pp. 293–340). Hillsdale, NJ: Lawrence Erlbaum Associates.

Emery, R. E. (1982). Interparental conflict and the children of discord and divorce. *Psychological Bulletin, 92*, 310–330.

Feldman, S. S., & Wentzel, K. W. (1990). Relations among family interaction patterns, classroom self-restraint and academic achievement in preadolescent boys. *Journal of Educational Psychology, 82*, 813–819.

Forehand, R., Long, N., Brody, G., & Fauber, R. (1986). Home predictors of young adolescents' school behavior and academic performance. *Child Development, 57*, 1528–1533.

Frank, S. J., Pirsch, L. A., & Wright, V. C. (1990). Late adolescents' perceptions of their relationships with their parents: Relationships among deidealization, autonomy, relatedness, and insecurity and implications for adolescent adjustment and ego identity status. *Journal of Youth and Adolescence, 19*, 571–588.

Galambos, N. L., & Silbereisen, R. K. (1987). Income change, parental life outlook, and adolescent expectations for job success. *Journal of Marriage and the Family, 49*, 141–149.

Grotevant, H. D. (1983). The contribution of the family to the facilitation of identity formation in early adolescence. *Journal of Early Adolescence, 3*, 225–237.

Grotevant, H. D., & Cooper, C. R. (1985). Patterns of interaction in family relationships and the development of identity exploration in adolescence. *Child Development, 56*, 415–428.

Harmon, L. W. (1989). Longitudinal changes in women's career aspirations: Developmental or historical? *Journal of Vocational Behavior, 35*, 46–63.

Hauser, R. M., & Featherman, D. L. (1977). *The process of stratification: Trends and analyses.* New York: Academic Press.

Hauser, S. T., & Greene, W. (1992). Passages from late adolescence to early adulthood. In G. Pollock & S. Greenspan (Eds.), *The course of life* (Vol. 4, pp. 377–405). New York: International University Press.

Hauser, S. T., & Levine, H. (1993). Relatedness and autonomy in adolescence: Links with ego development and family interactions. In S. C. Feinstein (Series Ed.) & R. C. Marohn

(Vol. Ed.), *Adolescent psychiatry* (Vol. 19, pp. 185–227). Chicago: University of Chicago Press.

Hauser, S. T., Powers, S. I., & Noam, G. G. (1991). *Adolescents and their families: Paths of ego development.* New York: The Free Press.

Haveman, R., Wolfe, B., & Spaulding, J. (1991). Childhood events and circumstances influencing high school completion. *Demography, 28,* 133–157.

Hetherington, E. M., & Martin, B. (1986). Family factors and psychopathology in children. In H. C. Quay & J. S. Werry (Eds.), *Psychopathological disorders of childhood* (pp. 332–390). New York: Wiley.

Hill, J. P., & Holmbeck, G. N. (1986). Attachment and autonomy during adolescence. *Annals of Child Development, 3,* 145–189.

Hill, M. S., & Duncan, G. (1987). Parental family income and the socio-economic attainment of children. *Social Science Research, 16,* 39–73.

Hodge, R. W. (1966). Occupational mobility as a probability process. *Demography, 30,* 19–34.

Hoffman, J. A. (1984). Psychological separation of late adolescents from their parents. *Journal of Counseling Psychology, 31,* 170–178.

Hoffman, J. A., & Weiss, B. (1987). Family dynamics and presenting problems in college students. *Journal of Counseling Psychology, 34,* 157–163.

Hoffman, L. W. (1984). Work, family, and the socialization of the child. In R. Parke (Ed.), *Review of child development research: Vol. 7. The family* (pp. 223–282). Chicago: University of Chicago Press.

Hoffman, L. W. (1989). Effects of maternal employment in the two-parent family. *American Psychologist, 44,* 283–292.

Hogan, D. P., & Astone, N. (1986). The transition to adulthood. *Annual Review of Sociology, 12,* 109–130.

Hollingshead, A. F. (1975). *Four factor index of social status.* Unpublished manuscript, Yale University, New Haven, CT.

Holmbeck, G. N., Paikoff, R. L., & Brooks-Gunn, J. (1995). Parenting adolescents. In M. H. Bornstein (Ed.), *Handbook of parenting: Vol. 1. Children and parenting* (pp. 91–118). Mahwah, NJ: Lawrence Erlbaum Associates.

Ihinger-Tallman, M. (1982). Family interaction, gender, and status attainment value. *Sex Roles, 8,* 543–556.

Josselson, R. (1987). *Finding herself: Pathways to identity development in women.* San Francisco: Jossey-Bass.

Kahl, J. A. (1953). Education and occupational aspirations of "common man" boys. *Harvard Educational Review, 23,* 186–203.

Kenny, M. E. (1987). The extent and function of parental attachment among first-year college students. *Journal of Youth and Adolescence, 16,* 17–29.

Kenny, M. E. (1990). College seniors' perceptions of parental attachments: The value and stability of family ties. *Journal of College Student Development, 31,* 39–46.

Kobak, R. R., & Sceery, C. (1988). Attachment in late adolescence: Working models, affect regulation and representations of self and others. *Child Development, 59,* 135–146.

Lamborn, S. D., Mounts, N. S., Steinberg, L., & Dornbusch, S. M. (1991). Patterns of competence and adjustment among adolescents from authoritative, authoritarian, indulgent, and neglectful families. *Child Development, 62,* 1049–1065.

Lapsley, D. K., Rice, K. G., & Shadid, G. E. (1989). Psychological separation and adjustment to college. *Journal of Counseling Psychology, 36,* 286–294.

LeCroy, C. W. (1988). Parent–adolescent intimacy. *Adolescence, 23,* 137–147.

Levinson, D. J., Darrow, C. N., Klein, E. B., Levinson, M. H., & McKee, B. (1978). *The seasons of a man's life.* New York: Ballantine.

Lopez, F. G. (1991). Patterns of family conflict and their relation to college student adjustment. *Journal of Counseling and Development, 69,* 257–260.

Lopez, F. G., & Andrews, S. (1987). Career indecision: A family systems perspective. *Journal of Counseling and Development, 65,* 304–307.

Lopez, F. G., Campbell, V. L., & Watkins, C. E., Jr. (1988). Family structure, psychological separation and college adjustment: A canonical analysis and cross-validation. *Journal of Counseling Psychology, 15,* 402–409.

Lopez, F. G., Campbell, V. L., & Watkins, C. E., Jr. (1989a). Constructions of current family functioning among depressed and nondepressed college students. *Journal of College Student Development, 30,* 221–228.

Lopez, F. G., Campbell, V. L., & Watkins, C. E., Jr. (1989b). Effects of marital conflict and family coalition patterns on college student adjustment. *Journal of College Student Development, 30,* 46–52.

Maccoby, E. E., & Martin, J. A. (1983). Socialization in the context of the family: Parent–child interaction. In P. H. Mussen (Series Ed.) & E. M. Hetherington (Vol. Ed.), *Handbook of child psychology: Vol. 4. Socialization, personality, and social development* (4th ed., pp. 1–101). New York: Wiley.

Mare, R. D., & Chen, M. D. (1986). Further evidence on sibship size and educational stratification. *American Sociological Review, 51,* 403–412.

Marjoribanks, K. (1989). Environments, adolescents' aspirations and young adults' status attainment. *Educational Studies, 15,* 155–164.

Masselam, V. S., Marcus, R. F., & Stunkard, C. L. (1990). Parent–adolescent communication, family functioning, and school performance. *Adolescence, 25,* 725–737.

Moore, D. (1987). Parent–adolescent separation: The construction of adulthood by late adolescents. *Developmental Psychology, 23,* 298–307.

Nakao, K., Hodge, R. W., & Treas, J. (1990). On revising prestige scores for all occupations (GSS Methodological Rep. No. 69). Chicago: National Opinion Research Center.

Nakao, K., & Treas, J. (1990). Computing 1989 occupational prestige scores (GSS Methodological Rep. No. 70). Chicago: National Opinion Research Center.

National Center for Education Statistics. (1993a). *The condition of education, 1993.* Washington, DC: U.S. Government Printing Office.

National Center for Education Statistics. (1993b). *Digest of education statistics.* Washington, DC: U.S. Government Printing Office.

Paikoff, R. L., & Brooks-Gunn, J. (1991). Do parent–child relationships change during puberty? *Psychological Bulletin, 110,* 47–66.

Penick, N. I., & Jepsen, D. A. (1992). Family functioning and adolescent career development. *Career Development Quarterly, 40,* 208–222.

Peterson, J. L., & Zill, N. (1986). Marital disruption, parent–child relationships, and behavior problems in children. *Journal of Marriage and the Family, 48,* 295–307.

Rehberg, R. A., & Westby, D. L. (1967). Parental encouragement, occupation, education and family size: Artifactual or independent determinants of adolescent educational expectations? *Social Forces, 45,* 362–374.

Rice, K. G., Cole, D. A., & Lapsley, D. K. (1990). Separation-individuation, family cohesion, and adjustment to college: Measurement validation and test of a theoretical model. *Journal of Counseling Psychology, 37,* 195–202.

Rumberger, R. W. (1983). Dropping out of high school: The influence of race, sex, and family background. *American Education Research Journal, 20,* 199–220.

Rumberger, R. W. (1987). High school dropouts: A review of issues and evidence. *Review of Educational Research, 57,* 101–121.

Rumberger, R. W., Ghatak, R., Poulos, G., Ritter, P. L., & Dornbusch, S. M. (1990). Family influences on dropout behavior in one California High School. *Sociology of Education, 63,* 283–299.

Sewell, W. H., & Hauser, R. M. (1975). *Education, occupation and earnings: Achievement in the early career.* New York: Academic Press.

Sewell, W. H., & Shah, V. P. (1968). Social class, parental encouragement, and educational aspirations. *American Journal of Sociology, 73,* 559–572.

Steinberg, L. (1990). Interdependence in the family: Autonomy, conflict, and harmony in the parent–adolescent relationship. In S. S. Feldman & G. L. Elliott (Eds.), *At the threshold: The developing adolescent* (pp. 255–276). Cambridge, MA: Harvard University Press.

Steinberg, L., Elmen, J. D., & Mounts, N. S. (1989). Authoritative parenting, psychosocial maturity, and academic success among adolescents. *Child Development, 60,* 1424–1436.

Strodtbeck, F. (1951). Husband–wife interaction over revealed differences. *American Sociology Review, 16,* 463–473.

Youniss, J., & Ketterlinus, R. D. (1987). Communication and connectedness in mother– and father–adolescent relationships. *Journal of Youth and Adolescence, 8,* 265–280.

Youniss, J., & Smollar, J. (1985). *Adolescent relations with mothers, fathers, and friends.* Chicago: University of Chicago Press.

V

SUMMARY

Adolescent Transitions in Context

Julia A. Graber
Jeanne Brooks-Gunn
Teachers College, Columbia University

Anne C. Petersen
University of Minnesota

Since the mid-1980s, several volumes (e.g., Adams, Montemayor, & Gullotta, 1989–1993; Feldman & Elliott, 1990; Gunnar & Collins, 1988; Lerner & Foch, 1987; Levine & McAnarney, 1988) have been devoted to advances in the study of development during adolescence. In addition, some books have been devoted to the compilation of findings from single, seminal longitudinal studies of adolescents (e.g., Simmons & Blyth, 1987; Stattin & Magnusson, 1990; Werner & Smith, 1992). Still other volumes have focused on specific topics in the field of adolescent development such as health promotion (Millstein, Petersen, & Nightingale, 1993) or stress and resilience (Colten & Gore, 1991; Furstenberg, Brooks-Gunn, & Morgan, 1987; Haggerty, Sherrod, Garmezy, & Rutter, 1994). Along with delineating the current state of the field, the amassing literature on adolescent development has highlighted many avenues for continued study as illustrated by the chapters in this volume. This book focuses particularly on adolescent transitions and their impact on developing young people.

Although noted as an important period of development throughout the history of psychology, until the mid-1960s, the unique experiences of adolescents were only occasionally studied. Historically, the first conceptualizations of adolescence, from Aristotle to G. Stanley Hall, have been as times of upheaval, storm, and stress. Although it was these views that shaped the early research in the field, this work did not substantiate beliefs about universal storm and stress (Offer, 1987) nor premises about major discontinuities in behavior (Lerner et al., chap. 1, this volume;

Nesselroade & Baltes, 1974) at adolescence. As Lerner and his colleagues noted, amidst the changes of adolescence is the continuity of many other aspects of the adolescent's life and environment. In fact, in some cases discontinuities in development experienced during adolescence may result in an improvement in behavior and adjustment rather than a decrement in functioning or upheaval. Across the historical and recent perspectives on adolescent development, however, this period has been conceptualized as a time of transition.

Embedded in the framework that adolescence is a time of transition is the idea that transitions result in changes in roles taken on by adolescents. Lewin (1939; Bronfenbrenner, 1977a) was perhaps one of the first to note that the changes of adolescence are inherently defined by the social context and the individual's interaction with and behavior in that context. Within these social contexts are roles and expectations for behavior based on identification or membership in a social group. Of particular psychological significance during adolescence is that the change in role from child to adult occurs over a period of time, in part because full membership status in the social group of adults in most developed societies is delayed significantly beyond the entry into adolescence. Issues of group membership, including role changes as evidenced by new behaviors and self-definitional changes as a member of a new group, and development occurring within the context of interactions between the individual and the environment, have continued as themes for understanding the development of adolescents.

TRANSITIONS

The importance of adolescence as a period of transition and in fact as being defined by a series of transitions (e.g., puberty as one of many markers for the entry into adolescence, starting a new job as one of many markers for entry into young adulthood) has led to the testing of models of development around the issues of transition. Models of development that focus on the impact of transitions have been discussed in depth elsewhere, notably by Lerner and his colleagues in chapter 1 of this volume as well as others (Elder, 1985; Pickles & Rutter, 1991). Pickles and Rutter (1991) identified transitions as "events or happenings that bring about the potential for long-term psychological change" (p. 133). Despite the breadth of such a statement, it has the simplicity of being applicable to a range of experiences with an emphasis on the potential for lifelong influences of the changes experienced by adolescents.

Of interest to researchers interested in developmental transitions (as well as others who share an interest in this topic) is identifying how and under what circumstances the experience of a transition has pervasive influence and what the nature of that influence is. Hence, the experience of a transition is not considered equivalent across individuals. The goal of research is to explain individual differences in outcome based on differences in how a particular transition was experienced (Pickles & Rutter, 1991). Factors associated with individual differences in the experience of transitions include the individual's development prior to the transition, the timing of the transition within the individual's life course, and the interaction of the transition and the psychological experience of it in the social environment.

Transition periods are intriguing to investigators in part because the outcome can be so diverse. For example, Pickles and Rutter (1991) reported that the choice of marital partner can be a potent factor in getting onto a better mental health trajectory for adolescents who had a prior history of problems. Marriage resulted in a "turning point" for some individuals, helping them change their negative trajectories. For others, partners merely reinforced and perpetuated previous behavior patterns. Individual differences in choices resulted in discontinuities in behavior (with positive consequences) for some young adults, and continuities in behavior for others (with negative consequences).

In other research, it was demonstrated that transition periods accentuated existing behavioral patterns (Block, 1982; Caspi & Moffitt, 1991). Caspi and Moffitt (1991) examined changes in behavioral problems in girls in association with the timing of their pubertal development. In this case, girls who had behavioral problems in childhood and went through puberty earlier than their peers experienced a worsening of their prior problems in the mid-adolescence years. Neither early-maturing girls who did not have prior problems, nor girls with prior problems who matured at the same time or later than their peers, exhibited the same frequency and severity of problems as the early-maturing girls with prior problems. For some girls, accentuation of behavior in association with passage through a transition resulted in continuity (along with worsening) in a pattern of poor adjustment rather than the onset of new problems.

During the time of a transition, it has been suggested that individuals respond with an initial decrement in adjustment until they adapt to the new roles and contexts (Stewart, 1982). Stewart (1982) suggested that initial self-evaluations are poor during transitions due to feelings of incompetence or being overwhelmed; with adaptation, these feelings change, resulting in the ability to make more integrated emotional responses and to embark on courses of action. Empirical work has supported this model for responses to marriage and birth of first child, at least for women (Stewart, Sokol, Healy, & Chester, 1986). (See also Brooks-Gunn & Chase-Lansdale, 1995, for a description of a similar process for teenage parenthood.) Hence, it might be expected that with each transition there is some moderate upheaval and the impression that an individual is experiencing pervasive problems may be the result of spacing of the multiple transitions at adolescence. In fact, Simmons and her colleagues (Simmons & Blyth, 1987; Simmons, Carlton-Ford, & Blyth, 1987) suggested that simultaneity of adolescent transitions is one source of individual differences in adaptation to adolescent transitions with adolescents who experience simultaneous changes rather than sequential changes being at risk for behavioral and affective problems.

Particular transitions occurring in adolescence provide opportunities for closure of behaviors that existed in a specific context. School changes in particular have been found to be times of behavioral change (Simmons & Blyth, 1987). For example, survey studies have found that frequency of drinking increases in the post-high-school years (predominantly due to increased alcohol use by college students) but that at the same time, adjustment in terms of depressive affect improved in those years (Aseltine & Gore, 1993). Similarly, drug use declines in young adulthood, again, in association with the transition to marriage (Bachman, Johnston, O'Malley, & Schulenberg, chap. 5, this volume). Interestingly, both graduation from high school and marriage have culturally defined ceremonies that clearly distinguish these events as transitions that mark the end of one period of life and the beginning of a new period. The behaviors that are acceptable for individuals prior to the event or transition are not the same as the behaviors that are expected after the transition in both cases.

The complex interactions of individual development within a social context at the time of transitions and how these interactions of person and environment relate to behaviors in several domains is described throughout this volume. We consider the social contexts of adolescents ranging from those closest to the individual such as family and peers to school contexts at the classroom and school-system level to the contexts of the workplace, neighborhood, and larger community—in many ways exemplifying micro-, meso-, exo-, and macroenvironments in Bronfenbrenner's (1977b) ecological model. More importantly, the interaction of these systems in shaping adolescent development is also evident. Throughout the domains of development, family influences on outcomes of transitions are pervasive, as seen in their connection to school contexts and to young adult transitions to work and further education. We consider two transition points— entry into adolescence and entry into young adulthood—in this volume.

Entry Into Adolescence

Prior research and reviews have described the numerous transitions in physical development, family and peer relations, and school changes occurring in early adolescence. As indicated, in studying or understanding the navigation of developmental transitions, the individual differences that predict positive and negative adaptations must be considered. In the area of research on puberty (Graber, Petersen, & Brooks-Gunn, chap. 2, this volume), we described some experiences such as menarche that are momentarily stressful for many individuals but are followed by adaptation; this pattern parallels the process described by Stewart (1982). Longer term effects are a product of the aspect of pubertal development under consideration (e.g., hormonal changes or growth spurt) and the context of these changes (e.g., timing of the transition; see Graber et al., chap. 2, this volume) or timing relative to other stressful transitions such as school change (Petersen, Sarigiani, & Kennedy, 1991; Simmons & Blyth, 1987).

This paradigm might also "fit" phenomena occurring within the family. For example, conflict with parents over rules, such as curfew, occurs as adolescents take on more adultlike and independent behaviors in response to the expectations of impending adulthood; initial perturbations in parent–child relationships seem to lead to adaptations to the new roles on the part of each member of the family system (Laursen & Collins, 1992; Paikoff & Brooks-Gunn, 1991). With the transition into adolescence and the pressures (both internal and external) on the adolescent to behave more autonomously come increasing demands by the adolescent for a role in decision making—a common source of conflict between parents and adolescents (Montemayor, 1983; Smetana, 1988). Longer term effects of conflict or continuation of the conflict are related to individual differences in families and adolescents (as was the case for pubertal effects on behavior); that is, only some families continue to have difficulties. Holmbeck (chap. 7, this volume) specified a detailed model for studying the complex correlates that ultimately predict outcomes for relationship change in early adolescence. Navigating periods of increased conflict is dependent on prior relational behaviors and dispositions of each member of the relationship and the skills of each member at resolving conflict as well as numerous other environmental and interpersonal factors. Despite the fact that prior skills and interactions are likely to influence the success of parents and adolescents in resolving conflicts, it is noteworthy that the conflicts of adolescence are, in fact, new experiences for the participants in the conflict in most cases. Of course, as Holmbeck (chap. 7, this volume) noted, parent–adolescent conflict is merely one aspect of parent–child relationships during the adolescent decade and across the life course. The saliency and primacy of parental and family influences on behavior pervade areas of activity other than conflict or parent–child interactions, and influence many domains of the adolescent's life often implicitly if not explicitly.

At the same time that family relations are changing, the peer environment is also changing. Despite common beliefs that the increasing importance of peers is at the expense of the importance of parents, especially as an influence on deviant or risk behaviors, Berndt (chap. 3, this volume) reported that peer influences on adolescent behavior (especially risk behaviors) are not as widespread and detrimental as previously suggested in the literature. In fact, peers are an increasing source of support during adolescence as young people have more independence in deciding with whom they spend time, and how much time they spend with these individuals. These individuals form the network and context for social supports and increasingly intimate relationships.

However, along with potential positive influences, the peer group does form the context for exploring or engaging in behaviors that parents and society, more generally, often consider undesirable, especially for younger adolescents (e.g., intercourse), or behaviors that are not condoned for individuals at any age (e.g., drug use). Both Rodgers (chap. 4, this volume) and Bachman and his colleagues (chap. 5, this volume) noted the importance of peers and intimate relationships in predicting behavioral change during adolescence and young adulthood. In the case of sexual activity, the prevalence (or *perception* of the prevalence) of sexual activity in an adolescent's peer group was a strong determinant of age of onset of intercourse. In this case, it would seem that peers have a negative influence on the adolescent but sexual behavior becomes much more accepted by society (if not parents) once an adolescent is older. Developmental correlates of the timing of intercourse are critical to study in order to assess potential negative impact on adolescents (Rodgers, chap. 4, this volume). Interestingly, for drug and alcohol use, historical trends suggest that usage of particular substances is associated with the general acceptability of the drug at the time and may wax and wane with popular opinion as well as campaigns to inform the public on health risks (Bachman et al., chap. 5, this volume). For example, the social context of the college dormitory may at one time be very tolerant of marijuana use and at another time promote alcohol use instead. As noted earlier, forming a strong bond such as marriage with another individual was associated with decreasing these activities. Overall, peer relations in early adolescence and the social context that they form take on new dimensions and continue to shape development throughout the life course.

The school environment is also central to an understanding of the intersections among transitions, behavior, and context. Eccles, Lord, and Buchanan (chap. 10, this volume) applied the stage–environment fit model to school transitions. They documented the importance of the immediate context of teachers and parents in influencing school achievement. Related to the behavior of teachers in the middle school years are broader structural issues imposed by the school and educational systems. At the educational system level, approaches to teaching that emphasize control rather than decision making and interaction are in direct opposition to the needs of most early adolescents who are experimenting with greater independence. In fact, this period of development has been the target of several school-based programs designed to teach decision-making, social, and coping skills (see Cook, Anson, & Walchli, 1993, for a review of several programs and Petersen, Leffert, Graham, Alwin, & Ding, in press, for a description of a program to teach effective coping skills).

Entry Into Young Adulthood

Pressures to curtail education and adolescence result in entry into adulthood often prior to the individual being adequately prepared to take on the full responsibilities of that role. As with the entry into adolescence as signaled by pubertal development or by school transition, the timing of the transition into adulthood is likely to have an impact on how the transition is experienced and what the long-term effect of the transition ultimately is.

Most researchers have examined a series of role changes as defining the transition to adulthood. The developmental tasks associated with this transition are completing one's full-time education (or dropping out), starting full-time employment, supporting oneself and living on one's own, getting married, and beginning a family of one's own. In contrast with entry into adolescence and the onset of puberty and the entry to middle school, these series of transitions that have been used to define becoming a person with full role status in adult society are less obligatory; that is, individuals may make some but not all of these transitions and still function as an adult. (See Graber & Dubas, in press, and Sherrod, Haggerty, & Featherman, 1993, for recent volumes on leaving home and the transition to adulthood, respectively.) Again with each of these transitions, roles and relationships are restructured (Cohler & Musick, chap. 8, this volume; Maughan & Champion, 1990; Pickles & Rutter, 1991), and the outcome of the transition is influenced by prior developmental experiences and prior restructuring of roles (Sherrod et al., 1993).

Clearly, the transitions that define leaving adolescence and becoming an adult are not independent of one another but are interrelated. For example, the timing of finishing one's education will influence the success and timing of entering the work force. Modell and Goodman (1990) delineated historical changes in these transitions, noting that for men, education and work transitions usually preceded marrying and starting a family, with the gap between these sets of transitions narrowing over the past few decades. Women enter marriage earlier and spend more of their lives married and as parents in comparison to men across historical periods (Watkins, Menken, & Bongaarts, 1987). Recent studies report that college students and college-bound adolescents expect to begin their first full-time job during their early 20s, later than youth who do not expect to attend college (Bingham, Stemmler, Crockett, & Petersen, 1991; Graber & Brooks-Gunn, in press-a; Hogan & Astone, 1986).

These patterns of young adult transitions increasingly describe fewer and fewer of the experiences of adolescents in U.S. society today. Research on the transition to young adulthood must also account not only for the present patterns of transitions and how they are experienced by most adolescents but also the effects of out-of-synch and off-time adult transitions as they are experienced by subgroups of adolescents (Sherrod, in press). Notably, the alternative patterns are more frequently experienced by adolescents from lower income and poor families and adolescents from cultural backgrounds other than mainstream, White, middle-class America.

The transition from school to work may be particularly stressful for those adolescents who make this transition after dropping out of high school (Hess, Petersen, & Mortimer, 1994). The effect of competing roles and multiple demands on an adolescent are apparent in the discussion of dropping out of school (Ianni & Orr, chap. 11, this volume). As Ianni and Orr pointed out, the decision to drop out of school may be active or passive and is often the result of family, school, and community deficits that result in adolescents discontinuing their education prematurely. Such deficits may be the result of numerous factors such as the type of school structure and environment documented by Eccles and her colleagues (chap. 10, this volume) or competing demands from the family to become a worker and contribute to the support of the family (Newman, chap. 12, this volume). Notably, Ianni and Orr conducted extensive work on prevention and intervention of school dropout that recognizes the needs of adolescents, and provides supports in the school, family, and community environments when possible, to counteract prior deficits. Because the rates of dropping out do not differ substantially among urban, suburban, and rural communities but rather are influenced more by school, the importance of accounting for the nature of the particular school and community context can not be overemphasized in countering this problem.

Even for adolescents who complete high school, those who do not go on to college or continue with technical or trade training make the transition into the labor force with less education and fewer marketable skills, as well as less opportunity for financial support for additional training (Commission on Work, Family, & Citizenship, 1988). Youth growing up in poor families are overrepresented in the pool of unemployed youth—those youth having the most difficult transition into the workforce (Hess et al., 1994).

Newman's detailed ethnographic data on the work experiences of low-income wage earners in Harlem (chap. 12, this volume) documents effects of transition into the workforce in a sample of older adolescents and young adults. Many studies have found that working while still attending high school can have a negative effect on school performance and promote engagement in problem behaviors (Steinberg, Fegley, & Dornbusch, 1993) as well as increase adolescents' reports of fatigue (Carskadon, 1990); often for these adolescents the jobs were an additional support to educational goals and a method for distancing oneself from drugs and crime in the neighborhood. For adolescents growing up in very poor families, the funds earned were a resource for buying educational supplies and adding to family funds, still providing for personal spending. Perhaps more importantly, the work environments became contexts for development—they provide social supports, role models, and training in work ethics. Despite the low social value (as Newman described it) of the job outside of the work environment, the adolescents themselves felt a sense of pride in "being a worker." Given the scarcity of jobs in the adolescents' neighborhoods, such a label may be a potent sign of success for these young adults. Unfortunately, as Newman noted, these jobs do not result in a simple transition into better jobs. The probability of finding a job that provides a better standard of living is not high in the absence of additional job skills or education (Bell, Allen, Hauser, & O'Connor, chap. 13, this volume; Hess et al., 1994).

The broader context of poverty that has shaped the lives of adolescents working in low-wage jobs in Harlem provides a very different transition into adulthood than that described by Bell and her colleagues (chap. 13, this volume). The two studies clearly focus on different factors that influence adolescents' transition to work as well as different types of transitions; although, had similar factors been studied in both samples, similar associations may have been found. The adolescents studied by Newman seemed to immerse themselves in the environment of work; it is this context and its influence on other aspects of life that form the picture of their lives. In contrast, Bell and her colleagues considered the pervasive influence of family relationships at each step in the transition into the labor force. As with prior adolescent transitions, the nature of parent–adolescent interactions was predictive of outcomes of the transition into work. Specifically, adolescents' expression of autonomy in the context of support from parents as exhibited in mid-adolescence was associated with completing high school as well as ultimate educational attainment. The nature of parents' interactions with one another also predicted young adult occupational prestige.

Many factors in the family environment are predictive of adolescent educational and occupational success. (See Bell et al., chap. 13, this volume; Ianni & Orr, chap. 11, this volume; and Eccles et al., chap. 10, this volume, for reviews of these literatures.) These factors include parenting behaviors as exhibited in interactions, expectations, and transmission of values as well as modeling expected behaviors (e.g., working, having a college degree). Given the salience of the family context in shaping the transition to work and the salience of adolescent work experiences, at least for some adolescents, studies integrating the relationship among these domains of influence are needed.

Yet another path to the world of work was described by Sullivan (chap. 6, this volume) in his comparison of patterns of criminal behavior in late adolescent boys growing up in three different neighborhood environments. Whereas engagement in criminal activities is not itself an accepted "career" or "work" transition, it is particularly interesting that some adolescent boys discontinue these activities and make the transition into the world of work, whereas others continue with criminal behaviors. Sullivan's delineation of the life-course experiences and influences on these adolescents is notable for the inclusion of neighborhood contexts and self-reported influences that shape the decision to make a change. Through the study of similar behaviors exhibited by the young men who were observed in different neighborhood contexts, Sullivan documented the strong influence of networks within a community that exert forces on an individual's behavior and guide the transition to work. Specifically, White adolescents who were engaged in criminal activities were more likely ultimately to obtain legal employment than were African-American or Hispanic adolescents; obtaining legal employment was associated with better opportunities for employment along with connections to those jobs via older working men in the neighborhood. In addition, young men in the White, lower and working-class neighborhood were likely to receive pressures from community members and family friends to discontinue their illegal activities. These changes also happened in conjunction with getting married and/or starting a family. Hence, multiple social interactions influenced the success in making the transition to work for young men.

As indicated previously, the completion of education and entry into the workforce are two of the adult transitions that happen earliest for most individuals, especially men. In contrast, adolescents themselves expect to begin a family of their own in the mid- to late 20s with adolescents from rural communities expecting to make this transition a few years earlier than adolescents from suburban communities and more affluent families (Bingham et al., 1991; Graber & Brooks-Gunn, in press-a) and with women across communities expecting to marry and have children earlier than men (Bingham et al., 1991; Hogan & Astone, 1986).

For adolescents who become parents in the teen years, the normative sequence of these transitions is disrupted and the transition to parenthood is markedly off time. The effects of making the transition to parenthood during adolescence have most often been examined in the lives of girls

(Brooks-Gunn & Chase-Lansdale, 1995; Cohler & Musick, chap. 8, this volume; Merriwether-de Vries, Burton, & Eggeletion, chap. 9, this volume) with some recent work examining the lives of young fathers and the nature of the relationship between adolescent mothers and fathers (e.g., Merriwether-de Vries et al., chap. 9, this volume; Sullivan, 1993).

As Cohler and Musick (chap. 8, this volume) noted, the importance of new and competing roles is apparent in the experience of teen parenthood. As with adolescents who drop out of school (some of whom do so because of pregnancy or parenthood), the demands of other roles are in competition with the more normative tasks of adolescence. As has been discussed extensively, the role change by an adolescent to "new mother" forces a redefinition of roles on her mother, or both parents, as they take on the role of grandparent (Brooks-Gunn & Chase-Lansdale, 1995; Merriwether-de Vries et al., chap. 9, this volume).

SUMMARY

Throughout the discussions of the different adolescent transitions from puberty through young adulthood, issues of role change and timing are pervasive. Examining the spacing and number of different types of transitions and subsequent adaptations that must be made during the adolescent decade, it is not surprising that this period becomes overwhelming for some adolescents as exhibited in increases in mental health disorders during this time. (See Millstein, Petersen, & Nightingale, 1993 for recent statistics on adolescent mortality and morbidity.) In addition, successive and sometimes simultaneous transitions in adolescence do not happen independently of one another, such that having a particular type of transition may predispose an individual to have a similar experience with the next transition. For example, it has been found in some studies that girls who go through puberty earlier than their peers are also more likely to have sexual intercourse earlier than their peers. Furthermore, girls who have intercourse earlier than their peers become pregnant at even earlier ages than older girls because girls who have sex at younger ages are less likely to use contraception than older girls. Finally, girls who become pregnant in adolescence are more likely than other girls to drop out of school, incurring many potential lifelong disadvantages for success in employment. Of course, not all girls who go through puberty early follow this pattern of transitions.

Factors that predict who will make successive healthy transitions versus who will make successive unhealthy or risky transitions are becoming increasingly better defined. For example, the adolescent's pre-existing repertoire of coping and adaption skills upon entry into adolescence is clearly a factor in whether problems will be accentuated by the transition (e.g., Caspi & Moffitt, 1991). Simultaneity of transitions has also been documented as a predictor of subsequent adjustment in adolescence (Petersen et al., 1991; Simmons & Blyth, 1987). Interestingly, both of these conceptual models have been applied effectively to the pubertal transition but could easily be models for studying transitions across adolescence and the life course.

Recent research that has combined developmental and health psychology has identified reproductive transitions as potentially critical periods in understanding mental and physical health outcomes across the life course. The hypothesis under investigation is that "experiences of stress during periods of physiological change may be qualitatively different and have different effects on girls' and women's health than during a time of stability" (Graber & Brooks-Gunn, in press-b). The assertions underlying this hypothesis are that:

> (a) stress encompasses a broad range of environmental influences on the individual, (b) stress affects health, both physical and mental, (c) large individual differences exist in responsivity to stress and, hence, the ultimate health outcomes of the stress, (d) reproductive transitions are unique developmental periods when the physiological system is particularly vulnerable to stress, (e) stress actually affects the physiological system differently during these periods, and finally (f) the most significant changes in health outcomes are likely to occur due to the accumulation of stress during a reproductive transition. In combination, evidence points to periods of reproductive transitions as being crucial times when the nature of those experiences is likely to predict individual differences in subsequent mental and physical health outcomes. (Graber & Brooks-Gunn, in press-b)

Models such as this may be particularly useful in future research on adolescent development especially when linking pubertal development with subsequent transitions such as pregnancy. Whereas the first tests of this model are being done in studies of women's health, broader application to boys' development may be made and may form a useful contrast for explaining gender differences in health trajectories, as observed in depression and heart disease, from adolescence through adulthood.

Although numerous areas for further research in understanding development in adolescence exist, the wealth of knowledge that has accumulated in the past several decades has been instrumental for motivating prevention and intervention programs as well as better understanding on the part of the public as a whole on the nature of adolescence. Cumulatively, the current knowledge base demonstrates the need for a systems perspective in understanding and explaining the complex causes and consequences in adolescent development. In practical terms, this means that future research must emphasize: (a) multidisciplinary research that combines different research strategies and researchers who have a range of training experiences and expertise; (b) the involvement of participants from diverse ethnic, racial, and social class groups; and (c) the study of the multiple contexts that make up an individual's life. It is notable that the study of adolescence, as highlighted in this volume, is making meaningful progress on each concern.

ACKNOWLEDGMENTS

The first two authors were supported by a grant from the National Institute of Child Health and Human Development (NICHD) during the writing of this chapter. The authors also wish to acknowledge the influence of Karen Matthews, Judith Rodin, Nancy Adler, Joyce Bromberger, Judy Cameron, Ralph Horowitz, Bruce McEwen, Marielle Rebuffe-Scrive, and Elizabeth Susman, members of the Reproductive Transitions Working Group of the John D. and Catherine T. MacArthur Foundation Research Network on Health-Promoting and Disease-Preventing Behaviors, in some of the ideas presented.

REFERENCES

Adams, G. R., Montemayor, R., & Gullotta T. (Series Eds.). (1989–1993). *Advances in adolescent development* (Vols. 1–5). Newbury Park, CA: Sage.

Aseltine, R. H., & Gore, S. (1993). Mental health and social adaptation following the transition from high school. *Journal of Research on Adolescence, 3*(3), 247–270.

Bingham, C. R., Stemmler, M., Crockett, L. J., & Petersen, A. C. (1991). *Community-contextual differences in adolescents' expectations for the timing of adulthood transitions.* Unpublished manuscript, The Pennsylvania State University, University Park.

Block, J. (1982). Assimilation, accommodation, and the dynamics of personality development. *Child Development, 53*, 281–295.

Bronfenbrenner, U. (1977a). Lewinian space and ecological substance. *Journal of Social Issues, 33*, 199–212.

Bronfenbrenner, U. (1977b). Toward an experimental ecology of human development. *American Psychologist, 32*, 513–531.

Brooks-Gunn, J., & Chase-Lansdale, P. L. (1995). Adolescent parenthood. In M. H. Bornstein (Ed.), *Handbook of parenting: Vol. 3. Status and social conditions of parenting* (pp. 113–149). Mahwah, NJ: Lawrence Erlbaum Associates.

Carskadon, M. A. (1990). Patterns of sleep and sleepiness in adolescents. *Pediatrician, 17*, 5–12.

Caspi, A., & Moffitt, T. E. (1991). Individual differences are accentuated during periods of social change: The sample case of girls at puberty. *Journal of Personality and Social Psychology, 61*, 157–168.

Colten, M. E., & Gore, S. (Eds.). (1991). *Adolescent stress: Causes and consequences.* Hawthorne, NY: Aldine de Gruyter.

Commission on Work, Family, & Citizenship. (1988). *The forgotten half: Pathways to success for america's youth and young families*. Washington, DC: William T. Grant Foundation.

Cook, T. D., Anson, A. R., & Walchli, S. B. (1993). From causal description to causal explanation: Improving three already good evaluations of adolescent health programs. In S. G. Millstein, A. C. Petersen, & E. O. Nightingale (Eds.), *Promoting the health of adolescents: New directions for the twenty-first century* (pp. 339–374). New York: Oxford University Press.

Elder, G. H., Jr. (1985). Perspectives on the life course. In G. H. Elder, Jr. (Ed.), *Life course dynamics: Trajectories and transitions, 1968–1980* (pp. 23–49). Ithaca, NY: Cornell University Press.

Feldman, S., & Elliott, G. (Eds.). (1990). *At the threshold: The developing adolescent*. Cambridge, MA: Harvard University Press.

Furstenberg, F. F., Jr., Brooks-Gunn, J., & Morgan, S. P. (1987). *Adolescent mothers in later life*. New York: Cambridge University Press.

Graber, J. A., & Brooks-Gunn, J. (in press-a). Expectations for and precursors of leaving home in young women. In J. A. Graber & J. S. Dubas (Issue Eds.), W. Damon (Series Ed.), *New directions for child development: Leaving home*. San Francisco: Jossey-Bass.

Graber, J. A., & Brooks-Gunn, J. (in press-b). Reproductive transitions: The experience of mothers and daughters. In C. D. Ryff & M. M. Seltzer (Eds.), *The parental experience in midlife*. Chicago: University of Chicago Press.

Graber, J. A., & Dubas, J. S. (Eds.). (in press). *New directions for child development: Leaving home*. San Francisco: Jossey-Bass.

Gunnar, M., & Collins, W. A. (Eds.). (1988). *Development during transition to adolescence: Minnesota symposia on child psychology, Vol. 21*. Hillsdale, NJ: Lawrence Erlbaum Associates.

Haggerty, R. J., Sherrod, L. R., Garmezy, N., & Rutter, M. (1994). *Stress, risk, and resilience in children and adolescents: Processes, mechanisms, and interventions*. New York: Cambridge University Press.

Hess, L. E., Petersen, A. C., & Mortimer, J. T. (1994). Youth, unemployment and marginality: The problem and the solution. In A. C. Petersen & J. T. Mortimer (Eds.), *Youth unemployment and society* (pp. 3–33). New York: Cambridge University Press.

Hogan, D. P., & Astone, N. M. (1986). The transition to adulthood. *Annual Review of Sociology, 12*, 109–130.

Laursen, B., & Collins, W. A. (1992). Interpersonal conflict during adolescence. *Psychological Bulletin, 115*(2), 197–209.

Lerner, R. M., & Foch, T. T. (Eds.). (1987). *Biological-psychosocial interactions in early adolescence*. Hillsdale, NJ: Lawrence Erlbaum Associates.

Levine, M., & McAnarney, E. R. (Eds.). (1988). *Early adolescent transitions*. Lexington, MA: D. C. Heath.

Lewin, K. (1939). The field theory approach to adolescence. *American Journal of Sociology, 44*, 868–897.

Maughan, B., & Champion, L. (1990). Risk and protective factors in the transition to young adulthood. In P. B. Baltes & M. M. Baltes (Eds.), *Successful aging: Perspectives from the behavioral sciences* (pp. 296–331). New York: Cambridge University Press.

Millstein, S. G., Petersen, A. C., & Nightingale, E. O. (Eds.). (1993). *Promoting the health of adolescents: New directions for the twenty-first century*. New York: Oxford University Press.

Modell, J., & Goodman, M. (1990). Historical perspectives. In S. Feldman & G. Elliott (Eds.), *At the threshold: The developing adolescent* (pp. 93–122). Cambridge, MA: Harvard University Press.

Montemayor, R. (1983). Parents and adolescents in conflict: All families some of the time and some families most of the time. *Journal of Early Adolescence, 3*, 83–103.

Nesselroade, J. R., & Baltes, P. B. (1974). Adolescent personality development and historical change: 1970–1972. *Monographs of the Society for Research in Child Development*, *39*(1, Serial No. 154).

Offer, D. (1987). In defense of adolescents. *Journal of the American Medical Association*, *257*, 3407–3408.

Paikoff, R., & Brooks-Gunn, J. (1991). Do parent–child relationships change during puberty? *Psychological Bulletin*, *110*(1), 47–66.

Petersen, A. C., Leffert, N., Graham, B., Alwin, J., & Ding, S. (in press). Promoting mental health during the transition into adolescence. In J. Schulenberg, J. Maggs, & K. Hurrelmann (Eds.), *Health risks and developmental transitions during adolescence*. New York: Cambridge University Press.

Petersen, A. C., Sarigiani, P. A., & Kennedy, R. E. (1991). Adolescent depression: Why more girls? *Journal of Youth and Adolescence*, *20*, 247–271.

Pickles, A., & Rutter, M. (1991). Statistical and conceptual models of 'turning points' in developmental processes. In D. Magnusson, L. R. Bergman, G. Rudinger, & B. Torestad (Eds.), *Problems and methods in longitudinal research: Stability and change* (pp. 133–165). Cambridge, UK: Cambridge University Press.

Sherrod, L. R. (in press). Leaving home: The role of individual and familial factors. In J. A. Graber & J. S. Dubas (Issue Eds.), W. Damon (Series Ed.), *New directions for child development: Leaving home*. San Francisco: Jossey-Bass.

Sherrod, L. R., Haggerty, R. J., & Featherman, D. L. (1993). Introduction: Late adolescence and the transition to adulthood. *Journal of Research on Adolescence*, *3*(3), 217–226.

Simmons, R. G., & Blyth, D. A. (1987). *Moving into adolescence: The impact of pubertal change and school context*. New York: Aldine.

Simmons, R. G., Carlton-Ford, S. L., & Blyth, D. A. (1987). Predicting how a child will cope with the transition to junior high school. In R. M. Lerner & T. T. Foch (Eds.), *Biological-psychosocial interactions in early adolescence* (pp. 325–375). Hillsdale, NJ: Lawrence Erlbaum Associates.

Smetana, J. G. (1988). Adolescents' and parents' conceptions of parental authority. *Child Development*, *59*, 321–335.

Stattin, H., & Magnusson, D. (1990). *Paths through life: Vol. 2. Pubertal maturation in female development*. Hillsdale, NJ: Lawrence Erlbaum Associates.

Steinberg, L., Fegley, S., & Dornbusch, S. M. (1993). Negative impact of part-time work on adolescent adjustment: Evidence from a longitudinal study. *Developmental Psychology*, *29*, 171–180.

Stewart, A. J. (1982). The course of individual adaptation to life changes. *Journal of Personality and Social Psychology*, *42*, 1100–1113.

Stewart, A. J., Sokol, M., Healy, J. M., & Chester, N. L. (1986). Longitudinal studies of psychological consequences of life changes in children and adults. *Journal of Personality and Social Psychology*, *46*(1), 143–151.

Sullivan, M. L. (1993). Culture and class as determinants of out-of-wedlock childbearing and poverty in late adolescence. *Journal of Research on Adolescence*, *3*(3), 295–316.

Watkins, S. C., Menken, J. A., & Bongaarts, J. (1987). Demographic foundations of family change. *American Sociological Review*, *52*, 346–358.

Werner, E. E., & Smith, R. S. (1992). *Overcoming the odds: High risk children from birth to adulthood*. Ithaca, NY: Cornell University Press.

Author Index

Subject Index

A

Adolescence
  cognitive ability, 8
  crime, 141–161, 378
  culture conflict, 300–301
  delinquency, 141–161
  friends' influence, 57–80
    age changes, 65–66, 71, 78
    best friends, 59–60
    cliques, 62
    coercive power, 72–73, 79
    confidant, 62
    conformity, 71
    educational aspirations, 67
    expert power, 74–75
    friend selection, 67–68
    gender differences, 64–65
    group status, 63
    increased interaction frequency, 62
    informational influence, 74–75
    legitimate power, 75
    mutual process, 69
    negative perspective, 57–58, 68–72, 78
    observational learning, 74, 77
    outcomes, 66–69
    parental relationship and, 63, 66
    peers, 59–63
    persuasive force, 74
    positive perspective, 58, 71–72, 78–79
    referent power, 74
    reward power, 73–74
    romantic partners, 66
    susceptibility, 63–64, 79
    transitions, 70–72, 77–78
  identity formation, 295–296
  low-wage employment, 323–342, 377
    autonomy, 327–328
    education, 330–331
    immigrants, 328–329, 336–337
    motivation, 326–332
    personal responsibility, 341
    pooled household income, 328–330
    social network transition, 337–340
    social relationships, 339–340
    work ethic, 335–336
  nonfriends relationships, 62–63
  onset of, 23
  peer pressure, 58, 72–75
  peer rejection, 62
  poverty, 141–161
  psychological development, 296–297
    frustration self-esteem model, 296
  self-oriented process, 218